Francophone Postcolonial Studies

Francophone Postcolonial Studies

A critical introduction

Edited by

CHARLES FORSDICK

James Barrow Professor of French
University of Liverpool

and

DAVID MURPHY

Lecturer in French
University of Stirling

A member of the Hodder Headline Group
LONDON
Distributed in the United States of America by
Oxford University Press Inc., New York

First published in Great Britain in 2003 by
Arnold, a member of the Hodder Headline Group,
338 Euston Road, London NW1 3BH

http://www.arnoldpublishers.com

Distributed in the United States of America by
Oxford University Press Inc.,
198 Madison Avenue, New York, NY10016

British Library Cataloguing in Publication Data
A catalogue record for this book is available from the British Library

Library of Congress Cataloging-in-Publication Data
A catalog record for this book is available from the Library of Congress

ISBN 0 340 80801 2 (hb)
ISBN 0 340 80802 0 (pb)

1 2 3 4 5 6 7 8 9 10

Typeset in 10/12pt Sabon by Phoenix Photosetting, Chatham, Kent
Front cover illustration: 1931 Exposition Coloniale poster © ACHAC
Back cover photo: Ben Radford, Getty Images/Allsport
Printed and bound in Malta

What do you think about this book? Or any other Arnold title?
Please send your comments to feedback.arnold@hodder.co.uk

Contents

PART II   LANGUAGE AND IDENTITY IN THE FRANCOPHONE WORLD

PART III   POSTCOLONIAL AXES: NATION AND GLOBALIZATION IN CONTEMPORARY FRANCOPHONE CULTURES

PART IV   POSTCOLONIAL THOUGHT AND CULTURE IN THE FRANCOPHONE WORLD

Contributors

Chris Bongie teaches in the English Department at Queen's University, Canada. He is the author of two books, *Exotic Memories: Literature, Colonialism and the Fin de Siècle* (1991) and *Islands and Exiles: The Creole Identities of Post/Colonial Literature* (1998), and is currently completing a translation/critical edition of Victor Hugo's novel about the Haitian Revolution, *Bug-Jargal* (to be published in 2004).

Rosemary Chapman is Senior Lecturer in French at the University of Nottingham. Author of *Siting the Quebec Novel* (2000) and co-author of *Francophone Literatures: a Literary and Linguistic Companion* (2001), she has published articles on Tremblay, Hébert, Ouellette-Michalska, Théoret and Roy. Her current research focuses on Gabrielle Roy.

J. Michael Dash, Professor of French and Director of Africana Studies at New York University, has worked extensively on French Caribbean writers. His publications include *Literature and Ideology in Haiti* (1981), *Haiti and the United States* (1988), *Édouard Glissant* (1995). His most recent books are *The Other America: Caribbean Literature in a New World Context* (1998), *Libète: A Haiti Anthology* (with Charles Arthur, 1999) and *Culture and Customs of Haiti* (2001).

Anne Donadey is Associate Professor of French and Women's Studies at San Diego State University in California. She is the author of *Recasting Postcolonialism: Women Writing between Worlds* (2001) and of a number of articles on Francophone women writers, the politics of racial representation, and anti-racist feminist education.

Laurent Dubois is Assistant Professor of History at Michigan State University. His publications include *Les Esclaves de la République* (1998) and *A Colony of Citizens: Revolution and Slave Emancipation in the French*

Caribbean, 1787–1804 (2003). He is currently completing a history of the Haitian Revolution.

Elizabeth Ezra is Senior Lecturer in French at the University of Stirling. She is the author of *The Colonial Unconscious: Race and Culture in Interwar France* (2000) and *Georges Méliès: The Birth of the Auteur* (2000), and is co-editor with Sue Harris of *France in Focus: Film and National Identity* (2000). She is currently writing a book, with Martine Beugnet, on French cinema and colonialism.

Charles Forsdick is James Barrow Professor of French at the University of Liverpool. He is author of *Victor Segalen and the Aesthetics of Diversity* (2000) and editor of *Travel and Exile* (2001). He has published articles on exoticism, travel literature and postcolonial theory, and is currently completing a study of travel and the persistence of cultural diversity in twentieth-century literature in French.

Azzedine Haddour is Senior Lecturer in French at University College London. He is the author of *Colonial Myths: History and Narrative* (2000), co-editor of *City Visions* (2000), co-translator of Sartre's *Colonialism and Neocolonialism* (2001) and editor of the forthcoming *Fanon Reader* (2003).

Alec G. Hargreaves is Director of the Winthrop-King Institute for Contemporary French and Francophone Studies at Florida State University. He is the author of numerous publications on post-colonial minorities, editor of the journal *Expressions maghrébines* and co-editor, with Mark McKinney, of *Post-Colonial Cultures in France* (1997).

Eileen Julien is Professor of French and Comparative Literature and directs the David C. Driskell Center for the Study of the African Diaspora at the University of Maryland. She is completing a study on Senegalese culture, *Modernity and Multiple Imaginaries in Literature and the Arts*, and is co-editing a volume, *The Locations of African Literature*, investigating the complex relationship of African literary texts to the social sciences and their uses in social scientific disciplines.

Roger Little retired from the Chair of French (1776) at Trinity College Dublin in 1998. His principal research interests are in modern French poetry and in the (self)representation of the Black in French-language literatures. General editor of Grant & Cutler Critical Guides to French Texts, he also directs L'Harmattan's series *Autrement Mêmes*. His latest book is *Between Totem and Taboo: Black Man, White Woman in Francographic Literature* (2001).

Maeve McCusker is Lecturer in French Studies at Queen's University, Belfast. She specializes in the contemporary Caribbean novel in French, and has published articles on gender, orality and the representation of history. She is currently preparing a book-length study of Chamoiseau's work.

John McLeod is Lecturer in Commonwealth and Postcolonial Literatures, School of English, University of Leeds. He is the author *of Beginning Postcolonialism* (2000) and was guest editor *of Kunapipi: Journal of Post-Colonial Writing*, 21.2 (1999). His essays have appeared in the *Journal of Commonwealth Literature, Interventions, Moving Worlds*. A new monograph, *Postcolonial London: Metropolitan Culture after Empire*, is forthcoming.

David Murphy is Lecturer in French at the University of Stirling. He has published widely on African – particularly Senegalese – culture, and on the relationship between Francophone and Postcolonial Studies. He is the author of *Sembene: Imagining Alternatives in Film and Fiction* (2000), and is co-editor, with Aedín Ní Loingsigh, of *Thresholds of Otherness/Autrement Mêmes: Identity and Alterity in French-Language Literatures* (2002).

Aedín Ní Loingsigh is Lecturer in French at the University of Edinburgh. Her main research interests lie in Francophone African fiction, and her work has focused on the theme of exile as well as the contribution of African literature to new developments in travel writing. She is co-editor with David Murphy of *Thresholds of Otherness/Autrement Mêmes: Identity and Alterity in French-Language Literatures* (2002).

Gabrielle Parker is Pro-Vice-Chancellor and Dean of the School of Arts at Middlesex University, London. Her research into the politics of French language and culture (with particular emphasis on Francophonie) is informed by earlier engagement with contemporary feminist theory; she completed a doctoral thesis on the novels of Michèle Perrein.

Marilyn Randall is Associate Professor of French at the University of Western Ontario, Canada. Her current research in the field of Quebec studies concerns the cultural representations of the 1837–8 Rebellion in Quebec. She has recently published a study of literary plagiarism, *Pragmatic Plagiarism: Authorship, Profit and Power* (2001).

Mireille Rosello teaches at Northwestern University, Chicago. She has written on surrealism (*L'Humour noir chez André Breton*, 1987), on Tournier (*L'In-différence chez Michel Tournier*, 1990), on Caribbean literature (*Littérature et identité créole aux Antilles*, 1992) and on contemporary women writers (*Infiltrating Culture*, 1996). Her latest books are *Declining the Stereotype* (1998) and *Postcolonial Hospitality: The Immigrant as Guest* (2001).

Andy Stafford is Lecturer in French at Lancaster University. He researches modern French writing and visual culture, especially the essay and Francophone literature. He has published on Barthes, Begag, Chraïbi, Césaire, Glissant, and Sembene. His interests are the Black Atlantic, North African literature, the writing of photography.

Julia Waters is Lecturer in French at the University of Bath, specializing in recent French and Francophone literature. She is the author of *Intersexual Rivalry: a 'Reading in Pairs' of Marguerite Duras and Alain Robbe-Grillet* (2000) and is currently working on Duras's (post)colonial representations of Indochina.

Heather Williams has been Lecturer in French at the University of Wales, Aberystwyth, since 2000. She has published articles on Mallarmé in journals including *Nineteenth-Century French Studies* and *Romance Studies*, and now also researches representations of Brittany in French-language literature, from 1789 to the present day.

Patrick Williams is Professor of Literary and Cultural Studies at Nottingham Trent University. His publications include *Colonial Discourse and Post-Colonial Theory* (with Laura Chrisman, 1993), *Introduction to Post-Colonial Theory* (with Peter Childs, 1996), *Ngugi wa Thiong'o* (1999), *Edward Said* (2001).

Winifred Woodhull teaches at the University of California, San Diego. She is the author of *Transfigurations of the Maghreb: Feminism, Decolonization, and Literatures* (1993) and has written widely on French and Francophone film and literature, including the literature of immigration, considered in a global frame.

Acknowledgements

The editors would like to thank for their assistance in the preparation of this volume: ACHAC, Christine Dutton, Sam Haigh, Nick Harrison, Eva Martinez, Aedín Ní Loingsigh and Elena Seymenliska. We also acknowledge the support of all our friends and colleagues in Stirling and Liverpool, and are most grateful to the contributors, whose work helped us greatly in writing the introduction. More generally, we are grateful to all those pioneers in the field of Francophone Postcolonial Studies whose work we aim to consolidate and develop in this volume.

David Murphy would like to thank the British Academy and the Leverhulme Trust for their financial support, which allowed him to carry out much of the research for his chapter. Charles Forsdick would like to thank the AHRB for its generous support of a project devoted to 'New Approaches to Twentieth-Century Travel Literature in French', from which a number of his reflections included in this book emerged.

The reflections in Laurent Dubois's chapter are based on a history of the Haitian Revolution – whose working title is *The Story of the Haitian Revolution* (Cambridge, MA: Harvard UP) – that he is currently writing. Eileen Julien would like to thank Susan Andrade, Biodun Jeyifo, Micheline Rice-Maximin and Kalidou Sy for their comments on her chapter. Julia Waters's chapter appeared, in an earlier form, in *Remembering Empire* (Society for Francophone Postcolonial Studies, 2002), pp. 98–115.

Note on quotations from French
When a French-language text exists in a readily available English-language translation, we have endeavoured to provide the title and other quoted material from this. In all other cases, quotations are provided in the original French, with a translation provided by the author of each individual chapter.

Introduction: the case for Francophone Postcolonial Studies

BY CHARLES FORSDICK AND DAVID MURPHY

In 1989, François Maspero and the photographer Anaïk Frantz undertook an unorthodox voyage by rail through the Parisian 'banlieue' [suburbs]. The account of their journey, *Roissy-Express* (1994 [1990]), describes the effects of unexpected deceleration as the travellers disrupt the customary commute down the suburban RER-B line, restricting their movement to one stop a day, alighting and exploring the area surrounding each station. Maspero, best known as the publisher of radical anti-colonial authors such as Frantz Fanon (see Maspero 2002), undermines in his text the spatial homogeniza-tion that results from a traditional Paris–banlieue split. The city's peripheral spaces are re-endowed with a diversity – historical, cultural, ethnic – that official versions of them tend to deny. The account restores dignity to marginalized populations of immigrant origin and represents a sustained reflection on the ethics of postcolonial hospitality (Ben Jelloun 1984; Rosello 2001, 68–81). That Maspero takes seriously France's status as a postcolonial nation is striking, for the journey occurs against the backdrop of the bicentenary of the French Revolution, the first of a rash of assertively national commemorations by which the last decade of twentieth-century France was characterized.

In 'Entre histoire et mémoire', the 1984 introduction to his monumental collection of essays *Les Lieux de mémoire*, Pierre Nora had called for a reassertion of popular memory in the forging of national identity (1997, I, 23–43); by the time he came to write his postface, 'L'Ère de la commémora-tion', in 1992, his initial optimism had been tempered by a sense that the unevenness of historical process had in the late twentieth century been transformed into the consensus of commemoration (1997, III, 4687–719). What Nora fails to acknowledge – and what a number of critics have subsequently pointed out (Tai 2001; Derderian 2002) – is the contribution of his own selection of 'sites of memory' to a particular aspect of this consensus. For Nora's concept of Frenchness is nation-centred, tied closely to the geography of the Hexagon; there is only fleeting recognition of the role played by colonial expansion in the formation of national and Republican identity (Ageron 1997). In this way, Nora's volumes reflect French commemorative practice. Certain aspects of twentieth-century colonial history – the 1931 Exposition coloniale at Vincennes (discussed by several contributors to this volume: Forsdick, Ezra, Hargreaves, Chapters 4, 5 and 13 respectively, and reflected in the illustration on the cover), the massacre of North African demonstrators by the Parisian police on 17 October 1961, the independence won by Algeria in 1962 – have been remembered in France only reluctantly, with attempts at commemoration (or, more accurately, recovery from amnesia) marked with controversy; and although more distant events, such as the abolition of slavery in 1848, have been deemed worthy of official commemoration, celebrations have tended to propagate a one-sided, specifically French version of them. The 1998 celebrations of the 150th anniversary of abolition, for instance, presented the end of slavery as the product of metropolitan philanthropy, conveniently forgetting both the slaves' own agency and the fact that this was abolition for the second time. As the contributions by Little and Dubois to this volume remind us (see Chapters 1 and 2), slaves were freed for the first time under the Convention in 1794, but the 200th anniversary of this event (subsequently deemed historically inconvenient) was eclipsed by commemoration of the Liberation in 1994. Indeed, it was the two European wars that dominated late twentieth-century French memory, so much so that the historian Henri Rousso identified an almost obsessive 'Vichy syndrome' (1987) that has been seen by some commentators as the result of an active suppression of colonial memory (Donadey 1996, 218). These two strands of contemporary history do meet – in events such as the massacre in Sétif in 1945 or the trial of Maurice Papon for crimes against humanity – but, despite the efforts of filmmakers such as Ousmane Sembene (*Camp de Thiaroye*, 1988) or Bertrand Tavernier (*La Vie et rien d'autre*, 1989), the colonial dimension of the First and Second World Wars – as well as the contribution of colonial troops to French war efforts – has itself been largely ignored.

These uneven processes of recollection and amnesia are symptomatic of more general questions relating not only to contemporary France and other French-speaking cultures but also to the ways in which knowledge about them is constructed (see Tévanian 2001, 109–33). For such Eurocentric (or France-centred) versions of history are dependent on similarly subjective and selective epistemic orthodoxies. Although, after the Evian Accords of 1962, France and Algeria might for very different reasons have longed to present the end of the war as a clean-break settlement allowing the divergence and subsequent autonomous existences of former colonizer and former colonized, such aspirations were clearly utopian. Although both countries were henceforth chronologically 'post-colonial', their relationship remained a 'postcolonial' one, influenced by continued demographic displacement, by the pressures of neocolonial politics, by the troubled legacy of the French language, by a reluctantly shared history repressed and yet constantly threatening to return (Stora 1991). As the illustrations on the cover of this volume suggest, the interplay between the colonial past and the post-colonial present reflects unfinished processes of representation and remembrance. In this context, various commentators have noted that the discourse surrounding France's World Cup victory in 1998 – with star player Zinedine Zidane, son of Algerian immigrants, leading the way – contained strong echoes of the discourse of Empire, which praised those of France's 'foreign' peoples who contributed to the glory of 'la Plus Grande France' [Greater France] (Ezra 2000, 145–53; Blanchard *et al.* 2001, 49).

The specific circumstances of the Franco-Algerian relationship are supplemented and illuminated by a series of other colonial and postcolonial axes suggesting that in the wake of the French Empire there remains a complex network of French-speaking (or, in certain cases, partially French-speaking) regions, countries and communities which together form a Francophone space. As Gabrielle Parker's contribution to this volume shows (Chapter 8), the official French version of this phenomenon – or at least of a substantial part of this phenomenon – is 'la Francophonie', a group of French-speaking countries/regions through whose cultural, diplomatic and commercial connections France maintains its opposition to what it perceives as the ever-increasing influence of English-speaking cultures. Derek Walcott's attack on what he styles 'Franco-phoney' reflects criticism not only of this institution but also of France's attitude to its former colonial possessions. Use of the epithet 'Francophone' itself – in phrases such as 'littérature francophone' [Francophone literature], referring to all literature written in French except that produced in France itself – suggests a neo-colonial segregation and a hierarchization of cultures that perpetuates the binary divides on which, despite the rhetoric of a 'civilizing mission', colonialism depended for its expansion and consolidation.

Over the past few decades, many scholars – both in France and elsewhere – have begun to address the issues outlined above, not only exploring colonial culture and history from a post-colonial vantage point but also addressing the socio-political and linguistic situations or cultural products that have emerged before and after the formal influence of French colonialism was replaced by more complex interrelationships. The essays that make up this volume have been commissioned to reflect the principal new directions in this scholarship. At the same time the book offers consolidation of, and a certain coherence to, the diverse lines of enquiry that make up this field. We have decided to divide the project of a Francophone Postcolonial Studies into four main strands. A fifth, involving postcolonial comparatism and implicit in a number of chapters here (such as Ní Loingsigh, Chapter 14, or Stafford, Chapter 15), is a logical extension of this collection's aims and will be outlined below. Part I is devoted to the exploration of the historical perspectives necessary for an understanding of current postcolonial issues, outlining a more complex and chronologically ambitious genealogy of Francophone postcoloniality than is often admitted; contributions will address material spanning a period from the sixteenth century to the present day (from Montaigne to the work of the contemporary Caribbean 'créolité' movement) and covering many of the principal geographical regions touched by French colonial expansion. Part II, central to a volume whose principal focus is language-specific, explores the role of the French language in postcolonial debates, considering not only the impact of indigenous cultures on this externally imposed means of communication but also the ways in which the external influence of decolonization has impacted on France's own marginalized minority languages. The language issue is especially important in relation to the colonial and postcolonial history of France, as a French-language education was seen as the key to France's 'civilizing mission' in the colonies (see Murphy, Chapter 20; see also Julien, Chapter 11, on the complex relationship between orality and French in Africa); the organization of a French 'commonwealth' around a shared linguistic identity in la Francophonie is a clear illustration of this. The tensions between nation and globalization, and the development of new postcolonial axes in contemporary Francophone cultures, are addressed in Part III; chapters here, considering the strains imposed on a postcolonial Republican identity, are complemented by others exploring the ways in which individuals and ideas 'travel' between different Francophone spaces, producing new cultural matrices and political contexts. Part IV, focused on postcolonial thought and culture in the Francophone world, combines attention to specific regions – Quebec, sub-Saharan Africa, North Africa, the Caribbean, 'Indochina' (this latter contribution also serving to problematize the postcolonial relationship between metropolitan France and one of its former colonies) – with a more general consideration of issues relating to theory and gender, as well as the evolution within a predominantly Anglophone postcolonial theory of concepts originating in a Francophone context.

For the discipline of 'Postcolonial Studies' has emerged predominantly within English literature departments over the past two decades. In the late 1980s, there was an attempt to produce a synthesis of this new field of research in the landmark text, *The Empire Writes Back* (Ashcroft, Griffiths, Tiffin 1989). The authors used the term 'post-colonial' 'to cover all the culture affected by the imperial process from the moment of colonization to the present day' (1989, 2), and included a wide range of former colonies – from the United States and Ireland to the recently independent nation states of Asia and Africa – within the remit of Postcolonial Studies. They went on to argue that '[post-colonial literatures] emerged in their present form out of the experience of colonization and asserted themselves by foregrounding the tension with the imperial power, and by emphasizing their differences from the assumptions of the imperial centre' (2). However, this extremely broad definition of Postcolonial Studies has been both enabling and highly controversial. Aijaz Ahmad, in particular, has argued that '"postcolonial criticism" privileges as primary the role of colonialism as the principle of structuration in [the colonized's] history, so that all that came before colonialism becomes its own prehistory and whatever comes after can only be lived as infinite aftermath' (1996, 281). This critique of *The Empire Writes Back* is also one that has often been levelled at Postcolonial Studies as a whole, namely that it produces an over-generalized, Eurocentric framework, which is inattentive to the specifics of colonialism in different imperial contexts. There have also been increasing criticisms of *The Empire Writes Back* from a 'Francophone' perspective: Celia Britton and Michael Syrotinski argue that the book's attempt to define the boundaries of a new academic subject within English Studies led to the exclusion of non-English material from the postcolonial paradigm (2001, 4–5). We shall return to each of these criticisms below.

The criticisms of Postcolonial Studies – from within and without the discipline – have often veiled the positive aspects of the development of this field. English literature departments have been engaged in a remarkable revision of the literary canon, opening up the study of literatures from, principally, Africa and Asia, thus leading to an effective decentring of English Studies. Critics have also returned to the 'classics' of nineteenth- and twentieth-century English literature, and not simply the 'compromised' texts of colonial adventure stories – following Edward Said's model in *Culture and Imperialism* (1993) – in order to assess the ways in which the discourse of empire informs their literary vision. The debates on the use of the hyphenated form 'post-colonial' to refer to that which comes chronologically after colonialism, leaving 'postcolonial' to refer to a contemporary assessment of the culture and history of empire from the moment of conquest, have shown a willingness on the part of Postcolonial Studies to refine the object of its research in the light of criticisms of earlier definitions (see Ashcroft 1996). Each of the chapters in this volume follows this distinction between the hyphenated and non-hyphenated forms of the word, while also seeking to problematize these definitions. Particularly difficult to establish is the chronological categorization. While most colonies gained their independence in the aftermath of the Second World War, Haiti and Canada ceased to be French colonies long before this. As Laurent Dubois argues in his chapter on the Haitian Revolution (Chapter 2), 'Haiti was post-colonial decades before much of the rest of the world was colonial' (see also Bongie, Chapter 3, and Dash, Chapter 21). The situation in Francophone Canada, in which a white, French settler population has been dominated by a white, British settler population for two centuries, is equally complex (see Randall, Chapter 7, and Chapman, Chapter 22). Finally, the situation of the DOM-TOMs, those former French colonies such as Martinique and Guadeloupe, which have chosen to be 'integrated' into the former colonial centre rather than opting for independence, provide a singular framework within which to discuss the attempt to forge 'post-colonial' identities (see McCusker, Chapter 10, and Dash, Chapter 21). As will be argued below, these cases are the result of very specific colonial histories, which do not seem to correspond directly to any equivalent history in the Anglophone world, and which must consequently be more carefully analysed in order to escape the worst generalizing tendencies of postcolonial theory.

Unlike other literary or cultural theories, it seems difficult to speak of a specific approach or key set of ideas that mark out a distinctive post-colonialism in the way that one might speak of Marxism, poststructuralism or feminism. In fact, postcolonial theory borrows heavily from other theoretical -isms, which it then applies to the field of Postcolonial Studies: as Jeannie Suk claims in her study of Francophone Caribbean writing, '"Postcolonial" then, becomes a contractual indicator of a practice of reading that accentuates the commonality of the problems that arise from colonialism' (2001, 19). Although our theoretical sympathies will no doubt appear obvious from our own contributions to this volume, we have sought to reflect the full range of Postcolonial Studies in our choice of contributors for this book.

Three main theorists have emerged as the leading figures within the field, representing different strands across the theoretical spectrum: Edward Said, Gayatri Spivak and Homi Bhabha. Through his major studies, *Orientalism* (1978) and *Culture and Imperialism* (1993), Said has been central to the reassessment of 'classic' texts from the Western canon (his work is discussed by Forsdick, Chapter 4, P. Williams, Chapter 16, and McLeod, Chapter 17). Said's work has been highly influential but his relatively 'traditional' historical readings of literary texts have met with much criticism from more 'theoretical' critics, particularly those engaged in poststructuralist reading practices, who have come to form the most important group within Postcolonial Studies over the past decade. Both Spivak and Bhabha belong to this latter strand of postcolonial thought, although Spivak's work is in fact very difficult to pin down, owing debts to Marxism, feminism, and deconstruction (for a discussion of Spivak's work, see McLeod, Chapter 17, and Donadey, Chapter 18). An English-language translator of Derrida, Spivak often appears the archetypal post-Marxist, who is highly attentive to issues of class, but refuses to prioritize this over issues of race or gender, and whose work is centrally concerned with the problematic nature of representation. Finally, Homi Bhabha is perhaps the critic whose work has been most central to the development of postcolonial theory in the past decade. His essays are deeply informed by Lacanian psychoanalytical theory and Derridean deconstruction, and his work has consistently promoted the notion of 'hybridity' – as did the authors of *The Empire Writes Back* – as the central concern of Postcolonial Studies. (This excessive focus on 'post-colonial hybridity' has been heavily criticized: see Ahmad 1992; Shohat 1992; and several contributors to this volume.)

In recent years, many critics have come to argue that the rise of the Said–Spivak–Bhabha triumvirate, consistently anthologized in Postcolonial Studies readers, is a sign of the potential stagnation of the field. In this view, the development of a 'star-system' of critics is mirrored by a 'star-system' of authors – Rushdie, Naipaul – whose work is seen as quintessentially 'postcolonial'. The dangers of Postcolonial Studies becoming trapped in a process of anthologization/exoticization, or what Graham Huggan has called 'marketing the margins' (Huggan 2001), is a very real one. However, we would argue that the main problem with Postcolonial Studies is its (often unacknowledged) focus on the British colonial experience. As it is currently constituted, Postcolonial Studies refers almost exclusively to 'Anglophone' Postcolonial Studies, or, to cite Harish Trivedi's stinging rebuke, 'the postcolonial has ears only for English' (1999, 272). In an incisive (posthumously published) overview of Postcolonial Studies, the French critic Jacqueline Bardolph rightly highlights the assumptions made even by insightful Anglophone critics such as Elleke Boehmer about the applicability of their ideas to a non-Anglophone context (Bardolph 2001, 8; see also Apter 1995; Britton and Syrotinski 2001, 5; Forsdick 2001a; this point is also echoed in many chapters in this volume).

It is this assessment of the Anglophone 'bias' of Postcolonial Studies that has guided us in choosing the title of this volume, and more widely of the field we are attempting to outline, a field in which the 'Francophone dimension' of Postcolonial Studies can be fully explored. However, coupling the word 'Francophone' with 'postcolonial' may at first seem slightly problematic, as in much current usage the two terms are used to describe parallel fields, as though 'Francophone Studies' was a completely separate field of research to 'Postcolonial Studies'. On the contrary, we would argue that Francophone Studies is engaged in the same intellectual pursuits as Postcolonial Studies, exploring 'postcolonial issues' in relation to France and its former colonies (this has largely been the understanding of Francophone Studies in North America, throughout the past decade). The term 'Francophone' is in itself highly problematic, as it is used interchangeably in so many contexts – political, linguistic, cultural – that its precise meaning is unclear and elusive for many people (see Parker, Chapter 8; see also Murphy 2002). As was argued above, despite the 'inclusive' impulse of many working within Francophone Studies who seek to promote the study of non-metropolitan 'French' cultures, the use of the term 'Francophone' has often involved an 'exclusionary' gesture, which is used to emphasize ethnic or racial 'difference' from a perceived 'French norm', with metropolitan France rigorously excluded from deliberations of Francophone Studies. This constitutes heavy baggage for the word but we would argue that this is precisely the moment to 'decolonize' the term, emphasizing that 'Francophone' refers to all cultures where French is spoken, including, of course, France itself (Murphy 2002). In so doing, we aim to develop a genuine dialogue between Francophone Studies and Postcolonial Studies. If the latter has largely ignored Francophone material, the former has often been deeply suspicious of postcolonial theory, which has been seen as an 'Anglo-Saxon' (i.e. North American/British) cultural model. Consequently, many works on the 'Francophone world' have primarily been based on geographical or linguistic criteria, and do not attempt to theorize the legacy of French colonialism (Combe 1995; Beniamino 1999). The suspicion of 'postcolonialism' is exemplified by the attitude of the French cultural activist and travel writer Michel Le Bris, who dismisses Said's *Orientalism* as 'l'hystérisation de toute pensée, le refus de toute complexité, de toute nuance' [the hystericization of all thought, the refusal of any complexity or nuance] (1995, 197). As Antoine Compagnon has perceptively argued, after the theoretical revolution of the 1960s and 1970s, many French literary critics (and more generally critics in the French-speaking world) have focused on establishing standard, 'universal' practices of textual analysis. They have accordingly been deeply suspicious of 'radical, Anglo-Saxon' theories such as postcolonialism, queer theory and cultural studies, with their 'historical' and often overtly committed readings of literary works (Compagnon 2000).

   One of the ironies of this 'French' reluctance to engage with postcolonial theory is that the postcolonial debate was, in part, launched by anti-colonial French-language writers such as Aimé Césaire, Frantz Fanon, Albert Memmi and Jean-Paul Sartre, and there is an ongoing (if not always acknowledged) dependence on Francophone material, as is witnessed by the reliance on poststructuralist thinkers such as Derrida, Foucault and Lacan. There are signs that Anglophone postcolonial critics are beginning to address this Francophone dimension of their discipline. In an important new development, the prominent postcolonial critic Robert Young has recently attempted to uncover these 'Francophone origins' of postcolonial theory by situating the work of theorists such as Fanon within their original historical context rather than assuming that theirs are 'free-floating' ideas applicable in all contexts, as has often been the case in Postcolonial Studies (Young 2001). Young has also sought to uncover the 'postcolonial location' of the work of important poststructuralist critics such as Derrida, Cixous and Foucault, each of whom has been central to much postcolonial theory. John McLeod's contribution to this volume (Chapter 17) takes issue with Young's stance, however, claiming that the attempt to restrict such theories to the 'original meaning' of their Francophone context is deeply flawed, and ignores the work of Said (1991 [1983], 2000 [1994]) and others on the ability of such theories to 'travel' and take on new meanings. While welcoming Young's manoeuvre, we at least partially share McLeod's reservations, which have also been expressed by Celia Britton and Michael Syotinski, who stress that: 'The point is not that we need to uncover hidden genealogies allowing us to trace the roots of both postcolonial theory and *francophonie* to shared French origins, but rather that it is important to resist assumptions about its identity, and the contexts to which it can or cannot apply' (2001, 5). The chapters in this volume accordingly seek to define and reassert the Francophone dimension of Postcolonial Studies, seeking to test the assumptions of Anglophone postcolonial theory against the 'realities' of the Francophone world, while also exporting its own ideas – see for example the chapters by Dash (Chapter 21) and Donadey (Chapter 18), which present important Francophone theories on identity in the Caribbean and on feminist history that are not always well known in the Anglophone world. This volume seeks to launch this dialogue, not least by providing a valuable source book for those working in English who are not always aware of developments in the Francophone world, and who often only have access to the small number of texts available in translation.

Developing this dialogue will inevitably necessitate the widening of the debate to include more French scholars. One cannot underestimate the role of Republican ideology in shaping French resistance to postcolonialism. Since the French Revolution, French national identity has rested on the abstract notion of citizenship, which claims to transcend issues of race, gender and class, in order to create a society of equal citizens. Many French intellectuals are deeply distrustful of any cultural development that appears to threaten the cherished 'universal' values of the Republic – as is argued by Rosello (Chapter 12) and Hargreaves (Chapter 13) elsewhere in this volume. In presenting the case for Francophone Postcolonial Studies, we are not simply advocating the unproblematic adoption of an 'Anglo-Saxon' multicultural model (French scholars sometimes think that postcolonialism is just a vague, liberal, 'politically correct' movement that is uncritically in favour of multiculturalism). Multiculturalism has its own inadequacies, and these have been charted by many within Postcolonial Studies (JanMohamed and Lloyd 1986). However, just as the problems of 'multiculturalism' have been addressed, so too must those of Republicanism, which has often supported exclusively white (male) notions of Frenchness. As Alice Conklin has argued, French Republicanism was partly shaped by the French colonial experience and this tension between universalism and ethnocentrism has yet to be examined fully (Conklin 1997). Conklin's work has heavily influenced the French historians in ACHAC (Blanchard *et al.* 1998, 2001, 2002; Bancel *et al.* 2002), and, more widely, there has been a growing exploration of the legacy of colonialism on French culture (Ross 1995; Mouralis 1999; in this volume, see Laurent Dubois's arguments about the influence of the Haitian Revolution on French conceptions of Republicanism, Chapter 2, and H. Williams on the influence of anti-colonial theory on regional movements in France, Chapter 9).

It is extremely revealing to examine the parallel developments of Francophone Studies and Postcolonial Studies over the past two decades. In France itself, Francophone Studies remains a marginalized field of activity within French Literature departments – indeed, it is often relegated to Comparative Literature departments – and its development has been dependent on the activities of committed but often isolated individual researchers whose work displays many parallels with Anglophone postcolonial criticism (although some of these critics would themselves reject the epithet 'postcolonial' for their work): on sub-Saharan African literature, see Borgomano (1998), Chevrier (1974), Mouralis (1984, 1993) and Nkashama (1989, 1997); on North African literature, see Bonn (1974, 1985), Brahimi (1998), Gontard (1981, 2000) and Khatibi (1983a, 1987; his work is discussed by Woodhull, Chapter 19); on Caribbean literature, see Antoine (1992), Condé (1979) and Fonkoua (2002); on the representation of 'other cultures' in French literature, see Moura (1992a, 1992b), Todorov (1993 [1989]) and Yee (2000). However, only in the past few years have French critics begun to engage seriously with 'postcolonial theory'. Jean-Marc Moura's introductory survey (1999) was an important development, providing French-language critics with their first overview of this field, although, perhaps due to the breadth of his task, his vision of Postcolonial Studies is in places slightly schematic, and does not always take account of the internal questioning of the discipline that has taken place. Jacqueline Bardolph's brief, but extremely incisive, account of postcolonial theory (2001) offers a clearer glimpse of the potential for dialogue between Anglophone and Francophone critics (interestingly, Bardolph worked within English literary studies in France, which has often been heavily engaged in postcolonial debates).

French departments throughout the Anglophone world have made greater efforts than their French counterparts to open themselves to non-Hexagonal 'French' cultures over the past two decades (although Francophone Studies has often been seen as a supplement to traditional 'French' courses, bearing little relation to 'French Studies', rather than as a questioning of our understanding of what the object and parameters of French Studies should be). Anglophone critics of Francophone cultures have also been more active in engaging with postcolonial theory than their Francophone counterparts (no doubt, in part, due to the limited access to postcolonial texts in French translations): however, the vast array of introductions to Postcolonial Studies, as well as postcolonial readers, that now exists within English Studies, and which is perhaps the clearest indication of the by now established position of Postcolonial Studies on undergraduate programmes – see, to name but a few of the best works, Williams and Chrisman (1993), Boehmer (1995), Moore-Gilbert (1997), McLeod (2000), Young (2001) – is not yet matched by a similar depth of work in Francophone Studies.

None the less, there does now exist a large body of work exploring the 'postcolonial' problematics within Francophone Studies. Much of this work was pioneered in North America by critics such as Emily Apter (1999) and Françoise Lionnet (1989, 1995a). Interestingly, Lionnet's concern with gender issues helped to place feminism at the heart of much Francophone postcolonial thought, whereas Anglophone Postcolonial Studies has often been accused of overlooking issues of gender. For example, in the mid-1990s, leading English-language scholars contributed to a volume that sought to explore the links between postcolonial women's writing in a wide range of Francophone spaces (see Green *et al.* 1996; see also Woodhull 1993; Hitchcott 2000; Haigh 2000; Donadey 2001; gender issues are dealt with in many of the chapters in this volume). Equally, in Britain (and other Anglophone countries), interest in Francophone Postcolonial Studies has hugely expanded in the past decade. Several years ago, Alec Hargreaves and Mark McKinney (1997) brought together North American and British academics to explore postcolonial issues in relation to contemporary French culture, and we see our volume as a continuation of those efforts, but opening them up to a wider field of enquiry. The experts gathered together in this volume represent some of the leading figures in the field, and their work illustrates the growing complexity and variety of research in this area. As well as outlining the geographical boundaries of the postcolonial world, there have been efforts to develop a more complex genealogy of Francophone Postcolonial Studies: see for example, Roger Little's *Autrement Mêmes* series (published by L'Harmattan), Azzedine Haddour's translation of Sartre (2001 [1964]), Christopher Miller's work on the 'prehistory' of Negritude (Miller 1998), or Bill Marshall's 'French Atlantic' project (his *Encyclopaedia of the French Atlantic* will be published in 2004), each of which attempts to recover work ignored by Anglophone and recent Francophone postcolonialism. Perhaps, most importantly, we are now witnessing the emergence of theoretical works by authors within Francophone Studies, which provide a comparative analysis of postcolonial concerns in relation to works from both Anglophone and Francophone contexts. For instance, in his excellent study of postcolonialism, Nicholas Harrison (2003) shifts between discussion of Joseph Conrad, Assia Djebar and Driss Chraïbi, and consistently stresses the need to analyse the differences between different experiences of empire, as well as the gap between colonial rhetoric and colonial 'realities'.

A number of Francophone paradigms have gained a dominant position in postcolonial discussions. The notion of 'créolité' that has been developed in the French Caribbean is one of the few Francophone theories to have been integrated into the Anglophone postcolonial debate. Understandably, Algeria, with its long, interlaced history with France has been the object of much attention, particularly in France (see Cixous 1996, 1998; Daeninckx 1984; Derrida 1998a [1996]). Also, as was mentioned above, Canada and Haiti offer two extremely distinctive postcolonial models that do not allow easy generalizations regarding the meaning of the 'postcolonial'. However, it is important to avoid a situation whereby there is a theoretical reliance on a small number of dominant models – as is often argued about the preponderance of Anglophone theories based on Indian experiences of empire. It is vital that Francophone Postcolonial Studies engages with the full diversity of the Francophone world, including 'marginal/peripheral' Francophone sites such as 'Indochina' (see Yeager 1987; Cooper 2001; see Waters, Chapter 23, for an important exploration of the postcolonial relationship between France and 'Indochina'), and the island cultures of the Pacific (Devatine 1998; Scemla 2001; regrettably, the chapter we commissioned on 'Indochina' and 'Francophone island cultures' had to be omitted from this volume due to circumstances beyond our control).

There is a risk, therefore, that just as (Anglophone) Postcolonial Studies has been dominated by certain theoretical or regional paradigms, so might the fully diverse potential of Francophone Postcolonial Studies be eclipsed by prominent trends in scholarship that, although specific to the circumstances of their production, are granted more of a portability and general applicability than their detail permits. Yet the emergence of Francophone Postcolonial Studies as a discrete field entails another potentially more serious pitfall of which the editors of this volume are acutely aware. Until recently, much scholarship on the Caribbean archipelago – with some notable exceptions – has tended to be produced according to the dominant languages spoken within the region, with the result that a polyglossic, pan-Caribbean space is fragmented into smaller spaces still defined along transatlantic axes in relation to their former colonial occupiers. Michael Dash has advocated the more sustained recognition of 'the Other America' (1998), a Caribbean space described, in the light of Édouard Glissant's thinking, in relational and cross-cultural terms. There is a risk that Francophone Postcolonial Studies might repeat the practices of Caribbean scholarship, but with this separatist tendency writ large, i.e. that a parallelism might be suggested where in fact comparatism is essential.

This volume has only aimed to map territory and suggest directions for future research. We have already stressed above that a major development in the future of Francophone Postcolonial Studies must involve the dialoguing with – or 'travelling' towards – work in other postcolonial traditions that John McLeod advocates in his contribution to this collection (Chapter 17). The more active promotion of a comparatist dimension in postcolonial criticism is a logical development. For the commonly accepted foundational text of postcolonialism discussed above, Edward Said's *Orientalism*, is itself the work of a comparatist heavily influenced by French-language material whose indifference to postcolonial theory (and hostility to its excesses) is well documented (Williams 2001). What Said's ambiguous position vis-à-vis postcolonial thought suggests, however, is that the epistemic shift implied by this body of work emerges itself from a comparatist tradition. Susan Bassnett (1993) was one of the first to present postcolonialism as comparative literature's contemporary avatar, and Franco Moretti (2000) has at least outlined a comparatism that moves beyond its traditionally Eurocentric focus. Their comments are illuminated by responses to the 1993 Bernheimer report on 'Comparative Literature at the Turn of the Century' – and especially by those made by scholars instrumental in the emergence of Francophone Postcolonial Studies, such as Emily Apter and Françoise Lionnet (see Bernheimer 1995). One of the first explicit efforts to offer a comparative postcolonialism (Bery and Murray 1999) results more in the juxtaposition of intellectual traditions rather than their interpenetration, although some insightful historical research has endeavoured to compare colonial practices and traditions (see, for example, Baumgart 1982; August 1985; Cooper and Stoler 1997; Clancy-Smith and Gouda 1998).

It is the comparative project that casts light on the usefulness of Francophone Postcolonial Studies, for this appellation ultimately does not apply to a discipline in competition with Postcolonial Studies or to a mono-lingual subfield of that discipline. Francophone Postcolonial Studies exists as a challenge to any exclusive definition of the postcolonial. The acknowl-edgement of a Francophone postcoloniality allows sustained attention to the non-European cultural contexts and products that have emerged from French imperialism; it encourages at the same time, as works such as Jane Bradley Winston's *Postcolonial Duras* (2001) demonstrate, the re-visiting of material once considered exclusively metropolitan (see Haddour, Chapter 6, on Camus, and Waters, Chapter 23, on Duras); and it also permits, as Jacqueline Bardolph suggests (2001), comparison of situations emerging from different colonial traditions, attenuating the risks of generalization and ensuring the grounding of postcolonial reflections in specific situations.

This volume is inspired by such aspirations. Far from representing a quixotic effort to reclaim postcolonial theory for French-language specialists, it aims to highlight the Francophone contribution to the emergence of this body of thought, while also suggesting the ways in which a more rigorous application of postcolonial thinking to French-language material might allow a more coherent understanding of Francophone post-coloniality to emerge. Postcolonial theory, like its objects of study, cannot be a pure product. It is, in Robert Young's terms, a 'franglais mixture' (2001, 18) whose internationalist origins in the struggles of decolonization have been supplemented by Marxist theory and poststructuralist thought. Postcolonialism has 'travelled' in the Saidian sense of the word (Said 1991, 226), and the Francophone dimensions of these constructive journeys – international, transatlantic, transcontinental – highlight the appropriateness of applying the critique of knowledge it permits to French-language products and contexts. (The contributions by Forsdick, Ní Loingsigh and Stafford, Chapters 4, 14 and 15 respectively, emphasize the importance of 'travel' as a key trope of Postcolonial Studies.) The urgency of such an enterprise can be seen in the first volume of the journal *Interventions*, in which there is one article on 'Postcolonialisms and the Latin Americas' (Vieira 1999), but where the one Francophone contributor notes that there is not 'in the francophone arena any delimitation of a special discipline that would correspond to "postcolonial studies"' (Hountondji 1998, 28).

This book is part of a continuing effort to prise open postcolonialism and move beyond the Anglophone stranglehold that processes of anthologiza-tion – Peter Hallward, for instance, describes a rapidly ageing discipline, generating 'academic souvenirs' (2001, 336) – imposed on the field in the late 1990s. One of its aims is to present French and Francophone Studies as an exporter of ideas rather than the net importer it is usually understood to be. Its principal aim, however, is to instigate and sustain dialogue between those working in the varied and often hitherto autonomous areas of post-colonialism. The range of contributors reflects this primary ambition, for, although many are indeed associated with French and Francophone Studies (itself of course an interdisciplinary site of enquiry), others have approached the Francophone postcolonial problematic from an Anglophone post-colonial perspective. In the first issue of the journal *Postcolonial Studies*, the editors claimed: 'postcolonialism is not a new discipline, nor an entirely identifiable field of research. [A] gesture rather than a demarcation, [it] points not towards a new knowledge, but rather towards an examination and critique of knowledges' (Seth *et al.* 1998, 8). This volume is cast in the spirit of this definition, suggesting that its implications ultimately contribute not only to disciplinary shifts but also (and much more importantly) to an ongoing epistemological evolution. In bringing together critics from a range of disciplines and with a range of approaches, its collaborative aspiration has been, to borrow Jonathan Arac's terms (1997), not to present a 'shop window' of individual contributions but to suggest a more experimental 'laboratory' from which we hope might emerge new ways of approaching material that is specifically French-language or more generally postcolonial – or both of these. Postcolonial Studies must be truly comparative if it is to develop, opening itself up to, among others, French, Dutch, Spanish, Belgian, Portuguese, Japanese, Turkish experiences. We must look beyond certain triumphalist discourses of a globalized, Anglophone uniformity in order to understand better the complexity and diversity – linguistic, cultural, political – of the world in which we live. As the rhetoric of empire seems increasingly to occupy a prominent place in public discourse, the urgency of such a project becomes ever more apparent.

PART

I

HISTORICAL PERSPECTIVES: FROM SLAVERY TO DECOLONIZATION

1

Seeds of postcolonialism: black slavery and cultural difference to 1800

BY ROGER LITTLE

Postcolonialism is an intellectual fashion, and like all 'isms' will in due course become a 'wasm'. Scholars disagree about its scope and meaning: its life will be shorter if, as a critical tool, it is perceived as unclear and confusing, or longer if it appears to reward continuing clarification and exploration.

The term presupposes a viewpoint prompted by the end of colonialism, the high period of which, for France, was roughly 1870–1920. Many have assumed that only texts written after that time (and particularly those by colonized peoples, as in the Negritude movement) – or even after the independence of former colonies – deserve their attention. This is to confuse postcolonialism as a critical stance and post-colonialism (with a hyphen) as a historical era. France embarked on colonization towards the middle of the seventeeth century, so there is every reason to suppose that postcolonialism can profitably explore the colonial and post-colonial from that time onwards. And since colonization was an adventurous encounter with, and an exploitation of, the Other, it was in turn preceded and accompanied by Europeans who stayed at home and reflected on the nature of individual, social and cultural identity. Their stance, one still often found today, used the Other as sounding-board, giving priority to their own preoccupations, something which postcolonialism endeavours to turn on its head. But postcolonialism has probed such earlier relationships to good effect and highlighted authors and writings traditionally excluded from the canon. Such revision is salutary and stimulating: it legitimizes the present study as well as the fresh consideration (and therefore republication) of previously neglected texts.

The interactive evolution and particular dosage of theories of economics, justice, religion and politics have, at any given time and place in human history, determined attitudes taken towards the employment of slaves. Only the strong-willed have ever bucked the general trend of the moment. In the ancient world, where citizenship was not dependent on skin colour, slaves were, by force of circumstance, predominantly indigenous. Later, closing ranks, Christians avoided taking slaves of their own persuasion, a position enshrined in law in the sixth century by the emperor Justinian. During the crusades, Saracens and Mahometans were therefore legitimate grist for both slavery and conversion. True to this logic, and supported by spurious arguments drawn from the Book of Genesis (9: 22–5, where Ham is cursed by his father, Noah, for seeing him drunken and naked, as if that were Ham's fault, and as if it were proven that black Africans were descended from Ham), popes had no qualms in declaring Blacks subject to a similar double whammy. The great commercial opportunity came after 1492, when Columbus 'discovered' America – the inverted commas encapsulating the postcolonialist problematization of discovery.

That event, epoch-making in so many ways, was psychologically momentous in that, to echo Malvolio, Europeans had alterity thrust upon them. They were to react as Columbus did from the outset: on the one hand, a new world was revealed to be marvelled at and converted to Christianity, while, on the other, temporal sponsors needed satisfying and there was prospect of gold aplenty. On his second voyage, Columbus already had a coffle of slaves on board. In 1517, at the request of Las Casas, a Dominican prelate, 'Charles V authorised the export of 15,000 slaves to San Domingo, and thus priest and king launched on the world the American slave-trade and slavery' (James 1963 [1938], 4). Commercial motives were tricked out with humanitarian ones. It was purportedly to relieve suffering as well as to save souls that church and state colluded to have slaves taken to the new world from Africa to work the mines and replace the indigenous Caribs who had already succumbed to the rigours of forced labour.

This commercial speculation underpins the imaginative speculation reflected in what primarily interests us here, but some background facts are worth recording. In 1626, the first African slaves were held by the French in the West Indies (Munford 1991, II, 362). Following the creation of the Compagnie française des Îles d'Amérique in 1635, the French landed in Guadeloupe and Martinique, slavery in the West Indies being authorized by Louis XIII the next year. Colbert, Louis XIV's energetic minister, was instrumental in establishing trading companies which led to further colonization. In 1664, for example, he formed the Compagnie du Sénégal et de Guinée, the better to organize the slave trade. It is scarcely surprising that accounts of travel in both Africa and the new world proliferated exponentially and were read avidly as contacts developed from the sixteenth to the eighteenth centuries. They fixed the representational paradigms and stereotypes which remained largely in place until the advent of postcolonialism.

Although France was not historically the first to engage in the exploitation of Blacks in settlements and planter colonies in the Americas, not doing so indeed on any scale until the last quarter of the seventeenth century, after Guadeloupe and Martinique had been declared crown property, it became second only to Britain in what was known as the triangular trade. At its height in the eighteenth century, this was an immensely profitable circuit, and colossal fortunes were made. Each stage brought handsome returns: on the African coast, guns, alcohol, iron bars and trinkets from Europe were traded against prisoners captured in internal wars; the 'middle passage', terminal for them, took them as mere commodities across the Atlantic to be sold to planters; and what they produced – gold rapidly being replaced by coffee, tobacco and, the most labour-intensive, sugar – returned to Europe, where a snobbish fashion for sweet coffee became a habit and a necessity. However much it cost the consumer, it cost the workers who had produced it, quite literally in Helvétius's striking image (*De l'esprit* [1758], Chapter 7), popularized by Voltaire in *Candide* (1759, Chapter 19), an arm and a leg.[1]

Meantime, in 1571, a law had been passed whereby 'there are no slaves in France' (Peabody 1996), mainly meaning that on French soil medieval serfdom had officially come to an end, but also covering the case of imported slaves. Its force would be whittled away only towards the end of the eighteenth century (whereas Granville Sharp introduced just such a law in Britain in 1772). What regulated relations between master and slave in the French colonies was the *Code Noir*, promulgated in 1685, the year of the Revocation of the Edict of Nantes. Just as the latter was intolerant towards Protestants, so the former, under the guise of neutral jurisdiction, gave rights to owners which included violent physical punishment and even the death of their slaves. It is a clear-cut case in which justice and the law are two quite different things. Successive modifications to the *Code Noir*, made largely under pressure from the slave traders and plantation owners, articulate in their own interests, tended towards even greater limitations on slaves who, being illiterate anyway, remained unaware of any rights they might have. The law was not repealed until 1794, only to be reinstated by Napoleon in 1802. Not until the final abolition of slavery in the French colonies, in 1848, did it finally disappear from the statute books.

Legal, commercial and religious attitudes combined to entrench a sense of the white man's superiority, with consequences that still resonate today. Both inferiority and superiority complexes are damaging to psychological and social health. While regulatory laws passed an ocean away could be ignored when found inconvenient, and the benefits of naked self-interest be allowed to override humane considerations on the grounds of an arguable common weal, the greatest paradox lay in the opposing forces, seemingly irreconcilable in the exploitation of black slaves, of Christian principle and

---

[1]   Well-known and frequently republished texts are not listed in the bibliography. Further details may be found in the bibliographies given in Chalaye (1998), Cohen (1980), Hoffmann (1973), Little (2001a), Munford (1991), Seeber (1937) and Todorov (1993 [1989]).

practice: spreading the Word 'legitimized' the spreading of power. The ordinance to convert as many heathen souls as possible and the precept of loving your neighbour as yourself held no sway against the forces of capitalism, itself supported by the biblical parable of the talents (Matthew 25: 14–30). Only Quakers managed to square the circle, acting with exemplary humanity, providing education and decent conditions which proved to be entirely compatible with successful profits (Jones 1911). Ultimately, in all other cases, a minor but manifest biological difference, that of skin colour, reinforced by the deeply rooted symbolism of blackness as evil, was allowed to dominate all other considerations. Although exploitation would take other forms and a legal framework be put in place to guarantee liberty and equality, the persistence of this attitude shows how difficult it is to legislate for fraternity.

The principles of the French Revolution alluded to here are clearly at odds with the ownership and enslavement of other human beings. They are, however, ideals, and they were developed over decades of preliminary debate conducted between, on the one hand, those with vested interests in belittling Blacks, considering them as less than human beings, and, on the other, the 'philosophes' who, even if they sometimes had shares in the slave trade, argued as a matter of principle that, in the terminology of the Revolution still current today, they had human rights. There is and always has been a chasm between Republican idealism and the reality of French policies (see Dubois, Chapter 2).

The most powerful eighteenth-century representations of Blacks and of the arguments surrounding them figure in the literary writings of philosophes and of their like-minded precursors and followers. Montaigne, for example, had shown a willingness to tackle concepts of property and, notably in his essay 'Des cannibales' (1580: *Essais*, I, xxxi), to conduct a sympathetic discussion into the status of otherness, launching irony as an appropriate literary mode for such questions. Lahontan placed the Other at centre stage and injected a new dynamism into the debate about cultural difference. His *Dialogues [avec] un sauvage de l'Amérique* (1990 [1703]) were the result of time spent in North America, and they had a major influence on subsequent debate by the philosophes. Montesquieu, in *Lettres persanes* (1721), likewise gave the Other a voice and, with his greater literary talent, set a powerful fashion. Two foreigners in Paris critique and satirize French society. The famous remark 'Comment peut-on être Persan?' [How can one possibly be Persian?] implying incomprehension at otherness became a catchphrase and resonates to this day. Diderot's *Supplément au voyage de Bougainville*, written in the 1770s, in which Tahitian civilization is shown to be admirable in many ways, continues and reinforces the tradition. Extensively studied by Todorov (1993 [1989]) in *On Human Diversity*, these texts are major stepping stones in the forging of a cultural identity. Even if such writings were more a critique of contemporary French society than a fully informed exposition of another culture, they may fairly be seen from our present perspective as of legitimate interest to a post-colonialist discourse.

While the thrust of financial and imaginative speculation was directed towards the new world, which provided the model for Rousseau's (and, later, Chateaubriand's) noble savage and the object for anti-slavery pleading, Africa remained the largely unexplored origin of wealth-creation. The widespread supposition that Blacks were inferior to Whites and that slavery was somehow their natural condition diverted attention away from Africa to the region where slavery was massively practised. Traders kept to a narrow coastal belt of West Africa. Only in 1799, at the very end of the period covered by this essay, did the world learn of Mungo Park's *Travels in the Interior of Africa* of 1795–7, the first foray into a vast hinterland. Overland journeying to 'black' Africa was blocked by the Sahara; there was no Suez canal; all traffic went by sea down the west coast. Where Portuguese navigators had shown the way in the fifteenth century, other European nations sailed in search of trade and profit, with occasional subsidiary hints, in increasingly numerous travel narratives, of disinterested discovery. It was not until 1639 that France set up its first West African trading post, near the mouth of the Senegal river.

A hundred years later, despite the anonymous author's wayward sense of geography, it is clear that the first black African hero in a French novel, *Histoire de Louis Anniaba* (2000 [1740]), returns to reign over an area upstream from Saint-Louis du Sénégal. In 1724 and again in 1736 and 1738, royal decrees had increased the severity of the *Code Noir*, adding new restrictions on Blacks. One of these was a ban on interracial marriage, and the extraordinary tale of Anniaba, based on historical fact, has him travel to France and after many adventures marry a white Frenchwomen. Cocking a snook at royal edicts in this way doubtless prompted the author's anonymity, but the courage of his convictions stops short of foolhardy confrontation: his hero belongs to a relatively pale-skinned ethnic group (the Fulani, or Peuls) which does not have negroid features and can therefore be taken as Mediterranean in type; and, rather than denouncing the law head on, the author extols the principle of tolerance through various episodes, culminating in a stout defence of religious toleration in Anniaba's kingdom. In other words, the author's preoccupation is less with the Other as such than with attitudes in France. What is most surprising to the modern reader, perhaps, is the complete lack of racism evident in the novel. While we recognize that this is integral to the book's didactic purpose (though it remains primarily a romp of adventure, suspense and derring-do), we may fairly assume that racism as we now understand it was not endemic to eighteenth-century French society (Little 2001a). Rather it took the form of a principled assumption that the Black was non-Christian, then sub-human, then anthropometrically 'proven' to be inferior.

This is clear in Marivaux's play *La Dispute*, first performed in 1744, where black guardians are employed to bring up four children in a state of nature so as to help resolve a dispute – never resolved of course – about whether men or women were the first to be unfaithful. This play-within-a-play had a direct influence on a celebrated modern novel, *La Planète des singes* by Pierre Boulle (1963), not just through its form and its interplay of races, but also through the very name of the key character Mesrou/Mérou (Little 2001b), showing its abiding relevance.

Less ambiguous black heroes entered the field of French awareness shortly after Anniaba, and did so via translation, a factor often neglected in considering the development of preoccupations and tastes. Just as material drawn from Spanish sources had given some of the earliest images of the new world, so the arrival in French, in 1745, of Othello and Oroonoko from Shakespeare and Aphra Behn respectively marked a sea change. As so often happens, the more simplistic hero had the greater impact. Oroonoko became the model of the black rebel leader, his characteristics and even his name being echoed in the representation of Blacks to the present day (see Seeber 1937; Little 2002b). Shakespeare's problematic Caliban has been revived and transformed, especially among West Indian writers, and become an almost inevitable point of reference for postcolonialist scholars. Hard on English heels came one of the hardest-hitting theoretical indictments of slavery in Montesquieu's *De l'esprit des lois* (1748, Book XV), building on his critique in *Lettres persanes*. From the middle of the century onwards, as they became increasingly synonymous with slaves, Blacks would be fore-grounded more and more in philosophical debate and in all the genres of literature.

The purposes of exploring cultural difference, a factor with which post-colonialism has engaged centrally, were well served by a succession of anti-slavery writings and noble savages, the latter acting as a kind of ultimate litmus test for 'civilized' society in the way that extraterrestrials do in modern science fiction. One of the most influential of them, himself influenced by Oroonoko, was Ziméo, the eponymous hero (with an initial Z as marker of his exoticism) of Saint-Lambert's tale of 1769, purportedly narrated by a Quaker. To the time of the Revolution, he provided the model both for subsequent black heroes and, through the first edition's closing authorial 'Réflexions sur l'esclavage', which neatly encapsulate the aboli-tionist position, for much of the ensuing debate, not fully critiqued until James (1963). Those remarks, reprinted in the widely read periodical run by Du Pont de Nemours, *Ephémérides du citoyen, ou Bibliothèque raisonnée des sciences morales et politiques*, include what we now recognize as unscientific old chestnuts but also other points which have not lost their validity (Saint-Lambert 1997 [1769], 21–3).

Hard-headed slave owners generally proved impervious to the blandish-ments of soft-hearted abolitionists, just as realpolitik ignores political idealism. Economic arguments against slavery, intended to strike at the very heart of capitalists' thinking and operations, were frequently deployed. But, as Seeber writes, 'the illusory appeal of free labor was not easy to dispel'

(1937, 93). The eighteenth-century impulse towards classification and categorization led scientists to explore (but never to explain satisfactorily) why Blacks were black (or occasionally albino, an unsettling 'aberration': see Little 1995), why they should be classed as nearer monkey than man, and why therefore they were by definition inferior creatures. Even the embryonic science of genetics could not explain the origins of difference. Many a writer, even those sympathetic to anti-slavery arguments, saw Blacks as fit for work in the tropics in a way that Whites were not, believing on biblical authority that Blacks were 'scorched by the sun' (*New English Bible*, Song of Songs, 1: 6), and felt that the American colonies would have to be abandoned if slavery were abolished. So science, 'reason' and capitalism reinforced each other against Blacks, a phenomenon that continued well into the twentieth century. Montesquieu was eloquent in his principled denunciation, on economic grounds, of such a position, and many 'philosophes', from Mirabeau to Du Pont de Nemours, followed his lead, forcefully echoed in Bernardin de Saint-Pierre's *Voyage à l'île de France* (1773, Chapter 12). Only in 1776, however, did Hilliard d'Auberteuil elaborate the first concerted programme of emancipation (Williams 2002), while the fullest economic argument was presented by Condorcet in his *Réflexions sur l'esclavage des nègres* (1781; Williams 1999). The cost of purchasing and maintaining slaves for a short working life and limited returns, it was demonstrated, exceeded that of even indentured labourers, who drew a wage but were neither bought nor housed, clothed or fed at the landowner's expense.

A hugely influential work went through no fewer than thirty-four editions in half that number of years, expanding as it went and becoming increasingly abolitionist in its stance. That was the *Histoire philosophique et politique du commerce des Européens dans les deux Indes* (1770), its contents reflecting its ambitious title, of which the abbé Raynal was the prime mover but to which Diderot in particular contributed major anti-slavery components. It became a point of reference and a quarry for telling episodes to be recycled in other forms. Pigault-Lebrun, for example, opens his preface to *Le Blanc et le Noir* with the words: 'J'ai lu Raynal, & j'ai écrit cet ouvrage' (Pigault-Lebrun 2001 [1795], 3).

Two enlightened long-term observers of the American scene whose names reveal that their origins lay in France, Hector Saint-John de Crèvecœur and the Quaker Anthony Benezet, were particularly influential among French abolitionists in the 1780s. The former's translation of his *Letters from an American Farmer* (1784) introduced the French to the writings of the latter and included comments on the fact that, since the 1776 Declaration of Independence, emancipation laws had been passed in some states while the importation of negroes had been banned in others (Seeber 1937, 119). Various Abolition Societies were founded, and further writings by French visitors to the United States were to reinforce the impact of American independence on political events in France.

Britain too provided a model driving force against slavery and the slave trade through the powerful writings and activities of abolitionists such as Granville Sharp, Thomas Clarkson and William Wilberforce, and specifically through their creation in 1787 of the Society for Effecting the Abolition of the Slave Trade. The Société des Amis des Noirs was created in Paris the following year by a like-minded group including Brissot de Warville, Mirabeau and the abbé Grégoire, all of whose writings, despite their ambiguities, contributed among others to the gradual change in their compatriots' thinking about the trade in and exploitation of their fellow humans. The 1780s saw an extraordinary proliferation of writings about Blacks, the pendulum swinging increasingly towards respect and all its consequences. The argument drawn from the biblical curse on Ham was increasingly seen as pious nonsense; intellectual inferiority, demonstrated to be the result of slavery rather than of nature, was firmly disproved by negroes and mulattos (still dismissively assimilated to 'Blacks') showing competence in medicine, astronomy, music, fencing, politics, poetry and so forth (though there are no slave narratives in French as there are in English; see Little 2002a); even writers who continued to support the principle of slavery argued for better treatment in the interest of richer returns.

New, better-informed, and more thoughtful books and pamphlets flooded the market towards 1789. Lecointe-Marsillac's *Le More-Lack* (1968 [1789]) is typical in that it encapsulates the point of view of the Société des Amis des Noirs. Its first part has a slave recount his tribulations, whereas the second allows the authorial voice both to rail against injustice and make practical (if at times contentious) proposals for ending it. One such promoted the case for transporting African women in greater numbers not just to satisfy slaves' sexual needs but also to have ready-acclimatized children who would grow into slavery and so save the cost and hassle of importing more. In parallel at the time came libertine novels affording Blacks more central roles than had previously been the case. The presumed animality of negroes led to fantasies about their sexual prowess, so giving rise to a subsidiary form of exploitation in titillating pornography (Little 2001a).

Against this background of fierce argument and increasingly muffled counter-argument came major political developments. The uprising in Saint-Domingue horrified many by its bloody brutality and became the focus of heated debate (on the Haitian Revolution, see Dubois, Chapter 2). (The highly problematic issue of anti-colonial violence would be tellingly revisited by Fanon among others.) It was to have resonances in literature which continue to this day. For strategic reasons, the French envoy granted abolition there in August 1793, scarcely expecting perhaps that it would be generalized by the Convention in February of the following year: 16 pluviôse an II (Biondi and Zuccarelli 1989). But direct representations in the Assembly by articulate mulattos put the seal on the prolonged, intensive lobbying by abolitionists and won the day over the commercial interests of the slavers.

In the proliferation of literature representing Blacks in the decade after the Revolution, no feature was found more consistently than the cruelty meted out to slaves: it provided a foil for dramatic contrast and the lively presentation of articulated argument. Typically, the scenario of Pigault-Lebrun's play, *Le Blanc et le Noir*, has a hands-off plantation owner employ a hands-on manager to ensure his slaves' docility and productivity. No less typically, there emerges from among the negroes an articulate rebel hero, Télémaque. Slaves' names, both real and fictional, were often those of biblical or classical heroes, reminding us particularly that parallels were often explicitly drawn between ancient civilizations and 'barbaric' ones, as in Lafitau's *Mœurs des sauvages américains comparées aux mœurs des premiers temps* (1994 [1724]). Modelled on Ziméo (an approximate anagram of Moïse) and the Spartacus-like black rebel envisaged by Louis-Sébastien Mercier in *L'An 2440, rêve s'il en fut jamais* (1771) – whom others were to see as an anticipation of Toussaint Louverture, the former slave who led the Blacks in Saint-Domingue towards independence as Haitians in 1804, but who, through Napoleon's treachery, never reached that promised land – Télémaque is supported by the soft-hearted (some would say soft-headed) planter's son. His uprising is successful, but his heart is in turn softened by his partner, Zamé, so the planter's life is spared.

Bernardin de Saint-Pierre's play *Empsaël et Zoraïde* – written around 1793 – bucks this trend by reversing the roles: the subtitle is *Les Blancs esclaves des Noirs à Maroc*, irony still serving the enlightened relativist cause well (Bernardin 1995 [1818]). Set in what we now call Agadir, in the kingdom of Marrakesh ('Maroc' as distinct from 'Le Maroc', Morocco), where Bernardin had probably stopped over on his return journey from Mauritius, the plot echoes historical fact. Empsaël, the real prime minister to Moulay Ismaël, was a negro captured in West Africa and transported to Saint-Domingue before escaping back to Africa. There, he participated in the national sport of capturing infidels approaching or leaving the Straits of Gibraltar. We find him surrounded by women so taken, including his French wife, Zoraïde. They and various men are standard representatives of a panoply of nationalities and religious persuasions – French, English, Dutch, Russian, Italian; Muslim, Jew, Catholic, Protestant, Quaker, free-thinker – wordily debating the rights and wrongs of slavery from their different perspectives. Captured one day is Empsaël's former master from Saint-Domingue, now served by Empsaël's brother, whereby the debate is brought to a head. Zoraïde's calming influence prevents bloodshed and everything ends happily. As a convinced abolitionist, Bernardin thus presents the range of sectarian arguments about slavery and encourages humane coexistence.

Abolition was to have no happy ending, at least for the time being. By the time Napoleon reinstituted the *status quo ante* in 1802, the issue was off the agenda. The abbé Grégoire's voice was raised virtually alone until, around 1820, the anti-slavery position was reinstated, to a limited extent, in both political and literary debate. As the nation state swung into a century of

masculine selfishness – self-satisfied productivity and mechanical inventiveness – the humanitarian aspect of exploring cultural difference also took a
back seat, most often occupied by women, whose compassionate percep-
tiveness was little valued. The centralization of Louis XIV's France was reinforced by the sense of the 'République une et indivisible' and a macho
mentality, which had imperial leanings. Rampant colonialism excluded
postcolonialism by definition. As the virgin territory of the dark continent –
as Africa was called, only to become Freud's metaphor for women – was
more intensively 'penetrated', so cranial measurements and the like led to
'scientific' racism. From a postcolonialist viewpoint, the sympathetic
interest in the Other shown in early, often forgotten texts may be no
substitute for giving that Other a full and equal (not to say dominant) voice,
but it would be churlish not to acknowledge the generosity of the impulse
and foolish to ignore the fertile soil in which the seeds of postcolonialism
grew.

2

In search of the Haitian Revolution

BY LAURENT DUBOIS

Where is the Haitian Revolution?

The complex web of suffering and redemption that carries the name of the Haitian Revolution is invoked regularly in some quarters, but conspicuously overlooked in others. It has been, and continues to be, simplified and romanticized, forced to do certain work in broader narratives of slavery, slave resistance, and nationalism, even when it is ill-suited for such work. The lack of archives and historiography on the subject is regularly mentioned, and often exaggerated, even as the existing rich tradition of research and writing on the subject remains little-known or referenced. And the many important lessons to be learned about the Haitian Revolution – about the history of European colonialism, the nature of colonial rule and colonial violence, and the central place of rich traditions of resistance within and against colonialism in the broader history of political culture – are only beginning to take their rightful place in broader debates in colonial and postcolonial studies.

If it is difficult to find, the Haitian Revolution itself is certainly to blame. It rudely undermined the basic assumptions held by many in Europe and the Americas about the nature of enslaved people and the role they had to play in the societies in which they lived (Trouillot 1995). Although it was and remains the ultimate example of slave resistance – indeed the only successful slave revolt in the history of the Americas – it has also been the prisoner of its own success, for the victory of the slaves, and the struggles that followed in its wake, raised many complicated issues not suggested by the many more slave revolts that were crushed. Because it exploded slavery, the Haitian Revolution permits us to see the many differences and fissures that existed within the slave population, militating against easy coherence and any sense that we have finally understood what this institution was, what it did to masters and to slaves, and what courage and imagination were necessary to survive and outlive it.

Facing this history, it is easy to feel overwhelmed, for understanding it requires an understanding of many perspectives: those of the Kongolese who were the majority among the slaves in the colony, along with those who had lived in different parts of West Africa (Thornton 1991 and 1993; Barthélemy 2000); those of the slaves who had been born in the colony; those of men and women who had been slaves in their lifetimes, but were free at the time of the Revolution; those of the men and women of African descent who were born free into a colony saturated with racial discrimination; those of administrators and merchants on both sides of the Atlantic who were often at odds with white planters; those of these white planters who struggled for profit even as their identities were profoundly shaped by their interactions with slavery and slaves. Saint-Domingue was a small colony, but within it were individuals from throughout the world, shaped by broader economic and intellectual processes that were reshaping Europe and the Americas. How are we to find our way through this labyrinth, let alone know where to catalogue it?

It is no accident that two major works about the Haitian Revolution were written by men preoccupied with attacking twentieth-century colonialism. C.L.R. James and Aimé Césaire both thought through the connections and parallels between the event and the anti-colonial struggles in Africa that took place during their own lifetimes (James 1963 [1938]; Césaire 1981 [1961]). They understood that the Haitian Revolution was the first great black anti-colonial revolution, one that struck a major blow to European imperialism, a precursor, as well as a cautionary tale. Haiti was the second nation ever to break away from its European colonizer, but unlike the United States its revolution led to a profound social transformation in the order that had been set up through colonialism. The rulers of independent Haiti had, in many cases, themselves lived as slaves, and they ultimately destroyed the French administration and drove out or killed most of the French residents who had brutally imposed the state on them and the masses of the colony's people. And, although rulers like Toussaint Louverture, before independence, and Christophe and Dessalines afterwards, sought to maintain many aspects of the plantation regime, the ex-slaves struggled, often successfully, to create an independent life for themselves that set in motion a broad economic and social transformation that was ultimately unstoppable. In other words, the Haitian Revolution was both a political and a social revolution, and in this sense a precursor to the Revolutions that many twentieth-century anti-colonial activists hoped (often in vain) would be realized in Africa and Asia – revolutions that not only expelled the colonizing power but also created a radically new, and more equitable, order.

But colonial Saint-Domingue was not twentieth-century Africa. Although the Haitian Revolution was in many ways an African revolution – the majority of those who participated in and lived through it were African-born – they were all exiles, in a world shaped obsessively by the exigencies of the Atlantic plantation economy. They had to make alliances across borders by crafting spaces of autonomy in a colony whose landscape itself was overwhelmed by the slave system. And, when they finally created a new nation, there could be no fantasy of a return to what had come before. Although Haiti's founders sought to reach back to a time before the horrors of European colonialism by using the indigenous Taino name for the island – Ayiti – their very presence there was of course the result of the history they were trying to exorcize. The future of the independent island was circumscribed by the fact that its population and landscape had been shaped to sustain an industrialized plantation zone tied to the Atlantic economy. The racial dynamics of colonial Saint-Domingue continued to shape life in independent Haiti, as conflicts simmered and barriers persisted between lighter-skinned and darker-skinned Haitians. Colonialism haunts post-colonialism everywhere, but it did so in a particularly fierce way in nineteenth-century Haiti (Sheller 2000; Trouillot 1990; Woodson 1990).

In its political culture the Haitian Revolution was in fact quite at home in the eighteenth century. Although the fact that many of its protaganists were slaves, and illiterate, has tended to obscure this fact, it was very much an Enlightenment Revolution. Indeed, it represented the pinnacle of Enlightenment universalism, for it challenged the most extreme and brutal form of oppression in the Atlantic world, and ultimately created a world in which liberty and citizenship were granted to all, regardless of race. As Susan Buck-Morss writes, during the decade of the 1790s, 'the black Jacobins of Saint-Domingue surpassed the metropole in actively realizing the Enlightenment goal of human liberty, seeming to give proof that the French Revolution was not simply a European phenomenon but world-historical in its implications' (2000, 835–6).

As in France, the promise of the revolution was rarely fully realized, and brutality arrived on the same train as egalitarianism and Republicanism. Administrators seeking methods to maintain plantation production found ways to retract rights almost as quickly as they were granted. But this should not overshadow the major political achievement of the Haitian Revolution. Out of individuals who were legally considered property, who had no control over their bodies and over the society that controlled them, it made citizens. While many ex-slaves were unable to exercise their rights, there were large numbers who did, and many who were able to expand the limited rights they were given. It was in Saint-Domingue that the universalism that is usually understood as the inheritance of the French Revolution found its most radical, and perhaps truest, form. It was there that it showed its dramatic promise as a force that could override and transform even the most deep-seated and profitable forms of tyranny. Indeed, the radical universalism that is usually understood as the inheritance of the French Revolution – and which would be used as a justification for French colonialism in the nineteenth century – was deeply shaped by the slaves who struggled for freedom in the Caribbean (Dubois 1998 and 2000; see also Rosello, Chapter 12, for a discussion of universalism). This contribution was screened out and forgotten, and in many ways remains 'unthinkable' (Trouillot 1995). But one can imagine that, in a different configuration of historical knowledge and disciplinary power, the Haitian Revolution would be taken as one of the foundation points for the emergence of human rights and democracy in the modern world.

But how did this remarkable victory come about? The road from slavery to freedom and ultimately national independence was a complicated one, and it encompassed two very different political directions. Starting in the 1760s, and throughout the rest of the eighteenth century, there was a strong push for autonomy on the part of many planters in Saint-Domingue. They chafed against strict metropolitan regulations regarding trade, which forced them to sell their products to France, and regularly flaunted these regulations by engaging in illegal trade with foreign merchants (Frostin 1975). Many were inspired by the achievement of the American Revolution. After 1789, many planters saw the French Revolution as an opportunity to push for more local control, forming local assemblies. One island-wide assembly that met at St Marc in 1790 granted itself the right to make decisions about trade policy, quite a bold move for the time. And they pointedly refused to call themselves a 'colonial' assembly, choosing instead the name 'general assembly', as a way of asserting that they were an autonomous political body that controlled a territory with its own needs (Garrett 1916, 60–1).

Starting in the late 1780s, dreams of increased political independence were propelled by planters' nightmares about the possibility of abolition. The French abolitionists who emerged on the political scene in Paris included several men who came to play an important role in the early years of the Revolution, and many planters saw the metropolitan government of the Revolution as a menace to their world. A strong planter-merchant lobby resisted the abolitionists in Paris, and stalled any action on the question of slavery until after the uprisings in Saint-Domingue in 1791. But they had less success in stopping the demands of free people of African descent from Saint-Domingue who wanted political rights and an end to racist legislation (Geggus 1989b; Benot 1989). Despite the fact that the free-coloureds who were demanding rights were wealthy slave-owners themselves, and for the most part invested in the existence of slavery, most planters saw any breach in the colour line as an inevitable weakening of all of colonial society, and they resisted tooth and nail, refusing to accept even a very limited extension of rights to this group passed by the National Assembly in May 1791. The actions of the National Assembly in favour of free people of colour pushed many planters in Saint-Domingue, who saw the action as a prelude to emancipation, to declare openly that they should seek protection from the British (Geggus 1982).

Before 1789, and during the early years of the Revolution, it was therefore the community of slave-owners that harboured desires for political autonomy, and even independence, from colonial authority. It was the class of white planters that supplied the activists who fought against a metropolitan government that, especially after 1789, they saw as a threat to the existence of slavery, and to their power as slave-holders. In resisting metropolitan authority, they opened the way for an alliance that was ultimately to carry out the destruction they had so feared.

The slave revolt that broke out in August 1791 was remarkable in its organization, speed and spread, and quickly took root in the richest part of Saint-Domingue, the Northern province. Whites, bewildered by the extent of the attack, rallied and fought back, and many expressed confidence that the slave rebels would be defeated within a few months. But, aided by the access to arms they had across the border with Spanish Santo Domingo, and soon by concrete assistance from the Spanish, the slave rebels managed to hold on and defeat the missions sent against them. Divided before the revolt, white society in Saint-Domingue began to disintegrate in the face of it. Already distrustful of the National Assembly and the administrators it sent to the colony, planters increasingly turned to the British for aid, some openly offering to hand the colony over as a way of preserving slavery. Metropolitan administrators who arrived in 1792, particularly one named Léger Félicité Sonthonax, shored up their power by working closely with free people of colour, which angered whites even more. Then, during the course of 1793 a remarkable alliance was forged between Sonthonax and home-grown rebel leaders. Facing the threat of losing the colony to either the Spanish, aided by the slave insurgents they had recruited, or the British, aided by local whites, Sonthonax offered liberty and citizenship to those slave rebels who would fight for him. And, within a few months, he ultimately declared slavery abolished in the North of Saint-Domingue, a declaration soon expanded to the whole colony. In the process, he saved the colony from counter-revolution from within (Fick 1990). Thus, it was the alliance between slave rebels and metropolitan colonial officials that led to the abolition of slavery in Saint-Domingue. This same alliance, celebrated in front of the National Assembly in Paris in February 1794, inspired the abolition of slavery throughout the French colonies (Gauthier 1995).

Liberty was won by the slaves of Saint-Domingue, then, not by attacking French metropolitan authority but by making an alliance with it against planters who were resisting colonial power. Slave rebellion found its ally in metropolitan colonial power. In the process, Republican rights were expanded to those who had been completely excluded from all legal rights. After 1794, France and its colonies were united, in principle, under one set of laws that were understood as truly universal, as applicable on both sides of the Atlantic regardless of social or economic differences. For a time, racial hierarchy was defeated by assimilationist universalism. Racially integrated armies defended French colonies against the British, and even attacked British colonies in the Eastern Caribbean, playing a crucial role in the worldwide conflict between the two imperial powers (Dubois 2003).

How, then, did this configuration ultimately lead to a struggle for national independence? It was the retreat of the French government from the policies of emancipation, which started in the late 1790s but was accelerated with the rise of Napoleon Bonaparte after 1801, and the move towards an ultimately short-lived peace with the British in that year. French rulers sought to hide their intention to crush the black armies that had emerged in the Caribbean, but many understood what was happening. Still, the road to outright resistance was a complicated one, and many of the key anti-colonial leaders, such as Jean-Jacques Dessalines, who declared Haitian independence in 1804, were for a time allied with the French before ultimately turning against them. It was only in 1803 and 1804, with Toussaint Louverture tricked into imprisonment and locked away to die in France, that a true war of national liberation was fought and won in Haiti. By then planter power had been crushed, replaced by a new elite of military generals. The victory of 1804 was, of course, a rejection of colonial power, but it was also the defence of a project of liberation that had been created through an alliance with a now vanished Republican metropole. Slave liberation, won through this alliance, had to be defended against a changed metropole through the creation of an independent nation.

Having gained its independence, Haiti precociously experienced many of the difficulties that continue to be faced in Latin America and Africa today. It has the dubious distinction of having been a pioneering target for neo-colonial and imperial policies that continue to shape our world. Isolated by France and a fearful United States in the early nineteenth century, its elite rulers ultimately made a deal in 1825 that allowed its ports to be opened up to trade with France. In return, however, the Haitian government granted France the payment of a massive 'indemnity'. What were the Haitians paying France for, precisely? Former slave owners and plantation owners from Saint-Domingue had, for decades, been lobbying the French government for compensation for the economic losses they had suffered during the Haitian Revolution. Much of what they calculated as having lost, of course, had been invested in the very bodies of those who had won their freedom by revolting during the Revolution. The 'indemnity' levied in 1825 was literally a fine for revolution, to be collected from the descendants of those men and women who had gained their freedom through rebellion a few decades before. Unable to pay the 'indemnity', the Haitian government borrowed money from French banks, and spent the next century contributing a good portion of its revenues to service this debt. The payments to French banks were eventually taken over by another benevolent power, the United States, which occupied Haiti from 1915 to 1934 in the process rewriting the Haitian constitution to open the way for foreign investment. The Haitians who rebelled against the occupation in what was later officially called the 'Second War of Independence' were crushed by the US troops. The twenty-year occupation left many legacies, including the formation of an internal security force that became the foundation for the Duvalier regime, and a vexed relationship with the United States that continues to this day (Schmidt 1985 [1972]; Trouillot 1990).

Where does the Haitian Revolution fit in the broader history of colonial, and post-colonial, history? Aimé Césaire wrote in 1961: 'Saint-Domingue est le premier pays des temps modernes à avoir posé dans la realité et à avoir proposé à la réflexion des hommes, et cela dans toute sa complexité sociale, économique, raciale, le grand problème que le XXème siècle s'essouffle à résoudre: le problème colonial. Le premier pays où s'est noué ce problème. Le premier pays où il s'est dénoué' [Saint-Domingue was the first country in modern times to have posed in reality, and to have proposed to the reflection of men, in all its social, economic and racial complexity, the great problem that the twentieth century is trying to resolve: the colonial problem. It was the first country where the problem was woven, and the first where it was unwoven] (Césaire 1981 [1961], 24). Saint-Domingue was, indeed, one of the eighteenth century's great colonies, a motor of profit for France, a jewel at the heart of the burgeoning Atlantic economy. The single-minded pursuit of profit, and the intensive focus on the production of plantation commodities for export, created a heavily industrialized and segmented economy. It also created a nightmare for the slaves who were the backbone of the system. The forms and advantages of colonialism, along with its brutal consequences, were powerfully condensed in the short history of Saint-Domingue.

It is not surprising, therefore, that when slave revolution exploded there it posed a great challenge to the contemporary understanding of the colonial order. The challenge came from whites seeking autonomy, but more powerfully from slaves who demanded, and ultimately won, rights within empire. The Haitian Revolution transformed the French colonial order for a time, creating an experiment in racial equality and emancipation within that order. In this sense the Haitian Revolution was the ancestor of later struggles for rights within empire through which the colonized demanded that the promise of democracy and equality that justified their subjecthood be fully applied, making them citizens. As was the case for the colonial reforms that followed the Second World War in the French empire, such attempts to transform the order from within led, perhaps inevitably, to struggles for complete independence. In both cases, however, the struggles for justice and equality within empire deeply formed the course and content of struggles for national independence. In Saint-Domingue turned Haiti, in other words, the contradictions of a racial order were made readily apparent, and a unique attempt to overcome this racial order – first through a profound reform in the colonial system, and then through a rejection of that system – made its way into the world.

The impact of the Haitian Revolution on modern political culture was enormous, though much of the work of tracking this influence has yet to be done. Susan Buck-Morss has argued recently that the events of the Revolution, well-known in Europe, shaped the thinking of Hegel in important ways. As she notes, this kind of exploration has no safe place in the academy – 'there is no place in the university in which the particular research constellation "Hegel and Haiti" would have a home'. But, as she suggests, remembering beyond traditional boundaries opens the way for telling important 'undisciplined stories' (Buck-Morss 2000, 822, 865). Although the wind of fear that slave revolution sent through the Americas and Europe is well known (Geggus 2001), the broader ways this dramatic struggle for freedom shaped the meaning of universalism and democracy is still for the most part ignored – and ignorable – for the continuing lack of detailed study on the question. This is unfortunate, for understanding the place the slave uprisings of the 1790s, particularly in Saint-Domingue, had in shaping the political culture of French Republicanism is crucial to a broader understanding of French colonial and post-colonial history.

A voracious consumer of slaves brought across the Atlantic, eighteenth-century Saint-Domingue helped prepare the terrain for Europe's eventual expansion into Africa. But it reached its height as a colony almost a century before French colonialism in Africa and Asia began in earnest, and Haiti was post-colonial decades before much of the rest of the world was colonial. Nineteenth- and twentieth-century empires have tended to dominate historiography and criticism in colonial and postcolonial studies, to the detriment of an engagement with the colonial processes which created Europe and the Americas simultaneously from the sixteenth through to the eighteenth centuries. But truly to understand the history of European colonialism – its discourses, ideologies, institutions, practices – it is vital to understand its multiple stages, and the ways the expansion of capitalism in the seventeenth and eighteenth centuries, and the ultimate defeat of empire in the late eighteenth and early nineteenth centuries, set the stage for the next period of colonial expansion (Coronil 1997). The Haitian Revolution represents a nodal point in this broader history, for it was at once a foundational moment in the history of French Republicanism and an event that defined and came to symbolize the possibilities – or, from another perspective, the dangers – of anti-colonial revolt. The achievement of the Haitian Revolution became a part of the political culture of Republicanism, even as the nation it created was expelled from the 'West', and indeed used as 'proof' of why European tutelage was ultimately necessary for 'inferior races'. In the paradox of Haiti's symbolic destiny we can see the broader paradox of imperial Europe, shaped by its interaction and confrontation with other cultures even as it presented itself as separate from and superior to them.

There is redemption to be found in searching for the Haitian Revolution, for in its story lie lessons about the racial orders that continue to haunt us and about ways to confront them. Within it lies a history of how a powerful economic system that made profits on both sides of the Atlantic was defeated by individuals armed mostly with the tools they had been given to work the cane fields. And within it is a crucial chapter of the history of how the idea of rights came to be understood as universal, as something that could not be quarantined and constrained. In this sense the Haitian Revolution is, indeed, everywhere.

3

'Of *whatever color*': (dis)locating a place for the creole in nineteenth-century French literature

BY CHRIS BONGIE

The word 'creole' is a notoriously slippery signifier, one that both defies racial characterization and calls it forth. It is a word, as Christopher Miller notes, that 'opens the question of race while distinctly providing no answer to it' (1985, 93). Its meaning changes with location, and in each of these locations this meaning has changed over time. It has been, and remains, a hotly disputed term. To take but one example: in the French Antilles, during the early days of colonization, the word referred to everyone born on the islands but originating from elsewhere, be it Europe or Africa. Over the course of the eighteenth century, however, the noun became virtually the exclusive property of the 'békés', island-born whites of 'pure' European descent, although as an adjective 'creole' was still used to describe other peoples and things (slaves, animals, cuisine). Recently, the authors of the influential *Éloge de la créolité* have attempted to contest this béké 'monop-olization' of the word (see Bongie 1998, 130–1), arguing for an all-inclusive vision of creole identity grounded in the syncretic (creolized) culture which, 'dans le creuset des îles ouvertes, a mélangé tout le Divers monde' [in the melting pot of open-ended islands, has mixed all the world's Diversity together] (Chamoiseau and Confiant 1991, 13).

As a general argument, the *Éloge*'s appeal to creolization has attracted academics in France and North America dissatisfied with identitarian politics and looking for 'a chance to break away from the dangerous and destructive patterns that were established when the rational absurdity of "race" was elevated into an essential concept and endowed with a unique power to both determine history and explain its selective unfolding' (Gilroy 2000, 14). And yet, as critics have not been slow to remark, praising an inclusionary creole identity at the expense of overtly exclusionary identities like 'black' or 'white' involves not (just) a rejection of the absurdity of raciological thinking, an opening out onto new and less dangerous patterns of thought, but (also) an ambiguous doubling and recalling of such thinking, a reopening of the identitarian terms beyond which the word seemingly points. 'Creole' is a double-edged word, which is why it can provide no answers to the vexing question of race: it both does and does not assert a fixed identity; it both is and is not entangled in the logic of race.

While this inherent ambiguity is essential to a general understanding of the word, it does not convey the whole story. For specific speakers, in specific locations and at specific points in history, the word has had very precise meanings: a béké in the nineteenth century, for instance, would be in no doubt about what he meant by 'creole'. Local context often clarifies (but can also muddy) the word's meaning, attenuating (or heightening) the uncertainty with which it necessarily confronts non-local readers. The potential tension between context-specific vernacular meaning(s) and a general understanding of the word is itself an important aspect of the word's ambiguity, and one must remain attentive to this tension when considering literary representations of creole cultures (see Lionnet 1998); that said, however, 'creole' predominantly functions in nineteenth-century French texts without regard to its localized contexts, as indeed it does in many current academic discussions of creolization.

This is not to say that these nineteenth-century French representations do not have a specificity of their own. I would suggest, indeed, that at the end of the eighteenth century the general connotations of the word underwent a veritable paradigm shift: by the turn of the century its inherent ambiguity became exacerbated as a response to the French and Haitian Revolutions. The revolutionary era effected a massive disruption of stable sign systems, providing 'a compelling demonstration that no eternal reality guaranteed the eternal truth of representations of the real' (Petrey 1988, 50). The referential instability of 'creole' took on a new significance in the opening decades of the nineteenth century, functioning as a metacritical marker of what was happening to language, and society, as a whole. In a world turned upside down, this multivalent word would come to bear a double burden of disavowal and desire, depending upon whether an author disapproved of or supported the 'forward' course of revolutionary history.

The word 'creole' became fraught with historicity, in line with a broader transformation of the French exotic tradition during the 1790s. As Léon-François Hoffmann has pointed out, 'avant la Révolution française, la vie coloniale telle que la représentaient les hommes de lettres paraît se dérouler hors du temps et en marge de l'histoire' [before the French Revolution, colonial life as it is represented by men of letters seems to unfold outside of time and on the margins of history] (1973, 101). The global ramifications of the Revolution bring France's colonies inside time, drawing them into relation with the 'centre' of history, which results in the emergence of two opposing textual approaches to the non-European world: on the one hand, an 'exoticizing exoticism', which figures 'other' worlds as 'a possible refuge from an overbearing modernity' (Bongie 1991, 16–17), disavowing revolutionary history and impossibly seeking in New Worlds the primitive and the aboriginal (Chateaubriand's *Atala* [1801] is an early example of this approach); on the other, a colonial exoticism that actively engages with history, be it approvingly or disapprovingly. This engagement will involve, among other things, attempting to locate a place (be it for purposes of containment or celebration) for the 'creole' and the ambiguities of a modernity with which it is henceforth associated.

The referential instability of 'creole' – its ability to exclude and include, to name and unname, to fix boundaries and to cross them – takes on a different nuance with every text in which the word is inscribed. Generalizations are possible, but dangerous; close readings are a necessity. The nineteenth-century text that I would like to focus on here is a novel published one year before *Atala*, Jean-Baptiste Picquenard's *Zoflora, ou La bonne négresse* (1800, English translation 1804). As did *Adonis, ou Le bon nègre* (1798), the first novel by this disciple of Bernardin de Saint-Pierre, *Zoflora* relates a tale – part 'conte philosophique', part lurid melodrama – about the early days of the Haitian Revolution. Here, the link between revolutionary upheaval and creole ambiguity, which will be the implicit subtext of representations of creoles in subsequent decades, could not be more explicit.

The novel tells the story of the virtuous Frenchman Justin who arrives in the flourishing colony of Saint-Domingue in 1788. During his stay on the island, he wins the devotion of a black slave girl Zoflora, but falls in love with Amicia, daughter of Zoflora's owner (and would-be seducer), the wicked planter Valbona. The twists and turns of this love triangle are interwoven with a chronologically hazy account of the slave insurrection, with historical figures like the rebel leaders Biassou and Boukman playing key roles. *Zoflora* ends happily, with Valbona disposed of by the insurgent slaves, and Justin back in a tranquil, post-revolutionary France with Amicia and Zoflora (who has sublimated her love for him): 'They all live together in a charming retreat beneath the finest climate of France; far from intrigue and noise' (Picquenard 1804, II, 233). In this muted version of what Françoise Vergès has termed the colonial 'family romance' (1999), the worlds of black and white are joined together at the end in fraternal/sororal friendship, and eighteenth-century ideals such as 'sensibility and humanity' (the novel's last words) are triumphantly (re)asserted.

Of the many uses of the word 'creole' in *Zoflora*, I will focus on two in particular, inclusive and exclusive: the first vividly demonstrates the word's ambiguity as a marker of 'racial' identity, while the second puts into play its stable, eighteenth-century meaning (at least in the French Antilles), denoting peoples of European descent born in the colonies. What unites both uses is an intense mixture of desire and disavowal that will typify later representations of creoles and creolized cultures during 'the racially conscious era of

French social Romanticism, in the late 1820s, 1830s, and 1840s' (Jenson 2001, 187).

The first, hesitantly inclusive, use of the word comes early on, when Justin – freshly arrived from France, his hopes for an inheritance thwarted by unforeseen circumstances – receives a lecture from an innkeeper, 'father Simon', on how to get ahead in the colony and yet still lead a virtuous life. Simon, a 'man of true philanthropy', is a patriarchal figure of wisdom, a throwback to the age of Enlightenment, peddling the commonplaces of Rousseau and Bernardin de Saint-Pierre. But, as the lecture concludes, his calm philosophical certitudes make way for rather more agitated claims: because Justin is approaching that age 'in which the development of your passions will make a total change in your being' (a change aggravated by the heat of the climate and the strength of the young man's constitution), Simon feels obliged to caution him concerning 'the women of this island'. By that expression, he clarifies that he means 'the creoles of whatever color' (Picquenard 1804, I, 62). These creoles, he continues,

> devote themselves, not to the cultivation of their minds nor even of those gifts which they have received from nature, but to acquiring the art of awakening transient desires, the gratification of which leaves behind in the recesses of the heart, at least satiety, weariness and disgust; if it does not give birth to more poignant regrets. In short they are real voluptuaries, but, it must be confessed, of the most sensual kind. (I, 63–4)

Simon then notes that Europeans visiting the island at first react negatively to these women because their 'color, form, and attainments differ so widely from those of their [the Europeans'] own country', but that this initial impression is soon replaced by a more favourable one: 'The creoles by their little attentions, their insinuating flatteries, their infantine jargon, and their pleasing caresses, soon find means to conquer it, and to have themselves preferred to the women of Europe who come over here. They are a sort of syrens [sic], by whose songs, when once heard, it is very difficult to escape being fascinated' (I, 64–5).

This passage invokes any number of stereotypes concerning creoles: their lack of mental cultivation, excessive sensuality, childish jargon, and so on. But the most important issue it raises involves the question of colour: who exactly is being described here? The phrase 'creoles of whatever color' seems unambiguously to refer to 'white' and 'black' women (as in other phrases like the 'colonists of all colors' [I, 73], 'planters of all colors' [I, 152]). But this provokes the 'natural' question of how the colour of (white) creole women could differ so widely from their European counterparts as to provoke distaste. In fact, the visible difference of (white) creoles was a commonplace assumption of nineteenth-century literature (one thinks of the 'singularly sallow' complexion of Bertha Mason's brother in *Jane Eyre*), and the emphasis on this difference cannot but interest contemporary critics because of the way it 'makes whiteness strange': it helps us see, as Richard Dyer states in a critique of the label 'people of colour', that 'we need to recognise white as a colour too, and just one among many, and we cannot do that if we keep using a term that reserves colour for anyone other than white people' (1997, 11).

The recognition in this passage of otherness within sameness, of 'coloured' whiteness, evidently provokes some anxiety on Picquenard's part, for the comment about fascinating 'syrens' is supplemented by a footnote in which he partially redirects the all-inclusive assumptions generating Simon's speech about 'creoles of whatever color' toward a more exclusive perspective. To speak of these creoles exercising a 'fascination', the note points out,

> may appear like exaggeration to Europeans who have never resided in the islands, and who judge of all women of color by those they sometimes meet with in Europe. To say the truth, from a whimsicality of circumstances, for which I cannot account, almost all those which I have ever seen in France, are not only ugly, but hideously disgusting, and very well calculated to give an unfavorable idea of the sex in the Antilles. But, be not deceived my good country-men! the American islands contain a number of creoles of all colors extremely handsome, and particularly, remarkable for tall, slender, and elegant figures, for the plumpness and firmness of their flesh, for the faultlessness of their forms, the whiteness of their teeth, and the lustre and expressive vivacity of their eyes. (I, 65)

This note vacillates dramatically in its vision of colour. At the beginning, where Picquenard is specifically addressing Europeans, 'women of color' is apparently being used as a label for 'mixed race' subjects, like the 'men of color' referred to later in the novel – 'the individuals of the intermediate population between the whites and blacks, that is to say, all those born of an intermixture of these classes, all who were called mulattoes, mestize, samboes, guadroons, &c.' (II, 63–4). By the end, though, Picquenard has returned to a more inclusive account, based both on local knowledge (derived from eyewitness – indeed, scopophilic! – experiences during his years in Saint-Domingue) but also on humanist Enlightenment assumptions that overlook the colour line in the name of 'universal' concepts such as a 'beauty' that can be shared by the entire human race, as when he later praises Zoflora for her 'beautifully regular' features and 'that charming plumpness which gives to the female form those graceful contours with which nature adorns the sex, whatever be the color', and remarks that beauty is 'of all countries, all complexions; it is not arbitrary as some have been pleased to assert [for] it ever bears a sacred and indelible stamp which through all the wide expanse of nature exacts and forces admiration and homage' (I, 159–60).

The troubling lability of the word 'creole' is very evident in this example, but has to be situated contextually in order to gain its full resonance. The tensions at work generating Picquenard's confrontation with creole ambiguity stem from the historical crossroads at which he is writing. He is poised between several ideas of colour, conflicted in his allegiances. On the one hand, he desires, in the manner of eighteenth-century mentors like Bernardin, to speak in terms of 'universals', to uphold a sensibility and humanity that can be accessed even by the most heartless of individuals, such as the rebel leader Biassou (see Bongie 1998, 245). On the other, he is aware of the racial hierarchies that structure social relations in the Antilles, and feels obliged for motives of realism to convey his knowledge. This local knowledge about 'race' and colour had already, in turn, for some decades been filtering back to Europe (Picquenard's novel is, indeed, part of that transatlantic process), providing the building blocks for the scientific racism that would come to dominate nineteenth-century European thinking, neutralizing the colour of whiteness and justifying racial hierarchies in hitherto unthinkable ways. Picquenard's vacillating representations of creoles – his shuttling between creoles of all colours and creoles of colour – are the product of a transitional moment in history, anticipating but not yet fully affected by 'the arrival of scientific racism toward the end of the eighteenth century' when 'confused and unsystematic race-thinking aspired to become something more coherent, rational, and authoritative' (Gilroy 2000, 31).

The second use of the word 'creole' that I want to look at here, an emphatically exclusive one, also needs to be understood as generated by a moment of historical transition. Here, in the descriptions of the sadistic Valbona, the accent is not on desire – as when 'father Simon', the benign voice of reason, found himself troubled enough to confess to the fascinating voluptuousness of the creole 'syrens' whom he is attempting to warn Justin against – but on disavowal. Valbona, whose very name signals his allegiance to the pre-revolutionary world not of *Paul et Virginie* but of *Les Liaisons dangereuses*, is introduced as 'a creole himself, and son to a creole, [who] had all the blemishes, all the ridiculous points of character peculiar to his country' (Picquenard 1804, I, 107). Just as Simon's fascinated desire makes itself heard only briefly amid the general condemnation of his creole voluptuaries, so too one cannot help registering a certain libidinal energy at work in Picquenard's ostensibly disapproving portrait of the villainous slave owner and libertine: 'He kept at each of his houses and at prodigious cost a sort of seraglio, composed of women of all colors; he had private theatres where plays were performed, kept a lodge of freemasonry at his own house, and made frequent excursions of pleasure' (I, 109). Much later on in the novel, Valbona's despicable actions toward 'the unfortunate victims of his luxury and his barbarity' provoke an authorial footnote that, unlike the note 'clarifying' Simon's comments about 'creoles of all colors', simply confirms the text's condemnation of him: 'The imagination of the reader will find it difficult to conceive, or his mind to give credit to so many enormities, but those who are acquainted with the corruption and barbarity of the creolian character [caractère créole], when given up to its native unrestrained violence, will be astonished at nothing they hear on that subject', as is immediately confirmed through the further example of that 'monstrous' white woman, a 'female creole of Leogane, so notorious for her crimes [...] who was made a horrible example of justice by the negroes during the time of one of their insurrections' (II, 186–7).

In these descriptions of Valbona, 'creole' and 'creolian character' refer only to Europeans of 'pure' white descent. What is being accomplished through this highly negative representation of (white) creoles, which intersects, but is also at odds, with the fascinated injunctions against creole 'syrens' of all colours? I would suggest that here the (white) creole is being used as a figure through whom both the Ancien Régime and the French Revolution are being disavowed. Valbona the libertine slave owner patently functions as a representative of the Ancien Régime: he is the bad father whom – as noted by François Vergès (rehearsing Lynn Hunt's argument) – French revolutionaries sought to delegitimize, 'reduc[ing] the place of the father in the family romance' in order to 'establish the legitimacy of the romance of fraternity' (1999, 38). The French Revolution thus, as it were, de-creolizes France and its colonies, ridding them of paternal despots. But, as the reference to freemasonry hints, the slave owner Valbona may be a stand-in not simply for the Ancien Régime but for the violent excesses of the Revolution as well – excesses that could be regarded at the time Picquenard wrote his novels (at the end of the Directory and the beginning of Napoleon's reign) as mercifully over and done with. Picquenard's (white) creole thus figures France's recent past, both monarchical and Republican, as something to be disavowed from the perspective of the ideological compromise between the two political orders seemingly achieved by Napoleon.

A further contextual explanation helps account for Picquenard's scathing disavowal of Valbona: in 1800, as the reference to the 'negroes during the time of one of their insurrections' suggests, Saint-Domingue did not – at least for a humanist like Picquenard – offer the spectre of black insurrection and independence but proof that progress toward racial equality was possible within the framework of French colonialism. Saint-Domingue, after all, was still a French colony: a decade of insurrection and internecine strife was over; Toussaint Louverture had emerged as supreme leader, bent on preserving liberty for his fellow blacks but also on giving sympathetic whites a leading role in restoring the plantation economy to its former glory. Only in 1802, when Napoleon brazenly attempted to restore slavery, was this rejuvenated, black-led version of the old colonial order destroyed; by the beginning of 1804, Napoleon's army would be driven from the island and Haiti's independence declared. Picquenard, in other words, is writing during a brief interregnum between the abolition of slavery and its attempted restoration, when it was still possible to imagine the reform/re-formation of French rule in Saint-Domingue.

Picquenard's double representation of creoles in *Zoflora*, with its particular admixture of desire and disavowal, is a product of this optimistic time. After the loss of Saint-Domingue (as well as, soon after, Louisiana and Mauritius), and the successful restoration of slavery in France's remaining 'old colonies' (Martinique, Guadeloupe, Cayenne, Réunion), creoles and creole cultures would become indissociable not only from the problem of slavery but from the aborted history of its abolition and, by extension, the aborted history of the Revolution in France (and of French rule in Haiti). In novels written during the Restoration and the July Monarchy (1814–48), 'creole' becomes a codeword signalling this unfinished history, provoking either disgust (on the part of counter-revolutionaries) or desire (on the part of those who wished for the logical conclusion of what 1789 began). The word's importance to French literature during this period is matched by its relative unimportance after 1848, when slavery was abolished: from this point on, 'creole' lost its coded historical resonance, taking its ideologically neutral place in the lexicon of 'exoticizing exoticism'.

Having provided a close reading of the sort that is necessary if one is to go beyond general comments about the word's inherent ambiguity, there is little space left here to provide an overview of representations of the 'creole' in nineteenth-century French literature. Indeed, it should be clear that no such overview is, strictly speaking, possible: individual representations of creole cultures cannot and should not be made to coalesce into a stable pattern; if there is such a thing as what I have referred to as 'creolist discourse' (Bongie 1998), it exists only in each individual enunciation of this discourse. Having said that, however, it might be ventured that two distinct approaches to representing creole cultures hold sway in key texts from the period 1814–48, generated either by disavowal or desire depending on the author's attitude toward the (uncompleted) French Revolution.

Nowhere is the disavowal of creole cultures more evident than in Victor Hugo's novel about the Haitian Revolution, *Bug-Jargal* (1826), directly influenced by Picquenard's *Adonis* and written at a time when the young Hugo was still an ultra-royalist rather than the masthead of Republicanism into which he would later fashion himself. *Bug-Jargal* offers deeply negative representations of creoles, of whatever colour. When the young French protagonist Leopold d'Auverney is asked by the rebel leader Biassou, 'Are you Creole?', Leopold proudly replies 'No ... I am French' (Hugo 2004 [1826]) – and thus confirms, even for the ruthless Biassou, Leopold's essentially honourable nature as opposed to that of the non-French (white) creoles. Virtually all other occurrences of the word 'creole' in the novel are as an adjective attaching to negroes and their 'patois' or 'jargon' (a word also used to characterize the arbitrary neologisms of the Jacobins). Hugo's novel is saturated with a repugnance for 'creole jargon' and the mixed (up) world it represents – a far cry from Picquenard's generous account of Zoflora, who speaks French 'with fluency and correctness; from time to time however enriching her narrative with those simple images of nature with which the creolian idiom [l'idiôme créole] abounds' (1804, I, 161–2). Hugo's muted critique of (white) creoles as harsh slave owners is swamped, in *Bug-Jargal*, by a virulent attack on (mulatto) creoles such as Biassou (see Bongie 1998, 231–61), who is carefully distinguished from the (black) African Bug-Jargal, d'Auverney's worthy but tragically doomed double.

Where Hugo disavows, George Sand desires, fervently identifying with her creole heroine in *Indiana* (1994 [1832]), who becomes a sounding board for (the ambiguities of) her revolutionary sympathies. Sand's feminist novel grounds itself in an analogy between being a woman and being a slave, asserting the need for their mutual liberation – an analogy also found in Picquenard, when Valbona's unfortunate wife laments to Zoflora, after the latter has witnessed him being particularly odious to his spouse, 'All slaves have not black skins, as thou mayest perceive [...]. Women, whatever be their color, their education, or their fortune, can seldom escape that melancholy state' (Picquenard, 1804, I, 170–1). Sand's novel depends upon this analogy, but as Deborah Jenson has pointed out, 'the marriage/slavery and love/slavery analogies' ultimately result in a certain 'erasure of race' (2001, 199). What does a white woman know of slavery? What does a Frenchwoman know of the creole cultures of the Île Bourbon (present-day Réunion), home not only of her upper-class white protagonist Indiana but of Noun, Indiana's chambermaid of indeterminate race, 'creole in the fullest meaning of the term'? (Sand 1994, 253) To identify with someone is not to share an identity, and this lack of common identity between the two terms of Sand's analogy (wife/lover, slave) is reflected in the anxious doubling – the resemblance and dissimilarity – of Indiana and Noun, who 'seem virtually to divide up between themselves the disjunctive extremes of the clichés of Creole identity, along the axes of Indiana's unhealthy psychological suscep- tibility (encoded as white) and Noun's sexual red-bloodedness (encoded as mixed race)' (Jenson 2001, 194), but who none the less prove strangely indistinguishable from one another at key points in the novel. The uncanny doubling of Indiana and Noun – both 'creoles' and yet obviously separated by class and, possibly, 'race' – signals the problematic nature of Sand's revolutionary analogy, and her at least partial awareness of the problem. As Jenson summarizes, 'One can hypothesize that Sand [...] wanted her use of the slavery analogy to be emancipatory but had a premonition of the same anxieties that would haunt the fields of feminism and African American studies in the wake of identity politics: the anxieties of authenticity, of a realism of identity, of "firsthand" phenomenological experience' (2001, 206). Just as Hugo, despite himself, is forced to give vivid expression to the revolutionary, creolized history that he wishes to disavow, so Sand is compelled to register her second-hand relation to the creole world(s) with which she desires to identify herself.

Doubling the anti- and pro-revolutionary positions exemplified by French writers like Hugo and Sand is a third representational approach, or set of approaches, that needs mentioning in closing: namely, what I have referred to as the native strain of 'creolist discourse' (Bongie 1998, 295–6). Flourishing in the period between 1833 – when the equal rights of all free people, regardless of colour, were acknowledged in the old colonies – and 1848, this literature adds a new twist to the problem of 'realism of identity' and '"firsthand" phenomenological experience'. Are the novels and poems written by creoles during this period just bad imitations of French literature about creoles, or does their near doubling of metropolitan representations exemplify a productive mimicry that, in Homi Bhabha's words, 'poses an immanent threat to both "normalized" knowledges and disciplinary powers' (1994, 86)? While repeating the moves made by authors like Hugo and Sand, this literature produced by creoles can be read as shifting the colonial terms of discussion, albeit slightly, and thereby anticipating the poetics of creolization promoted by the authors of the *Éloge*. Since, as I argued at the outset, inclusionary visions of 'creole' cannot be disentangled from exclusionary ones, to take the mimicry of these creole writers seriously, in Bhabha's sense, would entail reading all of them in relation to one another rather than simply privileging those on the 'right' side of post-colonial history and the colour line. In other words, we need to read these creole writers with an eye not only to their differences but also to their similarities: both 'whites' such as Hugo's Martiniquan friend Louis Maynard who, in *Outre-mer* (1835), disavows revolutionary ideals of equality and limits creole identity to his own caste (see Bongie 1998, 287–316); and writers 'of colour' like the Réunnionais Louis Houat who, in *Les Marrons* (1844), radicalizes the 'family romance' with which Picquenard's novel concluded, envisioning (if only in a dream, and only through a 'foreclosure of the native woman') a creolized future in the symbolic form of a 'mulatto' child produced from the union of a black maroon and his white creole wife – a resolution that offers 'the representation of the métis as a redemptive group [...] that would not rest on one "extreme", whether black or white' (Vergès 1999, 51, 24).

Four years after the publication of *Les Marrons*, the revolutionary project of abolition was finally 'completed' in the early months of the Second Republic: not only was slavery abolished, but French citizenship was granted to all inhabitants of the old colonies along with voting rights for all male citizens. The most radical dimensions of the 1848 legislation would soon be curtailed (colonial representation was suppressed by Louis Napoleon in 1852, for instance), but the 'problem' of creole identity in the old colonies was – with slavery abolished and French nationality secured for all 'creoles' – effectively regulated. The burden of colonial history, in subsequent decades, shifted to the new colonies in Africa and Asia, where more advanced technologies of surveillance and discipline would go hand in hand with increasingly Manichean distinctions between colonizer and colonized, ensuring that the sort of confusions surrounding 'creoles' and their hybrid cultures would be, if not entirely obviated, then at least relocated from the centre to the margins of colonial and anti-colonial discourse.

A century and a half after this shunting of creole ambiguity to the margins, it is tempting to interpret the new-found, post-*Éloge* centrality of creolized cultures in postcolonial theory as a laudable step forward on the road to 'putting into question all continental forms of identity, be they French, African, or Indian, and reconstructing them as hybrid, insular, and local' (Lionnet 1998, 78). But, if the ambiguities to which I have tried to give expression here have anything to teach us, it is precisely that no such determinate reconstruction of creoleness is possible: 'hybrid, insular, and local' identities can only be one part of the (dis)located story that the 'creole' has to tell – a story that both includes and excludes the margins and the centre, the minor and the major, the island and the continent, but that can only be told from an undetermined place between these two regrettably, if inescapably, identifiable locations.

4

Revisiting exoticism: from colonialism to postcolonialism

BY CHARLES FORSDICK

In summer 2002, an unexpectedly bitter controversy attracted prominent coverage in the Belgian media. Eight Baka pygmies from Cameroon had been brought to Belgium by the charity Oasis-Nature to sing and dance for tourists in a mock-up of an indigenous village built in the grounds of a private zoo at Yvoir (Stroobants 2002). Louis Raets, organizer of the spectacle, claimed that he had conceived the exhibition as a means of raising money for the construction of wells, pharmacies and schools in south Cameroon; what he had not foreseen was the fierce disapproval (accompanied by demonstrations and legal action) that his would-be humanitarian gesture would provoke. Anti-racist activists, human rights groups and representatives of Belgian immigrant groups claimed that the exhibition was 'racist and neo-colonial', 'degrading and voyeuristic' (Osborn 2002), arguing that there was little to distinguish this display from those in colonial France and Belgium in which colonial subjects were put on display like – and even in cages with – animals in a zoo. Parallels between the historical situations were not difficult to find, ranging from the unfortunate choice of a wildlife park as setting to claims that the pygmies' movement outside the park was heavily restricted. Even publicity literature echoed the 'denial of coevalness' (Fabian 1983) by which colonial exhibitions justified their displays, relegating the Cameroonians to a precivilizational, almost prehistorical moment with no links to the Western present: 'Help these people who live at the start of the third millennium as we did 2000 years ago' (cited in Osborn 2002).

Thus a seemingly trivial *fait divers* not only triggered memories of past events that the organizers of the exhibition had perhaps naively or conveniently forgotten, but also created a series of uneasy associations between the colonial past and the post-colonial present, suggesting that any neat division between the two is little more than imaginary. One of the main criticisms at which Raets baulked was the claim, made by the Mouvement des Nouveaux Migrants, that his exhibition was a 'zoo humain'. This transformed a poorly prepared and ultimately ill-advised humanitarian gesture into post-colonial prolongation of a centuries-long stage-management of European claims to racial superiority. The 'human zoo', a phenomenon whose complex and diverse history is fully explored in a recent collection of essays (Bancel *et al.* 2002; see also Hargreaves, Chapter 13), was rooted in the Renaissance and Enlightenment practice of sporadically bringing indigenous people to colonial capitals where they were paraded as exotic curiosities; in the nineteenth century, allied to colonial expansion and the domestic propaganda on which this depended, this practice was transformed into a systematic exhibiting of 'savage' otherness. At the beginning of the century, displays of non-Europeans were largely entrepreneurial affairs, as the tragic case of Sarah Baartman – more commonly dubbed the 'Hottentot Venus' – clearly illustrates (see Badou 2000); by the end of the century, the growth of colonial ethnography and the proliferation of national, international and colonial expositions had given the living indigenous diorama a much more official standing, with the hazily exotic status granted to representatives of other cultures at the beginning of the century replaced by more clearly racialized versions at its end. Linked to the perceived right to colonize, which guided nineteenth-century international relations, was the claim to an associated right to displace and exhibit colonized cultures and peoples.

The mention of a 'human zoo' linked allusively the contemporary Belgian stage-management of Baka culture to an earlier and explicitly colonial tradition of exotic display. Its organizers had failed to take into account deep-seated and highly sensitive issues of representation relating to the portrayal or actual display of non-Western or 'exotic' peoples in Europe. On the one hand and in a general sense, the presentation of black Africans undertaking activities deemed 'traditional' or 'authentic' triggered memories of earlier processes of colonial exhibition; on the other hand and in a more specifically national context, the pygmy show served as a reminder that, unlike in France, Belgians during the colonial period rarely saw colonial (i.e. Congolese) subjects unless they had actually travelled to Equatorial Africa (Jacquemin 2002), and they relied as a result on secondhand and often imaginary sources of information, on the filters provided by images and texts. At stake in the Yvoir incident – and in other similarly controversial 'African village' incidents, such as that at the Safari Parc in Nantes in 1994 – were, therefore, unresolved elements of colonial history and culture linked to exoticism and the processes of exoticization on which this depends. Moreover, reactions to the display served as a reminder not only that exoticism is an element of past representations of other cultures, but also that the means by which people, objects and places have been portrayed in the past have an impact on present representations.

Exoticism often describes an imagined quality or essence of difference (mystery, savagery, eroticism, cruelty) ascribed by one culture to another radically different (and often threatening) culture that falls outside its customary domestic frame of reference. Without conflating the complex range of representational practices bound up in the term, exoticism might be seen as the process occurring in a colonial context whereby the foreign is absorbed into a home culture, essentialized, simplified and domesticated in order to be presented not in the light of its original context but instead according to understandings imposed by the culture into which it is received (understandings often constructed from that culture's deep-seated fears and desires). The authors of *Key Concepts in Post-Colonial Studies* include 'exotic/exoticism' in their glossary of terms recurrent in postcolonial studies. Explaining the initially neutral sixteenth-century uses of the epithet 'exotic' (as a synonym for 'foreign'), they track its semantic drift towards more subjective and fixed colonial understandings:

> During the nineteenth century, however, the exotic, the foreign, increasingly gained, throughout the empire, the connotations of a stimulating or exciting difference, something with which the domestic could be (safely) spiced. [...] Isolated from their own geographical and cultural contexts, they represented whatever was projected onto them by the societies into which they were introduced. Exotics in the metropoles were a significant part of imperial displays of power and the plenitude of empires. (Ashcroft *et al.* 1998, 94–5)

The concise nature of the volume in which it is included dictates the shorthand of the definition, but this summarizes postcolonial understandings of the term. In the Francophone context, the alliance of exoticism to 'imperial displays of power' has privileged the 1931 Exposition coloniale at Vincennes as a case study or an exemplary site of exoticist practice to which many recent studies have been devoted either in part (Cooper 2001; Lebovics 1992; Norindr 1996) or in full (Hodeir and Michel 1991; Morton 2000). A mass-culture event, attended by over eight million visitors in the seven months its gates were open, the Exposition's impact on the collective imagination was as a result substantial – although, as Ageron makes clear (1997, 505), difficult to quantify with any precision.

Underpinning the geography of the Exposition was a process of exoticist reduction, a presentation of the French Empire in miniature so that, in the terms of the event's advertising material, the visitor could undertake 'le tour du monde en quatre jours' [a journey round the world in four days]: underlining the potential efficiency of a visit to the exhibition site, it added: 'Pourquoi aller en Tunisie quand vous pouvez la visiter aux portes de Paris?' [What is the point of going to Tunisia when you can visit it at the gates of Paris?] (Ageron 1997, 502). The reduction of an imperial expedition to a domestic journey, of the world to the scale of Vincennes was not merely, however, a matter of efficiency. The stage-management of a range of colonial locations on the Exposition site presented not the French Empire but an exoticized version of it. Colonial cultures were not presented as they were – divided, hybrid, unevenly developed, combining acculturated 'évolués' [literally, those who had 'evolved'] with subjects whose contact with the 'mission civilisatrice' [civilizing mission] was limited or non-existent – but as colonial propaganda demanded they should be. Exoticism was used at Vincennes to disseminate as widely as possible a sense both of the West's right to colonize and of the justness of imperialism. The processes of exoticization were employed to create a popular justification of owner-ship of elsewhere inherent in imperial expansion; the aim was to demon-strate who was civilized and who required civilization. Roland Barthes describes the ways in which exoticism denies history (1957, 165), pre-empting the anthropologist Johannes Fabian's identification (1983) of the tendency in Western representations of other cultures to situate the non-Western in a temporally distinct moment and to supplement geographical displacement with a chronological distance. In presenting colonial cultures in fixed, stereotypical forms, the organizers of the Exposition presented versions of those cultures that erased the effects of colonization while accentuating aspects of them to suggest the need for colonial intervention. Joël Dauphiné (1998) has produced a detailed account of the experience of the New Caledonian contingent at Vincennes, and a recent fictional inter-pretation of their treatment (Daeninckx 1998) reveals how educated Kanak were obliged to masquerade in their enclosure, situated in the Jardin zoologique d'acclimatation, as 'sauvages polygames et cannibales' [polyga-mous savages and cannibals] while many of their number were despatched for exhibition in Germany. A fictional account of the Exposition by a Senegalese author (Socé 1937) casts colonial reporters and lecturers as 'fabricants d'exotisme' [manufacturers of exoticism] (66) and describes in detail the mechanisms of this 'colonial exoticism'. For Socé, colonial exoti-cism is characterized by preconceived effects (90), not rooted in accurate observation but associated with the expedient accentuation of minor or imagined traits. One of the principal implications of the Exposition's reliance on such processes is seen in the contemporary inability to recognize or understand the anti-colonial sentiment existing not only outside the gates (Norindr 1996, 34–51) but also in embryo even among its indigenous players (Ageron 1997, 506–8); similarly, the fragmentation of colonial cultures according to differing exoticist strategies eclipsed the already rumbling resistance to colonial authority that was beginning unexpectedly to link colonies in a 'dynamic counter-modernity' (Young 2001, 2). Whereas many saw the Exposition as the acme of Empire and as a propagandist coup, a study of the exoticism on which it relied reveals a more nuanced picture in which exoticist (mis)representation creates a false sense of security and disguises the increasing fragility of colonial relations.

The relationship between exoticism and postcolonialism is on the whole antagonistic, which is little surprising given that the critique of colonialism from which much postcolonial theory has emerged is itself a robust indictment of colonial exoticism (Forsdick 2001b). Three Martiniquan critics illustrate this point. Aimé Césaire demands in his *Discourse on Colonialism* that the new societies that would emerge from anti-colonial struggle should be projective, not retrogressive, rejecting any return to a pre-colonial moment: 'It is not a dead society that we want to revive. We leave that to those who go for exoticism' (1972 [1955], 31). Exoticism is accordingly associated in Césaire's analysis with what Renato Rosaldo has dubbed 'imperialist nostalgia', the Western desire to resurrect what colonial contact has already destroyed (1993, 68–87). In *For the African Revolution*, Fanon goes on to claim that exoticism simplifies, objectifies, neutralizes and ultimately mummifies the colonized culture by denying its dynamism, complexity and depth (1970 [1964], 36). René Ménil is similarly dismissive, seeing Western exoticism as a perpetuated influence on the self-representation of (formerly) colonized peoples. He claims: 'il faut dépasser l'expression poétique contre-exotique qui est contaminée par cela même contre quoi elle veut se dresser' [we must move beyond a mode of poetic expression that is counter-exotic for this is contaminated by what it is supposed to be reacting against] (1999, 26).

   This rejection – or even vilification – of exoticism is repeated in the work of postcolonial critics, with Homi Bhabha for example proposing, as a paradigm of postcoloniality, 'an *inter*national culture, based not on the exoticism of multiculturalism or the *diversity* of cultures, but on the inscription and the articulation of culture's hybridity' (1994, 38; emphasis in original). Bhabha's comment – and in particular his dismissal of 'diversity' – reflects the risks of any prescriptive anti-essentialism and the limits of any universal application of theories of cross-culturality and creolization. As Michael Dash makes clear in this volume (Chapter 21), the transformation of a non-relational understanding of hybridity into a self-referential postcolonial orthodoxy has often been to the detriment of specific regional considerations. Similarly, the outright dismissal of diversity and the privileging of hybridity – the rejection in favour of liminality of a model of intercultural exchange that recognizes, initially at least, specific aspects of cultures in contact – fails to account for the complex range of practices and encounters that 'exoticism' (not reduced to its purely colonial form) conceals. In a defence of the term, Ron Shapiro criticizes 'postcolonialism's puritanical fumigation of language', claiming that 'critical terms like exotic [...] are subject to a merciless grinding down to a single ideological edge, thereby sharply reducing the range of different contexts in which such words might retain some usefulness and flexibility of meaning' (2000, 43). His position is polemical, caricaturing what might be seen as extreme, derivative applications of postcolonial theory, but it reveals at the same time an aspect of exoticism that is customarily eclipsed in denunciations of the concept – i.e. the notion that 'some degree of exoticism is intrinsic to the cognition of otherness since otherness is, by definition, constructed from a single position' (42). It is not so much exoticism, then, as a specifically colonizing, assimilative, one-way form of the process that postcolonialism tends to target. It is possible, therefore, as Victor Segalen suggests (2002 [1978]), to view exoticism as a reciprocal process involving the generation of mutual knowledge and associated with processes of inter-cultural contact alternative to those of colonialism. Once these aspects are acknowledged, the need for a re-exploration of the field of the exotic becomes increasingly apparent (Forsdick 2002), for exoticism is not a static, ahistorical practice exemplified by European attitudes towards otherness in the late nineteenth and early twentieth centuries, but one whose dynamics are rooted in diverse chronological and geographical contexts.

A number of exemplary studies have already begun this process of elaborating a more complex genealogy of exoticism, either in ambitious overviews associating the concept with the allied concepts of relativism, rac(ial)ism and nationalism (Todorov 1993 [1989]) or in more focused case studies exploring its operation at a particular historical moment (Porter and Rousseau 1990; Robbins 2002). As critiques of Orientalism subsequent to Edward Said's exploration of that practice have revealed, it was not so much rehabilitation of the concept that was necessary as its further attenuation – an attenuation in which French-language sources, with which *Orientalism* and *Culture and Imperialism* already engage closely, have proved invalu-able, despite apparent French antipathy to Said's work (Murphy 2002, 180–1). Indeed many of the points raised by the more perceptive early readers of *Orientalism* are applicable to exoticism itself: the need to view questions of Orientalist misrepresentation in relation to issues of the (un)reliability of representation in general (Clifford 1988); the recognition of the polyphony inherent in Orientalist accounts and evident in texts right back to the twelfth-century Franco-Italian travel account of Marco Polo (Porter 1983); or an awareness of the heterogeneity of Orientalist discourses and their progressive transformation according to historical circumstances (Lowe 1991).

Aijaz Ahmad dismisses *Orientalism* as an 'Aeschylus-to-Kissinger narrative' (1992, 183), portraying Said's thesis as a seamless one, a strait-jacket imposing a monolithic understanding of representations of elsewhere. The charge is unfair, ignoring the genuine complexity that emerges from the tensions of Said's narrative (Moore-Gilbert 1997, 43–4), although it might accurately be made against some of his less rigorous exegetes. Ahmad's accusation of a decontextualized ahistoricism is one that might similarly be applied to certain understandings of exoticism, as might be the concerns (addressed subsequently by Said himself in *Culture and Imperialism*) that the process inevitably silences indigenous voices and suppresses dissent among those seeking alternative ways of engaging with otherness. Despite these similarities, exoticism has not attracted commentaries as substantial as those devoted to Orientalism, at least not among postcolonial critics or scholars in the English-speaking world, and there is a tendency to conflate the two terms, with the power imbalance inherent in the former cast (para-doxically perhaps, in a move from the hazily particular to the general) as a more widespread version of the latter. As Santaolalla has argued (2000, 10–11), however, there is a need to distinguish between the two: Orientalism and exoticism are not synonymous and do not follow the same patterns. Not only is exoticism less geographically determined; but also, often disrupting the mono-directional and essentially colonial nature of Orientalism with what Santaolalla casts as its 'multidirectional and polyvalent' potential (2000, 13), exoticism provides a much more versatile means of understanding intercultural contact and the mutual implications of the interaction of cultures. As Longley has claimed, both the reflexivity of the 'exotic' as a category and the diverse range of processes contained in the term 'exoticism' have major implications for those interested in exploring collective identity formation, the instability of identity when faced with radical difference and the means whereby cultures negotiate such a challenge: '[exoticism] not only marks the culture's limits but points to the endless spaces beyond its boundaries from which the culture is viewed by others' (Longley 2000, 30).

In the light of such an understanding of the term as the brokering of mutual incomprehension, the negotiation of the gap between often radically different value systems, exoticism is usefully understood in relation to a definition that presents it as a process of translation of elsewhere. Such a definition requires that the term be stripped of the fixed value judgements with which its semantic field is customarily saturated and returned to the more neutral, original understanding of 'exotique' that the epithet's etymology implies (Maigne 1985). Segalen proposed such a reassessment of 'exotisme' in the early twentieth century, despite his hesitation over the retention of a 'bloated and compromised word, abused, ready to explode, to burst, to empty itself of everything' (2002, 56). Like 'travel' (hooks 1992, 173), 'hybridity' (Young 1995) or a number of other terms that despite colonial connotations have been revitalized by postcolonial usage, exoticism retains what Clifford calls a 'historical taintedness' (1997, 39) that far from compromising the term is a constant reminder of the need to avoid its abstraction and ensure its historicization. If exoticism is cast as translation – with translation understood here not as a purely linguistic or technical matter, but as a more general process by which diverse groups such as travellers (Cronin 2000) or postcolonial authors (Bassnett and Trivedi 1999) make sense of other cultures – the issues with which this chapter is concerned become central to debates about emergent fields such as Intercultural Studies. With the emphasis on degrees of transformation, the issue is no longer authenticity, fidelity or accuracy; the often cited if less frequently analysed Italian adage – 'traduttore–traditore' – fades from view. André Lefèvre describes translation instead as 'a channel opened [...] through which foreign influences can penetrate the native culture, challenge it and even contribute to subverting it' (cited in Bassnett 1993, 159).

Understanding exoticism as process of translation encourages us to explore what happens when one culture – or, more accurately, its representative(s) – comes into contact with a radically different culture and attempts to bring an account of it home to an audience whose attitudes might range from paranoid fear to unbridled enthusiasm. At the same time, however, as Victor Segalen's account of early missionary activity in Tahiti written from a purportedly Polynesian perspective attempts to show (1995 [1907]), if exoticism is to be understood as a reciprocal, two-way process, then it also potentially encompasses the ways in which non-Western cultures process and represent the jolt inherent in contact with other cultures, whether that experience involves active travel (e.g. Dadié 1959; Kpomassie 1981) or occurs, as in Segalen's example, 'sur place'. Here, in what is a reaction to the perceived impasse of colonial discourse, we must proceed with caution, stressing the need not only for meticulous contextualization (historical, geographical and cultural) that takes into account the imbalance of power relations in any given encounter, but also for avoidance of any critical practice that conflates the radically different processes of exoticism that emerge from such encounters. In her study of the Swiss tradition of 'human zoos', Brändle claims that without such detailed 'micro-études', overgeneralized, pan-European uses of the notion risk collapsing into redundancy (2002). There is a need for similar caution in more general considerations of exoticism – a need to avoid generalizations that impose a blanket understanding of exoticism transcending the period, place and circumstances in which different cultures come into contact.

Although recent readings of exoticism have been influenced by an apparent bifurcation between English-language and French approaches to the area – one heavily influenced by the overdetermining postcolonial dismissal of the notion (to which I have alluded above), the other often underestimating the role of colonialism as a result of the rejection of postcolonialism by many French-language scholars – there have nevertheless been a number of recent works that have begun to map the territory outlined already and offer critical engagements with exoticism that emphasize its instability and unevenness. Chris Bongie has proposed a binary distinction between 'imperialist' and 'exoticizing' exoticisms, the first ethnocentric and appropriative, the second characterized by a chronic extroversion that privileges elsewhere as a 'possible refuge from an overbearing modernity' (1991, 16–17).

Definitions offered by Jean-Marc Moura and Roger Célestin depend more on sliding scales. Moura (1992b, 16–25) describes a range of exoticist practices whose extremes are 'fantaisie exotique' [exotic fantasy] (dependent on cliché and stereotype) and 'écriture de l'altérité' [writing alterity] (in which there is a genuine engagement with and perpetuation of otherness). In the work of Célestin, the scale ranges from 'exemplification' to 'experimentation', the former characterized by the total domestication of the exotic object, the latter (at its extreme) by the evaporation of observing traveller-subject absorbed into the radical otherness of the exotic periphery (1996, 5–7).

All three respond to the early twentieth-century critique of exoticism by Victor Segalen, and it is with a consideration of his work that this chapter will conclude. Naval doctor, poet, novelist, travel writer and essayist, Segalen died prematurely in 1919. His writings emerged slowly in the post-war period until he became a major point of reference for a number of postmodern and postcolonial critics. His primary reflections on exoticism are a series of fragments jotted between 1904 and 1918 (Segalen 2002), and his notion of an 'aesthetics of diversity' is a common point of reference for scholars of exoticism seeking a convenient definition of the term. Although Segalen is better known through decontextualized quotation than as a result of sustained engagement with his work, his early twentieth-century struggle with 'le Divers' [Diversity] is invaluable to any exploration of exoticism not because it provides such portable and universally applicable definitions, but because it performs a series of contradictions central to our understanding of the concept.

As I have already suggested above, Segalen's reconsideration of the semantic field of the exotic – his refusal to reduce it to 'the tropics or coconut trees, the colonies or Negro souls' (2002, 46) – results in a reorientation of exoticism and its extension beyond a narrowly defined set of primitivist clichés and Orientalist stereotypes. Linked to this terminological shift is a more robust conceptual grasp of the operation of exoticism, dependent on the interaction of radically different cultures. It is in following the logic of this stipulation of radical difference that Segalen's reflections are often, for early twenty-first-century readers, uncomfortable reading. Borrowing the vocabulary of thermodynamics, Segalen identifies a process of global 'entropy' (2002, 48) whereby as a result of various aspects of modernity (colonialism, tourism, the mechanization of transport, feminism, the democratization of public life) individual cultures are drifting towards a unified monoculture: if there is a progressive levelling of diversity, he asks, how might the distances on which exoticism depends be perpetuated? Although in his essay and in correspondence, bemoaning the spread of 'métissage' [hybridity], Segalen fails to provide a positive answer, the formal innovation of his creative work – e.g. the 'Tahitian' novel *Les Immémoriaux*, or the 'Chinese' poetry collection *Stèles* – by attempting to present non-Western cultures from indigenous perspectives, or by transforming the page into a laboratory of intercultural contact, suggests ways in which new forms of exoticism might emerge.

Popular with 1950s authors, such as Glissant and Khatibi, seeking to think through the cultural implications of decolonization (Forsdick 2000), Segalen proposed a sense of indigenous identity, separate from colonial influence or interference. It is in a postcolonial frame that his apparently strict binaries, opposing hybridity with diversity, become more challenging. For in his own colonial context Segalen posed a series of questions with postcolonial import: does diversity inevitably depend on essentialism and the regulation of cultural interaction? Does hybridity inevitably erode the possibility of individually distinctive cultures? Does contact between cultures – or, by extension, representation of one culture by another – inevitably entail the assimilation of the weaker by the stronger, or might new configurations (or new modes of representation) emerge? These questions, ignored when Segalen was writing, are now central to postcolonial criticism, and this is why the contradictions of Segalen's work might usefully be more closely explored by postcolonial critics – as opposed to being rapidly dismissed, as is the case in the work of Said (Forsdick 1997). As Glissant's ongoing engagement with Segalen has revealed, a postcolonial understanding of Diversity – rooted in each culture's right to resist transparency, to be opaque (Glissant 1990, 203–9) – is central to reflections on cultural relativism, to considerations of the possibility of non-hierarchical relationships between cultures, of the subaltern's self-articulation (and self-determination), of resistance to often overwhelming forces of cultural assimilation. It is negotiation of the relationship between Diversity and 'métissage' that poses the greatest challenge, and Segalenian exoticism leaves unresolved the tension, in Khatibi's terms, between 'identité aveugle' [blind identity] and 'différence sauvage' [savage difference] (cited in Gontard 1990, 168), between the crippling introversion of a hermetically essentialist view of culture and the chronic extroversion of a free-floating, decontextualized hybridity. With paradigms such as James Clifford's 'travelling cultures' (1997) or Mary Louise Pratt's 'transculturation' (1992), we move beyond the restrictions of such a polarized view, finding new ways of articulating the patterns of diversity in a postcolonial world. Exoticism has travelled a long way from reductively colonial understandings of the term with which this chapter began. No longer simply dismissed as an adjunct to colonial discourse, it emerges as a concept central to postcolonial criticism and worthy of very serious consideration.

|5|

Empire on film: from exoticism to 'cinéma colonial'

BY ELIZABETH EZRA

From the turn of the twentieth century to just before the Second World War, colonial culture in France was at its apogee, or what Raoul Girardet refers to as its 'apothéose' (1972, 175). The colonial empire expanded dramatically in the first decades of the Third Republic, a military expansion that was soon accompanied by an unprecedented proliferation of colonial imagery in official and popular culture. The novels of Pierre Loti and Pierre Mille, like many of the exoticist novels of Flaubert and poems of Baudelaire before them, inspired dreams of faraway lands complete with abundant raw materials and compliant natives. As the new century dawned, however, popular culture became increasingly visual. The paintings of Paul Gauguin conjured up colourful images of the (French) tropics, and lavishly illustrated reviews such as *Le Petit Journal* and *L'Illustration* inspired a generation of budding colonial officers to don dashing white uniforms and travel to distant lands. In 1889, the advent of photo-offset printing gave rise to the booming trade in picture postcards depicting scenes of colonial life (which often featured scantily clad North African women), and advertising campaigns for *Banania* breakfast drink featured, first, a Caribbean version of Lady Bountiful, and then, after the First World War, the 'Y'a bon' Senegalese soldier whose grinning face soon became a cultural icon. In the period leading up to what became known as the Jazz Age, modernist fascination with the 'primitive' was embodied in representations not only of French colonial subjects, but also of African-Americans, who played a significant role in the shaping of France's exoticist visual culture.

One of the most popular cultural events of the late nineteenth and early twentieth centuries was the colonial exhibition, sometimes presented on its own (as in 1915, 1922 and 1931), and sometimes in conjunction with the great world's fairs (as in 1889, 1900 and 1937). The colonial exhibitions purported to offer visitors a glimpse of life in the colonies, as crowds gathered to watch imperial subjects displayed like living museum exhibits in their 'natural habitats', or French-designed reconstructions of native villages. Designed to combine the fruits of the newly developed science of ethnography with entertainment, the exhibitions anticipated the vogue for 'info-tainment' by nearly a century. Walking through these colonial villages, or being propelled by means of rickshaws or, as in 1931, a little purpose-built train that conveyed them around the Bois de Vincennes, visitors could feel as though they had travelled to the ends of the earth without having left Paris (see Forsdick, Chapter 4, for further discussion of such practices).

This emphasis on the spectacular in colonial culture found a powerful form of expression in the new medium of cinema, which created imagined communities through moving images. The illusion of mobility in stasis cultivated at the exhibitions was perfected in film, as viewers could look in on the colonies from the comfort of their cinema seats. This medium at first complemented, but would eventually supersede, the exhibitions as a means of circulating images of France's colonial empire. Like the exhibitions, representations of the colonial in film offered both entertainment and the trappings of ethnographic investigation. Exoticist cinema served as a means of identification and as a marker of acquisition, as did the displays at the colonial exhibitions, which showed the French what (and whom) their country had appropriated, bringing to their doorstep all that had become part of 'La Plus Grande France'. Cinematic displays of empire gave French visitors a sense of control over alterity, as it was brought to them in a contained form, in which potentially threatening difference was domesticated.

Film in the silent era did not often engage overtly with colonial issues, but the implicit assumptions that underlay many films with exoticist themes, and especially those that depicted Africans (or African-Americans), contributed to what I have elsewhere called France's 'colonial unconscious' (Ezra 2000), paving the way for the adventure epics of the 1920s, and culminating in the 'cinéma colonial' of the 1930s.

Exotic origins

From its very beginnings, cinema was fascinated by colonialism. The 'fathers of cinema', the Lumière brothers, were also the fathers of 'cinéma colonial', which is as old as cinema itself. Two Lumière films made in 1896, just months after the first public screening of the 'cinématographe', reveal the desire for control and mastery displayed in most colonial representations of the period. The first, *Baignade de nègres* (July 1896), was filmed at the Jardin d'Acclimatation in Paris, where subjects of the French colonial empire had been transported for centuries in order to be displayed before a curious public. In this 'village colonial', a group of adolescent African boys wearing knee-length shorts jump and dive into a lake, then wade back to the shore and jump in again. In the background, African men paddle in canoes back and forth across the small lake. The whole scene is observed by white spectators, some with parasols, who stand at the water's edge; a white man appears to dictate the action from the side of the lake, motioning the Africans in and out of the water, hurrying them along. In the second film, titled *Coolies à Saigon* (December 1896), a French colonial officer in white uniform walks across a street with his back to the camera, followed by a Vietnamese man. Regimented rows of Vietnamese men march across the frame diagonally, pulling a large vehicle with a single, monolithic wheel, carrying a long piece of wood that appears to be either a kind of building material or a weapon. When the cortège is out of frame, the colonial officer, followed by his native companion, crosses the street again, this time toward the camera – thereby 'framing' the labour.

In both films, a white man controls the activity depicted, as if 'directing' the scene, whether by instructing the African boys and men to enter and leave the water in *Baignade de nègres*, or, in the case of *Coolies à Saigon*, by marching across the street authoritatively before and after the Vietnamese pull their heavy load past. In this way, the colonizer presents himself as both the source and destination of the labourers' activity. A similar technique is used in a film the Lumière brothers shot in Annam (today Vietnam) in early 1900, *Le Village de Namo: panorama pris d'une chaise à porteurs*. This film follows in the tradition of the popular panorama film originated as early as 1896 by Zecca cameraman Promio, and continued by Méliès in his 1898 *Panorama pris d'un train en marche*, in which the camera was attached to a moving vehicle, giving early audiences a sense of exhilaration and movement. In the Lumière film, small children are shown running towards the camera head on, as it moves backward, all the while laughing in curious delight. Two men walking behind the children towards the camera carry a long object, which appears to be a canoe, between them on a stick across their shoulders. The children eventually scatter out of frame, and, as the film ends, the men carrying the canoe continue towards the camera. Once again, in this film, the Western camera operator is controlling the scene, directing everyone toward the viewer, as if to say that these children can be made to come to you, the centre of the world, as can these strapping adult men who are capable of performing heavy labour. In many ways, these early films set the scene for films depicting 'exotic' subjects through the next three decades, by depicting the appropriation, containment and domestication of alterity.

Ethnography and entertainment

At the turn of the twentieth century, looking at people became a means of sizing them up, classifying them in the racial categories devised by the new science of ethnography, which was intended both to facilitate and to justify colonial domination. Ethnography, which was based on observation, made early use of visual media such as photography and cinema. In 1895, the photographer and amateur ethnographer Félix Regnault took a series of photographs at the Exposition Ethnographique in Paris of West Africans engaged in various ordinary physical activities such as running, jumping, carrying children and cooking (Rony 1996, 48 *et passim*). He used a chronophotographic device developed by his mentor Étienne-Jules Marey, a pioneer of pre-cinema. Regnault's images served to identify and classify features of the 'African gait', in order to help French troops improve their own agility. Since much of West Africa was under French control, this amounted to domination by means of imitation. Many of the films made in the pre- and early sound period reflect this colonial strategy of importing and appropriating the skills of the colonized for the purposes of containment and control. Regnault's photographs of African bodies in motion, like other ethnographic footage of traditional dance, prefigured films that featured Africans (or, as was often the case, African-Americans) dancing. In many of these films, white French people are shown performing a dance associated with Africans. For example, in 1903, two films were made celebrating the arrival in France of the cakewalk, which had originated with American slaves: *Le Cakewalk infernal*, by Georges Méliès, and *Le Cakewalk chez les nains*, made by the Pathé company. Both films show Africans transferring their knowledge of the cakewalk to Europeans. Ironically, by appropriating this dance, the French were participating in a *mise en abîme*, because the cakewalk was already a parodic imitation by blacks of white slave owners' gait.

In *Le Cakewalk infernal* (1903), Méliès plays the role of the devil who is taught how to do the cakewalk by two African-American dancers in blackface (as was the tradition in American minstrelsy). When the devil dances, first his legs, then his arms, detach from his body and dance independently of their owner. The film, one of the most euphoric and energetic that Méliès ever made, ends in a riotous dance sequence, as the devil's female minions join him in frenzied abandon. The spectacle of the black dancers is rendered exotic by association with the supernatural through the film's infernal setting as well as by the special effects – a novelty in this period – that created the devil's disarticulated limbs. The devil and his minions, played by white dancers, take over the dance, ending the film in a frenzy of high kicks. In *Le Cakewalk chez les nains*, a top-hatted magician, apparently of African origin, watches over two miniature dancers of apparently European origin, dressed in old-fashioned shepherd and shepherdess costumes, doing a traditional European dance. The magician makes the couple disappear and reappear again dressed in more modern clothes; this time, the couple does the cakewalk, a skill apparently imparted to them by the African magician. The magician makes the couple disappear a second time, appearing himself, now in miniature, in their place, doing the cakewalk.

In *Le Cakewalk chez les nains*, dance is associated metonymically with magic, and with the supernatural powers suggested by means of special effects such as substitution splicing. The cakewalk is presented as a phenomenon as fantastical as the magic implicit in the sudden appearances, disappearances, and changes in size. Similarly, the diabolical setting of *Le Cakewalk infernal* adds a layer of the fantastic that goes beyond 'mere' magic, which was an ordinary feature of Méliès's films, since the filmmaker was first and foremost a professional magician. In both films, the cakewalk is represented as something alien, transgressive and indeed transformative, transmitted to Europeans by African-Americans. As the African magician enables the European couple to perform the cakewalk in the Pathé film, he also transforms their old-fashioned costumes into contemporary clothes, suggesting an African influence in the construction of European modernity. This suggestion, which anticipated the modernist vogue for negrophilia in the 1920s (epitomized in Paul Morand's best-selling 1927 short story collection, *Magie noire*), would inform the depiction of Africans in many films of the silent era.

The colonial-modern aesthetic

Dance, the exotic and a self-conscious modernity also converge in another film produced near the end of the silent period, *Charleston* (1927) by Jean Renoir, also known under the title *Sur un air de Charleston*. Like the cakewalk films that had depicted the earlier dance vogue, also of American origin, *Charleston* plays on the eponymous dance form's status as an import. In this short fantasy, an explorer from the future (2028), played by African-American dancer Johnny Hudgins, lands in Paris following an apocalyptic war that has destroyed the city and decimated nearly all its inhabitants. When the explorer disembarks from his spherical flying saucer, he encounters a wild woman, played by Catherine Hessling, accompanied by her pet gorilla. The woman immediately pursues the explorer, chasing him and finally pinning him to a post, where she ties him up and forces him to watch her perform the Charleston. Horrified, the explorer at first tries to shield his eyes, but little by little, he becomes intrigued, and then fascinated, by the strange dance. He announces in an intertitle, 'I have discovered the Charleston, a dance originating with the white races'. The woman then proceeds to teach the dance to the visitor, who, after a few awkward attempts, masters the technique. At the end of the film, the woman joins the explorer in his flying saucer, as an intertitle declares: 'And thus was imported to Africa a new fashion: the Culture of the Indigenous Whites' (capitals in original).

As in Méliès's *Cakewalk infernal*, the African in *Charleston* is made to seem alien by virtue of his association with the supernatural: in this case, in a science fiction fantasy set in the distant future. The whole film is structured on a reversal: black invades white, observes and learns from white, then takes white back with him, in an inversion of the slavery model. It is the African who appears gauche, without rhythm or natural grace, whereas the white woman appears to have mastered the dance; it is the African who is timid, whereas the white woman is threatening and sexually aggressive. Like the special technical effects in Méliès's and Pathé's films that dazzled their contemporary audiences, Renoir's film highlights (albeit in satirical mode) technological progress. The film's setting in the distant future ostensibly compels viewers to rethink notions of modernity and the primitive. But the film ultimately reinforces the very stereotypes it inverts. According to Martin O'Shaughnessy, the actor Johnny Hudgins's 'American origins link him to a New World modernity that threatens to overtake a decadent ruined Europe while his Africanness helps to defuse the threat by making his modernity a joke' (2000, 63). As in the cakewalk films, the 'civilized' observer is taught how to move by a 'savage', who is eventually whisked back to the explorer's homeland, presumably to help import the new dance to the people at home.

This pattern of colonial appropriation is repeated in the films of the late silent and early sound period starring Josephine Baker. Having arrived in Paris in 1925 with a black dance review from the United States, Baker stayed in France, and soon became an icon of the Jazz Age. Despite hailing from St Louis, Missouri, she was most often identified with the French colonies in her films and stage shows: her biggest music-hall success was the title role in *La Créole* (1935), and her most celebrated song began, 'J'ai deux amours, Paris et mon pays' – the implication being that her 'country' was a French colony, rather than the United States.

Baker's earliest film, *La Sirène des tropiques* (Henri Etievant and Mario Nalpas, 1927), plays on modernism's appropriation of the cultural artifacts of societies deemed 'primitive'. Near the end of the film, Baker dances before an awe-struck crowd after ripping off her sequined evening gown (anticipating a similar climactic scene in the 1935 *Princesse Tam-Tam*) to reveal a modernist geometric-print outfit that looks like something Léger would have designed. Not uncoincidentally, this 'modernist' outfit is identical in cut (scoop neck, tank top, skirt that ties sarong-like in the front, lengthening diagonally down each leg, with a long fringe) and very similar in design to the outfit the Baker character earlier wears in the tropics when dancing outside a grass hut with other villagers. In a similar arrangement to that of the modernist geometric shapes, the tropical version of the outfit sports polka dots and a large flower, as if to suggest that the 'primitive' becomes modern(ist) when transplanted to the 'métropole', like the Oceanic sculptures that ended up in Picasso's private collection in Paris. The 'primitive' body in motion, it is implied, has inspired the modernist aesthetic, as dancer Loïe Fuller's swirling movements had inspired the curves of Art Nouveau. The modernist observation of the 'primitive', as evidenced in its appropriation of the latter's iconography, enables Western culture to contain the 'other', much as the Lumière films described earlier equated looking with control. The domestication of alterity is the underside of modernism's surface abandon in music, clothing, art, and dance. This move to contain and control underpins the apparent rapprochement through imitation in the colonial–modern aesthetic.

Colonial appropriation is also evoked in the 1934 *Zouzou*, when the eponymous heroine, played by Baker, is 'discovered' while doing a dance in which she poses like a soldier shooting – like, in fact, a 'zouave', from which the name 'Zouzou' derives. The term 'zouave', which originally referred to Kabyle troops who fought for France, was adopted by the French army to refer to battalions composed entirely of French nationals dressed in 'exotic' uniforms. First, the Kabyle warriors themselves, and then their dress and even their name, were taken over by the French, while the original 'zouaves' themselves were 'literally and figuratively eliminated from that army corps, dispossessed of their own name and reassigned to other army units' (Norindr 1999, 118). Josephine Baker's soldier pose in *Zouzou* thus explicitly invokes the colonial appropriation of the colonized; like the cakewalk, this appropriation is shown to come full circle, as Zouzou, a colonial subject, reclaims the zouaves' history in both image and name.

This moment of 'revanche' is brief, however, as Zouzou ends the film perched in a giant birdcage, pining away for her lost homeland in a music-hall number. The image of Zouzou as a caged bird, literally imprisoned behind bars, recalls an early Pathé film, the 1907 *Mésaventures d'une mission nègre à Paris*, which ends with the king of a visiting African delegation (played by white actors in blackface), having created all kinds of mayhem and shocked Parisian passers-by with his antics, locked up behind bars. These images of imprisonment are apt metaphors for the containment of colonial alterity.

When alterity cannot be controlled or contained, however, it must be eliminated, as certain films of the early sound era demonstrate. In *Le Blanc et le noir* (Robert Florey, 1930), based on the play by Sacha Guitry, a white woman has an adulterous affair with an African-American singer, which results in the birth of a black baby. The woman's husband, who sees the baby before she regains consciousness after childbirth and realizes what has happened, takes the baby to the Assistance Publique and exchanges it for a white baby before his wife wakes up. The man is portrayed as a hero for standing by his wife and raising the white child as his own. In this morality tale of 'acceptance', what drops out of the equation is the black baby, whose absence is the prerequisite for the white couple's happiness. In *Dainah la métisse*, a Jean Grémillon film made the following year, the elimination of the problematic 'other' takes a more sinister turn when a woman of African descent literally disappears from a luxury cruise ship, presumably having been pushed overboard. In *Princesse Tam-Tam* (Edmond Gréville, 1935), Josephine Baker's second sound film, the 'other' is merely left behind in her native Tunisia, instead of relocating to Paris with the French novelist for whom she has been a source of inspiration. The implication is that Tunisia is where Aouina belongs, and that any attempt to integrate into French society is doomed to failure.

Cinéma colonial

Baker's arrival in Paris and her brief film career came at a time when exoticist cinema was undergoing a transformation. Throughout the inter-war period, cinema showed an increasing interest in the French colonial empire, as emphasis shifted from representations of sub-Saharan Africa(ns) to depictions of North Africa. The empire ceased to be forbiddingly alien, and instead became 'un espace familier, pétri de toutes les influences de la civilisation européenne' [a familiar space steeped in the influence of European civilization] (Benali 1998, 35). In the 1930s, according to Dudley Andrew, 'the exciting and robust adventure tales of Africa common to the silent screen became transformed into quieter, more desperate films' (1995, 242). Colonial cinema itself became appropriated by official colonial institutions and reordered into a rehearsal of familiar domestic anxieties.

The vogue for colonial adventure films was ignited by Jacques Feyder's 1921 film *L'Atlantide*, which was based on Pierre Benoît's 1919 bestselling novel, and which became a huge blockbuster both at home and abroad. Before the Rif War came to a head in 1925, most colonial films were shot in Morocco, but in the late 1920s and the 1930s changing Moroccan labour conditions, combined with offers of assistance from the Algerian-based Foreign Legion, made it more economical to film in Algeria. Films shot in Morocco bear the imprint of Marshal Hubert Lyautey, who 'pacified' the region in 1912, and whose policy of 'association', or indirect rule, was reflected in sympathetic (some would say paternalistic) portrayals of Berbers (Slavin 2001, 58–83). Many of these films would be remade in the sound era, including, most notably, *Les Cinq Gentlemen maudits* (1919 and 1931), as well as *L'Atlantide* (remade in 1932 by G.W. Pabst); *Les Hommes nouveaux* (1922 and 1936); *L'Aventurier* (1924 and 1934); *La Maison du Maltais* (1927 and 1938); and *L'Occident* (1927 and 1937). The remakes often differed significantly from the originals, reflecting the tensions and concerns of the era in which they were produced (see Slavin 1996; Ungar 1996; Benali 1998, 37–50).

Key colonial films from the 1930s include Jacques Feyder's *Le Grand Jeu* (1934); Marie Epstein and Jean-Benoît Lévy's *Itto* (1934); Marcel L'Herbier's *Les Hommes nouveaux* (1936); Léon Poirier's *L'Appel du silence* (1936); Pierre Chenal's *La Maison du Maltais* (1938); Jacques de Baroncelli's *L'Homme du Niger* (1939); and Julien Duvivier's *Les Cinq Gentlemen maudits* (1931), *La Bandera* (1935), and *Pépé le Moko* (1936). These films take a variety of generic approaches to their subjects, ranging from romantic melodrama (*Le Grand Jeu* and *La Maison du Maltais*) to battle epic (*La Bandera*) to film noir (*Pépé le Moko*) to explicit propaganda (*Les Hommes nouveaux, L'Homme du Niger, L'Appel du silence*). Stock characters in colonial cinema include the small-time crook or failed hustler fleeing France to start over in the Foreign Legion; the once-successful businessman, ruined by his love for a bad woman, hoping to leave his past behind; the humanitarian doctor or valiant colonial officer working to fulfil France's 'mission civilisatrice' [civilizing mission]; and the bored society woman looking for a little adventure. In the 1930s, the colonial empire is portrayed as a means of escape from the turmoil and perceived decadence of a France divided by political conflict. The colonies appear to offer these characters a chance for redemption, but invariably cement their ruin. Although the majority of films of this period were grounded in the construction of stark oppositions between colonizer and colonized, some painted a more ambiguous picture of the colonial project, blurring, or at the very least complicating, preconceived notions of clear boundaries between colony and 'métropole'. *Pépé le Moko*, for example, has been singled out by many scholars for its portrayal of hybridized racial and sexual identities, especially in the figures of Pépé and Slimane (Morgan 1994; O'Shaughnessy 1996; O'Brien 1997; Vincendeau 1998). The sound version of *La Maison du Maltais*, too, has been shown to undermine the idea of a stable colonial identity (Ungar 1996). The cosy images of the 'Hexagone' conjured up by expatriates in these and other films of the era were rooted in nostalgia for a place that was either a distant memory or had never existed in the first place.

In films of the 1930s, the colonized, usually relegated to an indistinct mass, are often referred to as 'les salopards' [the bastards], and are almost always either absent from the film credits, or featured much less prominently than the importance of their roles would indicate (Lagny *et al.* 1986, 127–76). Marie Epstein and Jean Benoît-Lévy's *Itto* (1934) has often been cited as an exception to these practices, because of its use of authentic Berber dialogue and its penultimate scene, in which a white French woman is shown breastfeeding a Berber baby alongside her own child. Hailed by some critics as a celebration of universalist Republican values, the film has also, however, been read as a glorification of the 'Berber myth', which aligned this group with the French against the Arabic peoples of the Maghreb (Slavin 2001, 115–17). At best, then, colonial cinema portrayed natives of North Africa in a paternalistic light that aimed to advance colonial objectives.

One of these objectives was a didactic one. In the last decades of the Third Republic, feature films often depicted the colonized as ethnographic objects of contemplation in didactic, documentary-style vignettes, such as those featured in *Les Cinq Gentlemen maudits* (which opens with footage of tribal dance and a possession ceremony) and *Pépé le Moko* (in which voice-over is used to describe the Casbah and the various groups that inhabit it). Charles O'Brien argues that these 'unsettling' moments 'exceed the representational capacities of the official culture' (1997, 223), while Dudley Andrew contends that their subversiveness is subsumed in the reassuring generic conventions of the 'cinéma colonial', which 'sought to erase the line between the genres so as to produce a homogeneous experience, the experience of classic French film', which generated 'cinematographic comfort' (1997, 233, 234). As unsettling as these stylistic incursions are, however, the documentary representational forms they invoke were certainly already familiar to the French filmgoing public, who had flocked to films such as *La Croisière noire* (Poirier, 1926), which followed the Citroën-sponsored car rally from Algeria to Madagascar; Marc Allégret's *Voyage au Congo* (1927), based on André Gide's travelogue; and the US import *Africa Speaks* (Paul Hoefler and Walter Hugger, 1931). The staging of difference, in other words, was in itself a source of 'cinematographic comfort' for a public accustomed to the ethnographic gaze in both documentary and fiction films, in a tradition that extended back to the birth of cinema.

Instead of separating 'pure' spectacle designed to entertain from an ethnographic representational style, French exoticist cinema, like the colonial exhibitions, has always combined the two. Documentary moments in the 'cinéma colonial' – like the Lumières' actuality footage – point to a self-consciously pedagogical dimension to the films that mirrors the function of the colonial exhibitions, whose explicit aim was to 'educate' as well as entertain. In the latter half of the 1930s, the lesson being imparted was, as ever, that of the usefulness of the colonies (in terms of manufacturing, commerce, and tourism); what was changing, however, was the use envisaged for them. As the Second World War approached, depictions of the appropriation, containment and reordering of colonial subjects served to bolster French self-confidence about the country's military capabilities. The 'cinéma colonial' reminded the French (and, to some extent, the rest of the world) that the 'troupes coloniales', who had served so well in the First World War, could again be useful in any impending conflict with Germany. Though it often eschewed scenes of overt violence, colonial cinema none the less glorified French military prowess. And the role of the colonized, as it had been since before the beginning of cinema, was to be appropriated for use in the service of French global ambitions.

6

The Camus–Sartre debate and the colonial question in Algeria

BY AZZEDINE HADDOUR

Camus's anti-colonialist stance in the essays collected in *Actuelles III* (1965 [1958]) is at odds with his fictional writings which, despite his avowed refutation of colonialism, either disavow the issue of colonialism or replicate the thrust of its racist language. Arguably, with the exception of his short story 'The Guest' (1962 [1957]), Camus's work is ahistorical, bearing no relation to the historical context from which it emerges. Taking my cue from Macheray, I shall argue that between the œuvre and history there is necessarily a relation of reciprocity (Macheray 1978, 128); this relation in Camus's œuvre is not immediate and spontaneous, but is dissimulated. To determine what is reflected through the speculum of Camus's representation and what is suppressed, I shall analyse Camus's political views in *Actuelles III* and those of Sartre in *Colonialism and Neocolonialism* (Sartre 2001 [1964]; see P. Williams, Chapter 16, for a discussion of Sartre's absence from postcolonial theory), contrasting their respective positions vis-à-vis the Algerian crisis (see Drake 1999), I shall also study Camus's novel *The Plague* (1948 [1947]) and 'The Guest', two texts which mediate Camus's contradictory views.

Published as a series of articles in *Alger républicain* in June 1958, *Misère de la Kabylie* raises three issues: famine, unemployment and illiteracy. Initially, these articles cover the itinerary of famine that plagued Kabylia in the 1930s. Camus maintains that Kabylia was an overpopulated region that consumed more grain than it produced (1965, 905). Relying completely on agriculture, Kabylia was in the grip of a natural calamity, and famine was the price to be paid for its debts to an unyielding land: emigration was the only outlet to alleviate the plight of its people (905). However, the economic crisis that affected France after the great depression limited the job opportunities available to the Kabyles. In 1935 measures were put in place to prevent immigration, forcing them to return home. These restrictive measures left the Kabyles with no option but to starve in an immiserized Kabylia (906). Half of its population was out of work, which benefited the 'gros colons' [wealthy colonists] who exploited the famished Kabyles and paid them starvation wages (917). Illiteracy was another issue that aggravated their condition. Nine hundred thousand children in Algeria were deprived of education; about 80 per cent of Kabyle children did not go to school. The failure to educate them represented for Camus the failure of the doctrine of assimilation (923; for a discussion of assimilation in sub-Saharan Africa, see Murphy, Chapter 20). This failure, together with the measures that prevented immigration, denied the Kabyles the opportunity to better their condition. Camus advocates a politics that would guarantee the 'administrative emancipation' of the Kabyles and would improve their economic condition (928). He denounces the laws which stipulated that indigenous Kabyles and Arabs must renounce their Muslim status in order to become naturalized as French, arguing that it was the colonial administration that imposed on them this status (929). To find a solution to the plight of the Kabyles, Camus proposes that the French government must tackle unemployment, reform education to cater for the needs of their children, and remove restrictions on immigration (930).

The Second World War and its legacy brought more misery to colonized Algeria. Scores of Algerians served under the French flag in the fight against Nazism. On VE Day, 8 May 1945, the indigenous population was allowed to parade and to commemorate those who had given their lives in the French war effort. Thousands appeared carrying anti-colonial banners: for indigenous Algerians one repressive regime – Nazism – had been defeated, but colonialism still remained. The demonstrations culminated in massive repression throughout the country and the massacre of over 45,000 civilians by French police in Guelma, Kharata and Sétif. It was one of the ironies of history that the 'Free France' which found a refuge against Nazism in Algeria turned out to perpetuate Fascism in its colony (see P. Williams, Chapter 16, for a discussion of similar ideas in Césaire's *Discourse on Colonialism*). The 1945 crisis was a landmark in the history of the colony, announcing the beginning of the end of French Algeria.

Camus was sent by *Combat* to investigate the circumstances of the uprising. In *Crise en Algérie*, written in response to the 1945 uprising, he contends that the political landscape of colonial Algeria was dominated by two opposing tendencies: those (i.e. the nationalists) who exaggerated the severity of the crisis, inciting the French government to deploy repressive measures, and those (i.e. the settlers) who were indifferent to the plight of the natives, and who had in fact opened a wedge between French and Algerians (941). Camus argues that Algerians had always wanted to be assimilated, but after 1945 they relinquished this desire (950). However, the doctrine of assimilation was never coherent: it was always proposed but never implemented; it met, principally among the 'gros colons', with a hostility that could not be denied (950–1). Although he refers to the failure of the politics of assimilation and the political marginalization of the colonized under French laws (952), much of his discussion centres around

Algeria's problems, which were, in his view, primarily economic. Famine, he maintains, was a plight always feared in Algeria where harvests were as capricious as the rain (944). Grain was the staple food of its people, millions of whom suffered because of the failure of their crops.

Like the earlier *Misère de la Kabylie*, Camus interprets a political crisis as a natural calamity, namely famine. In fact the uprising had marked colonial Algeria with a political awareness that challenged colonial oppression. François Quilici astutely remarks that *Crise en Algérie* mystified the political dimension of the crisis by suppressing its nationalistic impetus (cited in Siblot and Planche 1986, 160). In response to Quilici, Camus argues that his project is of reconciliation and not of obfuscation. In two articles, signed *Combat*, dating from 23 and 25 May 1945, Camus dismisses Quilici's inflamatory language. Camus's silence on the issue of the repression that claimed the lives of more than 45,000 people could be interpreted as a deliberate strategy to avoid heightening tension, and as an attempt to reconcile the conflicting parties. Some critics, however, levelled against him the charge of silencing political conflict.

In 'Lettres à un militant Algérien' addressed to Azziz Kessous at the height of the Algerian War, Camus reiterates some of the views expressed in *Misère de la Kabylie* and *Crise en Algérie* suggesting that France could no longer keep a silenced mass of people under the shadow of colonial hegenomy, forever denied and subjugated (964). In 'Algérie 1958', he concurs with the nationalists' denunciation of the abuses of French colonialism, deploring the exploitation, dehumanization and psychological degradation of the colonized; injustices which were bound up with colonialism, its history and its administration (1012). The critics of French colonialism in Algeria, he maintains, failed to differentiate between the 'gros colons' and the French Algerians, 80 per cent of whom were not 'colons' but belonged to the working class, and, though more privileged than the colonized, were worse off than the working class in mainland France (974). He refuses to offer the 'pieds noirs' as the expiating victims of French colonialism (898, 945, 974), instead charging the metropolis with colonial greed. Essentially, he represents the French Algerians, like the colonized Berbers and Arabs, as victims of the colonial system. He proposes a round table to bring the opposing factions together (971). In 'Le Parti de la trêve', he denounces colonial repression which denied the existence of the colonized's culture, and also rejects the demands of the nationalists for independence, which would mean the repatriation of over one million French Algerians (986). In 'L'Algérie nouvelle', he supports Professor Marc Lauriol's proposal outlining constitutional reforms to set up in the French Assembly a mainland section (comprising French and French Algerians) and an Algerian Muslim one – reforms which could, in Camus's view, put in place the necessary political structures for the establishment of a federalist state, akin to that of Switzerland, in which different ethnicities would become imbricated within the same territory.

Camus does not approve of the politics that perpetrated the misery of the colonized people but he also warns against what he calls a 'politics of abandonment' which jeopardized the political interests of France in Algeria (891). He attacks the Right for rallying behind the banner of patriotism and for allowing the Left to occupy the moral high ground; and attacks the Left for legitimizing the excesses and abuses of an incendiary nationalism in the name of justice (895). Both tendencies represented this 'politics of abandonment' that failed to reconcile the opposing parties in the Algerian crisis (898). He fears that, while Europe acknowledged the necessity of decolonization, Russia on the other hand was busy annexing many peoples to its ideology and was expanding its empire to the shores of North Africa (Egypt and Algeria were its new targets). He also fears that the natives would espouse the causes of an ascending imperialist ideology advocated by Egypt and sponsored by the Communist USSR. A Pan-Islamic state in Algeria was, in Camus's view, a fanciful idea held by the nationalists but without a future (979–80).

To recapitulate, Camus rejects both the politics of pacification undertaken by the French army to reconquer Algeria in the era of decolonization, and the revolutionary causes of the FLN, perceiving the latter's anti-colonial project as a threat to the political existence of French Algeria (900). His views are *ipso facto* contradictory: France should relinquish its colonial endeavour in Algeria, but its presence must continue.

Jeanson's review of Camus's philosophical text *The Rebel* in *Les Temps modernes* triggered a bitter controversy between Sartre and Camus. In his review, Jeanson criticizes Camus for elevating human suffering to a metaphysical level and for overlooking the economic, historical and political conditions which determined this suffering (Jeanson 1952, 2077). In 'Réponse à Albert Camus', Sartre reiterates this position, arguing that Camus holds a peculiar view of history which ignores the concrete situation of rebellion and that he is selective in his condemnation of injustice (Sartre 1964, 93, 107). For instance, although he condemns state terrorism and totalitarian theocracy, which he associates with Stalinism, Camus is oblivious to the Malagasy people who were tortured by colonial police, to the Vietnamese who were drowned in napalm or to the Tunisians who were plagued by the 'rats' of French colonialism (Jeanson 1952, 2090).

The Algerian War provided a forum for the controversy to continue. In January 1956, Camus went to Algeria to issue his 'Appel pour une trêve en Algérie' [Appeal for a truce in Algeria]. A few days after Camus's meeting in Le Cercle du Progrès in Algiers, Sartre organized a conference in the Salle Wagram in Paris to denounce the mystification of neocolonialism. Camus thought that the future of French Algeria was not compromised by the war. Sartre, on the other hand, believed that French colonialism was infecting the political life of the mainland with its racism, and that the task of the French people was to put an end to it.

In 'Le colonialisme est un système', Sartre warns against 'neocolonialist mystification', alluding to Camus's journalistic reportages which cover the misery suffered by the indigenous people thus:

> This mystification consists of the following: you are taken around Algeria, you are obligingly shown the extreme poverty of the people, which is dreadful, you are told of the humiliation the Muslims suffer at the hands of the wicked colonists. And then, when you are really outraged, they add: 'that is why the best Algerians have taken up arms; they couldn't take any more'. (2001, 30)

Sartre raises the same issues as Camus: famine, unemployment, immigration, education and assimilation. Sartre is quick to reject the view that 'the Algerian problem is *first of all* economic. It is a question of providing, by means of judicious reform, food for nine million'; he is also quick to refute the claim 'that the problem is *social*: the numbers of schools and doctors must be greatly increased' (30; emphasis in original). Sartre dismisses as 'neo-colonial mystification' the view epitomized by Camus that the 'old Franco-Muslim fraternity' could be rediscovered if the socio-economic conditions of the Algerians were improved (31), a view that simply ignores the politics of the colonial system in Algeria.

Sartre argues that, in the nineteenth century, capitalism went through a process of transformation to become colonialist (33). Jules Ferry was to become the theorist *par excellence* of this new brand of capitalism, which sought new markets for industrial and commercial expansion. Sartre astutely shows that 'the capital with which France "is awash" will not be invested in under-developed countries. [...] Ferry is very clear: capital will not leave France, it will simply be invested in new industries which will sell their manufactured products to the colonized country' (33). The viability of this project depended on colonial settlements. A number of laws were drafted to make legal the dispossession of the Algerian fellahs, and also paved the way for colonial settlements. Under the pretext of indexing the communal land of the indigenous tribes, that is to say privatizing it, the senatus-consulte of 1863 expropriated most of the fertile land. The Warnier Laws (1873) implemented another spoliation on a massive scale. As Ageron says, the aim of the colonial laws was to hand the land of the indigenous peoples to European settlers (1968, 101). For Sartre, '[t]he so-called development thus relied upon a plundering of the inhabitants that continued for a century. The story of Algeria is the progressive concentration of European land ownership at the expense of Algerian ownership' (Sartre 2001, 34–5). French colonialism needed to create a new market in the colony:

> But the Algerians are not, nor can they be, the colonists' customers. The colonist must export to pay for his imports: he produces for the

French market. The logic of the system makes him sacrifice the needs
of the native population to those of the French in France.

Between 1927 and 1932, wine-growing increased by 173,000
hectares, more than half of which was taken from the Muslims.
However, Muslims do not drink wine. On this land that was stolen
from them they grew cereals for the Algerian market. This time it was
not only the land that was taken from them; by planting vines there,
the Algerian population was deprived of its staple food. (2001, 37)

Driven off the most fertile land in the North, the Algerians were forced to
farm on arid land. But, while their agricultural productivity was decreasing,
the population had trebled since colonization. As Sartre points out,
'concentration of land ownership [led] to the mechanization of agriculture'
(38). Effectively, the machine came to replace the dispossessed and exploited
fellahs:

Nothing demonstrates better the increasing rigour of the colonial
system: you begin by occupying the country, then you take the land
and exploit the former owners at starvation rates. Then, with mechanization, this cheap labour is still too expensive; you finish up taking
from the natives their very right to work. All that is left for the
Algerians to do, *in their own land*, at a time of great prosperity, is to
die of starvation. (2001, 39; emphasis in original)

Colonialism turned the dispossessed fellahs into an agricultural proletariat.
Is it not paradoxical, Sartre remarks, that by its ineluctable dialectics the
system forced the Algerians to seek in France the jobs that France denied
them in Algeria? Immigration could not be the solution to the plight of the
Algerians, as Camus intimates; but it was a symptom of the colonial
malaise.

Sartre also rejects the doctrine of assimilation. The senatus-consulte of
1865 stipulated that the colonized could be naturalized provided they
reliquished their Muslim identity. Not only did the Muslims reject this
proposal, but it was not endorsed by the colonial administrators either.
Subsequently, the Loi-Jonnart (1919) and the Blum–Viollette Bill (1935)
attempted to enfranchise the 'évolués' ['educated' Algerians] but not the
colonized masses. The mayors representing the settlers forced the French
government to repeal the 1919 law in 1920 by reinstating the 'code de
l'indigénat', and over a decade later they would boycott the Blum–Viollette
Bill. A glimmer of hope for possible reforms was raised by the 1947 laws
providing the abolition of the 'communes mixtes', the separation of religion
from the state and the establishment of two electoral colleges; but the rigged
elections of 1948 and 1951 dashed this hope (Chikh 1981, 47). The
doctrine of assimilation was nothing but a myth. Alluding to the 1919 law
and the Blum–Viollette Bill, Sartre writes: 'The status of Algeria is

monstrous in itself. Did the French government expect to mystify the Muslim population by granting the two-college Assembly?' (2001, 42). Colonialism never meant to assimilate the colonized. In fact, assimilation and colonialism are a contradiction in terms. The language of the colonized was relegated to the status of a foreign language; their culture was displaced but never replaced by the colonizer's. The separation of the state from religion was one of the prerequisites of Republicanism in France, but 'in Algeria', argues Sartre, 'the French Republic cannot allow itself to be Republican' (42). It was through the religious leaders, the 'maraboutists', who were the clients of colonialism, that France attempted to control the cultural institutions of the colonized and to maintain its colonial dominance. The universality of France's institutions was abandoned in the colonies where all 'men' were not equal. 'One of the functions of racism', Sartre elaborates, 'is to compensate the latent universality of bourgeois liberalism: since all human beings have the same rights, the Algerian will be made a subhuman' (45).

The colonists denied to the colonized the Republican/democratic rights that were enjoyed by mainland France. An ambivalent relationship developed between France and its colony: the latter sought its economic independence while it always relied upon the mother country to maintain its colonial dominance. Sartre describes these colonists as 'separatists [who] are also hyper-patriots': they are Republicans in France and Fascists in the colony who hate the Republic and its institutions but 'passionately love the Republican Army' (45). Sartre is adamant that:

> mainland France is caught in the trap of colonialism. As long as she asserts her sovereignty over Algeria, she is compromised by the system, [...] by the colonists who repudiate her institutions. [...] [C]olonialism obliges France to send democratic Frenchmen to their deaths to protect the tyranny that the anti-democratic colonialists exert over the Algerians. (45).

The solution is clear for Sartre: the system must be dismantled.

In *Crise en Algérie* and subsequently in *The Plague*, Camus seems oblivious to the fact that Republican France harboured Fascism in its colony. In *The Plague*, he universalizes tyranny and oppression but the imperative of his mythic vision blinds him to the consideration of another type of injustice, more concrete and pertinent to the settings of his work, namely the injustice perpetrated against the colonized Algerian people. *The Plague*'s mythic narrative distorts and dislocates its relation with history. By hiding behind the gloss of universalism, the narrative neutralizes the historical contradictions that inhere in its structure. These contradictions must be sought at the level of history and ideology, as well as at the level of the text's 'mise-en-forme' (Macheray 1978, 137).

In his article 'Albert Camus's Algeria', Quilliot interprets *The Plague* as a parable for the 1945 crisis. 'The rats [which] continued to die nevertheless, invading the gutters and the mouths of sewers', are victims of colonialism and its oppression. The carriers of the plague cannot be seen as 'the rats of colonialism, an old sickness that was dragging on in Algeria' (Quilliot 1962, 42). In Camus's text, Fascism is symbolized by the plague, and the struggle to combat it summons up the pharmaceutical operation to contain and remove the threat it posed to the order of the city. Critics such as Sartre perceive affinity between colonialism and Fascism. In *Crise en Algérie*, Camus silences the political dimension of the crisis – the struggle of the natives to free themselves from the shackles of French colonialism – while in *The Plague* he refers briefly to the misery of the indigenous Arabs but ultimately overlooks their plight. In *The Plague*, just as in *Crise en Algérie*, Camus silences the struggle of the natives against colonialism, and, more significantly, the repression they suffered at the hands of the French on VE Day, as well as the resonance which colonialism has with Fascism. In the narrative, the colonial city is a site in which the natives are contained and segregated. The text can be read as a trope encapsulating the exclusion of the colonized, their containment like the plague. In the texture of *The Plague*'s universalizing narrative, we can detect strategies comparable to those employed by Fascism.

Rambert's mandate as a journalist to investigate the condition of the natives in *La Peste* evokes Camus's visit to Algeria as a reporter for *Combat*. Neither Rambert in the novel nor Camus as reporter for *Combat* willingly investigates the causes of this misery. Camus ignores the problem of the colonized Arabs and the fact that the 'rats of colonialism' survive on their poverty. He is an unwitting accomplice to the agents of disease, for his universalism avoids the problems of injustice that originate in the French colonial occupation of Algeria. The polarity postulated between Camus's universalism and Fascism disintegrate in *The Plague* with the interposition of the Algerian question.

The colonial malaise, suppressed in Camus's universalizing narrative of *The Plague*, surfaces in 'The Guest'. (Camus plays on the ambiguity of the French word 'l'hôte', an ambiguity missing from the English translation.) The gendarme instructs Daru to bring to justice an Arab who murdered his cousin over the theft of some grain, a major offence when so many are victims of starvation. The Arab's crime is metonymically associated with the Arabs' revolt. Reluctantly Daru agrees to deliver the Arab to the police, after the gendarme tells him that he is implicated in the conflict. Though the Arab's crime revolts Daru, he treats his 'guest' with a certain respect. They eat of the same food and sleep in the same room. The Arab's surprise demonstrates that under colonial hegemony such equality is not usually observed. In the morning, Daru shows the Arab the way to the east, which leads to prison, and the way to the southern territory, and thus freedom. Daru wants the Arab to escape to the desert, but the Arab's choice to go east implicates him in a moral and political stance. The connection between famine, revolutionary politics and crime crystallize in the figure of the Arab. Although he is not identified as revolutionary, his 'brothers' at the end of the short story in their threat of vengeance certainly resemble the solidarity of men in revolt against a political system, striking against Daru.

Camus's narrative expresses the injustice of Daru's situation as the host of his brother, the Arab. Camus modifies the story of Cain and Abel, which issues in a double movement in the short story: the Arab (Cain) kills his cousin (Abel); Daru (Cain) is implicated in the inevitable death of the Arab (Abel). Camus also infuses a New Testament revisionism into his modernized version of the tale from Genesis. In Matthew 25: 34–46, shortly before the Last Supper, Christ gives an account of the Last Judgement. Clearly, this has implications for 'The Guest', since Daru takes in a stranger, the Arab, and gives him food, drink and shelter. Daru serves the Arab his 'last supper' before he meets his 'last judgement' in the French law courts. But Camus subverts the efficacy of the New Testament parable, which promises a reward for the hospitality of the host. In the imminence of the new kingdom – a new political entity in the Algerian nationhood which emerges from the old French colonial possession – Daru faces a reversal of roles, becoming the 'guest' rather than the 'host'.

'The Guest' covers 'that itinerary of famine' charted by Camus in *Misère de la Kabylie* and relates the problem of famine to political revolt. The context is ambiguous: the narrative conflates the historical specificities from which it emerges (the Algerian War) with the 1945 uprising. 'The Guest' also refers implicitly to *Crise en Algérie*. As we have seen, Camus explains in his reportage that Algeria's plight was economic: the majority of the indigenous population suffered from famine because they were at the mercy of bad crops as unyielding as the capricious rain, which threatens them with drought. In order to save these populations and to prevent the famished masses 'incited by a few mad criminals' from repeating the massacres of Sétif (1965, 946), Camus argues that urgent political reforms must be implemented, and hundreds of ships of wheat sent to Algeria. The ships of wheat that Daru expects are emblematic of the hand held out by the French to the indigenous population. In his position, Daru, the teacher, stands as a purveyor of the doctrine of assimilation. The French geopolitical map on the blackboard is a colonial symbol. In Algeria, the teaching of French history and geography are part of a programme to promote this colonial doctrine. However, the fact that the classroom has been turned into a granary during the famine is an indictment of the failure of France's 'mission civilisatrice'. The words inscribed on Daru's blackboard by the Arab's 'brothers', however clumsily executed, articulate a challenge to this doctrine and to the privilege accorded to the colonizer. Despite the rejection of the Blum–Viollette Bill, Camus perceives the politics of assimilation as the only way out of the impasse in which Algeria finds itself in 1945. He describes the politics of the colonial administration as lagging behind the times, attempting to block the movement of history. He laments its reactionary politics which thwarted the politics of assimilation, responding to the political demands of indigenous reformers with prison. Essentially, 'The Guest' mediates the trajectory from reform to revolt in Algerian politics. The decision of the Arab to head in the direction of the prison, the east where the 1945 uprising took place, reinforces this interpretation. The east of Algeria is the ideological location where the Algerian War is ignited.

As we have seen in *Misère de la Kabylie* and *Crise en Algérie*, Camus exposes the pauperization of the indigenous people but never attacks colonialism. In *Crise en Algérie*, he considers the political malaise of 1945 as a consequence of the failure of France to extend the rules of its democratic institutions to Algeria and promote assimilation (1965, 951). But Camus forgets that the colonial system installed by France could not at one and the same time assimilate the natives and expropriate them. In effect, impoverishment and famine are not unfortunate natural calamities, as Camus intimates. They are the result of France's colonial laws, which dispossessed the natives.

The pauperization of the colonized must be sought at the level of history and politics (Sartre 1976 [1960], 717). Violence, Sartre argues, characterized the encounter between colonizer and colonized. Colonization was achieved by military means; its project was to expropriate and dispossess the colonized. A number of laws were imposed on the colonized the better to rob them (1976, 717). Colonialism pulverized the social structures and the cultural institutions of the colonized but would not allow them to enjoy those of the colonizer. Poverty was consequent upon the dispossession and the exploitation imposed on the colonized by French colonial laws. In other words, violence was inscribed in the relation between the colony and mainland France: it was, in Sartre's terms 'exis' and 'praxis', a mediating agency between colonizer and colonized (718). There are two aspects to colonial praxis. Firstly, the colonialist did not coerce the natives to work for starvation wages, but colonialism gave rise to a set of conditions (galloping demography, famine, unemployment) which forced them to accept these wages. These conditions denied the natives any agency of resistance to create new ways of sociability which is free from this violence. Secondly, exploitation was realized as a process (721–2). Assimilation and colonialism are two contradictory concepts: conferring the rights of political citizenship on the colonized cancels colonial privileges. So, it is necessary that the colonized should be treated as nothing but objects to be exploited for less and less (722). In Algeria, colonialism produced institutions and political structures which refused to recognize France's liberal and Republican tradition; it enabled the colonizer as free citizen to exploit the colonized subjects and perpetrate violence against them.

In his 'Preface' to *The Wretched of the Earth*, Sartre argues that the colonial situation produced the native and the colonialist as a couple implicated in the same violence (Sartre 1967 [1961]). As was argued above, the violence to which the natives were subjected was experienced as a process of exploitation, produced and maintained by force. In order to overcome their objective condition, Sartre argues, the colonized must confront the total negation to which they were subjected by another negation, meeting violence with violence (1976, 733). This violence involving colonizer and colonized was the 'reciprocal interiorization of a single oppression': colonialism. The colonial system is not an 'abstract mechanism'; it is a reality 'embodied in a million colonists' (Sartre 2001, 44).

The points of view reflected in *Actuelles III*, *The Plague* and 'The Guest' are partial, in that they overlook the violence which is central to Sartre's account of colonialism. *Actuelles III* disregards the politics that installed the colonial system; *The Plague* silences the resonance colonialism had with Fascism; 'The Guest' is oblivious to the fact that famine was the outcome of expropriation. The contradictions at the core of Camus's œuvre are the product of a slippage of points of view, which necessitates a dual interpretation (Macherey 1978, 148). The first contradiction is between the text and the moment(s) of its production, the second is between Camus's liberal political views and the colonialist ideology of French Algeria. These contradictions are either manifest or latent in his narratives, operating smoothly, even when they are suppressed and displaced. The partiality of his views, that is the gaps between what his writings reflect, refract or obfuscate, give rise to these contradictions which structure his œuvre (Macherey 1978, 150). His writings, despite obfuscating their historical specificities, capture the historical process. These gaps articulate meaning or, as Macheray puts it, silence is eloquent in these texts (1978, 151). The multiplicity of Camus's points of view decentres his œuvre. The slippage, or in Derrida's parlance 'différance', makes the opposition between presence and absence possible; the gap between what is represented and what is excluded contains the possibility of the text's deconstruction (1976 [1967], 143–4).

7

Resistance, submission and oppositionality: national identity in French Canada

BY MARILYN RANDALL

Most critics would situate the postcolonial moment in French Canada during the period of the Quiet Revolution (1960–70), when young intellectuals in Quebec discovered and circulated the writings of Albert Memmi. A new edition of his *Portrait du colonisé*, published in Montreal in 1972, seemed to describe perfectly the state of French Canadian society for the dissatisfied young intellectuals of postwar Quebec who became convinced of the need for economic, cultural and political decolonization. In its most radical terms, this involved independence from the colonizer, a role which Canada (and American capitalism) had taken over from the British. Decolonization also implied a psychological cure for the French Canadian 'colonization complex' that had made them complicit in their own oppression and unable to conceive of their situation other than as preordained by an implacable providence. The term 'Canadien', which originally designated only the French, was supplanted after Confederation by 'Canadien français', an epithet whose connotations were later seen as expressing a double alienation. The term 'Québécois' emerged during the Quiet Revolution to describe a cultural, political and territorial specificity freed from reference to two colonizing 'others': France and Canada.

Between its French origins and its Canadian present, a third colonial situation complicates the postcolonial condition of French Canada. The French settler colony of Nouvelle France became British in 1760. Politically, economically and ideologically, oppositional forces to colonization, both in the nineteenth and twentieth centuries, focused on British, Canadian and American domination. Culturally, however, French Canada remained a settler colony of France until well into the twentieth century. In the ongoing struggle to establish and protect a national language as central to their national identity, French Canadians have had to fight against both the assimilating forces of a dominant foreign language and culture and the cultural inferiority complex common to settler colonies.

In order to test the postcolonial hypothesis for French Canada, it is necessary to accept two theoretical premises. Following Jorge de Alva, we consider that postcoloniality signifies 'not so much subjectivity "after" the colonial experience as a subjectivity of oppositionality to imperializing/-colonizing (read: subordinating/subjectivizing) discourses and practices' (cited in Loomba 1998, 12). In this sense, rather than posit a historical post-colonial moment for French Canada, we will examine the ways in which the development of French Canadian national identity demonstrates opposi-tionality – in the nineteenth century to the fact of its colonial status, and in the mid-twentieth century to the effects produced by the history of colo-nization. The evolution of 'Canadien' nationalism in the early nineteenth century, the resistance embodied in Parliamentary struggles against the British imperial government and the failed Rebellion of 1837–8 clearly allow us to study both the 'subjectivity of oppositionality' in the colonial period and the ensuing development of a national identity posited in oppo-sition to the colonial – and subsequently Canadian – governments.

A second difficulty in considering French Canadian claims to coloniza-tion is expressed in an exchange between Albert Memmi and a group of French students who objected to these claims both because of the apparent prosperity of Quebec and because the French themselves were a colonial power who colonized the native peoples. In Memmi's response, 'Toute domination est relative. Toute domination est spécifique' [All domination is relative; all domination is specific] (1972, 138), his use of the term 'domination' rather than 'colonization' foreshadows de Alva's use of the parenthetical terms 'subordination' and 'subjectivization'. While the Parisian students point to the anomaly of a settler colony of an imperial power claiming 'colonized' status, the history of the French in Canada does fulfil the three fundamental conditions that distinguish 'oppositional post-colonial' societies from white settler colonies: racism; a second language; and political struggle (Mishra and Hodge 1993 [1991], 286).

The 'Patriotes' who forged the 1837 Rebellion believed strongly that the injustices they suffered under British rule were even more intolerable for being perpetrated on European descendants and intellectuals who were in every way the equals of their conquerers. The 'Canadiens' were not the impenetrable 'Other' that constituted so many of the indigenous popula-tions of imperial colonies; the 'racial' differences between colonizer and colonized did not display the Manichean oppositions that guaranteed the 'natural' superiority of one over the other. These differences had to be con-structed by the process of colonization and, according to Lord Durham's Report following the 1837–8 uprising, were firmly in place by the time of the Rebellion.

In this chapter, we will read the colonial history of French Canada through the discourse of the 1960s 'decolonialists' who set out to trace in their history the source of their contemporary social, economic and psychological debilitation. In so doing, they identified the failed Patriot Rebellion of 1837 as an important cause of the subsequent attitudes of submission and inferiority which they identified among French Canadians. The Rebellion has also been seen by many modern historians as the single most significant event in French Canadian history, an analysis which is certainly borne out by its abiding importance in the popular imagination. The activists of the Quiet Revolution looked back to this less quiet one as a source of their present subjugation and as a model for future revolution. And the irony of modelling a future on a failed past was not lost on the more insightful of them.

What did modern French Canadians see when looking at their past and present through the enlightening lens of the theory of decolonization? According to separatist poet Paul Chamberland, French Canadians are so involved 'avec l'idéal canadien que nous nous confirmons dans notre rôle de minorité jusqu'à l'élever au rang d'une *vocation historique,* seule susceptible de réaliser notre être' [with the Canadian ideal that we confirm our own role of minority within it to the point of raising it to the level of a *historical vocation,* the only one capable of realizing our nature] (1983 [1964], 96; emphasis in the original). Chamberland locates within Quebec society every element of the condition of the colonized defined by Memmi – from the unhappy situation of colonial bilingualism, to the internalization of one's inferior position, to self-loathing, to the retreat behind core values which, in his Quebec, included religion, history, hockey and the tavern. And he situates the cause of this condition in the colonial past:

> Le groupe canadien-français devint une minorité, au sein du Canada, à peu près au même moment où il devient un peuple. De la conquête à la révolution manquée de 37, il formait la majorité de ce qui serait le Canada, mais il n'était pas à proprement parler un peuple; son existence politique se réduisait à celle d'une colonie 'd'outremer', il était la chose de la métropole britannique. Tout le long du dix-neuvième siècle jusqu'en 1867, il accéda [...] à un régime politique et social plus autonome. Mais la conjoncture démographique évolua nettement en sa défaveur de sorte que son sort demeure jusqu'à maintenant lié à celui du Canada anglais. C'est donc dire que la société canadienne-française fut toujours une société mineure, infériorisée; une société coloniale où le rôle du colonisateur fut joué d'abord par l'Angleterre puis par le Canada anglais. C'est une constante qui traverse les différents régimes.
>
> Collectivement, nous n'avons jamais connu la liberté; nous avons toujours été un peuple dépendant, colonisé. Nous n'avons jamais eu d'histoire: celle des autres nous en a tenu lieu. Cette condition de colonisés, de minoritaires, nous a faits ce que nous sommes, et c'est en elle que nous pouvons découvrir la raison première de notre aliénation. (1983, 94)

French Canadians became a minority within Canada at about the same time as they became a people. From the Conquest to the failed revolution of '37, French Canadians formed a majority of what would become Canada, but they were not strictly speaking a nation: their political existence amounted to that of an 'overseas' colony; they were subjects of the British metropolis. Throughout the nineteenth century until 1867, they enjoyed [...] a relatively autonomous political and social regime. But demographics evolved decidedly against them so that their destiny remains linked to that of English Canada. This is to say that French Canadian society was always a minor, inferiorized society; a colonial society where the role of colonizer was first played by England, then by English Canada. It is a common feature of the different regimes.

Collectively, we have never known liberty; we have always been a dependent, colonized people. We have never had a history; we have only had the history of others. This colonial, minority condition has made us what we are, and it is in this condition that we can find the cause of our alienation.

The conflicting interpretations of the 1837 Rebellion, seen variously as a defeat and as a victory, as a mistake and as destiny, are both the cause and the consequence of its abiding significance. Although the defeated Patriots eventually became immortalized as ambiguous national heroes, the negative force of this failed attempt at nationalist revolution was seen as producing a psychology, not to mention a politics and an economy, which demonstrated canonical symptoms of colonization:

> L'échec de l'insurrection de 1837 a profondément marqué le peuple canadien-français. Ce fut une ratification de la défaite. Une seconde fois, l'épreuve des armes se soldait par un désastre. [...] Le peuple canadien-français acquit alors un profond sentiment d'infériorité, con- cluant que la force serait toujours contre lui. (D'Allemagne 1966, 20)

> The defeat of the 1837 insurrection has profoundly affected the French Canadian people. It was a confirmation of the conquest. A second time, the recourse to arms ended in disaster. [...] The French Canadian people subsequently acquired a profound feeling of inferiority, concluding that the force of might would always be against them.

Historian Robert-Lionel Séguin announces in the preface to a pamphlet about the Rebellion: 'Ce petit livre est le premier d'une série que nous publierons pour que tous les Québécois, tirant les leçons des événements de leur histoire, entreprennent la dernière phase de leur libération' [This little book is the first in a series which we are publishing so that all Québécois, drawing lessons from the events of their history, may undertake the last phase of their liberation] (1964, 3).[1] If many agreed that 1837 contained important lessons for the present, it was for conflicting reasons. Some saw the defeat as a warning against the colonized mentality from which French Canadians still suffered; others saw a popular uprising fought by noble martyrs and heroes to be emulated. And, when the Quiet Revolution became less quiet, culminating in the acts of violence known as the October Crisis, the Manifesto of the Front de libération du Québec explicitly appealed to the Patriots as precursors: 'Il faut lutter, non plus un à un, mais en s'unissant, jusqu'à la victoire, avec tous les moyens que l'on possède comme l'ont fait les Patriotes de 1837–1838 (ceux que Notre Sainte Mère l'Église s'est empressée d'excommunier pour mieux se vendre aux intérêts britanniques)' [We must fight, not individually, but together, until we achieve victory, with all the means at our disposal, as did the Patriots of 1837–8 (whom Our Holy Mother Church did not hesitate to excommunicate the better to sell themselves out to British interests)] (Ferretti and Miron 1992, 188).

From resistance to submission

The 1837 uprising, which followed three decades of parliamentary resistance to British oligarchy, was not originally an ethnic conflict, but fostered a 'defensive proto-nationalism, insisting on the fundamental loyalty of French Canadians to Britain's empire' (Greer 1993, 123). Its principal architects, most notably the Patriot leader Louis-Joseph Papineau, were staunchly in favour of British rule, and wished only to gain the full advantages of British citizenship through responsible government. The resistance leading up to the Rebellion aimed at mobilizing public opinion in support of constitutional reform. Popular assemblies were held, where resolutions outlining conditions and demands were passed in favour of the Patriots. A fierce war of words raged in the partisan press, the Patriot newspapers vacillating between vociferous attempts to mobilize agitation and warnings against premature action. A boycott of imported goods was undertaken to weaken British revenues and increase local independence. The examples of the American revolution and the Irish struggle for independence were important reference points. The origins of the Patriot ideal were thus anti-imperial and anti-colonial but not narrowly nationalist – the enemy was a government whose crime lay not in its being British but in its increasing tyranny and perversion of those very liberties that British democracy championed.

---

[1] Séguin's use of 'Québécois' is, in 1964, a political gesture. The term is not yet generally accepted and denotes a separatist allegiance. Other separatists insist during the same period on the term 'Canadien français', in order to underline their continuing colonization.

Repeated rebuffs by London only served to radicalize a faction of the movement in favour of armed resistance. In the end, the Rebellion amounted to a series of local skirmishes for the most part easily trounced by British troops and volunteers. Reprisals in the form of burning whole villages, court martials for treason, exile and executions served to divide further an already divided populace between those who saw the British as bloodthirsty tyrants and those who regretted the rashness of armed revolt.

Debates are ongoing about whether the British forced the Rebellion, whether the people actually rebelled or acted in self-defence, to what extent the 'habitants' supported the Patriots, whether or not they were coerced or manipulated by a bourgeoisie primarily interested in their own advancement rather than in the common good – and whether the Rebellion was primarily a political or an ethnic conflict. While the majority of Patriots in Lower Canada were French, their ranks included democrats of British and European origins united against British colonial rule. But the economic and political ascendency of British Canadians in Lower Canada added a 'racial' element to the political struggle. In his report on the causes of and solutions to the problem, Lord Durham – 'Radical Jack', a liberal thinker for his time – propounds a racial analysis: 'I expected to find a contest between a government and a people: I found two nations warring in the bosom of a single state: I found a struggle, not of principles, but of races' (Durham 1963 [1838], 22–3). He also makes some infamously memorable diagnoses of the pitiful state of French Canada:

> There can hardly be conceived a nationality more destitute of all that can invigorate and elevate a people than that which is exhibited by the descendants of the French in Lower Canada, owing to their retaining their peculiar language and manners. They are a people with no history and no literature. The literature of England is written in a language which is not theirs; and the only literature which their language renders familiar to them, is that of a nation from which they have been separated by 80 years of foreign rule, and still more by those changes which the Revolution and its consequences have wrought in the political, moral and social state of France. (150)

His solution: 'It is to elevate them from that inferiority that I desire to give to the Canadians our English character' (149).

The Union of the two Canadas in 1841 followed by the Confederation of four provinces in 1867 sealed the minority status of the French and initiated a prolonged period of 'submission', conservatism and nationalist isolationism dominated by the clergy. But it is also in this period that we see the beginnings of a literary movement which, as Memmi and Fanon point out, is often a belated arrival on the colonial scene. It is here that the reference to France becomes important, inaugurating a long cultural debate pitting regionalists against universalists in much the same way that the political history of Quebec since Confederation opposes nationalists and federalists. The history of these debates has been recounted many times and we cannot do them justice in this chapter. But it is essential to point out the enduring centrality of the linguistic question and, significantly, that it was founded on a double resistance: not only to assimilation by the English, but also with reference to the cultural metropolis. In an important exchange of letters during the 1860s between the literary critic and cleric Casgrain and the poet Crémazie, the latter writes:

> Plus je réfléchis sur les destinées de la littérature canadienne, moins je lui trouve de chances de laisser une trace dans l'histoire. Ce qui manque au Canada, c'est d'avoir une langue à lui. Si nous parlions iroquois ou huron, notre littérature vivrait. Malheureusement nous parlons et nous écrivons d'une assez piteuse façon, il est vrai, la langue de Bossuet et de Racine. Nous aurons beau dire et beau faire, nous ne serons toujours, au point de vue littéraire, qu'une simple colonie, et quand bien même le Canada deviendrait un pays indépendant [...] nous n'en demeurerions pas moins de simples colons littéraires. (Cited in Gauvin 2000, 23)

> The more I reflect on the future of Canadian literature, the less I think of its chances to leave a trace in history. What Canada lacks is a language of its own. If we spoke Iroquois or Huron, our literature would live. Unfortunately, we speak and write, in a rather pitiful way, the language of Bossuet and Racine. Whatever we say and do, we will always be, from the literary point of view, simply a colony, and even if Canada were to become an independent country [...] we would still remain only a literary colony.

The impossibility of the colonial culture crossing the Atlantic and thus of becoming 'really' literary, lays out the only path available to Canadian literature, that of keeping intact 'le plus précieux de tous les trésors: la langue de ses aïeux' [the most precious of all treasures: the language of its ancestors] (cited in Gauvin 2000, 26).

In 'Le mouvement littéraire au Canada français' (1866), Casgrain, for his part, traces a cultural programme which will dominate well into the twentieth century. He has no doubt that there will be a Canadian literature; it is to be an expression of the people as shaped by the Catholic faith, which is the only *raison d'être* of both – 'our literature will follow our destiny':

> Ainsi sa voie est tracée d'avance; elle sera le miroir fidèle de notre petit peuple dans les diverses phases de son existence [...]. Elle n'aura point ce cachet de réalisme moderne, manifestation de la pensée impie, matérialiste. (Cited in Lamonde and Corbo 1999, 216)

> Thus its path is set out in advance. It will be the faithful mirror of our
> small people in the various phases of our existence [...]. It will not
> have a hint of that modern realism which is a manifestation of
> impious, materialist ideas.

This conservatism, or 'conservationism', was not only cultural but also
engendered a socio-political and economic programme designed to protect
the cultural legacy of the French language, the Catholic religion and the
tradition of agriculture and rural family life. Against the Anglo-American
superiority in commerce and industry, a theory of 'agriculturalism' based on
the natural affinities of peoples was developed. As late as 1900, at a time of
rampant industrialization, urbanization and emigration to the prosperous
northeastern States, nationalist politicans such as Henri Bourassa argued
that the English were economically superior because they had drunk
'l'instinct des affaires et du commerce avec le lait maternel' [the instinct for
business and commerce with their mother's milk] (cited in Vincenthier 1983,
103), and that the French in Canada would affirm 'leur véritable supériorité
en suivant les tendances de leur race' [their natural superiority in following
the tendencies of their race], which included keeping:

> ses fils à la charrue, ses filles à la chaumière [...] au lieu de les disperser
> dans les provinces lointaines et, surtout, de les envoyer dans les villes
> où ils perdent leur santé, leur robuste simplicité, souvent même leur
> honneur. (103)

> their sons at the plough and their daughters at the hearth [...] instead
> of sending them into far-off provinces, and above all into cities where
> they destroy their health, lose their robust simplicity, often even their
> honour.

Needless to say, Bourassa himself had never touched a plough. While the
economic dream of agriculturalism was definitively shattered by the industrial realities intensified by two world wars, it continued as a cultural and
symbolic force in the tradition of the 'novel of the land', which promoted
the agriculturalist ideal well into the late 1940s.

In opposition to conservative nationalists, a liberal political and intellectual class had survived since the nineteenth century. It is this class that the
Marxist analyses and those underpinning decolonization of the 1960s
would identify as the 'Negro kings' whose participation in the federal
government was denounced as collaboration with the oppressor. One such
Liberal was Wilfred Laurier, the first French Canadian federal prime
minister (1896–1911) who, in a speech before the Club Canadien in 1877,
was at great pains to explain that political liberalism was neither anti-
clerical nor 'a new form of evil, a heresy' (cited in Lamonde and Corbo
1999, 238). Explicitly evoking the tradition of Papineau and the 1837

Rebellion, he explains to a sceptical audience that, although French Canadians are indeed a conquered race and a minority, they have been guaranteed their rights and freedoms by the democratic constitution which is a legacy of British rule and, indirectly, of the Rebellion (in Lamonde and Corbo 1999, 239–40).

During the Quiet Revolution, this same intolerable ambiguity was embodied by Pierre Elliott Trudeau, the 'French Canadian' prime minister, who promoted internationalism over nationalism, condemned the fallacy of the nation state, and defended the role of Quebec within Confederation (1962). Separatist intellectual and novelist Hubert Aquin responded to Trudeau's pro-federalist argument in terms which are clearly inspired by the theory of decolonization:

> 'If Canada as a state has had so little room for French Canadians', writes Trudeau, 'it is above all because we have failed to make ourselves indispensable to its future.' Making ourselves indispensable to the destiny of others! Here we see the theme of cultural exorbitation expressed with rare precision. It consists in creating in the majority group a need for the minority, that 'indispensability' which immediately confers on us the right to the dignity of a minority; thus, in this scheme [...] which is familiar to all consumers of federalist French Canadian thinking [...] the existence of the French Canadian group can only be justifed if it remains grafted onto an English-speaking majority which can no longer get along without it. [...] In this scenario, French Canada would play a role, sometimes even a starring role, in a story it could never write itself (Lord Durham was right, in this sense, when he wrote that French Canadians were a people without history!). (Aquin 1988, 37–8)

The two questions raised in the Casgrain–Crémazie debate would not disappear: while the primacy of language for the definition of a nation would outlast that of religion, the opposition between regionalism and universalism – what today we would see in terms of periphery and centre – would animate cultural and political debate until the mid-twentieth century on two fronts: that of Quebec versus France, and Quebec versus Canada.

Submission as resistance

In *The Wretched of the Earth* (1967 [1961]), Frantz Fanon has described a three-stage evolution of colonized people from an initial posture of submission and desire for assimilation into the culture of the colonizer, towards a period of revalorization of the indigenous culture, and finally to active revolt against the colonizer. In attempting to reconcile the history of French Canada until 1960 with this framework, one finds an apparent reversal in which resistance precedes submission. The retreat from active resistance in favour of a conservative form of nationalism favoured by the political and clerical classes in Quebec only developed in the years following the definitive defeat of the Patriots and the assimilation of their less radical elements into the new federal government. This desire for insularity and for traditional values was pursued well into the twentieth century by opposition to federal government incursions into the autonomy of the province on the part of the arch-conservative and fiercely nationalist Premier Duplessis. Resistance to the forces of assimilation implied submission to a subaltern role within the larger economic and political context of Canada and North America, as well as to a determinist philosophy which promised rewards in heaven for virtuous poverty on earth. Political liberalism became synonymous with assimilation and was opposed to nationalism, defined according to traditional French Canadian and Catholic values. Even before the 1960s, these forms of 'resistance' were denounced as a retrograde pursuit of tradition which had kept the province in the 'Dark Ages'. But the theory of decolonization, while explaining how refuge in the past was a symptom of colonization, also revealed its oppositional nature:

> Fuite du présent, le repli sur nous-mêmes est donc une forme inconsciente de refus de l'Anglais et, à la limite, refus de la Conquête et des deux siècles qui en découlent. [...] Avant 1867, ce refus a été ouvert – jusqu'à la rébellion de 1837 – , mais après, n'ayant plus de raison d'être puisque l'Anglais nous faisait son semblable et son égal, il s'est intériorisé, est devenu maquis en nous, résistance souterraine. Refus de l'Anglais et refuge dans le passé, qui sont l'avers et l'envers d'un même retranchement, constituent la trame irrationnelle de ce que nous appelons notre nationalisme traditionnel. (Bouthillette 1997 [1971], 40)

> Our desire for insularity is a flight from the present which is, as well, an unconscious form of refusal of the English and even a refusal of the Conquest and the two centuries following it. [...] Before 1867, this refusal was overt – until the Rebellion of 1837 – but afterwards, having no more justification, because the English made us their brother and equal, the refusal was interiorized, went underground in us, became underground resistance. Refusal of the English and refuge in the past, which are two sides of the same retreat, make up the irrational texture of our traditional nationalism.

Quebec's long struggle for political and cultural self-definition demonstrates a double resistance consistent with its colonial history, that is further complicated by conflicting theories and visions of race, nation and state. In their evolution from 'Canadiens', to 'Canadiens français' and finally to 'Québécois', the French in Canada have been at times united against a common enemy and at others divided among themselves, occupying a confusing variety of subject positions within the range of colonial possibilities: colonizer and colonized; victim and political partner; collaborator in their own oppression and active rebel. We have attempted to expose the continual 'subjectivity of oppositionality' underlying this history from the early nineteenth-century resistance to political domination by the British to the later retreat from Anglo-Canadian economic and cultural hegemony which threatened to annihilate the French in Canada.

The economic, political, cultural and linguistic situation in twenty-first-century Quebec provides certain evidence that both resistance and submission were effective forms of opposition to the forces of colonial domination. But it was the emergence of the theory of decolonization in the mid-twentieth century which provided intellectuals not only with the historical explanation of their condition and a programme for revolutionary action, but also with an analysis of the past whereby successive defeats could be reread, if not as victory, at least as significant architects of a present that was no longer predestined, but historically produced. And, if history is constructed by men and women rather than ordained by God, it can also be deconstructed and, moreover, reconstructed.

LANGUAGE AND IDENTITY IN THE FRANCOPHONE WORLD

8

'Francophonie' and 'universalité': evolution of two notions conjoined

BY GABRIELLE PARKER

Francophonie: a geographer's notion, a political conceit

The notion of francophonie has acquired different meanings, depending on the geographical and historical context.[1] For Onésime Reclus, the geographer who coined the word in the late nineteenth century, it referred to those countries where French was spoken. Anticipating the definition adopted over a century later,[2] Reclus understood as 'francophones' all those who shared French (cited in Tavernier 2000, 14). By the end of the twentieth century, a collective identity was predicated on this notion, nurtured by common references and practices in order to generate a sense of belonging. Francophonie had become a political project conceived in order to bring diverse peoples and nations together on the basis of shared values. However, as a phenomenon, Francophonie is intimately linked with colonization: the coining of the word in 1880 coincides with the height of nineteenth-century colonialism, while the development of the notion coincides with the process of decolonization. 1880 is also the year when Jules Ferry, Minister of Education, declared French the sole medium of instruction and communication throughout the French Empire; thus the French 'imperium' ruled within France and without.

---

[1]   This essay follows Tétu's nomenclature (1997, 14): 'francophonie' (small f) designates the ensemble of countries and people who use French (consistently, or occasionally) as their language of communication; 'Francophonie' (capital F) refers to the official institutions that bring together governments, countries or official, international authorities using French.
[2]   The new definition of 'francophonie', 'pays ayant le français en partage', proposed by Maurice Druon, was agreed at the Fifth Francophone Summit (1993) held in Mauritius.

French had enjoyed an international status as language of power, culture and learning from the seventeenth century. Calvet (1999 [1987], 251) sees a turning point in the nineteenth century with the reversal of the demographic and economic strengths that had sustained French territorial, linguistic and economic expansion. Calvet notes two further symptoms of a loss of influence: a) the creation of the Alliance française in 1883 – a response to the notion that French needed to be defended and expanded; b) the creation of a multiplicity of artificial languages intended to have an international reach – a symptom of the erosion of the 'universal' character of French.

Another explanation might lie in the carving up of Africa by European powers at the Berlin Conference of 1884–5 and the reproduction and export of language rivalries to a new continent. In that same year, Jean Jaurès made explicit the link between the foundation of the Alliance française and the requirements of colonization. Then a young lecturer at the Faculté des lettres in Toulouse, Jaurès declared to the local Alliance française that only when they understood French would 'nos colonies' [our colonies] become French 'd'intelligence et de cœur' [in their hearts and minds] (cited in Girardet 1983, 94). His main concern was to compensate for the scarcity of French settlers in the colonies through the spread of schools and (French) literacy. Jaurès's discourse was a blend of realism and lyricism, advocating education for the 'indigènes' because an educated population would best serve France's interests, and because learning about France and her values was bound to kindle loving gratitude and admiration among the natives (Girardet 1983, 96). (Jaurès's approach – winning hearts and minds – would later find an echo in Senghor's evocation of a 'humanisme intégral'.)

A year later, on 28 July 1885, Ferry advanced a similar proposition, though with less lyricism than Jaurès. According to Todorov, Ferry presents economic, humanitarian and political arguments to justify colonization (1993 [1989], 260–2). It was not sufficient for France to be free; she must also be great, her greatness measurable by the degree of influence exerted over the destinies of Europe and of the rest of the world through 'sa langue, ses mœurs, son drapeau, ses armes, son génie' [its language, its customs, its flag, its arms, its genius] – that is to say, both territories and minds were objects of conquest, and language was identified as a key tool of conquest. As to the second component of the argument, the humanitarian strand, it rested on the 'mission éducatrice et civilisatrice' [civilizing and educational mission] trope. Western humanism was not just complicit with colonialism, it underwrote the project.

Just as the propagation of the French language had been explicitly described as a compensating measure for the scarcity of French settlers, the extension of the Empire itself was seen as a way of offsetting territorial losses at home. In the chapter 'L'Hexagone' in Pierre Nora's *Les Lieux de mémoire*, Weber cites Lavisse, a geographer, contrasting France's signal failure to acquire elusive 'natural' borders and her successful colonial conquests and policies (Weber 1997, 1183). To Lavisse, this was the clearest indication of the path to follow. Weber suggests that the notion of 'La Plus Grande France' had emerged after the loss of Alsace-Lorraine: a form of counteraction to blur the limits – and limitations – of metropolitan France and to provide new outlets for the spread of its influence. Similarly, the reinvention of Francophonie in the 1960s accompanied the process of decolonization and the loss of the very Empire that had constituted 'La Plus Grande France'. Its further redefinition in the 1990s coincides, politically, with a readjustment of influences at global level, with the fall of the Soviet Empire, the reunification of Germany and the new 'scramble for Africa' triggered by this new world order (Parker 2002b). It was also concurrent with the finalizing of World Trade agreements and the expansion of media empires – all Anglophone, bar a few exceptions such as Vivendi Universal or Hachette Filipacchi.

Referring to the third and last leg of the extension of francophonie, Philippe Lalanne-Berdouticq (1998) suggests that the future of French in the twenty-first century rests largely on sub-Saharan Africa: the region enjoys the highest population increase in the world; its enormous wealth is still largely unexploited; it adopted the French language upon becoming independent as a necessary shared common good, imposing unity in place of the diversity of its own 'dialects'. However, he emphasizes that this still only amounts to a potential, itself threatened by American expansionist, cultural and economic designs. Lalanne-Berdouticq's unreconstructed discourse reproduces the main colonialist tropes of a century before. The arguments in favour of empire/francophonie are compensatory: (French-speaking) people (an elite, a workforce, some troops), large territorial 'possessions' and economic potential, all to be deployed strategically in a renewed globalization of the European battleground.

Francophonie: an institutionalized construct

This plastic notion was given a concrete, institutionalized basis through the creation of 'La Francophonie'. It became an 'affaire d'État' in 1969, with the first conference of États francophones in Niamey, Niger – although de Gaulle did not attend, and sent his Minister for Culture André Malraux instead. However, the first 'Conférence des chefs d'État et Gouvernement ayant en commun l'usage du français' [Conference of heads of State and Government of French-speaking countries] did not take place until 1986 in Versailles, where 42 countries took part. It had taken almost two decades for the project to mature.

The Agence intergouvernementale de la Francophonie, a direct outcome of the Niamey conference, was created on 20 March 1970. Its website credits three heads of state – Léopold Sédar Senghor (Senegal), Habib Bourguiba (Tunisia), Hamani Diori (Niger) – for its existence. Just as Rivarol sought to give weight and authority to the notion of the universality of French by pointing out that this virtue was bestowed upon it by speakers of other languages, official French defenders of Francophonie have always taken care to emphasize the non-metropolitan origins of the concept. Returning the favour, Senghor attributed its paternity to de Gaulle.

A non-metropolitan narrative, that of Congolese linguist Ntole Kasadi traces the beginnings of what he terms 'la francophonie moderne' to Senghor's early proposal of a 'Communauté confédérale' in 1958 – a project that, besides France, included countries of the Maghreb, Indochina and sub-Saharan Africa; this Community was a new version of 1946's Union française, albeit one made up of independent countries and therefore cleansed of any (colonial) ulterior motive. (Alongside Senghor, Kazadi also reclaims a name often omitted from the short list of 'pères de la Francophonie', that of Felix Houphouët-Boigny, first President of the Ivory Coast.) The project was idealistic, or perhaps politically naïve. Kazadi notes that the idea appealed to Bourgiba and Sihanouk, raised some interest in Morocco, Laos and Vietnam, but found no resonance in France (1991, 49).

Indeed, Kazadi's whole narrative emphasizes Senghor's long travails and de Gaulle's initial detachment. By 1962, Senghor had given up the idea of a confederation and concentrated on francophonie, a notion he defined as 'humanisme intégral qui se tisse autour de la terre: cette symbiose des énergies dormantes de tous les continents, de toutes les races, qui se réveillent à leur complémentarité' [an integrative humanism weaving its way around the world: a symbiosis of all latent energies across the continents, of all the races, now alive to their complementarity] (50). In 1965, Senghor called for a Commonwealth 'à la française'. Kazadi recalls that some African nations were less than enthusiastic about these proposals: Sékou Touré (Guinea) in particular tagged Senghor's idea 'francofolie' [francofolly] (50); Algeria failed to see the attraction of a project underlining the ties binding France to its former colonies; Zaire was not anxious to join.

The proposal in favour of creating the ACCT (Agence de coopération culturelle et technique) – which Kazadi describes as a kind of francophone UNESCO – was an avatar of an earlier idea launched in 1953 in Montreal: l'Union culturelle française, later Union culturelle et technique de langue française (52). It was presented to the OCAM summit in 1968. In 1980, at the Franco-African Nice summit, Senghor presented a project for a 'Communauté organique de la francophonie'. This was in sharp contrast with the Commonwealth – a 'communauté d'allégeance à un souverain' [community of allegiance to a sovereign]. The proposed francophone 'communauté d'allégeance à une langue' [community of allegiance to a language] was designed as 'une Communauté qui embrassera, ensemble, les domaines politique, économique et culturel' [a Community that was to bring together within a single embrace the political, economic and cultural spheres] (56). It was François Mitterrand who gave the final push towards the creation of a Francophone Community in the 1980s, bringing francophone heads of state together in 1986 (57). This is post-colonialism (i.e. after colonialism) almost by definition – although the reader may not be entirely convinced by Kazadi's assertion that the new Francophonie was totally innocent of any neocolonial connotation, or that President Mitterrand was entirely free of all colonial baggage with regard to Africa.

Francophonie and 'universalité'

In the late eighteenth century, the universality of French was widely accepted, leading Rivarol to ask: 'Qu'est-ce qui a rendu la langue française universelle?' [What is it that has made the French language universal?] (Meschonnic 1997, 205). The sense that French was gaining ground and winning minds began to prevail much earlier. Fumaroli quotes Charpentier writing in 1676: 'La langue française est aujourd'hui la langue d'un grand Royaume; une langue qui n'est point enfermée dans les limites de la France, qui est cultivée avec ambition par les étrangers, qui fait les délices de la politesse de toutes les Nations du Nord' [The French language is nowadays that of a great Kingdom; a language that is not confined to the limits of France, is cultivated by ambitious foreigners, and delights polite northern nations] (Fumaroli 1997, 4666). This prevalence of the French language had been carefully constructed over several centuries.

The formation of national identities is achieved through the notion of sharing a common estate, a common language foremost among the components of that inheritance. Thus, in France, the sixteenth century's preoccupation with the establishment of French as the national language coincided with the deliberate constitution of a material and symbolic heritage, as well as with a vast territorial expansion and policy of conquest. The work done on language during this period mainly involved the construction of 'thesauri' – dictionaries, but also 'dicts', which constitute a material reference that is commonly shared. A 'cosmopolitan' streak is a feature of the seventeenth century (Brunot, cited in Chevalier 1997, 3400) – the spread of learned journals in French, the beginning of foreign-language teaching (in merchant navy schools), the creation by Colbert (1669) of l'École des Jeunes de Langues (subsequently l'École des langues orientales). The Jesuit missions also contributed to extend French to the Asian and American continents. The development of the eighteenth-century notion of the 'universal' applied to science, culture, thought; (French) language was the vector of this shared European culture. Another thesaurus was constituted: *L'Encyclopédie universelle*.

As Balibar points out, however, at the time of the Revolution, the new self-constituted members of the Assemblée nationale (15 June 1789) were not a socially homogeneous group: what they did have in common, though, was that they all mastered the same language – written, as well as spoken: 'La communication entre les lettrés était si profonde et si autonome qu'elle

se désignait naturellement par les termes d'"univers" et d'"universalité"
hérités du latin classique et impérial' [Communication between people of
letters was so deep and so autonomous that it referred to itself quite naturally using the terms of 'universe' and 'universality' inherited from the Latin
of classic and imperial times] (1985, 4). Consequently, the elite of savants
and writers considered themselves to be part of a 'république des lettres'.

The Revolution ensured that learning 'la langue nationale' became a duty
for all citizens, most of whom had been hitherto excluded from the 'common' culture. Parallel movements in the rest of Europe led to linguistic
homogenization within nations (including first and foremost France), and,
subsequently, the erosion of the 'universal' status of French. Grégoire saw
the 'langue universelle' as 'langue de la liberté' (1794), and Barrère could
state to the Convention (8 pluviôse an II/27 January 1794):

> Le français deviendra la langue universelle, étant la langue des peuples.
> En attendant, comme il a eu l'honneur de servir à la Déclaration des
> droits de l'homme, il doit devenir la langue de tous les Français.
> (Meschonnic 1997, 23)

> Because French is the people's language it will become the universal
> language. Meanwhile, because it has enjoyed the honour of being used
> for the Declaration of the Rights of Man, it must become the language
> of all French people.

The notion of 'universality' in the eighteenth century was restricted to
Europe and its 'société polie' [polite society], just as the universality of 'les
droits de l'homme et du citoyen' [the rights of man and the citizen] was to
exclude slaves (until 1848) and women (until 1944 when they received the
vote, then 1999, when 'equal access' for women to political representation
was added to the Constitution): 'Un scandale pour une nation toujours prête
à se donner en exemple au monde' [A scandal for a nation always ready to
set itself up as an example for the rest of the world to follow] (Picq 2002,
13; see also Rosello, Chapter 12, on 'parité' for women). France also lagged
behind other French-speaking communities with regard to 'féminisation' of
the language itself. Francophonie was no less tardy: its first Conférence des
femmes de la Francophonie had to wait until the threshold of the twenty-
first century (Luxembourg, February 2000).

Universality presents also a parallel with Catholicism, 'one and universal'
and a form of messianism – *pace* the 'mission civilisatrice' trope. The
semantic rapprochement does not end there: the zealous promotion of the
language recalls that of the 'Œuvre de la propagation de la Foi' [Work of
propagating the Faith]. France had been the official protector of missionaries, then the most important Catholic missionary power: 'En 1900, trois
missionnaires catholiques sur cinq sont français. [...] Un écrivain catholique
des années 1920 va même jusqu'à écrire que la langue française est l'une des

langues privilégiées des saints' [In 1900, three out of five Catholic mission-
naries are French. [...] A Catholic writer of the 1920s went so far as to claim
that the French language is one of the saints' privileged languages] (Cabanel
2002, 90).

Francophonie: a neocolonial concept?

In the twentieth (and twenty-first) century, Francophonie was to offer access
to a new universality, once again based on language. Jules Ferry's project
had succeeded, but at a price. Education in the colonies had reinforced a
sense of alienation. Consequently, it is not unreasonable to question
whether Francophonie is genuinely post-colonial, or whether it is yet
another avatar of colonialism. Francophonie remains a political organization on which France relies in order to get votes and support in international
fora. The Moncton Summit (September 1999) and the Third Conférence
Ministérielle sur la Culture (Cotonou, June 2001) offer an illustration of
this, since they enlisted the whole spread of member countries to support
and defend France's stance on 'l'exception culturelle' (i.e. the exclusion of
cultural 'production' from World Trade agreements).

'Coopération' remains the main platform for French action in its former
colonies and beyond. It is an ambiguous means of intervention within the
political, economic and cultural tissue of these countries. In a Report to the
National Assembly entitled *Du Global à l'universel: les défis de la francophonie*, the author states:

> [S]i à l'origine la francophonie était un mouvement de nature linguis-
> tique (promotion et défense de la langue), elle a été amenée, selon la
> volonté des pères fondateurs, à participer au développement du Sud.
> Progressivement, la langue est devenue, non plus un objectif, mais un
> outil de développement. On utilise le français pour faire de la coopéra-
> tion, de la concertation, de la politique, de la coopération économique.
> La francophonie est appréhendée comme un espace de coopération
> politique, de solidarité Nord–Sud et de prévention des conflits.
> (Tavernier 2000, 183)

> If francophonie was originally a linguistic initiative [...], it has come to
> participate in the development of the South, according to the wishes of
> its founding fathers. Eventually, language has turned from an end to a
> tool of development. French is used in order to enable cooperation,
> concertation, political and economic cooperation. Francophonie is
> now perceived as an area of political cooperation, of North–South
> solidarity, and of prevention of conflicts.

Yet, if French is deemed necessary for the 'development' of emerging economies, what does it say about their dependency and colonial continuities?

Some critics of Francophonie advocate a radical departure in educational matters based on ethical grounds, especially advocating education in the local vernaculars, as 'un instrument essentiel pour le développement économique et démocratique d'une société' [an essential tool for a society's economic and democratic development] (Renard 2000, 41). The mission, message and policies of Francophonie have in fact been changing since 1998, in line with the restructuring of the organization (Parker 2002a). There is a new sense that the promotion and propagation of French in the world are inseparable from an action in favour of plurilingualism to be pursued in France and the European Union, as well as at the levels of international organizations and through new communication networks such as the internet.

The change of focus applies within and without: within her own frontiers France has yielded to European policy-making and adopted a new liberalism vis-à-vis its regional languages; outside them, it is also committed to supporting plurilingualism. This policy change is based on the notion that to defend French is to defend the ability of individual nations to assert their own cultural identities. The ultimate concession is even contemplated: 'Ainsi la francophonie mérite d'être défendue. Elle est le support de la diversité culturelle. [...] Sa diffusion en tant que système de pensée doit être favorisée, *y compris par le biais de l'anglais* et des langues vernaculaires' [Francophonie thus deserves to be defended. It is the vector of cultural diversity. [...] Its propagation as a system of thought must be helped, *even through the use of English* and of vernacular languages] (Tavernier 2000, 184; my emphasis). Not for French the 'status' of lingua franca. 'L'universel' is part of the pedigree of French, whereas 'l'anglo-américain' is global.

Francophonie: new commitments, new communities?

In his message to the 2002 Journée de la Francophonie [Francophonie Day] M. Josselin, the Ministre délégué à la Coopération et à la Francophonie, stated: 'La Francophonie s'est affirmée comme une communauté de valeurs, une organisation à vocation universelle en prise avec les défis de son temps' [Francophonie has proven itself to be a community of shared values, an organization with a universal vocation tuned into the challenges of its time]. Outlining the main policy for Francophonie – 'solidarité' – he stressed that it rested on a two-pronged approach: 'approfondissement de la démocratie' and promotion of 'diversité linguistique et culturelle'. Regarding the latter: 'Son objectif est d'éviter que la mondialisation ne devienne une source d'aggravation des inégalités, mais qu'elle soit au contraire un facteur de développement et de dialogue des cultures' [The aim is to prevent globalization from becoming a source of worsening inequalities and conversely to turn it into a factor of development and dialogue between cultures].

Francophonie thus becomes the space where French is shared: the 'lieu commun' for all French speakers – although the extension of Francophonie membership does go beyond the 'logical' and the sharing of a common language (how did Bulgaria qualify as a member?); conversely, French interests extend beyond the former 'pré carré' [France's 'reserved' areas of 'influence', mainly in Africa] while English-speaking powers – and indeed Quebec – seek to extend their area of influence beyond language boundaries (Parker 2002b).

At the same time, the four decades elapsed since the end of decolonization have allowed for a de-dramatization of the 'drame colonial' evoked by Memmi, especially at the level of language (Memmi 1990 [1957]). Césaire had already declared: 'La langue française me colonise, je la colonise à mon tour' [French language colonizes me; in turn I colonize it] (cited in Gauvin 1997, 41).

Having interviewed a number of francophone writers from North and South, Europe and Africa, the Americas and the Mediterranean regarding their relationship to French, Lise Gauvin concludes that their questioning of language is a manifestation of their desire to question the very nature of language and the notion that a language 'belongs' to any one group (1997, 6). Patrick Chamoiseau seems to support her thesis: he believes languages are 'relativized' by a new generation:

> Les enfants ne sont plus comme nous; leur rapport à la langue, à une langue, n'est pas le rapport que nous avions qui était un rapport fondateur, constructeur, un rapport d'élévation, de lutte, de progression. [...] [L]a langue a pris des distances quant à la notion d'identité, c'est-à-dire que la langue ne sert plus à définir une culture, une identité. (Gauvin 1997, 37)

> Children are different from how we were; their relationship to the language, to a language, is not the one we used to have, which was a founding relationship, a constructive, elevating one, one of struggle, of progress. [...] [L]anguage has distanced itself from the notion of identity, that is to say, language no longer serves to define a culture, an identity.

Thus a generation or so after Memmi a form of reconciliation with the (colonized) self is in progress. In Gauvin's interviews, writers such as René Depestre (Haiti) and Tahar Ben Jelloun (Morocco) consistently claim the French language as part of their own cultural baggage. If this is the case, then I believe that Francophonie loses its imperialistic edge and does become post-colonial. Renard reaches a similar conclusion, advocating the construction of a 'genuine francophone identity'. The cement holding this identity together is the French language and the 'values' seen to be conveyed by it in the collective imagination of many populations: solidarity, respect for the rights of man, tolerance, democracy (Renard 2000, 289).

'Égaux, Unis, Différents':[3] towards a new francophonie

According to Stélio Farandjis, the Secrétaire-Général du Haut Conseil de la Francophonie, the tension between diversity and universality constitutes both the challenge and the attraction of the concept of francophonie (cited in Bloche 1999, 21). Perhaps, but even this thought betrays a monolithic view of France ('universelle' and unified in her values) and 'the rest' (diverse and heterogeneous). French discourse itself has to be interrogated in order to deconstruct the opposition between metropolis and 'the rest'. Critics might argue that cultural diversity is simply a concept appropriated by France in order to underpin or defend its policy of 'l'exception culturelle'. However, as with the very notion of F/francophonie, credited to 'others' in order to absolve France of any neocolonial intent, Tavernier reminds us that diversity and universality were the basis of the 'conception senghorienne du métissage culturel' within an 'humanisme intégral' (2000, 15). 'Métissage' is presented as preempting the uniformizing effect of globalization.

Perhaps the answer lies in the emerging notion of 'diversalité'. This hybrid word welds together the notions of diversity and universality, thus reconciling two hitherto antonymic world views. The Glissant/Confiant/Chamoiseau model is different from the 'métissages' hitherto advocated, since it suggests a juxtaposition in which each component remains identifiable. Based on an interpretation of 'créolisation', it allows for the happy cohabitation of diverse components within each individual. The strategy proposed by Raphaël Confiant (tinged with subversive humour?), at the Third Ministerial Conference on Culture in Benin in June 2001, is to besiege Paris, the bastion of the French language, and to recreate an Académie – the Académie francophone – to be located in Paris, the 'berceau historique' [historic cradle], as well as a number of Académies régionales, whose raison d'être is be to the production of a *Dictionnaire du français mondial*. The project also includes the creation of teaching materials for the teaching of Créole, Wolof, Bambara, Berber, Arabic, in order to nurture the multiple identities that will help combat the uniformizing effects of globalization.

Diversity can indeed be liberating. Depestre points out with relish that the expansion of French culture beyond French frontiers has generated not only a number of creole languages, but also religions and new ways of life: 'La France a fonctionné comme un métier à métisser le monde. [...] Toute nouvelle civilisation se constitue à partir de la multiplicité d'apports culturels tramés par divers peuples' [France has woven a colourful canvas across the world on its looms. [...] All new cultures are made from the web and warp of various cultures threaded through by diverse people] (Gauvin 1997, 90). Jean-Pierre Verheggen for his part suggests that Walloons and

---

[3]   The motto appeared in the form of a 'watermark' background on the Francophonie website in 2001. This background has now been changed.

Quebecois should reclaim their language (French), stop apologizing for their 'petit nègre' [pidgin French] and become 'grands Nègres' because 'Nous sommes Africains quelque part' [We are partly African] (Gauvin 1997, 172). He refers enthusiastically to Loïc Depecker's work, *Les Mots de la francophonie*, pointing out: 'Nous sommes les inventeurs de cette langue française *à venir*' [We are the inventors of *tomorrow*'s language] (Gauvin 1997, 172; emphasis in original), hence the guarantee of its future. In favour of an inventive approach to language, he asserts: 'Il faut faire entendre l'*inouïversel*' [We must ensure *the unheard of* is *universally* heard] (Gauvin 1997, 180; emphasis in original).

If the centre (France) is perceived as oppressive, francophonie can gain strength from solidarity. Whereas 'Francophonie institutionnelle' remains suspected of neocolonialism, the community of people/s who make up 'francophonie' can create an 'espace de solidarité', reconciliation, hybridity and identity/ies. This amounts to a reinvention of francophonie from the outside. If this is the case, then francophonie is postcolonial not so much because it comes into its own 'after' colonization is over, but because it goes 'beyond'.

9

'Séparisianisme', or internal colonialism

BY HEATHER WILLIAMS

France is the only French-speaking country that is officially monolingual, and speaks French rather than a particular variety of the language. And, while it is fine, indeed a matter of pride, for France to have, as de Gaulle famously put it, some 265 varieties of cheese, the country seems far from comfortable with the richness of its actual linguistic heritage. The controversy in 1999 over the signing of the European Charter for Minority Languages threw into sharp relief a longstanding problem: the French State's intolerance, or perhaps fear, of France's own indigenous regional languages. While French is the language of the One and Indivisible Republic, Alsatian, Basque, Breton, Catalan, Corsican, Gallo and Occitan are all taught today in French schools (Cerquiglini 1999), and support for them has arguably never been stronger. So, just like la Francophonie (see Parker, Chapter 8), the Hexagon itself is a mosaic of differences, and yet the Paris–Province axis has long been conceptualized as a centre–periphery relationship. This chapter investigates ways in which regionalist movements within metropolitan France are analogous to, proclaim solidarity with, and draw inspiration from Francophone postcolonial writers.

While French literature and political discourse alike have predominantly portrayed provincial regions as picturesque variations on a French theme, with their inhabitants proudly assimilated into 'Frenchness', the literary and political activities of these regions reveal a rather more complex situation. This is because French unity, as well as French grandeur, have never been more than a myth in the regions of France where indigenous languages are used as a defining characteristic of identity. These include Alsace, or Elsass, where a Germanic dialect is spoken; its tragedy is to have been torn between two states, with Alsatians unable to express their Frenchness under German rule, and prevented from expressing their German identity under the French. Somewhat similarly in the north of France, French Flanders is the home of a linguistic minority created by its geographical proximity to the Flemish-speaking parts of Belgium. The south of France contains strong cross-frontier identities in the form of the Basques and the Catalans; the Basque language is so ancient that it is believed to be unrelated to any other language still in existence. As the larger part of the Basque Country, or Euzkadi, is in Spain, its autonomist movement has focused its energies on that state, and the same is true of Catalonia, the largest part of which is in Spain. Offshore, the autonomist movement on the island of Corsica has certainly been making its voice heard in Paris in recent years. Brittany, the westernmost tip of France, was independent until 1532, and prides itself on its separate history, culture and literature, especially the Breton language. Most of the estimated 500,000 speakers live in Lower (i.e. western) Brittany, whereas the Romance dialect Gallo is also spoken by a much smaller number in the eastern part of Brittany. In the south of France, Occitania's precise definition is open to dispute, thanks to its own internal heterogeneity, but it, like Brittany, takes pride in its unique cultural heritage; it is unlike Brittany though in that it cannot look back to a former state for inspiration. Brittany's unbroken historical tradition accounts for the fact that it presents the most coherent body of texts and theory, and provides the most striking example of internal difference in France.

Regionalist writers have been pointing out for well over a century that the sense of national identity, shared heritage, and homogeneity necessary for the concepts 'France' and 'Frenchness' to exist were achieved at the expense of this rich internal difference. But it is only relatively recently that centralizing views of French history and French literature have been challenged in mainstream writing (Thiesse 1991, 1999; Ford 1993; Gildea 1994) and that France's intolerance of its indigenous languages has been discussed in terms of fear or a sense of insecurity in the context of the country's demise on the world stage (Ager 1999). Despite being referred to in the homogenizing singular 'la Province', the periphery of France is not only different from its centre, but the peripheral cultures of France are also different from each other. What unites them, though, is an accusation levelled at the centralized state, relating to cultural and linguistic persecution, economic underdevelopment, and the political domination of the rest of France by Paris – a situation that has been provocatively termed 'séparisianisme' (Champaud 1977).

The regionalist movements are also united by their internationalist outlook. This was an inevitability for Basques and Catalans as they are cross-border peoples, and similarly for Alsatians as they have shuttled between two states. But equally important were the connections between Celtic civilizations, which meant that the Breton movement naturally looked across the sea to Wales and Ireland to find points of reference. As a consequence of looking beyond France's borders, regionalists focused increasingly in the course of the twentieth century on France's role on the world stage; and it is when they came to scrutinize their state's record in an era of decolonization that the use of 'colonialism' as a point of comparison became common, leading to the term 'internal colonialism'. More than just a political slogan, this encapsulated a countrywide political and cultural movement, reaching a peak in the late 1960s and early 1970s, that was founded on renewed solidarity between the marginalized regions of the Hexagon. The movement was led jointly by Brittany and Occitania, whose links on the literary scene had been well established during the nineteenth-century Romantic revival of regional sentiment. More importantly, this new-found confidence was based on solidarity between regions of the Hexagon and other parts of the world that had been colonized by France, though this too was in fact an old framework, as regionalist movements had been anti-colonial from an early date.

Maurice Duhamel (1929) provides an early example of such thinking. His study attacks the so-called 'unity' of France as a myth, and uses its colonial record to highlight the country's culpability in the repression of its own regional culture. A similar attitude fills the columns of *Breiz Atao* from the 1930s; the mouthpiece of the Breton nationalist movement urged its readers not to take up the French government's offer of farms in Algeria (November 1936), and contained articles opposing French attacks on Ethiopia (September 1935, February 1936), and the policies of Blum in North Africa (April 1937). These are no exceptions; the very first editorial of *Le Peuple breton*, written by Joseph Martray in 1947, is devoted to Algeria, and such an outlook proves to be a guiding principle of this publication. Through the 1950s and 1960s the comparison between Brittany and Algeria in particular becomes routine. Yann Poupinot, in his *Les Bretons à l'heure de l'Europe*, could describe Brittany as 'une colonie qui s'ignore' [a colony that does not know it is one] in his direct comparison of economic underdevelopment in Brittany and Algeria (1961, 70), but by the end of the 1960s the situation had changed irrevocably, and all marginalized cultures were using the colonial framework to argue their case. Work on Arabic language and culture had appeared regularly in *Al Liamm* throughout the 1960s, with attention given, for instance, to comparisons of the status of Breton and Arabic on the radio (1962), to the place of Arabic in the education system (1964), to 'Arabization' in Algeria (1966), and to cultural decolonization in Algeria (1967).

The Algerian war was undoubtedly responsible for a sea change within the regionalist movements in France. In the Occitan movement, the term 'algérisation' was coined as a precise way of conveying the extent of the underdevelopment suffered by the French regions (Lafont 1974, 270). The Union Démocratique Bretonne (UDB) presents its mission statement – in a 1972 pamphlet entitled *Bretagne=colonie* – largely as a response to the war articulated by young Bretons. This is echoed by Morvan Lebesque in his celebrated *Comment peut-on être Breton?*, where he claims that it is essentially since the Algerian war that he has hated the French state (Lebesque 1970, vii). But, apart from this, there were also internal, or more local, catalysts. The term 'internal colonialism' was probably used for the first time in winter 1961–2, as a response to the strike of the Décazeville miners, an event which also led to the founding of the Comité Occitan d'Études et d'Action (COEA). Like the demise of the Hennebont metalworks in Brittany, Décazeville occupies a symbolic position in the history of internal colonialism. It is considered indicative of the behaviour of the French state by Robert Lafont, the most prolific theorist of the Occitan movement, in his key text *La Révolution régionaliste* of 1967. This study was the most cogent exposition of internal colonialism to date, and was soon joined by a document in the same vein about Brittany; the manifesto of the Front de Libération de la Bretagne (FLB), disseminated from Dublin by the Comité de la Bretagne Libre (CBL) at the very end of December 1968, set out the ways in which Brittany was in 'une situation coloniale type' [a classic colonial situation] (Caerléon 1969, 289–94). By 1972, when the UDB published the polemical pamphlet *Bretagne=colonie*, this analogy was more than just a title or definition, or even a mission statement; it had been gathering pace for years, and had now been built into a coherent doctrine with reference to Francophone theorists. In explaining how Brittany's case fulfilled the criteria for cultural colonialism, it made explicit reference to Albert Memmi's *Portrait of the Colonized*, and Sékou Touré is cited in the same piece as a source for the definition of the term 'colonisé' itself. The Breton movement had shifted its focus, and the regional question in France had finally been liberated from its right-wing connotations acquired in particular during the Second World War.

The framework provided by Francophone writers allowed the regionalist movement to rearticulate the problem, and explains the change in the discourse. Their influence was equally significant over a simultaneous development: the harnessing, or reharnessing of the power of poetry. Of course, the role of poetry in the nineteenth-century revival in regionalist feeling is well known, in particular La Villemarqué's *Barzaz Breiz* (1839) and Mistral's *Mireille* or *Mirèio* (1859). It can indeed be argued that the Breton movement would not have come into being without the *Barzaz Breiz* (Guiomar 1987, 553; Reece 1977, 26). More than a century later, the impact, on the political understanding of an individual, of rediscovering La Villemarqué's infamous collection of ballads is dramatically incorporated into Morvan Lebesque's energetic retelling of the history of Brittany in *Comment peut-on être Breton?* (1970, 28). There is no need to repeat here the importance of literature to Empire, and its effect on the formation of identities. It is widely accepted that places are invented in literature, as literature is where images, both positive and negative, are formed, refined and disseminated. The clichés associated with provincial regions are the legacy of Romanticism; and the rural idyll (in the case of Brittany peopled by druids and sailors) created by minor Romantics became the target of the self-styled poets of decolonization.

Rejection and subversion of these damaging clichés – which portrayed a docile, subservient and essentially backward province – became paramount and systematic in the work of Paol Keineg, Christian Keginer, Yann-Ber

Piriou and Yves Rouquette. Their stormy relationship with the poetry of
perfect cadences and regular rhythms is evident on every page; as the
Occitan poet Yves Rouquette put it:

> Fuir tout pittoresque
> Nous ne sommes pas
> Des poètes paysans
> Nous n'avons pas de sabots à poser à la porte d'aucune ferme
> Et les formules nous les avons oubliées (Rouquette 1972)

> Flee the picturesque
> We are no
> Peasant poets
> We have no clogs to leave at the door of some farmhouse
> And the set expressions have been forgotten

The Brittany described by Paol Keineg in a poem entitled 'Il est défendu de
cracher par terre et de parler Breton' [No spitting or speaking Breton] is
deliberately unfamiliar to the student of Romantic literature:

> Lèvres et yeux gommés
> os de la face éclatés
> gisements de sang froid dans les veines
> racines des doigts tranchées
> aubépine fanée de notre haleine (Keineg 1971)

> Eyes and lips erased
> face of scattered bones
> veins of cold blood
> fingers sliced
> breath of dying hawthorn

The picture revealed here is neither Celtic nor seafaring; it is perhaps savage,
but by no means noble. The state of humanity here is a sorry one, and the
only hint of the usually grand and inspiring Breton nature – hawthorn – is
in its death throes ('fanée').

    This image of exploitation and oppression is echoed in contemporary
Occitan poetry. In Marie Rouanet's 1971 anthology *Occitanie 1970: Les
poètes de la décolonisation/Occitania 1970: los poètas de la descolonizacion: anthologie bilingue*, a similar picture of an 'internal colony' is
presented, and the French are denounced as 'colonialist': 'le peuple occitan
et la terre d'Occitanie sont encore dans une situation coloniale' [the Occitan
people and their country Occitania are still in a colonial situation] (Rouanet
1971, 9).

The underlying comparison that led these poets to describe their home territory as a colony is drawn explicitly by Yann-Ber Piriou in his 1971 anthology *Défense de cracher par terre et de parler breton: poèmes de combat (1950–1970: Anthologie bilingue)*, where he asks: 'Où sommes-nous donc? En Bretagne, en Algérie, au Kurdistan ou au Vietnam?' [Where are we then? In Brittany, Algeria, Kurdistan or Vietnam?] (Piriou 1971, 14). Statements of solidarity between victims of colonialism are a leitmotif in the work of this period, as in this example from Paol Keineg:

> c'est un de nos villages qui brûle
> quand un de nos frères saccage un village vietnamien
> c'est nous tous qu'il assassine
> quand il fracasse le crâne d'un enfant algérien. (1969, 52)

> it's one of our villages that burns
> when one of our brothers ransacks a village in Vietnam
> it's all of us he is killing
> when he smashes an Algerian child's skull.

Keineg makes no distinction between different types of colony; his dedications and quotations range from the Basque separatist group Euzkadi ta Azkatasuna (ETA), 'victimes de la répression française et espagnole' [victims of French and Spanish repression] (Keineg 1969), to Malcolm X and Aimé Césaire. Similarly in Occitania Yves Rouquette cites Césaire in a poem about Béziers, 'Oda a Sant Afrodisi' [Ode to Saint Aphrodise, patron saint of Béziers], which satirizes the inertia of politicians at a time when industries were closing and unemployment rising. Solidarity and an internationalist outlook are necessitated by the nature of the problem, as France's crimes stretch from Béziers to Indochina:

> De Béziers à l'Indochine, tu as troué des peaux de toutes les couleurs. Tu as ramassé dans tes banques de l'argent de toutes les odeurs. Tu as entassé dans tes musées les souvenirs de toutes les horreurs. Qui dressera la liste de tes crimes? [...] France–Cancer. (Larzac 1972, 27)

> From Béziers to Indochina, you have slashed skins of every colour. You have hoarded in your banks money of every odour. You have piled in your museums memories of every type of horror. Who will draw up the list of your crimes? [...] France–Cancer.

What really cements the solidarity is not so much the economic similarities between internal and external colonies as the shared experience of state education: as Rouanet claimed, 'l'école est la même pour tous: Bretons, Africains, Arabes' [school is the same for everyone: Bretons, Africans, Arabs] (1971, 9).

The way the French education system inculcates a centralizing, biased account of history amounts to more than selectivity with the truth, it constitutes a lie. The major part of *Comment peut-on être Breton* is devoted to demonstrating how France has provided Bretons with a pseudo-history, and has just as deliberately robbed them of their mother tongue (Lebesque 1970). Language is so much more than a simple means of communication: a shared, standardized language is generally considered a prerequisite for the creation of a feeling of group identity. This symbolic importance is well illustrated in the case of French. It explains why the phrase 'le français est la langue de la République' [French is the language of the Republic] was added to the Constitution in 1992, on the ratification of the Maastricht treaty; even if this was intended to protect French from the perceived threat of English, its effect now is to act as a renewed threat to regional languages, and by extension to France's own cultural diversity. Suppression of language is one of the main instruments of colonialism, and especially after the 1789 Revolution, France's regional languages were persecuted, initially through being tainted by association with counter-revolution. A century later, the education reforms of 1882 were parallel in strategy to the assimilationist educational policy pursued in French territories overseas. As Louis-Jean Calvet argues in his critique of the whole concept of la Francophonie, there was essentially no difference between the linguistic policy of the French Revolution in the Hexagon, and that of the Third Republic in the colonies (1974, 15). Well into the twentieth century children who were heard speaking a language other than French in school were punished, and had to wear what was called the 'symbole' in Brittany, or the 'signal' in Occitania.

It was above all the fact that that they did not speak French, language of the Revolution and of progress, that incriminated Breton peasants in the eyes of the Parisian administration, and meant that in the nineteenth century they were routinely compared to the primitive inhabitants of the further-flung parts of the new world. Balzac voices the opinion of the time in his novel about the counter-revolutionaries in Brittany, *Les Chouans*; a typical description of a 'chouan' (a counter-revolutionary) reads:

> Il faisait croire à une absence si complète de toute intelligence, que les officiers le comparèrent tour à tour, dans cette situation, à un des animaux qui broutaient les gras pâturages de la vallée, aux sauvages de l'Amérique ou à quelque naturel du cap de Bonne-Espérance. (Balzac 1957 [1829], 22)

> He gave an impression of such a total lack of intelligence, that the officers compared him, in this situation, sometimes to the animals grazing the rich pastures in the valley, and at others to American savages or some native of the Cape of Good Hope.

Around the same time, Auguste Romieu, the sub-prefect of Quimperlé in western Brittany, wrote the following shocking recommendation:

> La Basse-Bretagne, je ne cesserai de le dire, est une contrée à part, qui n'est plus la France. Exceptez-en les villes, le reste devrait être soumis à une sorte de régime colonial. Je n'avance rien d'exagéré. (Romieu 1831, 153)

> Lower Brittany, I insist, is a land apart, which is no longer France. With the exception of the towns, it should be subjected to some sort of colonial regime. I make no exaggeration.

Even though the stereotype of the fierce 'chouan' is gradually replaced by the docile feminine figure of Brizeux's Marie (followed shortly by Mistral's Mireille in Occitania), even though the barren land comes to be described as a fashionable blend of the sublime and picturesque and the uncivilized peasant gives way to a native version of the noble savage, the sole 'petite patrie' [small homeland] allowed by Paris was still a backward one to which the only possible attitude was condescendence (Bertho 1980; Williams 2003). Patronizingly positive clichés are ultimately no better than viciously negative ones; and so it is clear why the poets of decolonization in Brittany and Occitania rejected Romanticism's legacy. But they did much more than replace the damaging clichés with positive ones; for these modern poets, there was a more subtle sense in which poetry was political, and this was inseparable from the issue of language loss. For these 'révolutionnaires', as they called themselves, a poetic utterance was a political act, as Christian Keginer explains in his 'Point de départ: une poésie révolutionnaire bretonne existe' (1972, 69–72).

Truly revolutionary poetry does more than put the revolution to music, or tell its story in rhyme; Keginer explores what happens when a poet employs the language that has been forced upon him (and his people) by their oppressor, and argues that Breton poetry in French is necessarily political and revolutionary. In order for this energy to be realized, the Breton poet writing in the French language must first be conscious of actually speaking Breton despite using French words, and this is achieved through political commitment to the people of Brittany. The theory is set out as a parallel to the case of the black poet who writes in French:

> le poète noir qui écrit en français doit *saisir* qu'il est Noir pour cesser d'écrire dans la langue française, et parler enfin dans la *langue noire*, même si c'est avec des mots français. (1972, 69; emphasis in original)

> the black poet who writes in French must *be conscious* that he is Black so as to stop writing in the French language, and to write at last in *black language*, even if using French words.

Poetic creation similarly works though doing violence to the French language from within:

> La poésie bretonne de langue française – c'est par cette *contra-diction* qu'elle est politiquement révolutionnaire – entretient avec la langue française des rapports incestueux et meurtiers: née de cette langue étrangère, quoique sa source soit ailleurs, elle s'y marie afin de la mieux détruire. (1972; emphasis in original)

> Breton poetry in the French language – and it is this *contra-diction* that makes it politically revolutionary – has an incestuous and murderous relationship with the French language. Born of this foreign language, despite its source being elsewhere, it merges with it so as to better destroy it.

So although this poetry takes colonial suffering as its main subject-matter, it is the subtle but radical linguistic achievement that makes it 'decolonizing' and revolutionary. Even so, one could object that these fiery statements belong mainly in the domain of the postcolonial literary critic. But the actual poetry produced was also conceived as a political act in the same sense as a tract, and was meant to be read or sung aloud at gatherings and to be immediately accessible to larger audiences in that way. Many poems were turned into popular songs when put to music by Glenmor, Stivell, Servat and Tri Yann in Brittany, and music was also an essential part of the protest in the Occitan movement. Perhaps, after all, this is the most real sense in which the poetry was politics.

The poets' cultural legacy, on the other hand, is long-lasting. Keineg and Keginer, in pursuing a policy of poetic decolonization, are also responsible for the first concerted attempt to define Francophone Breton writing; *Bretagnes*, a journal founded by them in 1975, became the main forum for discussion. As a result they have become a privileged point of reference in the work of postcolonial literary critics in Brittany. The question 'is there a Francophone Brittany?' is today being asked by *Plurial*, the journal of the Centre d'Études des Littératures et Civilisations Francophones at the University of Rennes. It has produced some key definitional studies, like Marc Gontard's survey article: 'Pour une littérature bretonne de langue française', in a 1995 issue entitled *Écrire la Bretagne 1960–1995*, and combines rereadings of poets such as Keineg with discussion of present-day debates in Francophone writing from around the globe. Bernard Hue argues in the same issue that modern Francophone Breton literature reveals the change that has come about in Brittany and in Breton identity, concluding that 'bretonnité=altérité' [Bretonness=otherness] (1995, 12). Another important issue from 1994, comparing Brittany, the Maghreb and Quebec, takes its conceptual frame from Tahar Ben Jelloun, presenting the idea of 'métissage' as a positive, forward-looking value: 'l'avenir est au métissage' [the future belongs to 'métissage'] (Hue 1994, 5).

As another recently founded journal *Hopala!: débats de Bretagne et d'ailleurs* confirms, the Breton movement prides itself on being: 'résolument ouverte sur le monde' [resolutely open to the whole world]; each issue featuring a 'culture invitée' [guest culture] either from elsewhere in France or from further afield. The direction of French regionalism is, and always has been, determined initially by looking at the rest of the world, and then by looking closer to home and revealing France's double standards. Why could and can France not embrace the values that it claims to promote in other countries or regions where French is one of the languages spoken, such as Quebec? Why has France failed to extend the values of 'liberté' and 'égalité' to its indigenous minority cultures? The call today is for France to change in order to be saved from itself: 'faisons entrer la France dans la francophonie' [let's include France in la francophonie], urges Cerquiglini (1999).

If Parisian writers of the eighteenth and nineteenth centuries were allowed to compare Brittany to a colony, and arguably treat it like a colony, then the 1970s claim that Brittany is like a colony, or even is a colony, seems only fair; and, by the same token, it is also difficult to argue with the 1990s claim that the analysis of Breton literature requires a postcolonial framework. It was a heightened awareness of the devastating effect of the loss of language, combined with an internationalist outlook, that led the poets of decolonization in the French regions beyond the rejection or subversion of a literary legacy, and towards a new understanding of poetic utterance as political act. Now we have, in the form of postcolonial criticism, a renewed interest in – and indeed engagement with – writers from around the Francophone world, with the journal *Plurial* taking the lead in an exciting new attempt to negotiate and interrogate France's internal difference.

|10|

'This Creole culture, miraculously forged': the contradictions of 'créolité'

BY MAEVE McCUSKER

Introduction: 'L'exception antillaise'

The French-speaking Caribbean islands of Martinique and Guadeloupe have produced some of the earliest and most influential theorists of colonialism and its effects, whose work both anticipates and contributes to the current postcolonial moment. Writers such as Frantz Fanon, Aimé Césaire and Édouard Glissant have become foundational reference points in the development of the varied and ever-expanding area that we now call 'postcolonial theory', and obligatory inclusions in its anthologies and introductory texts. Most recently the 'créolité' school, the focus of this chapter, has contributed a copious series of theoretical and fictional soundings of Caribbean identity (on this subject, see also Dash, Chapter 21). The confluence, on these small islands, of an unapologetically self-reflexive essayistic tradition and a vibrant and internationally recognized creative output is remarkable, and can be explained to a significant extent by factors endemic to the area as a whole. For the Caribbean was the site of a particularly brutal and traumatic form of colonialism, beginning with the genocide of the indigenous populations and sustained by the middle passage and the slave trade. Firstly, identity, a touchstone of postcolonial discourse generally, becomes a particularly obsessive theme in a society which has no continuous link to a pre-colonial era, and in which transportation has shattered any sense of a permanent or essential selfhood. Secondly, the inherently multilingual nature of the Caribbean makes it a 'contact zone' which nurtures the formulation and circulation of identitarian debate. A third, related factor, given the dominance of English in the postcolonial theoretical domain, is the geographical proximity of the United States, where the field of postcolonialism has flourished since the 1980s, and where such prominent Antillean writers as Édouard Glissant and Maryse Condé have held university positions.

But one glaringly anomalous factor may, ironically, be the key to the specific prominence of the French Antilles on the world stage of postcolonial writing. For it is a peculiar paradox that these islands have been at the forefront of a tradition of 'writing back' to a centre of which they are supposed to form an integral part. Since 1946, they have had the status of Overseas Departments of France, meaning, in theory at least, that they are as French as Brittany or Normandy – an identity simultaneously exalted and despised. It is no doubt largely because of, rather than despite, this double bind, that Martinique, the most fully assimilated of the Overseas Departments, and an island which has no political or institutional claim to the word 'postcolonial', has produced some of the key theorists of this expanding academic area. Indeed, the sheer volume and vitality of identitarian debate to have emerged from the French Caribbean in recent years would seem to mandate the more inclusive, less chronologically or politically determined sense of the term 'postcolonial', as suggested by Stephen Slemon: 'The concept proves most useful not when it is used synonymously with a post-independence historical period in once colonized nations, but rather when it locates a specifically anti- or *post*-colonial *discursive* purchase in culture' (1991, 3; emphasis in the original).

So geography and history conspire to make the French Antilles difficult to place, a truly interstitial space. The very etymology of their name, 'ante illum, before the continent' (Chamoiseau 1997, 234), gestures towards this liminal and 'in-between' perspective. Poised precariously between 'Old' World and 'New', between the continental expanses of Europe, Africa and North and South America, these islands have become a kind of parallel world, and the site of a curiously doubled identity. Not only were they among the first lands to be colonized by the French, but the general move towards decolonization has passed them by (or rather, has been voluntarily rejected). The 1960s, the key period of independence struggles and decolonization the world over, heralded in the Antilles an increasingly dependent relationship with France due to the collapse of the sugar industry. That their currency, since 1 January 2002, is the Euro is just another conundrum in the ongoing negotiation of a paradoxical and ambivalent relationship with the old colonial master. This is a relationship characterized more by the insidious silencing of dissident voices than by the brutal and overt repression of the decolonized state, a fact which haunts contemporary writers. In *Écrire en pays dominé*, Patrick Chamoiseau's acknowledgement of his relatively privileged position is tinged with ambivalence; the unnamed African continent serves both as a stark reminder of the brutal aftermath of decolonization, and simultaneously as a shame-inducing mirror, reminding the sterile and assimilated Antillean of his level of cultural zombification and throwing into question the very role of the writer (1997, 18–20).

The créolité movement is the most recent artistic response to this state of (alleged) cultural paralysis, and has dominated Antillean cultural and literary life since the late 1980s. In this chapter I will situate the tensions and paradoxes embodied in créolité within the context of the roughly contemporaneous rise of postcolonial studies.[1] As we shall see, créolité's rhetoric of hybridity, its (often audacious) interdisciplinarity and its polarized reception intersect significantly with the fate of the parallel, and equally fraught, arena of contemporary postcolonial theory itself (not least in the intensity and vitriol of the criticism it has provoked, much of which centres on the validity of the term itself). But it is precisely in the ambivalences and paradoxes which beset the créolité discourse, the points at which it goes against its own rhetorical grain, that it can be seen to inhabit a space between colonial and postcolonial subjectivity. In this respect, and precisely because of its contradications and internal incoherences, it can be considered the paradigmatic formulation of Antillean identity.

In the closing pages of the *Éloge de la créolité*, Creole culture is described as having been 'miraculously forged' (Bernabé *et al.* 1993 [1989], 116) over three centuries of humiliation and exploitation. In the attempt to move beyond a narrative of recrimination and regret, the plantation is figured as the crucible of a wondrous alchemical process, whereby the disparate elements of Caribbean culture are reassembled in a new configuration. But the choice of words nonetheless points to a paradox at the heart of the créolité mission. As we shall see, for all the emphasis on concepts such as 'true memory', 'foundations' and 'authenticity', créolité is in many respects itself a forgery, a fabrication or a literary construct which bears little relation to contemporary (or even historical) Antillean reality.

Créolité: a return to the native land?

It is now axiomatic, if somewhat schematic, to claim that Negritude, the earliest 'postcolonial' discourse to emerge from the Antilles, merely inverted the racist binaries it sought to contest (see Burton 1993). By fetishizing a mythical and ossified African continent, Negritude reinscribed an oppositional logic of exclusion, and failed to address the painful dislocations and transformations of the middle passage itself. The emergence of Édouard Glissant heralded an epistemological break with this over-simplifying binary opposition. In such influential texts as *Le Discours antillais* (1981) and *Poétique de la Relation* (1990), Glissant looks to the Caribbean itself as the crucial repository for Caribbean identity and proposes such interactive, non-hierarchical concepts as 'creolization' and 'Relation'. Thus, he rejects

---

[1]   The term 'postcolonial' is not generally used by the créolistes – indeed, it might have provided a welcome alternative to the litany of hyphenated terms rejected as obsolete by the authors in the *Éloge de la créolité*: 'Afro-Caribbean, Negro-Caribbean, Franco-Caribbean, French-Speaking Caribbean, Francophone-Caribbean' (Bernabé *et al.* 1993 [1989], 96–7).

notions of ancestral purity and racial authenticity, proposing the mobile and horizontally proliferating rhizome as a more appropriate metaphor of Antillean identity than the unitary root.

This anti-essentialist stance is taken up by the créolité movement, composed primarily of three Martiniquans: the Creole linguist Jean Bernabé and novelists Raphaël Confiant and Patrick Chamoiseau. (Two Guadeloupean novelists, Ernest Pépin and Gisèle Pineau are also, in certain contexts, admitted to the ranks, though the impetus remains largely Martiniquan and male.) The movement, which was marked from the outset by a strong côterie-building instinct, came into being with the publication of *Éloge de la créolité* in 1989 and was consolidated by the appearance of Chamoiseau's and Confiant's literary history *Lettres créoles* in 1991. The concept is given further exploration in the fiction of both these authors, and in their subsequent essays (see, for example, Confiant 1993a and Chamoiseau 1997). So, while the *Éloge* is the text which has attracted most attention (partly because of its openly provocative and polemical edge, partly because of its ideological and linguistic accessibility, being published in a parallel French/English format), créolité remains an ongoing point of reference for these authors, a discourse which they have been actively refining and promoting for well over a decade.

In its self-conscious address to future generations, and in its implicit claim to be the founding text in the establishment of an indigenous and authentic literary tradition, the *Éloge* has been compared to Joachim du Bellay's Renaissance manifesto, *Deffense et illustration de la langue française* (1549). The authors, however, approach their subject in a spirit of praise-giving and benediction rather than in defence; their celebratory tone marks a clear break with the images of the diseased or hideously wounded body which dominated the work of Césaire, and with the Glissantian trope of the infected mind. Indeed, the word 'illustration', in its Renaissance context, chimes appropriately with the aims of the manifesto – the objective of which is not only 'illustrer' in the sense of 'to demonstrate', but more significantly 'to ennoble', to render more illustrious, the denigrated Creole culture which it celebrates. The authors declare that they want 'to name each thing [...] and to declare it beautiful' (Bernabé *et al.* 1993, 101). Their starting point, as for Glissant, is not Africa but the plantation, which becomes the enabling condition of a new identity, encapsulated in the neologism 'diversality'. But the signatories of the text diverge from Glissant on two key points. They see créolité not as a Caribbean specificity but as an emerging condition of global culture more generally – 'the world is evolving into a state of Creoleness' (1993, 122) – and they consider the Creole language as the primary vector in the articulation of this new identity.

Creoleness is defined as an 'open specificity', an 'annihilation of false universality, of monolingualism, and of purity', and conceptualized as 'our primeval chaos and our mangrove swamp of virtualities' (1993, 90). Moreover, artistic expression must reflect this complexity: 'Exploring our

Creoleness must be done in a thought as complex as Creoleness itself'
(1993, 90). In such pronouncements, the *Éloge* clearly chimes with the postcolonial imperative to 'think beyond narratives of originary and initial
subjectivities', and to focus rather on the in-between spaces which 'provide
the terrain for elaborating strategies of selfhood – singular or communal –
that initiate new signs of identity' (Bhabha 1994, 1–2). The emphasis on the
endlessly porous, mobile and fecund interaction, born from an ever more
complex network of influence, is further developed in Chamoiseau's *Écrire
en pays dominé*:

> Amérindiens, békés, Indiens, Nègres, Chinois, mulâtres, Madériens,
> Syro-Libanais ... Nous voulûmes préserver d'originelles puretés mais
> nous nous vîmes traversés les uns par les autres. L'Autre me change et
> je le change. Son contact m'anime et je l'anime [...]. Chaque Autre
> devient une composante de moi tout en restant distinct. Je deviens ce
> que je suis dans mon appui ouvert sur l'Autre. (1997, 202)

> Amerindians, békés [white settlers], Indians, Negroes, Chinese,
> mulattos, Maderians, Syro-Lebanese ... We wanted to preserve
> original purities but we saw ourselves criss-crossed by each other. The
> Other changes me and I change it. Its contact animates me and I
> animate it. [...]. Every Other becomes a component of me while
> remaining distinct. I become what I am in my open support for the
> Other.

This *Poétique de la Relation*, to borrow the title of Glissant's essay, proposes
that in the space of the plantation the boundaries between self and other
were destabilized, if not irrevocably broken down, through an ongoing
engagement with the other. So in keeping with the current postcolonial
orthodoxy, créolité proposes that 'colonizer' and 'colonized' cannot be
viewed as separate entities, but that they are rather mutually constitutive,
mutually complicating and contaminating discursive positions. Césaire's
Manichean model of identity is apparently rejected in favour of an open-
ended, mobile, heterogeneous and unpredictable interaction, and the
rhetorical signatures of a recognizably contemporary postcolonial discourse, already present in much of Glissant's work, are furthered:
indeterminacy, hybridity and the reappropriation of the multiple histories of
the Creole world become primary objectives. The celebratory tone allows
the rhetoric of the postmodern to combine with the identitarian emphasis
of the postcolonial.

And yet the paradoxes in which créolité is entangled recapitulate the contradictions which define contemporary Martiniquan society, and point to
the tensions at the heart of postcolonial identity more generally. In the first
instance, the concept of the Creole advanced in the text is itself problematic,
an issue explored by Chris Bongie in his contribution to this volume (see

Chapter 3). As Bongie argues, by reclaiming the word 'Creole' from the white/béké monopoly on the term, the créolistes substitute an inclusionary definition of the Creole for an exclusionary one, a gesture which, in its own attempt at affirmative action, risks positively discriminating in favour of the hybrid. In other words, the old categories of racial stratification, which the authors claim to be shaking off, remain intact. Moreover, while the tract claims to embrace the entire population of the Antilles in all its ethnic diversity, whites and mulattos are almost entirely absent from the fictional world of Chamoiseau and Confiant, suggesting not only an essentialism which valorizes 'métissage' over purity, but one which only rates a highly selective form of racial mixing.

The adoption of the manifesto form, too, can be seen as a quintessentially French manoeuvre. The Saint Lucian poet Derek Walcott takes issue with the rhetorical exuberance of the manifesto, arguing that 'it echoes, in all its emphatic isolation, all those pamphlets outlining programs for new painting, a new poetry, that erupt from metropolitan ferment, and that, reaching out to embrace a public, baffle it by their vehemence' (Walcott 1998, 224; see also Mazama 1996). The question of the projected public for the tract is indeed perplexing, epitomizing the 'doubling' of the colonial subject whose desire is, as Homi Bhabha has shown, to be in two places at once. For the *Éloge* is in fact the text of a lecture jointly delivered by its three authors in the Parisian suburb of Saint-Denis in 1988. Ironically, then, this mission statement was delivered in the first instance to a metropolitan audience rather than to the Creole people whose cultural practices it somewhat arrogantly proposed to transform. Equally, while it sets as a key objective the rehabilitation of the Creole language, it was published in French, and is most readily available in a bilingual French/English (rather than French/Creole) format. As Mary Gallagher comments, 'For all the pious words in praise of the Creole language, the subtext of *Éloge de la créolité* suggests mere lip service or at the very least reluctant realism in relation to the language' (1994, 11). It is difficult not to see in certain aspects of the *Éloge* precisely the exteriority which defines the colonial subject, an exteriority which is strenuously denounced in the text for having 'determined a writing for the Other, a borrowed writing, steeped in French values, or at least unrelated to this land' (Bernabé *et al.* 1993, 76).

Moreover, the *Éloge*, like all of Chamoiseau and Confiant's (French-language) novels, is published by a prestigious metropolitan publisher, and both authors have been willing participants in the institutional apparatus of the French media. The award of the Prix Goncourt to Chamoiseau in 1992 for his novel *Texaco* is only the most high profile in a range of nominations and awards. Celia Britton links this phenomenon to the export-driven imperative of the colonial enterprise itself. She argues that, because the Antilles are too small to sustain a viable independent publishing industry, Antillean novels have become a commodity. Like rum, pineapples and avocados, they represent an economically significant export to metropolitan

France, and one which must conform to metropolitan tastes in order to sell successfully there (Britton 1996, 15). This circulation via the metropolis undercuts the explicitly anti-hegemonic rhetoric of the créolité movement, which is recuperated, as a commodity, by the centre against which it positions itself – a mainstreaming of the margin which is of course symptomatic of the condition of the postcolonial artist more generally. While the créolistes remain outspoken and hostile with regard to the neocolonial role of France in the post-departmentalized Antilles, they are inevitably complicit with, and reliant on, the centre.

Equally, créolité occupies an ambiguous position, caught, Janus-faced, between competing narratives of crisis and celebration. The *Éloge* looks forward to the past, in a sense, proclaiming a rehabilitated indigenous culture, but simultaneously looking elegiacally back to disappearing customs and traditions. While the tone is 'appealing, stimulating, energetic and hopeful' (Gallagher 1994, 18), the aspects of Creole culture which are upheld in the section of the *Éloge* entitled 'The thematics of existence', and again in the fiction, are relics of an (albeit regrettably) disappearing age: the Creole storyteller, folk tales, local medicine and cuisine, the marketplace. For critics such as Maryse Condé, this panders to an unpardonably nostalgic, even quasi-folkloric vision of the islands. Her frustration with the thematic emphasis of the movement is obvious: 'Are we condemned *ad vitam aeternam* to speak of vegetable markets, storytellers, "dorlis", "koutem"...? Are we condemned to explore to saturation the resources of our narrow land? We live in a world where, already, frontiers have ceased to exist' (Condé 1993, 130). It is not coincidental that so many of the fictional heroes are elderly men and women, a fact which facilitates the evocation of the island's past rather than its present. In many cases they are symbolically linked to one of these privileged, but threatened, aspects: the 'djobeurs' of the traditional market in Chamoiseau's *Chronique des sept misères*; Solibo Magnifique, the eponymous storyteller; Marie-Sophie Laborieux, guarantor of the Creole quarter in *Texaco*, and herself the child of elderly parents; the murdered stickfighter in Confiant's *Le Meurtre du Samedi-Gloria*. In almost every case, these heroes (and occasionally, heroines) are childless and they end up, to put it bluntly, literally and metaphorically dead. The pessimistic orientation of much of the fiction, which mourns the passing of these traditions and customs, while suggesting no real hope of their continuation in the future, sits uneasily with the forward-looking and projective tone of the *Éloge*.

More dangerously, perhaps, the free-floating signifier 'créolité' could be seen as something of a cover-up, an excessively celebratory gloss. The intoxicating fervour with which the apparently democratic ideal of créolité is upheld and celebrated could be said to distort the reality of contemporary Antillean society, characterized by mass unemployment, drug abuse, economic paralysis and the increasing stranglehold of France. In this respect, the créolistes have been accused of being 'complicitous with the celebration of a museumified Martinique, a diorama'd Martinique, a picturesque and plastified Martinique that promotes a "feel-good" nostalgia for people otherwise busy adjusting to a rapidly modernizing lifestyle' (Price and Price 1999, 138). Significantly, two of the privileged metaphors of créolité are the mosaic and the kaleidoscope: the appeal of both these artefacts, suggesting the fusing of disparate elements to emerge in new, beauteous configurations, is obvious. But both depend on a trompe-l'œil, a special effect more virtual than real. The individual shards of the mosaic never interpenetrate, but remain rather glued into a static configuration. Equally, the kaleidoscope depends for its effect on a mirror image, an optical illusion which merely gives the impression of endlessly renewable and mobile combinations. And, in any case, the extent to which contemporary Martinique can be seen to embody 'the world diffracted and recomposed' (Bernabé *et al.* 1993, 88) is highly suspect. Tony Delsham, a Martiniquan journalist and erstwhile collaborator with Chamoiseau on various local publications, argues that, with regard to the Antilles, France can congratulate itself on a uniquely complete colonization, achieved to an unprecedented extent. Taking issue with the image of the mosaic, he points out that the béké class continues to hold 80 per cent of the land on the island and that economic status is still directly linked to skin colour. Moreover, contemporary Antilleans remain profoundly conditioned by the libidinal economy of the plantation; black Antilleans persist in their determination to whiten the race while the béké caste, seeking their spouses in France, remain as white as the day they arrived on the islands. In other words, Delsham argues that, since depart-mentalization, the Antilles have been the site of an aborted creolization, and that the celebratory rhetoric of créolité is not only premature, but deeply bogus (Delsham 1998).

Delsham's reservations, working out of the specific context of the Antilles, echo those raised in a more general postcolonial context. Ella Shohat, for example, sounds a cautionary note when she argues that: 'A celebration of syncretism and hybridity per se, if not articulated in conjunc-tion with questions of hegemony and neo-colonial power relations, runs the risk of appearing to sanctify the fait accompli of colonial violence' (1992, 109–10). The risk is that, in the use of catch-all terms such as 'hybridity' and 'créolité', one might 'fail to discriminate between the diverse modes of hybridity, for example, forced assimilation, internalized self-rejection, political cooptation, social conformism, cultural mimicry, and creative transcendence' (Shohat 1992, 109–10). Créolité could be seen as a spurious signifier of a unified and harmonious condition, effectively homogenizing and eliding very real differences and inequalities. It is significant that any explicitly political argument is relegated to a two-page appendix at the end of the *Éloge*, entitled somewhat dutifully 'Creoleness and Politics'. Significant, too, that the section opens with the now obligatory denuncia-tion of Marxism (an ideology consistently derided in the fiction of both authors), and which is caricatured here as a movement 'which has it that cultural and therefore identity-related issues will find a solution once the revolution is achieved' (Bernabé *et al.* 1993, 115). Collective action and large-scale political mobilization are relegated to the sidelines in favour of an exclusively artistic, some would say elitist, agenda – again a charge which has been levied at postcolonial theory itself.

Finally, the créolité movement has been heavily criticized for its programmatic and prescriptive impulse with regard to the Creole language, which is established as a cornerstone of the literary agenda, and a key index of this authenticity. And yet a close reading of the texts themselves reveals an 'effet de créole', to rephrase Barthes, an invention which depends more on the subversion of standard French and the use of archaisms than it does, strictly speaking, on Creole itself. The interlectal space occupied by Confiant and Chamoiseau is a peculiarly literary arena, a construct, reflecting a highly wrought literary 'langage' that bears little relation to the Creole spoken on the streets of Fort-de-France. Thus, for example, words such as 'bailler' (to give), 'pièce' (none) and 'morne' (hill) inflect the narrative with an effect of strangeness, but this is an effect derived from the French lexicon. Where Creole is included, it remains largely distinct from the weave of the text itself. Creole insertions are usually translated immediately afterwards, reinscribing the extent to which the gaze of the authors is 'turned in two directions' (Ashcroft *et al.* 1989, 61). For as Ashcroft and his fellow authors have argued, these explanatory gestures on the part of the postcolonial writer 'represent a reading rather than a writing, primordial sorties into that interpretative territory where the Other (as reader) stands' (1989, 61). Moreover, the actual location of 'pure' Creole in the texts is in itself revealing. In the work of the authors discussed above, it most often forms part of the 'discours' rather than 'histoire', encapsulated in direct speech, or conveying spontaneous interventions and unmediated emotional impulses – see, in particular, the autobiographical texts: both volumes of Chamoiseau's *Une Enfance créole* (1993 and 1994), and Confiant's *Ravines du devant jour* (1993b). The 'authoritative' narrative voice of the 'histoire' (although, admittedly, the word 'authoritative' carries connotations of assurance and self-possession which are not entirely appropriate for the hesitant, polyphonous and often anxious narrators of the fiction) is predominantly French – although a deformed and hybridized French.

Given the debates outlined above, it is interesting that Chamoiseau's latest novel *Biblique des derniers gestes* (2002) marks a significant departure from the hallowed temporal and geographical territory of 'créolité'. It projects backwards in time (to the middle passage, and to the beginning of the world itself, in two of the multiple versions with which the novel begins) and outwards in space (the protagonist-warrior travels, implausibly, throughout the entire colonized world). Significant, too, that the creolization of the language that marked earlier works has fallen away. Moreover, the novel opens with a denunciation of the self-exoticizing moves of contemporary Martinique. Césaire's eightieth birthday provides the cue for a series of tourist-oriented spectacles to be consumed by the visitor and by the media. The novel goes on to suggest a fairly unnuanced distinction between authentic remembering and the artificiality of 'official memory'. It is divided into two sections, the 'Livre de la conscience du pays officiel' [Book of conscience of the official country] and the apparently more organic, authentic 'incertitudes [...] du pays enterré' [uncertainties [...] of the buried country]. The former explores the extent to which contemporary Martiniquan culture, founded originally on a production economy, has become a shabby forgery based on reproduction (slide shows, photocopied pamphlets, recordings and archives). The 'buried consciousness' (which is obviously approved of by the author) relies heavily on the supernatural heritage of the island, and is accessed, through the protagonist's journeys, by immersion in nature as a life-giving force and through communion with woman as nurturer and lover. In other words, and despite the broader geographical scale of the novel, the binary oppositions on which Negritude was founded (truth versus falsity, authenticity versus exoticism, nature versus culture) are reinscribed. Once more, Chamoiseau subscribes to the very modes he seeks to resist; the desire to explode the tenets of Negritude results in the propagation of a different, but potentially equally disempowering, set of stereotypes.

It is clear that all the major theories to emerge from the Antilles (Negritude, antillanité, créolité) qualify as 'postcolonial' in that, on the most basic level, they 'locate[s] a specifically anti- or *post*-colonial *discursive* purchase in culture' to return to the definition cited above (Slemon 1991, 3; emphasis in the original). But contemporary postcolonial theory is more concerned with notions such as the construction of the subject and the tropes of hybridity, multiplicity and indeterminacy. If, on an initial reading (or indeed, on taking the créolistes at their word), it appears that the transition from Negritude to créolité reflects the development of postcolonial theory itself (that is, from the modernist problematic of authenticity and selfhood to an anti-essentialist, hybrid and syncretic model of identity growing out of the poststructuralist theoretical tradition), a closer reading of both theory and fiction reveals that a much more ambiguous relationship obtains between these two Caribbean discourses. And yet, for all its contradictions and internal tensions, the créolité movement has undoubtedly rejuvenated cultural life in the Antilles and brought these islands to the forefront of contemporary intellectual debate. That the Creole community elaborated by the créolistes remains an imagined one should not detract from the power of the movement itelf. For French Caribbean identity has always cultivated ambiguities and contradictions – a factor which explains its already generously theorized and acutely self-referential status, and which legitimizes paradox and contradiction as theoretical points of entry to contemporary Antillean identity.

|11|

Reading 'orality' in French-language novels from sub-Saharan Africa

BY EILEEN JULIEN

Il y avait une semaine qu'avait fini dans la capitale Koné Ibrahima, de race malinké, ou disons-le en malinké: il n'avait pas soutenu un petit rhume …

One week had passed since Ibrahima Kone, of the Malinke race, had met his end in the capital city, or to put it in Malinke: he'd been defeated by a mere cold …

(Kourouma 1981 [1968], 3)

The question of orality and its place in French-language texts from Africa is aesthetic and cultural, and it is also political. Because fluency in French is correlated generally to wealth and social standing in the countries where it is spoken, because oral traditions and African languages are the means of expression of people who typically exercise little international socioeconomic or political power, the representation of these historically devalued forms and languages in Euro-language literatures, be they English or French, has everything to do with the fault lines of power – the international order, class, race and even gender.

A word about African oral traditions

For centuries the oral traditions of Africa, in Amharic, Bambara, Hausa, Lingala, Poulaar, Swahili, Twi, Wolof, Xhosa, Yoruba, Zulu and hundreds of other indigenous languages, have thrived in the form of proverbs, tales, epics, riddles and poetry – religious, ceremonial, political, occasional, personal. Now more than ever, thanks in part to new critical perspectives on performance and increasing recognition of the singular importance of African languages in the cultural and political life of the continent, there is a burgeoning scholarship on these varied and complex traditions, both historical and contemporary. In the West African context, for example, Karin Barber (1991) has written an important study of 'oriki', a form of praise poetry among the Yoruba of Nigeria; Stephen Belcher (1999), Bassirou Dieng and Lilyan Kesteloot (1997), and other researchers have over the years explored the contexts and meanings of Bambara, Fulbe, Mande, Songhay-Zarma, Soninke and Wolof epic cycles; Biodun Jeyifo (1984) has written about Yoruba theatre; Karin Barber, Alain Ricard and John Collins (1997) have published an anthology of popular plays performed in the coastal cities of West Africa – Accra, Lomé and Lagos; Lisa McNee (2000) has contrasted the autobiographical discourses of Senegalese women in Wolof and French.

Far from unchanging immemorial traditions handed down word for word from father to son, oral artistic forms are and have always been supple and absolutely contemporaneous. Professional and occasional performers are immersed in the political dynamics and social life of the communities in which they perform. Moreover the oral text is created in the moment of its enunciation and reception, the moment when an audience invests the narrative fabric with meaning. The oral text, writes Senegalese historian Mamadou Diouf, takes shape 'dans le décodage' [in its decoding] (Diouf 1991, 36). For this reason, oral traditions are, above all, of their time.

Traditions of writing existed historically alongside the oral traditions in several contexts. Early literary genres, as in the case of Amharic or Swahili, included hagiography or praise poetry for warriors or rulers. With colonization from the late nineteenth century until the mid-twentieth century, Africans took up the pen to write 'literature' in European languages also.

Intertextualities

What then is the relationship between the new French-language texts from Senegal, Ivory Coast, Cameroon and other 'Francophone' localities and the ancient oral traditions in African languages or contemporary traditions evolved from them? (This chapter focuses on the perception of 'orality' in French-language literature, but it is important to note that there are appropriations and allusions across modes and that oral traditions, print and audio-visual media have reciprocal impacts on one another.) In asking this question, we are not referring to transcriptions and translations of oral epics and stories, such as *Kaïdara*, the bilingual edition of the Fulbe initiation story (Bâ and Kesteloot 1969) or the Fulbe heroic narrative, *Silâmaka et Poullori* (Seydou 1972). Nor will we focus on texts that relate stories of oral tradition: Djibril Tamsir Niane's *Sundiata: An Epic of Old Mali* (1970 [1960]), which narrates the creation of the ancient empire of Mali in the thirteenth century under Sundiata, as told to Niane by Mamadou Kouyaté; Camara Laye's *Guardian of the Word* (1980 [1978]), a historical novel about Sundiata's birth and triumph; or Birago Diop's *Tales of Amadou Koumba* (1985 [1947]) that names in its title the performer-historian ('géwël' in Wolof; 'griot' in French) of the Diop family and that narrates stories widely known in West Africa. In this remarkable collection, Diop also constructs stories of his own in an 'oral' mode. It is in fact his skill as a writer – his digressive prologues, his portraiture, his humour and wit – that brings the stories alive and makes Diop a revered writer among Senegalese readers.

Rather, our focus will be on French-language texts that draw inspiration from, adapt or rework performance practices, oral stories or genres. Yambo Ouologuem's *Bound to Violence* (1971 [1968]) is the chronicle of a fictive West African empire and is recounted in a style reminiscent of the griot; Hampâté Bâ's novel *L'Étrange destin de Wangrin* (1973) elevates to epic grandeur his protagonist, an interpreter in the service of the French colonial administration in West Africa; Jean-Marie Adiaffi's *La Carte d'identité* (1980) reworks the initiation story in a neocolonial context to denounce cultural alienation; Aminata Sow Fall's *Le Jujubier du patriarche* (1993b) reveals the centrality of history and oral traditions in contemporary identities; Boubacar Boris Diop's *Le Cavalier et son ombre* (1997) is a meta-fiction on the nature of oral storytelling and the novel. It is these types of intertextual relationship, which blur or marry genres, that have been of greatest interest to readers and critics, because form is ultimately the most powerful vehicle of ideas.

Let us draw a distinction at this point between what writers do and the assessments that we – readers, teachers and scholars – make of what they do. This chapter is primarily about the latter, the interpretation of 'orality' in French-language texts specifically and Euro-language texts more broadly. What we will examine, then, is the critical discourse on the 'traces' of oral traditions and national languages in the novel which, for reasons that shall become apparent, is the genre at the heart of a debate around oral traditions and Euro-language writing. What I shall outline are the problems associated with two interpretations of indigenous resources in Euro-language novels. Each amounts to an investment in the notion of an essential African difference. Before addressing these issues, we should consider a brief history of the novel in its relationship to the colonized world.

A theory of the novel

Standard literary historiography holds that the novel arose in modern Europe, especially eighteenth-century England, as the literary complement to the rise of the middle class, Protestantism and an ethos of individualism. Not coincidentally, according to Edward Said (1993), the novel appears at the moment of colonial expansion. Many of the early British and European novels – *Manon Lescaut* (1731), *Atala* (1801), *Wuthering Heights* (1847), *Jane Eyre* (1847) – have ties to the colonies. The colonial space is more literary convention in this early period than reality, a place to which personalities troublesome to the social order may be sent off and from which they return, often having made their fortunes.

Later novels and travel writing such as Pierre Loti's *Le Roman d'un spahi* (1881), Joseph Conrad's *Heart of Darkness* (1902), André Gide's *L'Immoraliste* (1902) and *Voyage au Tchad* (1928), E.M. Forster's *A Passage to India* (1924), Louis-Ferdinand Céline's *Voyage au bout de la nuit* (1932), Graham Greene's *The Heart of the Matter* (1948) – all written at a time when Europeans had actually travelled to or lived in North and sub-Saharan Africa, Indochina and India – are more concrete than their predecessors in their depictions of local topographies and populations, and of expatriate life in the empire.

But contact with Arabs, Asians and Africans in the empire or colonies did not mean, of course, that writers necessarily left their ideological lenses at home. The European novel, as perhaps the most powerful and far-reaching literary form over the last one hundred and fifty years, was central to the creation of ambivalent representations of Africa as the primitive 'other' of European modernity – both as welcome supplement to European culture, an antidote to an aging bourgeois civilization, and as the measure of how far Europe, thankfully, had come. Standard literary history and theory hold that from its place of origin in Europe, the 'centre' of what is often called 'the world system', the novel travels to the colonial empires themselves, the 'periphery', where it becomes the primary means through which imperial and colonial subjects 'write back' to the centre to counter these misrepresentations.

There may be more illuminating ways to think about the novel's origins and global presence (Julien 2003). But what is important to note at this point is that there was a degree of compulsion in novel writing from the 1940s to the 1960s, the heyday of decolonization. Not only did the first African novelists take up the challenge to demonstrate, as Nigerian novelist Chinua Achebe declared, that African life was not one long saga of barbarism before the coming of Europe, but, as Deidre Lynch and William Warner claim, 'the new nations emerging out of empires [were] required to produce novels in order to certify their distinct and modern nationhood' (1996, 5). The novel was seen and is still seen as the quintessential literary genre of modernity. Like the nation state, development, democracy, the multi-party system, free speech, technology – all those institutions and forms associated with Western modernity, which most of us (Western, African or other) have come to view as the only modernity – the novel would have to be emulated in newly independent African, Asian and American nations. Thus the novel became one of several yardsticks that could attest to African modernity.

In fact, the genre arguably has been the most important vehicle for African self-representation beyond the continent and probably across the continent as well. Simon Gikandi argues that Chinua Achebe was the first to realize the 'archaeological' and 'utopic' possibilities of the novel. A writer can exploit the novel's capacity, on the one hand, to excavate African pasts hidden or invented by what V.Y. Mudimbe and others have called the 'colonial archive' – that is, the novels, travel writing, and reports by colonial administrators or by European tourists to which I referred above – and, on the other, to imagine new communities.

The novel is thus a sign of the universal modern, and, in the African context, the typical story it has told or been asked to tell is the supposed struggle between 'tradition' and 'modernity'. Similarly, there has arisen an aesthetic interest in those features of local indigenous artistic traditions that would give 'specificity' to such novels. For, if the novel – so this argument goes – is unlike poetry and drama, has no indigenous precedent, and is therefore a European form, arising in and belonging to a specific socio-historical context, propagating values of individualism, often advancing aesthetic or formalistic pleasures for their own sake, then how can it be appropriated by an African writer and be authentically African?

As I indicated above, there may be better ways to think about the novel's origins and presence in the world. But in the context of decolonizing nationalism, it is precisely an anxiety on the part of Western and African critics and scholars to demonstrate the authenticity of Euro-language African writing, novels in particular, that has generated a critical preoccupation with 'African orality' and its impact on and representation in texts.

There are in fact two critical discourses making claims from very different locations for the centrality of oral traditions and what are called local or national languages in Euro-language texts. The first is an essentialist – some would say 'nativist' – stance that oral traditions and indigenous languages are the quintessential signs of African identity, and therefore render authentic supposedly alien modern forms, such as the novel. The second emanates from postcolonial theory itself: it is the writer's marginality vis-à-vis the colonial language that is his or her source of creativity. It is thus in subverting that language through the use of orality and mother tongues that the writer effects the defiant postcolonial gesture. Ironically, both stances amount to an investment in the notion of an essential African difference.

Orality as black difference: between mimesis and authenticity

The question of orality and African languages has been central to the study of Euro-language African literatures, from Emmanuel Obiechina (1975) and Mohamadou Kane (1982) to Abiola Irele (2001). Orality in its many guises (pidgins, African languages, proverbs, tales within novels) has been seen, first, as an inherent and essential 'black difference' which would surface necessarily in Euro-language writing from Africa.

In the 1970s, Mohamadou Kane wrote: 'l'originalité du roman african doit être cherchée plus particulièrement dans ses rapports avec les formes de la littérature orale' [the originality of the African novel must be found more specifically in its relationship to forms of oral literature] (1974, 537). He expanded on these views in his later work, *Roman africain et tradition* (1982). Alioune Tine similarly asserts that 'la littérature africaine se définit comme une littérature située entre l'oralité et l'écriture. Cette idée a permis la réalisation d'un vaste consensus qui va des critiques africanistes aux écrivains' [African literature can be defined as a literature situated between orality and writing. This idea has given rise to a vast consensus that includes both Africanist critics and authors] (1985, 99).

Emmanuel Obiechina, a scholar of primarily Anglophone West African literature, makes a concise argument for this view, claiming that the African novel is particularly affected by indigenous orality for two reasons. Firstly, it is because the novel is mimetic (or realist) that it is or must be characterized by orality:

> it is impossible to ignore orality in a form that prides itself on a life-like portrayal of reality when exploring the life and experience of people more than seventy per cent of whom at any given moment live within traditional oral societies throughout the varied contexts of pre-colonial, colonial, and postcolonial history. (1993, 124)

It is true that most novels by Africans in the 1950s, '60s and '70s – Obiechina is referring, of course, to autochthonous Africans and their descendants, not, for example, to South Africans of Afrikaner descent – were mimetic in their intent. And, to the extent that they were, it would be hard to quarrel with his assessment. It seemed self-evident therefore to scholars, critics and perhaps many writers that realism was a natural mode for African writers. The dominance of the realist mode is not unrelated to the largely ethnographic readings that have been the lot of African novels ever since.

Secondly, Obiechina argues that writers strive to write 'authentic' works of literature: 'a return to the roots movement in African literature as a means of giving maximum authenticity to the writing made the writers look to their indigenous poetics to create works that will endure by drawing upon their living oral tradition to enrich forms, techniques, and styles received through literate education' (1993, 124). The 'story within a story' is a particularly common practice in 'the African novel', and Obiechina refers to it as a 'narrative proverb', since the 'African novel is not a sole product of an individual consciousness (even though the novelist is a conscious individual artist), but is mediated by communal consciousness and impulses arising from group sensibility' (125). The 'narrative proverb', like proverbs in oral communities, draws 'upon group habits of speech and narration as a means of giving shape to experience, drawing upon what could be called the populist impulse in art and life' (125). There are assumptions in Obiechina's claims to which we shall return.

Orality, postcolonial marginality and resistance

While Kane, Obiechina, and others see orality as a defining characteristic of African culture and therefore the quintessential sign of Africanity in Euro-language literatures, postcolonial theory per se has focused largely on the ways in which writers from the formerly colonized zones have sought through their writing to undermine the ideological underpinnings of the former colonial powers. In *The Empire Writes Back*, Ashcroft, Griffiths and Tiffin write that postcolonial literatures have foregrounded 'the tension with the imperial power and [emphasized] their differences from the assumptions of the imperial centre' (1989, 2).

Thus to the extent that written English and French have been associated with 'civilizing missions' and 'manifest destinies', based on notions of civilization, progress, rationality, masculinity, individualism, Euro-language writing inflected with oral traditions and indigenous languages has been read as expressive of different sensibilities – populism, communalism – and therefore as a deliberate strategy of resistance vis-à-vis the premises of European or Eurocentric culture and writing.

The trouble with difference and marginality

The problems with these particular readings of oral traces in novels are many. But let it be clear that the critique I outline does not constitute an argument against heteroglossic African novels. On the contrary, such novels constitute one of the most important and exciting dimensions of contemporary writing. I would argue, however, that a text's language is a matter of sensibility and instinct, based on feelings of identity and comfort, rather than a matter of obligation, principle or deliberate choice. 'Francophone Africa' is a set of heterogeneous spaces, shaped by interethnic tensions and global flows, making use of multiple languages (African as well as European) and registers (for an exploration of similar ideas, see Murphy, Chapter 20). Stories within stories, the use of proverbs, variously cadenced and metaphoric language do not constitute a refuge or bulwark within and against a supposedly universal or transcendent cultural form but suggest complexity, dynamism, energy, and creativity. This is what I read in Kourouma's *The Suns of Independence* (1981): a language that effects not two separate cultural spheres or layers, but a world in which French and, in this instance, Malinke are always positioned vis-à-vis each other. Each always recalls the other since both languages inhabit the same space, even when only one is voiced (or written).

Thus I take issue with the well-known assertion of Frantz Fanon, whereby 'to speak [...] this or that language means above all to assume a culture, [...] to support the weight of a civilization' (1986 [1952], 17–18). Even though it points to power relations embedded in language that we must recognize, this claim ultimately obscures other equally significant aspects of language. Toril Moi reminds us: 'though it is true to say that the dominant power group at any given time will dominate the intertextual production of meaning, this is not to suggest that the opposition has been reduced to total silence. The power struggle *intersects* in the sign' (1994, 158; emphasis in original). We may in fact interpret an Igbo turn of phrase popularized for the non-Igbo by Achebe, 'where one things stands, another stands beside it', to mean the same thing.

Orality: an imprecise concept

I see several risks in readings of orality as authentic and as subversive. Firstly, as I have argued elsewhere (Julien 1992), the concept of orality is a nebulous, homogenizing notion that has little to do with – in Mamadou Diouf's terms – the enunciation and reception of distinct oral performances. In many critical studies, orality is defined ahistorically and essentially – that is simply as the opposite of writing and the novel. It is sometimes viewed as the source of a novel's strength (Scheub 1985, 56–7) and sometimes as its weakness, as in Kane's remarks on Ferdinand Oyono's *Houseboy* (Kane 1982, 205–18; Oyono 1966 [1956]). What begins as an explanation in Kane's early work becomes in his later *Roman africain et tradition* an accusation of deficiency (Julien 1992, 35–9). In other instances, oral traditions may be read as an index of a narrative's (or culture's) 'childlikeness' or immaturity – as in the case of Amos Tutuola's *The Palm Wine Drinkard* (1952) – or of cultural wholesomeness – Achebe's *Things Fall Apart* (1958). Given the slipperiness of the concept of orality, criticism's role has often been to identify a Euro-language text's authenticating traces – proverbs, embedded stories, phrases in indigenous languages – naming and cataloguing these elements as though they were ends in themselves or making superficial comparisons that lead to blame or praise.

'African exceptionalism'?

A second problem with the readings of ahistorical 'oral' traces as authentic is that orality becomes a metonymy for 'African'. The binary opposition between 'oral' and 'written' fails to tell the whole truth, which is that alongside the extraordinary power and presence of spoken words in Africa we find powerful written ones as well. Thus, despite its very own investment in binarism, what can we make of Cheikh Hamidou Kane's *Ambiguous Adventure* (1972 [1961]), if we succumb to the hunt for authenticating orality? What of Mudimbe's novels, or those of Mariama Bâ? The search for the element that confers African authenticity becomes prescriptive and limiting for African novelists who do not allude to oral traditions or do not reproduce the cadences of indigenous languages. Their novels are not therefore less African.

The view of African language-inflected French, as in *The Suns of Independence*, as a natural and necessary African literary practice is one manifestation of a habit of thought that is sometimes referred to as 'African exceptionalism', a broad and problematic tendency to see Africa as profoundly different from the rest of the world, whereas Quebecois, Breton or Provençal novelists have also experimented with standard French. Neither is writing out of a communal ethos and sensibility unique to African writers; nor is it necessarily the primary impulse of all African writing – see Ahmad's critique (1987) of Jameson's ideas (1986) on this issue. Thus, as Alexie Tcheuyap writes with respect to the Antilles, 'not only is writing without "traces" of one's language *not* a sin [...] neither is it a fatality or a new essentialism to be tracked down absolutely in every literary text' (2001, 57; emphasis in original). Senegalese philosopher Souleymane Bachir Diagne argues similarly that Africanness may be less a matter of specific things or practices than 'a way of approaching' the world (Diagne 2001).

The recourse to mimesis (or realism) in the majority of African novels has also sustained the ethnographic bias that has guided their reception over time. Of course, African writers of the 1950s and 1960s in particular felt compelled to present African perspectives in response to the representations or misrepresentations, as it were, of African life that were rife in European novels, travel writing, colonialist social science and administrative reports. But their texts are quite precisely perspectives, which emanate from writers' particular experiences and identities. That these writings are positioned and are inquiries (i.e. epistemological statements) tends to be ignored, for many readers in America, at least, read with the expectation that these mostly mimetic narratives by Africans will reveal the 'real' Africa.

Thus one reviewer of *African Novels in the Classroom* (2000), a guide by twenty-four college teachers, all except three of whom are historians and anthropologists, praises the book overall but regrets that 'only two of its essays pay any significant attention to the literariness' of the novels, which therefore have been reduced to 'purely sociological or historical document[s]' (Ogede 2001, 224). Thus the use of novels in social science contexts may be a good thing, may help professors of history, anthropology and other social sciences think beyond narrow theories, provided that the situated, textual nature of novels is not forgotten. In any case, with new generations of novelists, such as Boubacar Boris Diop, Werewere Liking,

Tierno Monénembo, V.Y. Mudimbe and Véronique Tadjo, the longstanding view of mimesis (or realism) as the natural mode of African novels is increasingly challenged.

Ornamentation

Thirdly, the notion of a vast reservoir of indigenous resources available to, if not destined for, the Euro-language writer who will put them to use in modern Euro-language literature is reminiscent of evolutionist paradigms of the nineteenth century that viewed African cultural practices as an initial phase in a process of maturation that would lead to the emergence of true 'Culture'. When readers and critics refer to 'the passage from orality to writing', often enough we find lurking in the background the assumption that traditional oral forms will be superseded and transformed into supposedly modern forms, such as the Euro-language novel. Oral traditions become simple 'ornaments' of the apparently imported Western form. Thus the Kenyan writer, Ngugi Wa Thiong'o, who for many years has championed the development of African-language literatures, parodies Léopold Sédar Senghor's poem, 'New York' – from the 1948 collection, *Hosties noires* (Senghor 1990, 115–17) – and complains of the 'lengths to which we were prepared to go in our mission of enriching foreign languages by injecting Senghorian "black blood" into their [Western] rusty joints' (Ngugi 1981, 7). Likewise, Senegalese novelist Boubacar Boris Diop in a recent interview states with regard to the Malinke-inflected French of *The Suns of Independence*:

> Aesthetically, it's very interesting, but politically it's very dangerous. [...] It seems to me that African languages are dying into French, enriching it. [...] And I think the French love it. It saves the French language from grayness and monotony. (Sugnet 2001, 158)

There is a conservatism in these remarks that I do not share, but I cite them to indicate that what I have dubbed the ornamentation of the novel with oral forms or African languages or the prescriptive call for such practice can be read as *non*-subversive. Most importantly, it is contexts that matter: Stephanie Newell notes, for example, that South Africans writing for *Drum* magazine in the 1950s 'selected English as their medium as a gesture of defiance against the language and educational policies of the Afrikaner state' (2002, 2). Moreover, the spotlight we have placed on this particular practice risks obscuring several important facts. Firstly, not all texts, Euro- or African-language, arise from the writer's supposed sense of marginality vis-à-vis the 'centre'. Secondly, oral traditions (despite Diop's fears) have their own trajectories as contemporary vehicles of creativity, entertainment, inquiry, dialogue and debate (Ahmad 1987; Barber 1995).

Finally, the view of the happy marriage of local lore and European form reinforces a certain Eurocentric view of the world in which all things modern come from the outside (the so-called centre of the world system located in Western metropolises). What is left to the formerly colonized periphery, then, is imitation and local colour. This critical stance on the aesthetics of African novels seems to me to parallel a political view in which modern institutions and forms – democracy, good government – seen as arising in the West must be imported, while local customs are retained to ornament them and provide cultural continuity. Writing of India, Radakrishnan makes an argument that would apply to African states as well:

> Western nationalisms are deemed capable of generating their own models of autonomy from within, whereas Eastern nationalisms have to assimilate something alien to their own cultures before they can become modern nations. [...] [I]n particular 'Third World' nationalisms are forced to choose between 'being themselves' and 'becoming modern nations' as though the universal standards of reason and progress were natural and intrinsic to the West [...]. [T]his divide perpetuates the ideology of a dominant common world where the West leads naturally and the East follows in an eternal game of catch-up where its identity is always in dissonance with itself. (1992, 86)

I have been signalling patterns of essentialist or postcolonial readings of orality in African novels and their implications: the first ties the novel to mimetic, nationalist and ethnographic agendas; the second foregrounds language difference and estrangement from the centre as the writer's source of originality. Both readings hold the novel hostage to the demands or expectations of a hegemonic readership, and serve to confine writers. Moreover, a 'return' to oral traditions of proverbs, tales and epics in the novel as the mainstay of a counter-poetics, affirming an original, authentic identity within supposedly universal forms belies the complex, inventive, and – yes – playful appropriations of life on the ground. The 'French-language' text punctuated with proverbs and tales and refashioned by the cadences of oral speech, creoles and national languages may be read more profitably, in my view, as the inscription of a dynamic reality addressed equally and fully to a range of readers who, with our varying language competencies and differences in power, inhabit one world.

PART III

POSTCOLONIAL AXES: NATION AND GLOBALIZATION IN CONTEMPORARY FRANCOPHONE CULTURES

12

Tactical universalism and new multiculturalist claims in postcolonial France

BY MIREILLE ROSELLO

One of the simplistic ways of charting the complex and nebulous territory of French postcolonial cultural diversity would be to set up a binary opposition. On one side, you have the Republican(ist)s,[1] also called 'Jacobins' because their ancestors are the radical wing of the French Revolution. They are also called universalists because their main creed is the belief that citizens are best protected from tyrannical (religious or political) community allegiance when defined as abstract subjects whose racial, gendered, ethnic, religious or class difference is rendered irrelevant by the sacrosanct, or rather sacredly secular, 'Law of the Republic'.[2] On the other side stand the multiculturalists who propose to take into account the notion of cultural difference, and to move away from the type of stiff, universalist principles that stand in the way of a more democratic and egalitarian societal project for ethnic minorities, gays or women. But this opposition, in itself, is not a fruitful way of posing the problem because it does not take into account the historical imbalance between the two positions and the rapidly changing shape of the French debate.

Even if we ignore the strength of all -ism suffixes, multiculturalism cannot be reduced to the obvious fact that France is made up of diverse communities, a reality that makes 'monoculturalism' obsolete (Khosrokhavar 2001). If multiculturalism was the simple consequence of the coexistence between several cultures on the same soil, we could claim that it existed centuries before the Declaration of the Rights of Man and of the Citizen: Romans and

[1] The binary opposition is bound to conflate distinctions carefully maintained by scholars who view Republicanism as a 'dérive à la fois mythique et idéologique' [mythic and ideological distortion] of Republican principles (Wieviorka 1997, 23).
[2] Alain Finkielkraut insists on the value of disidentification and on the link between individual freedom and the ability to say no to the group's dictates (Finkielkraut 1987, 143 *et passim*).

Gauls had to live together even before the Renaissance promoted travel and exchange. If that were the case, there would be nothing either new or distinctively French about the interdisciplinary debate on cultural difference and multiculturalism.

However, even deciding upon what we call 'cultures' is already over-determined by the historical shape of the discussion. The fate of Italians or Poles who migrated to France at the beginning of the twentieth century can be compared to that of postcolonial postwar migrants only if sociologists, historians, politicians and the general public accept to treat their experience as something comparable. And, for multiculturalism even to exist in France, it needs to be recognized as a legitimate parameter of the political and cultural debate by the French themselves. Until ten years ago, the relationship between universalism and multiculturalism neatly coincided with the distinction between inside and outside: the prevalent myth was that the former was the 'French model' par excellence while the other – Anglo-Saxon, or American – was inferior and foreign.[3]

The tone of the discussion between intellectuals is still often passionate if not downright rancorous. Multiculturalists are accused of endangering the Republic, of promoting fragmentation, ghettoization, of aping the Americans.[4] And, as communities mobilize and make claims on the Republic, universalists get blamed for not acknowledging the glaring historical shortcomings of their doctrine, a grand philosophical and political hypocrisy whose extravagant claims have allowed if not justified regimes that enslaved people, denied women the right to vote, colonized continents. But what has changed is that French multiculturalism can now be described as a constellation of voices that emerged at the beginning of the 1970s and have crystallized in the last years of the twentieth century to become a powerful if often diverse braid of political and cultural forces. Their most sophisticated representatives are keen to refuse the artificial and self-defeating alternative between egalitarianism and communitarianism and call for a reconfiguration of the terms of the debate (Wieviorka 1996; Wieviorka and Ohana 2001; Touraine 1997).

This chapter proposes to observe how the debate is being reformulated within and beyond intellectuals' discourse. To do so, I would like to highlight another possible definition of the word 'culture', which would allow us not so much to reach a perhaps utopian point situated beyond the distinction between universalism and multiculturalism but to identify the cultural

---

[3]   This ahistorical, monolithic and phantasmatic America is a convenient scarecrow: Wieviorka points out that the adjective 'American' is used almost systematically to evoke a cultural and political apocalypse ['l'apocalypse culturelle et politique'] (Wieviorka 2001a, 8) that disallows the analysis of other types of multicultural models implemented by Canada, Australia or Sweden (Wieviorka 2001b, 82–101). See also Horowitz and Noiriel (1992).

[4]   Note the strictly polemical value of the adjectives used by journalist Christian Jelen who wrote in *Libération* that 'un multiculturalisme ravageur' [devastating multiculturalism] is often synonymous with 'un communautarisme débridé' [unbridled communitarianism] (1997).

work that this dichotomy performs in postcolonial France. Instead of defining 'cultures' simply as sub-national communities united by certain ethnic, racial, sexual or religious components (blacks, gays, women, Muslims, Jews), I will concentrate on the precise aims of individuals and groups when they mobilize their cultural identity (do they want to obtain naturalization papers, have more minorities hired, change a misogynistic law, protect their personal relationships from the intrusion of the state?). In other words, I wish to privilege cultural practices over cultural identification markers even if, sometimes, the markers constitute the tactical or essentialist layer of discourse behind the practice, the tip of the multicultural iceberg.

In France, what is thought to be desirable or undesirable about both multiculturalism and universalism is presented, and fought for, differently in different contexts. The new parameters of the debates are defining themselves not so much between cultures but between individuals or groups whose approach to the values symbolized by universalism and multiculturalism varies depending on their goal. There may not be more 'cultures' today on French soil than a few decades ago, and it will always be almost impossible to quantify the degree of cultural difference between these communities, but what is changing is the protocol of encounters between these so-called 'cultures'. And the quality of these encounters depends on types of configurations that, for the purpose of this chapter, I will also call 'cultures': when cultures (in the traditional meaning of the word) meet, they do so differently depending on the context of their coming together – via political culture, educational culture, institutional culture, employment culture or entertainment culture – especially if these cultures have to agree with or dispute the commonly accepted borders of what is public and what is private.

I would suggest that in each of these (political, institutional, artistic) cultures, the general values or short-term goals that a given subject defends in the name of universalism or multiculturalism are always coloured by his or her relationship to a network of (ethnic, gendered, religious) identification. The play between culture defined as an inherited set of traditions and culture as a node of enunciation or site of resistance is still very much in flux, and is not constant or even coherent as the same individual moves between these different spheres. Therefore, the perhaps surprising success of the long struggles in favour of 'parité' [parity] and of 'Pacte civil de solidarité' [Civil Pact of Solidarity, aka PaCS] is perfectly representative of the changing climate of the 1990s: after almost a decade of heated discussions, the French Republic finally agreed to rethink the ways in which the law deals with gender and sexuality.

The first article of the law on the PaCS, passed on 15 November 1999, stipulates that 'Un pacte civil de solidarité est un contrat conclu par deux personnes physiques majeures, de sexe différent ou de même sexe, pour organiser leur vie commune' [A civil pact of solidarity is a contract agreed upon by two adults, of different sexes or of the same sex, to organize their life in common].[5] The apparent banality of the legal jargon cannot hide this cultural revolution. But, from the point of view of universalism versus multiculturalism, there are at least two ways of describing this development. We can either consider that the law officially recognizes gay unions (the citizen is now a sexualized subject), or we can point out that the issue of gay rights has been subsumed under the more general subheading of 'solidarity'. Depending on which aspect of the law we wish to emphasize, the new law can be presented as a revolutionary victory for gay rights or as a typically universalist and egalitarian way of dealing with sexual difference. Clearly, the driving force behind the campaigns that finally led to the 1999 law had to do with homosexuality and its legal recognition. In 1996, a cluster of prestigious intellectuals had co-signed a text published in *Le Monde* in which they stated: 'Nous considérons qu'il est grand temps de mettre un terme à la discrimination légale et sociale qui touche les homosexuel(le)s' [We believe that it is urgent that we stop legally and socially discriminating against gay people] (Bourdieu *et al.* 1996). But the law that was finally voted is an intriguing compromise: it neither simply extends pre-existing rights to homosexuals (they cannot marry or enter into 'concubinage') nor does it create a law specifically designed for the gay community (heterosexual PaCs are not only possible but far from rare). The PaCS is one of the most visible examples of a hybrid form of universalist multiculturalism, or perhaps of a typically French tactical universalism used by communities that would seem better served by an overtly multicultural discourse. As Didier Fassin points out, 'My suggestion is that today in France it is possible (though difficult) to articulate the claims of the women's movement and of gay and lesbian liberation by using the language of equality, instead of sexual difference – for sexual difference is today the language in which the interest of women and homosexuals are pitted against each other' (2000, 63).

The 'parité' debate offers another example of what we might view as hybrid universalism. Because politics is the clearest instance of public culture – the site where each private individual is expected to embody the abstract citizen imagined by the Enlightenment – any attempt at introducing cultural difference in that particular sphere was bound to meet with strong resistance.[6] The 1999 Law on Parity, which compels political parties to present an equal proportion of male and female candidates on their electoral lists, was such a radical ideological turning point that it necessitated an alteration of the French constitution (Agacinski 2001, 8). In this case, the

---

[5] For the complete text of the law, see: http://www.assemblee-nat.fr/dossiers/pacs.asp.
[6] In 1992, when Françoise Gaspard, Anne Le Gall and Claude Servan-Schreiber published their manifesto, *Au pouvoir citoyennes!*, the idea of parity was still unthinkable. Ten years later, 'parité' is inscribed in the constitution. For a history of the movement, see Halimi (1994 and 1999).

reformulation of the debate on universalism and multiculturalism cuts right through the ranks of French feminists, pitting the advocates of 'parité' such as Sylviane Agacinski or Gisèle Halimi against those, like Elisabeth Badinter, who continue to believe that universalism has to be more scrupulously applied. As is often the case in this type of discussion, both sides agree on the description of the problem: the French National Assembly should not remain a scandalously obsolete bastion of male privilege with only a little over five per cent of women among the ranks of the elected in 1996. But, faced with the clearly flawed implementation of universalism, Badinter insists that the remedy of parity is worse than the disease. She analyses 'parité' as the introduction of essentialism into politics, reminding her readers that such distinctions have historically been used to exclude women. Moreover, 'parité' will unavoidably generate 'nouvelles revendications paritaires de la part d'autres communautés, raciales, religieuses, voire culturelles ou sexuelles' [new demands for parity by other racial, religious, cultural or sexual communities] (Badinter 1996, 15). In one of her passionate articles to *Le Monde*, 'Non aux quotas de femmes' [No to gender quotas], she evokes the familiar and stereotyped spectre of a tragically fragmented American society (1996, 15).

To this coherent, both tactically and ideologically, universalist position, the defenders of 'parité' oppose a more nuanced agenda that tries to alleviate French fears of 'communitarianism'. They clearly distinguish between gender and other cultural differences: unlike gays, or children of Maghrebi immigrants, for example, women never constitute a minority. Gender difference is different from all other differences, which seems to foreclose the possibility of other communities trying to use the model of parity to demand similar rights of representation. For Badinter, whose fears are precisely that the Republic will eventually become a fragmented mosaic of ghettoes, the distinction is desirable, but we may wonder how the members of the communities thus described as 'differently different' will react in practice, especially since they are usually inseparable in global definitions of multiculturalism.

If opponents of PaCS and 'parité' seem to toe the traditional Republican line, their adversaries seem to be negotiating with universalism and inventing a politically effective hybrid discourse that combines multicultural tactics and universalist philosophical values. We may wonder if this constitutes what Sophie Body-Gendrot calls the 'third path' between 'l'hypocrisie de l'universalisme' [the hypocrisy of universalism] and 'le séparatisme des groupes identitaires se servant de leur histoire spécifique pour légitimer leur authencité et imposer d'autres tyrannies et d'autres confiscations de pouvoir' [the separatism of identities that use their specific history to legitimize and impose other tyrannies and other confiscations of power] (2001, 45).

We may also wonder what happens to this hybrid discourse when other types of differences are mobilized in other contexts: how do new (rather than supposedly traditional) religious practices and traditional (rather than supposedly modern) forms of secularism interlace? Clearly, the ingredients of the 'parité' negotiations will not work across the board and the intertwining between multiculturalism and Republicanism will change when 'different differences' begin to make a difference: what happens, then, when gender interacts with categories such as ethnicity or religion, especially when the debate occurs in another highly charged context such as Republican schools – another archetypal public space that has rigorously excluded the expression of cultural beliefs. What happens, then, when Woman is a female child of North African parents whose religious faith makes her decide to wear, in public, a 'hijab' (or headscarf) that ostensibly marks her as Muslim? In this particular case, gender is interestingly subsumed under other cultural and religious differences and it is Islam, secularism and immigration, rather than the role of women in general, that get discussed.

In 1989, a few Muslim students who wore a 'hijab' at school were threatened with expulsion by their principal who ruled that the scarf was a religious symbol and therefore incompatible with 'laïcité' [secular principles]. A few such 'affairs' regularly made the headlines between 1989 and 1994 and they became a typically French national issue: intellectuals wrote brilliant manifestos either against the veil or in defence of the young students (see, for example, Badinter *et al.* 1989). The Minister of Education, François Bayrou, eventually intervened and a memo was circulated to heads of departments in September 1994, stating that what would continue to be banned was not the religious symbol per se but 'ostentatious' signs that constitute in themselves elements of proselytism and discrimination.

This moderate text that tries to preserve the interest of the young students as well as the principle of secularism introduces an interesting distinction between an 'ostentatious' and a 'public' display, underlining that what is at stake here is the absolute distinction between the private and the public. Recurring conflicts between families and school authorities show that this dichotomy, one of the pillars of the Republican edifice, also requires that groups agree on how religious practices are defined: suggesting that a Muslim woman wears the veil inside the privacy of her home and gives it up in public does not make much sense – for a Muslim. And it is true that some latitude has been granted to religious symbols that are not historically seen as a threat to secularism (Christian children sometimes wear a gold cross around their neck). Perhaps, the Minister's new ruling is less revolutionary than realistic: it reflects, more than changes, contemporary as well as old practices.

If we approach the issue from a feminist point of view, once again, differences will occur within communities who may be expected to have the same values and the same goals: it is well know that some (Muslim, Christian or secular) intellectuals object to the 'hijab' which they interpret as a sign of patriarchal oppression.[7] But their tactics generally differ: some will insist on a strict implementation of secular principles at school, arguing that a secular public space is the only chance for young girls to escape the constraints of their culture of origin. Others recommend that students be allowed to keep their scarf in the classroom precisely because the alternative is to deprive women of their access to education. Once again, the alternative is not between multiculturalism and universalism but between strategic choices that, in the end, try to preserve individual liberties in a changing France: as the authors of *Le Foulard et la République* put it: 'Le foulard est désormais un phénomène français' [The headscarf has become a French phenomenon] (Gaspard and Khosrokhavar 1995, 205). And, just as historical changes occur within universalist and multiculturalist philosophies, transnational religions such as Islam manifest themselves differently in Algeria or in Europe, in France or in Germany. Without putting their faith in a regressive nationalism, many believe in the emergence of 'un Islam de France' [French Islam] or even 'un islam sécularisé' [secularized islam] (Lamchichi 1999, 194) that could co-exist harmoniously with democratic ideals, and whose visibility (the construction of mosques, the training of Imams, the distribution of 'halal' products – especially the ritual slaughter of sheep) would not be perceived as a threat by a large percentage of the French population (Leveau *et al.* 2001).

The last and third discursive culture where I would like to trace the play between the Republic and multiculturalist claims corresponds, loosely, to the realms of the arts and entertainment. Unlike politics, these are domains where cultural differences are sometimes less controversial. They are more likely to be accepted, even by universalists, as long as they make no political waves (no struggle for legal recognition, for public funds, for rights).

Of course, conservatives will profess to be shocked by films representing, say, gay lifestyles. And, if a strong, internalized respect for the distinction between private and public life may explain why French homosexuals were (thought to be) less inclined to claim a gay identity than their Anglo-Saxon counterparts, a quick look at the popularity of annual Gay Pride parades or at the French cinema of the 1990s would convince the observer that a more culturalist vision has slowly but surely infiltrated mainstream French society. Not only do several comedies have gay characters, not only do their plots explicitly consider what it means to be gay or lesbian – Josiane Balasko's *Gazon maudit* (1995), Gabriel Aghion's *Pédale douce* (1996) – but at least one film directly confronts the issue of homophobia in the workplace. Francis Veber's *Le Placard* (2001) is about an employee who

---

[7]   Many analysts recognize, however, that the young women who choose to wear the headscarf are less interested in tradition than in new postcolonial identification practices: for some, the Islamic scarf may well constitute 'un des signes d'une nouvelle identité "bricolée" dans un monde où ne font sens que la consommation et l'ascension individuelle' [one of the signs of identitarian 'bricolage' in a world where only commodities and individual success matter] (Gaspard and Khosrokhavar 1995, 207). See also Mernissi (1991 [1987] and 1993 [1990]).

pretends to be gay to avoid being fired (the assumption being that the company will be afraid of being perceived as homophobic). Whether it is read as a cynical critique of the potential abuses of affirmative action or as a satire of what happens to homophobia when it can no longer express itself openly, the film bears the traces of the most contemporary debates on the relationship between identity and rights.

For one could assume that, as long as no demands are made, all cultures are welcomed by the Republic. When cultural difference means Vietnamese restaurants, raï music or even American cinema, the potential conflicts between the national culture and its others are often neutralized by commodification and exoticization. And yet the distinction between a supposedly casual expression of one's culture and the demand for more recognition is never so absolute as it seems. Commercial objects can be interpreted as foreign and dangerous for national cultures – Hollywood and its multi-million advertising campaigns are the predator against which French directors have mobilized – just as representation and visibility can become the object of demands by different social groups, especially when one particular problematic cultural marker intervenes: race, or we should say, more accurately, but no doubt less forcefully, ethnicity.

None of the case studies that we have thus far observed has been about race. Curiously, in the country that saw the birth of Negritude, race did not function as a test case in the twentieth-century universalist–multiculturalist debate. Historians might retort that that battle was fought and lost by deputy Aimé Césaire who, privileging 'departmentalization' for his Martiniquan native land, gambled that more universalism, true assimilation, or rather a genuine equality through assimilation, would eventually give black citizens their fair share of the national culture. But that was in 1946. In February 2000, the black woman who violently denounced the invisibility of non-white citizens was not speaking at the National Assembly but before an amphitheatre full of celebrities, actors and actresses, gathered at the twenty-fifth night of the Césars (France's equivalent of the Oscars). During a spectacular and apparently unrehearsed intervention, Calixthe Beyala, the famous novelist of Cameroonian origin, addressed the public on behalf of 'minorités visibles' [visible minorities] and urged them to empathize with black people who are consistently excluded from French television and cinema. She pleaded in favour of 'une véritable représentation de la réalité multiraciale de la France dans tous les médias' [a genuine representation of France's multiracial reality in all media].[8]

Although the contents of her speech would sound quite familiar to African-American theorists or British cultural critics, the rhetorical choices made by Beyala were remarkably new in France. They are remarkably

---

[8]   On stage, Beyala was accompanied by Luc Saint Eloi, co-founder of the 'Collectif Égalité' whose goal is to expose racial discrimination on television. Part of their intervention and a more elaborate argument appears in Beyala (2000). See also Freedman and Tarr (2000).

controversial as well. Some of the elements of her rhetoric are worth noticing for the sake of comparing her struggle with the political fight for 'parité' or PaCS: while ethnicity is considered as 'the other difference' by the advocates of 'parité' who refuse to equate gender with ethnicity, here, gender disappears altogether as an operative category. And yet, the representative of the movement is not, as if by default, a black male. This may be silently noted as one more sign of the times. Another significant element of this episode is that demands are confined to the world of French media, to the culture of entertainment. Beyala puts her faith in fiction, in the stories with which society amuses itself: 'Je suis intimement convaincue qu'un bon film avec une bonne distribution noire ou arabe, est un antidote contre le racisme beaucoup plus efficace que dix ans de manifestations contre ce fléau' [I am utterly convinced that a good film with a good black or Arab cast is a better antidote against racism than ten years of demonstrations against this evil' (2000, 81). Note that her tactic cannot be simply equated with American affirmative action measures that target the world of employment or higher education. Yet Beyala is one of the rare public figures to critique openly her compatriots' knee-jerk condemnation of what they call 'positive discrimination'. While many French Republicans interpret the fact that certain states no longer support affirmative action as evidence that even America is recognizing its errors, Beyala suggests that, if affirmative action is disappearing, it is because it has served its purpose: a new black bourgeoisie has emerged, and such measures are no longer justified (91). What is at stake here is not so much the truth of such sweeping and premature claims about the end of affirmative action in the United States as the reasons invoked to either justify or condemn the practice itself. Beyala goes as far as to use the taboo word 'quotas' and she even invents a daring acronym: 'des quotas à durée déterminée – QDD' [fixed-term quotas] (90). Although activists and social scientists would probably find her proposals disappointingly vague, Beyala argues that such revolutionary practices would 'débloquer une situation particulièrement difficile, héritée de notre passé colonial et esclavagiste' [unlock a difficult situation, our legacy of colonialism and slavery] (90).

Her allusion to the historical contradictions of a specifically French universalism is a good reminder of why it is necessary, at present, at least to bring into question the traditional intellectual framework of the French Republican model. After all, it could be seen as an aberration to study 'French' multiculturalism. Is multiculturalism, by definition, global and transnational, not likely to transcend national borders and to encourage us to adopt a different perspective about the national? The question is almost rhetorical. Yet, as European countries progressively learn how to belong to a supra-national entity, their citizens are also coming to terms with different types of cultural encounters. Each nation is inventing its own type of multiculturalism, having inherited, and now contesting, some of the myths and narratives that were originally mobilized to promote the idea of the national.

French multiculturalism is both obviously transnational and national already, but the history of France as a nation state colours this process of globalization. The encounters between different cultures on French soil did not occur in a transnational historical vacuum. If hybrid voices of tactical universalism or Republican multiculturalism are slowly gaining currency in France today, it is because they have learned the lessons of previous decades of struggle. They are processing the legacy left by the sexual revolution of the 1960s, by the feminist struggles of the 1970s (movements that were already implicated in a dialectical tension between nationalism and internationalism). They are also reacting to the multiple causes of international migrations. While much international travelling is linked to multinational corporations and tourism, French immigrants are a direct or indirect consequence of the country's colonial past (for French citizens or migrants of Algerian, Senegalese or Vietnamese origin, for example), or of recent European conflicts. People who live on French soil, whether they are from a given culture or whether they constantly negotiate with the constraints of a given discursive culture, know that they share a world of banalized international communications where no political and philosophical system is ever free of foreign influence and where 'elsewhere' cannot be exclusively measured by physical distance. Yet they know that they are different from each other and also that it would be irresponsible to confuse the jet setter with the refugee who desperately tries to cross the Channel illegally.

13

The contribution of north and sub-Saharan African immigrant minorities to the redefinition of contemporary French culture

BY ALEC G. HARGREAVES

In 1999, an anthology of new French writing was published in English translation in London (de Chamberet 1999). It gave pride of place to post-colonial minorities living in the socially disadvantaged multi-ethnic neighbourhoods known in France as the 'banlieues' (literally, 'suburbs'). Interviewed about the anthology in *Le Monde*, the French publisher Olivier Cohen confessed to being perplexed by it:

> À quelques exceptions près, on a l'impression que le roman français aujourd'hui, c'est les Blacks, les beurs, la banlieue, la drogue, les homosexuels … Un peu comme si on en faisait une littérature de minorités, ce qui est un contresens car cela n'existe pas ici, ou alors de façon très embryonnaire. (*Le Monde* 1999)

> With a few exceptions, it gives the impression that the French novel today consists of Blacks, Beurs, the 'banlieues', drugs and homosexuals … It makes it look like some sort of minorities literature, which is completely wrong, for there is no such thing here [in France], except in a very embryonic state.

Cohen's reflexes are typical of those of many majority ethnic cultural gate-keepers in France who regard multiculturalism as an Anglo-Saxon invention alien to France's assimilationist traditions. Gatekeepers of this kind have constructed a generally inhospitable environment for artists of immigrant origin seeking recognition within France. The literature, films and other art forms produced by France's post-colonial minorities have been studied and valorized far more extensively outside France – especially in the English-speaking world – than within the country in which their creators live. Gradually, however, these artists have been making inroads into the cultural mainstream. As this chapter will show, their most forceful impact has been in non-text-based cultural forms, especially film and music, where commercial considerations and generational transitions have outweighed the conservatism of more literary-based cultural milieux.

Artists of African origin have been present in France since well before decolonization, and their numbers have grown in the post-colonial period (Blanchard *et al.* 2002), but it is only in recent years that there has been any real discussion of their contribution to French (as distinct from 'Francophone') culture (Hargreaves and McKinney 1997). Initially, most were temporary residents who remained culturally rooted in their country of origin, to which they would sooner or later return. The founders of the Negritude movement, for example, were primarily concerned with liberating Africa and the Caribbean from colonial domination (for a discussion of Negritude, see P. Williams, Chapter 16, and Murphy, Chapter 20). In their emphasis on what distinguished and separated them from France and its cultural traditions, they shared in certain ways the perception that was widely held in France that artists of African origin would never truly become part of French culture. The terms in which that separation was marked out was of course less valorizing in majority ethnic perceptions than in the eyes of Africans themselves. From colonial times to the present, Africans in France have been viewed by the majority ethnic population through a series of perceptual screens that have exoticized, belittled or dehumanized them. In the early part of the twentieth century, performances in France by African-American artists such as Josephine Baker were seen as exotic spectacles the interest of which was defined by their distance from French normality (for a discussion of Baker's career in France, see Ezra, Chapter 5). Similar exoticist reflexes structured the manner in which 'native' artists were packaged for the consumption of visitors to colonial exhibitions, the most famous of which was that held in Paris in 1931 (Hodeir and Pierre 1991). At its lowest depths, packaging of this kind took the form of 'human zoos', which had the effect of suggesting that the men and women paraded within them were animals rather than humans (Bancel *et al.* 2002; see also Forsdick, Chapter 4, and Ezra, Chapter 5). In the post-colonial period, the concept of 'Francophonie' has served to delimit a cultural space outside that of France structured by the French language. When writers of African origin living in France are referred to as 'Francophones', they are by the same token positioned outside the national culture of France. Similarly, in popular cultural forms such as television advertising, people of colour still feature primarily as exotic figures selling products associated with distant places (Debost 1993).

Despite these deep-seated perceptions among the majority ethnic population, minorities originating in North and sub-Saharan Africa are now permanent and growing parts of French society. The extent to which creative works produced by these minorities are recognized as part of French culture has depended on a variety of factors, of which three are particularly significant. The first of these is the length of family settlement by different minorities, for the emergence of a second generation, born in France of immigrant parents, greatly increases the pressures for recognition of minority ethnic elements within the cultural space of France. In this respect, the relatively early settlement of migrants from former French colonies in the Maghreb (i.e. North Africa), compared with those of sub-Saharan origin, has been of major importance. A second generation of sub-Saharan origin comparable in size and age to that of the Maghrebi minority has yet to emerge. Literary and cinematic work by artists of sub-Saharan origin in France is still dominated by writers and filmmakers born in Africa, whose work retains strong referential links with the 'home' country even when, as is the case with the Cameroonian-born novelist Calixthe Beyala (1992; 1993), they write about youngsters of African origin who are now putting down roots in France (on the emergence of an 'Afro-Parisian' blend of writing among authors of sub-Saharan African origin such as Beyala and Daniel Biyaoula, see Thomas 2001). Secondly, some cultural imports are seen as less 'assimilable' than others. Islam, a key element in the cultural fabric of the Maghreb and also present in other regions including former French West Africa, is often perceived as particularly problematic. Thirdly, the institutional structures of certain cultural forms have been more or less porous than others. In the field of literature, for example, the network of publishing houses and academic institutions which play a fundamental role in categorizing and publicizing writers has been relatively slow to recognize minorities of immigrant origin as constituent elements of French culture. In other cultural spheres, such as popular music and cinema, the barriers have been less rigid.

Although the beginnings of labour migration from the Maghreb, especially Algeria, date back more than a century, it was not until the 1970s that the rise of family settlement transformed a previously temporary expatriate population into France's first significant post-colonial minority. It was during this period that the first creative works by second-generation Maghrebis began to appear. These were initially visible in the work of local theatre groups, amateur filmmakers and rock bands (Maatouk 1979; *Sans Frontière* 1985). Later a substantial corpus of narrative prose emerged (Hargreaves 1997). Smaller numbers of artists whose roots lay in migration from ex-colonies in sub-Saharan Africa and the Caribbean were involved in similar developments. The works produced by second-generation members of minority groups were very different from those produced by migrant writers who had been born and raised in Africa, whose country of origin remained a primary reference and who wrote at least in part for readers back 'home'. For second-generation members of minority groups, home is in France. Although they are often said to be divided between the dominant culture of France and the cultural heritage of their migrant parents, it should not be forgotten that France is the country in which they were born, the locus of their formative experiences and the main place in which they seek public recognition for their work.

During the 1970s their creative work was initially concentrated in performance arts. Rock concerts or theatre productions were staged for relatively small, local audiences which tended to be composed predominantly of minority ethnic spectators. When young writers of Maghrebi origin began seeking wider audiences through the publication of novels and other narratives, they were more or less compelled to work through a publishing industry dominated by the majority ethnic population. They lacked the financial resources to set up their own publishing houses, and, with high rates of illiteracy among migrant parents and generally low levels of educational attainment among their children, the Maghrebi minority in France did not constitute a commercially viable audience in its own right. Minority ethnic authors were therefore obliged to address majority ethnic audiences via essentially majority ethnic publishers.

This did not necessarily run against the grain of their aspirations. A prime feature of their work was a determination to demonstrate the legitimacy of their presence in France, using a variety of narrative strategies – foremost among them humour – to overcome or circumvent the prejudices of majority ethnic readers. The best known and most prolific of these authors is Azouz Begag, whose largely autobiographical narratives (Begag 1986, 1989) typify the cultural hybridity and social aspirations of many second-generation Maghrebis. Raised in France by Muslim parents, Begag and his semi-fictional alter egos feel affection and respect towards the older migrant generation, but are far more in tune with the secular values of their majority ethnic peers. They speak and write in French, albeit with a sprinkling of Arabic expressions, and are set on making a future for themselves within mainstream French society, rather than closing themselves off in some ethnic ghetto.

While this corpus of work is now substantial – since the early 1980s more than a hundred narratives have been published by second-generation Maghrebis (see Hargreaves 1997) – and heavily marked by a desire for recognition and acceptance among the majority ethnic population, it has yet to fully attain this objective. In many respects, it remains marginalized by the publishing, journalistic and academic communities who act as gatekeepers to the wider public.

The problematic status of this writing is evident in the ongoing debate concerning its categorization. Is it French, Maghrebi, both or neither? The most common label applied to it is that of 'Beur' literature. The neologism 'Beur' was first adopted during the 1970s as a self-designation by second-generation Maghrebis. It was a piece of 'verlan' (backslang) formed by inverting and partially truncating the syllables of the word 'Arabe', which in everyday French usage often carried pejorative connotations inherited from the colonial period. Initially confined to minority ethnic milieux, it entered general circulation during the mid-1980s, just as the first novels and full-length feature films produced by young Maghrebis were beginning to find majority ethnic audiences. Journalistic usage of the word soon became heavily intertwined with media coverage of the 'banlieues', which by the late 1980s had become synonymous in press and television reports with disadvantaged neighbourhoods featuring dense concentrations of minority ethnic groups and high crime rates (Hargreaves 1996). The negative connotations associated in this way with media coverage of 'Beur' youths living in the 'banlieues' led many second-generation Maghrebis, including a large proportion of the writers and other artists among them, to reject what had originally been a liberating term (on the evolution and semantics of this term, see Durmelat 1998).

This was not simply because the word was often (though not always) negatively connoted. It was also because, even when apparently more positively connoted, it appeared to place second-generation Maghrebis in a category separate from mainstream French literature. Writers, filmmakers and other artists interviewed by François Reynaert in 1993 were therefore vigorous in complaining that the 'Beur' label was being used to ghettoize them. As Reynaert observed, these artists were not motivated by a thirst for autonomy from France of the kind that had inspired the Negritude movement. On the contrary, they wanted recognition within the French cultural sphere, and 'contrairement au temps de la négritude, il n'y a ni groupe, ni programme, ni école de la beuritude' [contrary to how it was with Negritude, there is no 'beuritude' group, programme or school] (Reynaert 1993, 18).

Journalistic coverage of the so-called 'Beur' generation was not the only factor inhibiting the incorporation of second-generation Maghrebis into the mainstream of French literature. French academics have also been slow to incorporate the work of these writers into their research and teaching programmes. Where they have been studied in French universities and research centres, this has usually been in programmes or departments of comparative or Francophone literature. As the 'Francophone' label is shorthand for 'French-speaking but not part of France', this has implicitly positioned them outside the literature of France, a categorization confirmed by their almost total absence from the programmes administered by departments of French literature.

Among the many reasons which may have contributed to this marginalization, three in particular may be mentioned here. One is the old idea of assimilation, inherited from the colonial era, which has encouraged the assumption that artists of immigrant origin cannot become part of French culture until they abandon their ancestral heritage (the issue of assimilation is also addressed in Rosello, Chapter 12, and Murphy, Chapter 20).

Secondly, there is a widespread belief, again inherited to a considerable extent from the colonial period, that minorities of African origin, especially those originating in Islamic countries, are too different from the majority ethnic population ever to become truly French. Thirdly, compared with their counterparts in the Anglophone world, French academics have been slow to widen their objects of study beyond the traditional literary canon. Where Anglophone academics have embraced popular culture, both literary and audio-visual, alongside more classical literary texts, French intellectuals remain far more snobbish in their attitudes towards the mass media and non-textually based forms of culture. One of the most striking features of many works by writers of Maghrebi immigrant origin is precisely their seemingly oral quality. They are strewn with colloquialisms and slang, and often draw more on cinematic and televisual references than on classical French literary models. By the same token, they appear to many French academics to fall not only outside the national field of French literature but also below the threshold of literature 'tout court'.

The cultural forms in which African minorities have broken most effectively through these kinds of barriers are film and music. Where academic institutions are dominated by an older generation of gatekeepers steeped in traditional literary culture, the film and music industries are driven more by market demand from younger audiences who find audio-visual cultural forms more appealing than text-based art.

The first feature film directed by a second-generation Maghrebi was Mehdi Charef's *Le Thé au harem d'Archimède*, released in 1985. One of the most striking aspects of this and many subsequent movies in a similar vein is the way in which, while focusing on minority ethnic characters, they call into doubt the significance of ethnic divisions within French society. Majority ethnic racism is certainly a divisive force and it is often portrayed in these films, but they repeatedly show that the stereotypes and prejudices fuelling racist attitudes are unfounded. In movies such as *Le Thé au harem d'Archimède* the fault lines structuring social relations are shown to revolve far more around age, gender and above all class than around ethnicity. Where racism appears, it is primarily in the behaviour of older French characters. The young friends at the centre of the story are of mixed ethnic origins, with majority ethnic characters interrelating easily with those of immigrant origin. The main friends are exclusively male, and their relations with female characters are characterized by marked divisions of social space and gender roles. But uniting almost all the characters is the shared experience of social disadvantage. It is this that suffuses the run-down 'banlieue' where they live, that prompts the petty crime and drug abuse in which many of them engage, and that leads older French inhabitants to engage in racialized scapegoating.

The film drives this point home by featuring two co-protagonists, Madjid and Pat, who are respectively of Algerian and French origin. Unemployed and broke, they share the same social predicament and a deep-seated friendship. It is true that in Madjid's home we see a parental culture marked by the Islamic faith and the Arabic language, in obvious contrast with the cultural norms dominant in France. But the cultural heritage of his parents is of little more than marginal significance to Madjid, who speaks French far more readily than Arabic and who seems as uninterested as Pat in any kind of religious belief.

The friendship between Pat and Madjid has since been replicated and extended in numerous movies in the form of what has come to be known as the 'Black-Blanc-Beur' trio. The best known film of this kind is Mathieu Kassovitz's *La Haine* (1995), in which the three co-protagonists are Vinz (white and Jewish), Hubert (of sub-Saharan African origin) and Saïd (a second-generation Maghrebi). *La Haine* is in certain respects untypical of the body of cinematic work featuring trios of this kind. Most seek to reassure majority ethnic audiences that France's new immigrant minorities are no threat to them. *La Haine* is a much angrier movie, responding to police brutality in the 'banlieues' (perceived as emblematic of wider forms of social oppression) by adopting violent postures, a recurrent example of which is the gun pointed by Vinz straight at the camera, and thereby at the viewer. The violent nature of the movie is one of the reasons why it had such a huge impact in France. Through that impact, *La Haine* helped to focus attention on the problems of France's multi-ethnic 'banlieues' and to open up a cinematic space that is now a major part of the French movie industry.

During the 1980s, films directed by Charef and other second-generation Maghrebis had prompted talk of the emergence of a school or genre of 'Beur' cinema, a category that raised problems similar to those involved in the debate surrounding 'Beur' literature (*CinémAction* 1990). In addition to the danger of appearing to suggest that 'Beur' cinema was in some sense separate from 'French' cinema, it ran the risk of implying not only that films categorized in this way revolved primarily around ethnicity but also that they were mono-ethnic in focus. During the 1990s, especially in the wake of *La Haine*, the concept of 'Beur' cinema was to a considerable extent displaced by that of 'cinéma de banlieue'. While this in turn raised many similar problems of ghettoization and risked reinforcing negative stereotypes associated with the 'banlieues' (Jousse 1995; Konstantarakos 1999), it had the merit of shifting the terms of the debate away from ethnically based categories (as exemplified in 'Beur' cinema) to those of a wider range of social issues (including but not limited to ethnicity). Those issues – of poverty, discrimination and social justice – are not the concern of a single ethnic group. They affect minorities of sub-Saharan origin as much as those of Maghrebi origin. And, while post-colonial minorities suffer far more from discrimination than socially disadvantaged whites, the problems of the 'banlieues' are to a considerable extent common to all their inhabitants, whatever their ethnic origins.

While the films that initially brought artists of African immigrant origin to the attention of the majority ethnic public were mainly categorized as 'Beur' or 'banlieue' movies, in recent years minority ethnic actors and film-makers have been associated with a much wider range of cinematic work. But, here too, artists of Maghrebi origin are still more visible than those of African and Caribbean heritage. In an analysis of recent French movies, Videau (2001) counted more than thirty actors of Maghrebi origin in significant roles, compared with fewer than ten of African or Caribbean origin. The huge box office hits *Taxi* (1998) and *Taxi 2* (2000), car-action movies produced by Luc Besson, one of the most powerful majority ethnic figures in contemporary French cinema, are examples of this trend. They cast Sami Naceri, a second-generation Algerian, as the majority ethnic pro-tagonist, Daniel. Naceri's light skin colour enables him to play such a role convincingly. At the same time, many if not most French spectators are probably aware of the actor's real-life ethnic origins, and they may be tempted to import this knowledge into their reading of the movie, all the more so when, in *Taxi 2*, they see Daniel wearing a number ten Zidane soccer shirt, which could well be interpreted as a nod towards the shared Algerian ancestry beneath the shirt of the French soccer star on the one hand and the fictional persona donned by Naceri on the other. In this way, the *Taxi* films hint at the ethnic diversity present in France while at the same time de-problematizing that diversity, suggesting that it can be simply if not indeed magically transformed into an inclusive Frenchness.

Similar issues have given rise to a ferocious debate around France's biggest box office succees of 2001, *Le Fabuleux Destin d'Amélie Poulain*, and in particular the role played by the second-generation Algerian Jamel, a DJ, comedian and actor whose personal life history and stage material have been heavily rooted in the 'banlieues'. In *Amélie Poulain*, Jamel plays a greengrocer's shop assistant named Lucien working in the Montmartre neighbourhood where the movie is set. Jamel is such a well-known figure in France that few people watching the film can have been unaware of the actor's ethnic origins. As with Sami Naceri in the *Taxi* films, his casting as a majority ethnic character in *Amélie Poulain* may be interpreted in different ways. On the one hand, it could be read as a sign of integrated casting, demonstrating that talented actors can participate in successful mainstream movies such as *Amélie Poulain* irrespective of their origins. On the other hand, the almost total absence of any minority ethnic characters in the movie and the apparent obliteration of the ethnicity of the one actor who might have brought such a dimension to the film have angered some viewers. This more hostile view was typified by a reviewer in *Libération* who castigated the film's image of 'une France rétrograde, ethniquement nettoyée, nauséabonde' [a nauseous, backward-looking, ethnically cleansed France], which, he argued, exemplified the reactionary and racist dreams of ethnic purity championed by Jean-Marie Le Pen (Kaganski 2001). (Shortly afterwards, Jamel co-starred alongside Gérard Depardieu in another box-office blockbuster, *Astérix et Obélix: Mission Cléopâtre* (2002), the biggest-budget French movie of all time, in which he played an Egyptian working with a band of Gauls to outwit the ambitions of the Roman Empire.)

The incorporation of minority ethnic artists into mainstream French cinema clearly raises difficult questions that are as much ethical and political as aesthetic or technical. Similar issues have arisen in the field of French popular music, where artists of African origin have had a greater impact than in any other cultural sphere. Central to this has been the spectacular rise of rap and the associated range of performance arts known as hip-hop, combining music, rhymed speech and dance. Initiated during the 1970s by African-Americans living in ghetto neighbourhoods of large US cities, rap was taken up in the French 'banlieues' during the 1980s. Compared with the US, where until recently rap was practised almost exclusively by African-Americans, the French rap scene has always been much more multi-ethnic in character. While some of its biggest stars – most obviously the Senegalese-born MC Solaar, described by *Newsweek* (1996, 42) as 'the most widely known French recording artist in the world' – are of sub-Saharan African origin, many other ethnic groups, including West Indians, Maghrebis and majority ethnic French, are also active practitioners. Not uncommonly, rap bands feature multi-ethnic line-ups such as those of Suprême NTM (highlighting the majority ethnic Kool Shen alongside West Indian Joey Starr) and IAM (whose members are of Italian, Malian, Algerian and Spanish extraction). In parallel with recent movies, rap has helped to promote the slogan 'Black, Blanc, Beur', which served, for example, as the title of France's first daily rap radio show, launched in Lille in 1991 (Cannon 1997, 153–4).

Rap received a major boost during the mid-1990s with the introduction of a system of quotas which, paradoxically, was designed to protect French music from foreign (especially American) imports. Under the Pelchat amendment to the 1994 Carignon media law, commercial radio stations have been required to ensure that at least 40 per cent of the songs they broadcast are in French, and half of this quota has to feature artists in the relatively early stages of their careers. The rap bands which by the early 1990s had begun to sign contracts with French recording companies were the major, quite unintended, beneficiaries of this system, gaining huge exposure on radio stations such as Skyrock and NRJ, the market leaders among young listeners in France (Davet and Mortaigne 1996; Hare 1997). This helped to make rap what is now the most popular form of music among young people in France, including those of majority ethnic origin.

The enthusiasm with which majority ethnic youths have embraced rap is not simply an accident of the Pelchat amendment. It relates both to the American origins of rap and to the greater openness of younger audiences in France, compared with older generations, towards transnational cultural phenomena. In contrast with the generations who still dominate academic institutions, who were raised in a world where national boundaries and identities seemed of self-evident importance, young people in contemporary France are far more likely to see themselves within a global cultural dynamic in which the United States plays a leading role. The importing and adoption of rap is a paradoxical part of this process. Rap was originally developed as a form of counter-culture by African-Americans who were tired of being excluded from the American dream. It was taken up initially in France by minorities in similarly marginalized positions. But, alongside the subversive aspects of rap, its American origins give it a glamorous dimension in the eyes of young people outside the United States. In this way, a shared (but not necessary identically constructed) interest in American cultural references has been helping to bring together majority and minority ethnic youths within the French cultural sphere.

As in the cinema, musicians of minority ethnic origin who gain success in majority ethnic milieux are sometimes accused of 'selling out' by tailoring their work to mainstream audiences. It is unquestionably difficult to penetrate mainstream markets without adjusting in some degree to the codes and expectations of majority ethnic consumers. But that challenge has to be confronted if post-colonial minorities are to widen their cultural resonance together with the boundaries of French culture itself. Those boundaries are being gradually reshaped, and the forces pushing in that direction are gathering pace.

14

Immigration, tourism and postcolonial reinventions of travel

BY AEDÍN NÍ LOINGSIGH

In the context of French studies, discussion of immigrant literature has rarely managed to move beyond the questions of national and regional classification that over recent decades have dominated critical readings of non-metropolitan cultural production. At best, immigrant literature is loosely defined as a minor genre; at worst, it is presented as an illustration of a culturally specific thematic. Moreover, the discussion of migration is so frequently couched in socio-economic terms that the figure of the immigrant becomes trapped within a homogeneous and voiceless alterity that renders her/him incapable, it would seem, of any meaningful commentary on the contemporary cultural realities s/he has helped to forge.

Given tourism's intrinsic devotion to the pursuit of pleasure, it may appear disingenuous to compare tourists and immigrants. In modern-day Western societies, the 'right' to go on holiday is a clear manifestation of capitalism's success, contrasting sharply with the involuntary movement of migrants and the disastrous state of Third-World economies. However, despite undeniable status distinctions between tourists and immigrants, as well as the very different nature of their mobility, studying the convergences and divergences of their respective routes can be an extremely effective means of charting the uneven cultural mingling of post-colonial societies. Both of these figures incarnate to varying degrees the hybrid identity of the modern subject; both are bound up in different ways in the dynamics of consumerist capitalism; and both are seen as representatives of mass, rather than individual travel. Finally, attitudes to both tourists and immigrants tell us something about the impact of class, gender and race in cultural constructions, and reveal important continuities between the colonial and post-colonial worlds.

Yet how do we delineate a meaningful space for representations of tourists and immigrants within Francophone postcolonial studies? The

answer lies, I believe, in revisiting the terms 'travel' and 'traveller'. In recent
years, the role played by practices of mobility in cultural formations has
been increasingly acknowledged, and the language of critical theory in
general has become saturated with the vocabulary of travel. However, the
emphasis on abstract and metaphorical meanings of travel and displacement
has often obscured important issues. For example, theorization of the locus
of multiculturalism and of multicultural identities is frequently carried out
at the expense of individual histories of travel and migration. Moreover, a
critical tendency to conflate radically different types of travel has almost
certainly contributed to the insidious perpetuation of a colonial paradigm in
which travel is seen as the individual pursuit of white, male, adventurous
Europeans. This in turn explains why narratives of travel continue to be
read according to the norms and conventions of Western literary traditions.

This chapter will question such assumptions by examining some recent
French-language texts that use immigrant and tourist journeys as their
narrative impetus. This will allow a consideration of the ways in which the
post-colonial shift from individual to predominantly collective practices of
movement and migration forces us to consider new models of travel. These
not only allow us to uncover neglected practitioners of travel, but also invite
us to explore how travel, despite its frequently cited associations with
colonialism, gender and class privilege, is too diverse and multiform to be
reduced to any simple definition. This consideration of postcolonial reinventions of travel will be limited to journeys to and from France and Africa.
My focus on this axis of travel is by no means intended to deny the multiple
orientations that define the network of post-colonial travel exchanges. None
the less, the particularly rich textual inscription of Franco-African travel,
and the continued importance of France as a destination for African
travellers, mean that this axis is particularly suitable for charting 'the
continuing complicity between travel writing and cultural imperialisms [and
for analysing] new forms of travel narrative that resist these earlier models
and that explore the possibilities inherent in travel writing as cultural
critique' (Holland and Huggan 1998, 48).

It is interesting to note that the erosion of colonial power, the advent of
independence and the migration of Europe's former subjects to the erstwhile
centres of empire coincided with a critical tendency to chart a decline of
travel and travel writing as they had previously been known. In addition to
an underlying nostalgia, these negative assessments reveal a growing frustration with the progressive postcolonial destabilization of neat categories
relating to travel and its significance. Given that European voices of cultural
authority and superiority had for centuries spearheaded the textualization
of travel and discovery, it is hardly surprising that challenges to established
forms should have caused such dismay. What is more surprising, however, is
that, despite the serious critical attention afforded to narratives of travel in
recent years, the notion that African writers may have contributed to the
expansion of the genre of travel writing appears to be something of a critical

blind spot. This is particularly evident in readings of African texts from the colonia era documenting the 'journey to Europe' where the question of generic affiliation has been notably absent, and where form is seen simply as a convenient way of exploring socio-historic issues.

It is tempting to blame such critical shortcomings on African authors themselves, many of whom appear to waver in their desire to brand Africans in Europe as travellers. This is particularly apparent in early post-colonial texts dealing with first-generation immigration where the unremitting poverty and social alienation of immigrants exclude them from the established universal conventions defining the traveller. Although the immigrant journeys in these texts clearly imply travel from Africa to France, this international journey does not appear to qualify immigrants as travellers. Fictional portrayals of immigrants show them lacking the competence required of conventional travellers, and they suffer more than they benefit from their journeys.

Although these early representations of immigration tend to portray a sedentary reality, it does not follow that immigration is not travel. In fact, it is precisely this divergence between immigration and conventional understandings of travel that points to the possibility of identifying new ways of travelling as well as new meanings for travel (on this subject, see Forsdick, Chapter 4). What such texts illustrate is the danger of following the well-worn track of European definitions of travel and travel writing, or indeed of falling into a romanticized view of immigrant journeys. To take seriously the notion that the immigrant is a traveller is not simply to oppose her/him to the conventional figure of the Western traveller, but to recognize that for the immigrant the enriching potential of travel cannot be held distinct from pain and isolation. Post-colonial narratives of immigration also show that dissatisfaction with home and a subsequent longing to return to an idealized version of it are also important reasons for the seemingly endless movement of immigrant life. Indeed, it is this very 'dwelling-in-travelling' (Clifford 1992, 103), rather than descriptions of a series of locations, that frequently characterizes the structure of these new models of travel writing.

The 1978 co-authored novel *L'Homme qui enjamba la mer* provides an instructive example of a new form of travel narrative that points to the continually shifting boundaries of the significance of travel in the post-colonial world. The plot of this fantastical tale of largely African immigrant labourers in Paris revolves around an imaginary totalitarian coup d'état aimed at limiting any further dilution of French culture through immigration. As their situation becomes increasingly precarious, the immigrants are forced to flee the French capital and escape southwards. As its title – 'The Man who Stepped over the Sea' – implies, the novel minimalizes the importance of the immigrants' journey across national borders, and, once in France, racism and bureaucracy determine the extent to which the men profit from their journey. The highly regulated spaces where they work and live seem deliberately designed to prevent reciprocal contact with native

Parisians, and thereby protect the city's sense of cultural cohesion. The protagonists of *L'Homme qui enjamba la mer* are not, however, static beings. The novel's undeniable dynamism derives largely from the ceaseless criss-crossing of Paris by refuse collectors, labourers and unemployed men who journey between their places of residence, their workplaces and various cultural landmarks they have built. The horizontal perspective of these travelling labourers and unemployed 'flâneurs' ['strollers'] is in direct contrast to the promontory viewpoint identified by Mary Louise Pratt in her study of colonial exploration narratives. According to Pratt, this elevated position allowed colonial travellers to 'claim authoritativeness for their vision [and suggests there is] no sense of limitation on their interpretative powers' (1992, 217). Building on the ideas of de Certeau (1984 [1980]), recent studies of the relationship between power and spatial representation reveal a similarity in methods and perspective between this knowing colonial gaze and the aerial view of maps. In *L'Homme qui enjamba la mer*, attempts by the totalitarian powers to erase the city's cultural plurality (by burning the mosque and removing immigrants) and to impose a unified and smooth vision of French culture are reminiscent of cartographic processes that transform complex spatial realities into readable, tabular texts. The history of immigration in Paris is also effaced by another cartographic gesture: the project of denomination. Written into the French names of public monuments the immigrants have built is the implication that the constructed landscape translates the fixity of France's history and traditions. As moving, errant subjects, the immigrants are refused the right to name, and are thereby powerless to write their history on the cityscape.

However, anchoring the importance of travel and immigrants in the history and geography of Paris is precisely what Mengouchi and Ramdane achieve through their writing. The immigrants' journeys through the city provide a strikingly original demonstration of the importance of immigrant travel to Paris, and belie the notion that immigration is a purely economic activity detached from social and cultural practices. The novel's emphasis on Paris as seen through the eyes of these men evokes the centrality of the visual to travel and, like travellers, the immigrants are shown to be critical observers of foreign manners and morals who provide an alternative way of visiting the city. The final 'unmapping' of the French capital, and the destruction of the Montparnasse tower, rejects the notion that the official history of Paris is an unassailable construct, and posits the city's survival on its ability to accommodate the histories of different travellers.

In Jean-Didier Urbain's lively study of tourists, reference to the Montparnasse tower inadvertently reveals a point of intersection between immigrant and tourist routes (1993, 140). The tower, whose existence *L'Homme qui enjamba la mer* attributes to immigrant labour, is mentioned as one of several vantage points on the Paris tourist itinerary designed to satisfy the traveller's inevitable taste for the panoramic. What is striking here is the way in which the privileged colonial gaze mentioned above appears to have been converted into a specific modern-day tourist gaze. Both gazes like to posit the landscape surveyed as knowable terrain, and, in different ways, both tend to ignore, or misread, very immediate cultural realities. In the case of the tourist, the urban vantage point also provides a means to indulge in a primary purpose of tourist travel: escape from immediate realities. The growth of tourism, however, has meant that true escape is translated as distance, and foreign rather than local experiences of difference. As tourists strike ever further from home, the way they see and interpret their destinations needs to be questioned. In other words, to what extent do the various practices of tourism replicate, or encourage, the colonial gaze? And how, in turn, is immigrant travel shaped by the tourist's interaction with 'natives'?

Although J.R. Essomba's *Le Paradis du Nord* (1996) is primarily concerned with the various stages of an African immigrant's perilous journey to France, it also sees tourism's contact with native culture as central to our understanding of the ways in which post-colonial travel is inflected by questions of race, class and national location. Crucially, the novel's frame for the uncomfortable encounter of tourists and immigrants is a luxury hotel in Cameroon's capital, Douala, where the novel's principal protagonist is employed as a menial bar worker (in an obvious reference to the multinational chain, the hotel is called 'Sovotel'). Similar to James Clifford's description of the hotel lobby (1992, 101), the hotel bar functions as an important 'site of displacement, interference, and interaction'. Here, the penniless, illiterate Jojo's dreams of travelling northwards to an idealized France are fuelled by encounters with the prosperous tourists and businessmen he serves. The ostentatious wealth of these travelling residents becomes at once the motivation for and the solution to the African's journey. Not only do these travelling hotel residents support the industry that employs Jojo; they also unwittingly contribute to the African's travelling fund when he conspires with a friend to rob them. For Third-World employees of tourism like Jojo, encountering holidaymakers means confronting the failings of their own society and coming face to face with the fundamental privileges of the modern, capitalist economy in which they participate without reaping its benefits. Jojo's arduous journey northwards in travelling conditions that contrast sharply with the privilege, comfort and security of the travellers he serves is indicative of the desperate measures economic migrants are prepared to take in order to accede to the lifestyle and travel practices of Western tourism.

If, as Clifford suggests, hotels represent a meeting point for different cultural practices in the modern world, it seems clear that in Essomba's novel the ethos of luxury establishments and the consuming practices of their wealthy residents speak loudest. The status of the luxury hotel's resident is dependent first and foremost on purchasing power, on an ability to 'buy time [and] to avoid work and replace it with leisure or with other kinds of work' (Urry 1995, 131). The 'Sovotel' setting is also emblematic of the modern reincarnation of a certain tradition of privileged, patronizing travel where the ultimate goal 'is to set up sedentary housekeeping in the entire world, to displace the local peoples, or at least to subordinate them in the enterprise, to make them the "household" staff of global capitalists' (MacCannell 1992, 5). As well as serving them, the presence of these local employees also provides the moneyed hotel resident with the illusion that s/he is encountering the other in the comfort of a temporary home, removed from the reality of local life.

In his 1991 film, *Bezness*, Tunisian director Nouri Bouzid questions this perception of the Western tourist as cultural discoverer by shooting the film from the perspective of the victims of tourism's illicit practices. As in Essomba's novel, the intersecting paths of tourists and would-be immigrants are presented primarily as a source of alternative funding for a journey away from poverty towards the material privileges represented by Western tourists. Bouzid, however, reins in any uncritical discussion of tourism's benefits to developing countries by examining the issue through the vexed question of sex tourism. In order to finance his dream of travelling to the material comforts of the West, the film's protagonist, Roufa, turns to the lucrative yet uncertain 'bezness' of selling his body to European tourists (male and female) who have travelled to the coastal resorts of Tunisia in search of 'sea, sex and sun'. From a native perspective, the contact zone with tourists is shown to be a predominantly male domain, suggesting that women are involved differently in tourism. Indeed, despite the nature of this 'bezness', Roufa insists that his fiancée, Khomsa, remain true to Muslim codes of practice governing female sexuality. She, however, becomes increasingly frustrated by this containment of her sexuality and by her fiancé's moral double standards. Slowly, she allows herself to become involved in a game of seduction with the travelling French photographer, Fred, who is besotted both personally and professionally with her exotic 'otherness'.

Fred's camera is a potent reminder of the connection between travel/tourism, desire and voyeurism that Bouzid's camera, in turn, seeks to expose. Needless to say, the association of the exotic with the erotic, and the possibility of heterosexual and/or homosexual contact with the 'other', underwrite many classical French narratives of travel, particularly those dealing with North Africa. Like the writer and his/her pen, Fred no doubt believes that his camera provides a benignly artistic and intellectual means of looking that allows him to apprehend, and to represent, the 'other' space of North Africa. However, in the tradition of so many well-known colonial images, Fred's distinctively erotic photographic images of Khomsa reveal how the female 'other' is unveiled, objectified and appropriated for the gratification and consumption of the male gaze. Bouzid is careful none the less not to characterize Khomsa's encounter with the travelling photographer as one-sided or monological. Contact with another value system is seen to provide her with a choice, albeit one that involves compromising some of her own values. Fred's 'harassment' also prompts Khomsa to contemplate resisting, and to demand that both he and Roufa consider her subjectivity. Ultimately, however, this encounter involves a choice concerning her own right to travel to France with Fred or to remain within the familiarity of her own culture.

In Roufa's case, despite the privileged status bestowed on him by the gender politics of his own cultural sphere, he is shown to be powerless to subvert the power relations of the contact zone between would-be immigrant and tourist. Although he imagines his male identity and authority are reinforced by the tourist encounter, he too is shown to be demeaned by the exoticizing and exploitative practices of a certain form of tourist travel. While it could be argued that his 'bezness' is a form of intimate cultural exchange, and that these relationships are premised on the understanding that they are short-term, Roufa is, in fact, transformed into little more than a disposable commodity that allows Western tourists to indulge in the age-old myth of a hedonistic and sexually unrestrained North Africa. Finally, his encounters with tourists and tourism, which are relatively successful in material terms, fail to prevent Khomsa's seduction by Fred. In this respect, his 'bezness' can be said to reflect the double-edged benefits of tourism to the Third World: despite the cultural and economic gains of tourism, they invariably require damaging compromise and ultimately do little to challenge the seductive appeal of Western capitalism.

As we have seen in *Paradis du Nord* and in *Bezness*, distorted images of others and of other places are essential to an understanding of the unequal forces that determine tourist and immigrant practices of travel. By turning to an earlier exploration of this question, Michel Tournier's *La Goutte d'or* (1986), we can see the processes behind these distortions laid bare. The novel is essentially a portrayal of a young Berber's voyage of discovery that is structured according to a physical journey from the Sahara to the Parisian immigrant neighbourhood of the novel's title. Like *L'Homme qui enjamba la mer*, *La Goutte d'or* is an imaginative defence of the immigrant as traveller, and it has been accepted as an original and revealing insight into French perceptions of Arab identity. Here, however, I will consider the less frequently studied question of the novel's exploration of the relationship between tourism and photography.

Idriss, the novel's protagonist, differs from other immigrants because his decision to leave home is not motivated by economic necessity but by his determination to recuperate a photograph taken of him by a French tourist. Like the jeep in which the tourist and her male companion travel, their camera is symbolic of the contrasting wealth and travelling practices of tourists and immigrants. Interestingly, if photography can be said to structure the different stages of the tourist's journey (Crawshaw and Urry 1997), the different stages of Idriss's journey to – and throughout – Paris are marked by encounters with various photographers and image-makers who appropriate and distort his identity. These encounters invariably predicate a relationship of profit and control that benefits the observer, and transforms

Idriss, the observed, into a static product for visual consumption. In the French tourist's determination to capture Idriss in the desert setting, in the falsified advertising images of North Africa and its inhabitants, and even in the French-financed museum of desert life, we see how the Western traveller, and in particular the tourist, is thought 'to possess all-seeing eyes which are able to identify real, authentic local people and local customs' (Crawshaw and Urry 1997, 178).

Western tourism's obsession with photogenic landscapes appears to be disturbed by the character of Mustapha, the photographer whom Idriss meets in the Algerian town of Béchar. Calculating the tastes of consuming Western tourists, Mustapha offers a choice of highly stylized backdrops portraying exotic African landscapes against which his clients may choose to be photographed. These deliberately staged scenes are a pointed reference to tourism's commodification of place, and highlight the constructed reality of the industry's supposedly authentic representation of other places and peoples. These photos also hint at the superficial nature of certain types of tourist travel, and suggest that these travellers would be better off staying at home rather than travelling the predetermined routes of tourist brochures in search of clichéd portrayals of exotic landscapes and cultures.

Although we may admire Mustapha's entrepreneurial initiative, his photography business is also a grotesque illustration of how tourist destinations run the risk of becoming parodies of themselves by packaging what they envisage to be the desired experience of the all-consuming tourist (MacCannell 1992, 19). Rather than protecting his country's unique environment and cultural specificity through his business, Mustapha, like so many tourism employees, is in fact creating a setting, or a product, that is dictated by a global appetite for difference and the exotic. This last point leads us to another complex and under-explored effect of the omnipresence of images on travelling practices in the post-colonial world. Advancements in technology and global communications mean that images of the other can now be beamed into the most remote corners of the globe. Like the tourists and consumers in *La Goutte d'or* who stand mesmerized in front of museum showcases, sex shops, and the exotic displays of shop windows, the postcolonial armchair traveller is now assured of a close encounter with 'other' cultures and peoples merely by looking at a computer or TV screen.

Contrary then to the maxim that the camera never lies, the camera in *La Goutte d'or* does nothing but lie, manipulating and manipulated by post-colonial practices of travel. However, if the novel carefully and skilfully reveals the ways in which visual representations of the other are shaped by social and cultural practices, it is less successful at highlighting the author's own inevitably subjective view of the 'other'. Tournier's brilliant play with tropes of travel should not deter the reader from noting a problematic tendency on the part of the author to repeat some of the failings he condemns. Like many colonial narratives of other places and cultures, opposition between Western and Islamic civilizations in the novel is often crudely schematic. Furthermore, the absence of any real linguistic or material barriers in Idriss's journey lends at times to an almost romanticized view of immigrant travel. Finally, the portrayal of tourists and tourism in *La Goutte d'or* also points to an interesting paradox. Although the figure of the immigrant is by and large successfully individualized, Tournier fails to acknowledge the diversity of tourists. It is true that the African texts discussed earlier are also guilty of presenting tourists as a homogeneous group. However, as a European who frequently travels to Africa, Tournier's attitude to tourists is arguably less understandable. Tourism in his novel invariably operates as a highly conservative form of travel, designed primarily to satisfy the smug, middlebrow traveller whose pursuit of pleasure takes precedence over engagement with the other.

Tournier's portrayal of tourists draws attention to an interesting congruence between anti-immigrant and anti-tourist discourses (Amirou 1995; Urbain 1993). Needless to say, analysis of the true complexity and significance of these convergences lies outside the scope of this chapter. However, within the parameters of a purely generic discussion of travel, these discursive convergences offer an interesting insight into anxieties concerning postcolonial dissolutions of established borders and categories. For example, in different ways, tourists and immigrants are frequently perceived as a threat, rather than contributors to, and beneficiaries of, established 'authentic' cultural and social practices. One of these practices is of course travel itself, and critical neglect of tourist and immigrant journeys reveals an undeniable nostalgia for privileged, less democratic forms of travel. It is clear too that, like postwar nostalgia for authentic travel, anti-tourist and anti-immigrant discourses are both underwritten by a distinctive elitism that feels threatened by what it perceives as the mass, uncontrolled movements of immigration and tourism. Finally, without wishing to understate the significant differences between attitudes to immigrants and tourists, both figures are inevitably defined by their inalienable 'otherness'.

Interestingly, the only concession made to the inevitably homogeneous and collective identity of tourists and immigrants is broadly racial. Immigrants are thought to be non-Western, and tourists Western. Whatever the statistical and cultural justification for such associations, they fail to recognize how individual experiences of tourism and immigration are inevitably shaped by class, cultural origins and gender. The fixed identities of immigrants and tourists also fail to take into account the possibility of crossover between the two identities. Calixthe Beyala's novel *Maman a un amant* is significant precisely because it highlights the ways in which gender impacts upon immigration and travel. Furthermore, although Francophone African literature and cinema may have numerous examples of return journeys (many of which arguably represent a form of tourism), Beyala's text marks a new development as it imagines the possible consequences of a transformation from immigrant to Western-style tourist. The novel is in fact a sequel to Beyala's highly controversial and successful *Le Petit Prince de*

Belleville (1992), which introduced the immigrant Traoré family from Mali. As in many texts dealing with African immigration to France, details of the international journey the family has undertaken are gleaned through fleeting references to a past that M'am, the main protagonist of *Maman a un amant*, would rather forget. M'am's association of 'home' as a site of suffering and exclusion has been shown to be typical of a female perception that considers travel and migration to be a potential means of moving on and severing the roots that tie women to oppressive patriarchal structures. The conflicts and contradictions of M'am's particularly female immigrant route have already been the subject of incisive analysis (Hitchcott 1997). To conclude this chapter, I would like to consider briefly the significance of the physical journey M'am undertakes when she reverses the orientation of immigration, and takes her family on holiday to the south of France.

When her philandering husband is imprisoned for polygamy in *Le Petit Prince de Belleville*, M'am is forced to take on the traditionally male role as family provider. Her solution is to begin an ethnic jewellery business and fill a niche that has almost certainly been created by the cosmopolitan tastes of Western tourists. It is her entrepreneurial success that enables her to take her family on holiday. However, this journey raises important questions about where the immigrant-tourist is headed. Certainly, the novel successfully questions the view that immigrants can only envisage travel as having a serious purpose. It also shows that Africans' participation in tourism need not entail being workers or part of a destination's exotic attraction. Beyala's novel also provides a positive angle on tourism as a catalyst for exploring, rather than exploiting sexuality. Once in the south of France, M'am discards her African boubou and dons a bikini, the Western sartorial symbol of female emancipation and of the holiday's potential for sexual liberation. M'am's 'discovery' of her body ultimately leads her to have an affair with a fellow French tourist, with whom she has her first experience of sexual pleasure.

For all its emphasis on the positive aspects of the immigrant's transformation into tourist, *Maman a un amant* also exposes some worrying ambiguities. Firstly, rather than telling their fellow immigrant neighbours that they are going to a little-known provincial village, the Traorés insist that they are going to the supposedly more sophisticated destination of Cannes. This would suggest that integrating into French society, and becoming a tourist, means the immigrant must also adhere to the rules of travel, and recognize that ways of travelling and choice of destination are important markers of social position. The Traorés' clichéd observations on the rural simplicity of their holiday destination suggest that they have bought into tourism's discourse of rusticity, and relate to their surroundings in the manner of sophisticated Parisians. The various reactions of locals, however, reveal that the visitors continue to be perceived according to skin colour and racial stereotypes. Although the family appears to have crossed the boundary between immigrants and tourists, they are clearly not yet perceived as citizens with all the rights that this status entails. As an immigrant working in the informal economic sector, M'am also has no 'right' to the 'congés payés' [paid holidays] of French workers, suggesting that access to holidays continues to remain differential.

Maman a un amant, like the other texts examined here, exhibits various qualities that testify both to travel's multiple meanings and to the complex set of discourses that define postcolonial mobility. These different representations of travel reveal how the disjointed and fragmented cultures generated by international mobility erode, as they have always done, colonial accounts of national cultures. The directions taken in this chapter demonstrate the need to reclaim neglected practitioners of travel in order to ensure a more inclusive critical stance that takes account of travel's imbalances, contradictions and constant reinventions. The directions not taken illustrate the rich ground that exists for future considerations of the subject.

15

Frantz Fanon, Atlantic theorist; or decolonization and nation state in postcolonial theory

BY ANDY STAFFORD

O my body, make of me always a man who questions!

(Fanon 1986 [1952], 232)

Urgent tasks in describing the world (in order to change it) depend upon current circumstances. The rise of Fascism (linked to the European racist demonization of migrants) and the return of Imperialism (if not a new form of colonialism) dominate the political (and therefore, theoretical) horizon in this new millennium. Any postcolonial theory worth its salt is then, and rightly so, summoned to react, engage and debate in these two pressing concerns. What is difficult, however, is deciding which threat is the more urgent of the two to address. Naturally, the two are linked. Racism and discrimination feed on, and into, the West's imposition of (its own) order on various parts of the world.

Though not in any way wishing to neglect nor to underestimate the growth of racism, this chapter will consider the second of these pressing concerns. This does not imply an order or hierarchy of tasks, only a recognition that, though deeply linked, the two questions cannot be given justice in one chapter. The reader interested in racism in the recent Francophone context can refer to an important collection of essays on the threat of Le Pen in France (Collective 2002).

Thus it is to postcolonial theory's most recent accounts of decolonization that we must urgently turn. David Murphy (2000, 18) has rightly noted that the 'failings of the anti-colonial movement' should not be used as a way of denigrating liberation brought about by decolonization. However, though I sympathize with some of the comments by Peter Hallward decrying the worst excesses of contemporary postcolonial theory, there is something naïve in the belief that 'a reaffirmation of the nation state [is] essential [...] for any effective conceptualization of a progressive political practice' (2001, xx). Surely it is curious that, despite his critique of Neil Lazarus's 'permanent revolution', Hallward should end up with a similar view of the nation state. This study will try to transcend this contradiction by putting forward a supple (which does not mean lacking in rigour) view of attitudes towards the post-colonial nation state confronted now by global capital.

While drawing inspiration from the wave of anti-colonial struggles of the 1950s and 1960s, the analysis will put forward a theory of decolonization, which sees this (first?) decolonization process as 'deflected'. There is no better place to find this phenomenon than in Algeria, and through the writings and theories of Frantz Fanon. In other words, it is important that we explain not only the failure of the French Caribbean to liberate itself (some would, rather harshly, blame Aimé Césaire for this), but also the dire direction taken by Algeria since independence.

Fanon's postcolonial Atlantic

As the opening chapter of David Macey's magisterial biography (2000) points out, Frantz Fanon is barely remembered either in Martinique or Algeria. How, then, shall we remember him? As FLN spokesperson, speaking of liberation and equality, indirectly responsible for what has followed in Algeria's forty years of independence? As politically motivated postcolonial theorist, quoted endlessly to back up the most arcane and glib literary theory? Or (and this is Macey's suggestion) as an agent acting between two islands, one real (Martinique) and the other political (Algeria, in its struggle for liberation)?

Even though we must accept that Fanon needs to be rehistoricized (Gates 1991, 469–70), need this be at the expense of believing in a future world that is truly postcolonial? Here a 'dialogue' with Fanon is inevitable: if Fanon's own theories have been subject to what Said calls 'traveling theory' (2000 [1994]), in both time and space, then it is to the credit of these theories. Said's implication that theories, once removed from their historical juncture, take on a new form cannot be a smokescreen for reinventing the wheel. Thus we will note later the applicability of Fanonian theory to Palestine, as a sign of an exit from a purely Francophone transatlantic problematic.

To consider then Fanon's Algeria as an 'island' is, in a sense, to relegate his thought to that of the FLN leadership. Fanon, as much of his writing shows, was by far one of the most internationalist members of the political leadership across the Maghreb in the tumultuous period of the 1950s. Indeed, there was a deep-seated failure to establish a Maghreb unity, which, as Mohammed Harbi has pointed out, was a sign of a 'grande stérilité intellectuelle au sein des partis politiques des trois pays' [great intellectual sterility within the political parties of all three countries] (2001, 250–2). In this climate, Fanon's internationalism was all the more impressive.

However, one other danger in remembering Fanon is that of keeping his theories and writings 'en vitrine' [in a showcase]. Surely, the man who gave his life to Algerian liberation should be remembered generously as an actant for human liberation (then and in the future). Neil Lazarus (1999) has rightly defended Fanonian theory against critics such as Christopher Miller, who, with the luxury of hindsight, abstracts himself and Fanon from History; and Lazarus has consistently, and fraternally, pointed to errors of political judgment in Fanon's ideas. We could go further in considering Fanon's political heritage in the midst of the 1950s and suggest that, though not the theorist of 'the national question' in the mould of a Stalin, his thought (largely unconsciously it seems) has reformulated Marxism. This reformulation led inadvertently to disastrous consequences for liberation struggles, helping to inflect African and Arab Socialism towards a bankrupt Maoism.

Now, let it be said that a critical engagement with, and reappraisal, of Fanonian revolutionary theory is not an attempt to blame him for what has followed; indeed, Fanon has inspired liberation movements across the world. Rather, we should ask what is the political content of the Fanonian heritage? How might Fanon's liberationist commitment be redirected? One way is to consider his founding of an atlanticist internationalism.

Fanon's Atlantic travel is of fundamental importance to understanding his internationalism. He signs up in 1943 to fight against Nazi Germany, travelling via Bermuda to West Africa and then to North Africa, reaching Toulon and seeing action in the dying months of the Second World War. He returns to his native Martinique in 1945, via Le Havre, on a desperately cramped ship. A second circuit, to go to study in Paris and then Lyons, is begun in 1946, followed by another brief return to Martinique. Finally, he leaves Martinique for the last time in 1951. In the classic fashion of the triangular-circuit typical of Francophone West Indian intellectuals, he finds Africa and North Africa in Paris, but always via (what Édouard Glissant calls) a 'detour', that is Africa (Accra) and North Africa.

This 'triangular' consciousness is evident in Fanon's writings. The first chapter of *Black Skin, White Masks* considers Creole language in relation to French. Even *The Wretched of the Earth*, as Albert Memmi has suggested (1971), is written in the light of the unrest in Martinique between 1959 and 1961. In Caribbean terms, then, Fanon's writing shows the dilemma, even double bind, of Caribbean French subjects/citizens: either 'sell out' to French colonial oppression, or be compromised by the excluded language of Creole. In this sense, Fanon (and not Césaire) is, in Chamoiseau's and Confiant's words, the 'ante-creole' (see McCusker, Chapter 10). Indeed, creole and relational theorists of today – Chamoiseau, Confiant, Glissant – seem to follow Fanon's ethos of 'starting from scratch', of affirming, in similar voluntarist fashion, the spread and significance of Creole. Is the view of 'diversality' more Fanonian than Cesairian, with its aim to establish an authentic (if not national then linguistic) culture? Creole theorists believe that they have gone beyond the French-versus-Creole dilemma, by a voluntaristic promotion of creolization, which deploys globalization and poststructuralist rhizomatic philosophy as a sign of creolization. Hallward makes this point most cogently in relation to Glissant's trajectory, showing how Glissant's early nationalism has been replaced by a post-national relationality of totality (2001, 66–125).

Hallward's analysis of this post-national theme in Glissant's recent work is deeply political. However, not only does Hallward seem to contradict his own view that literature and politics should be kept separate – his close reading of Glissant's novels cannot be seen as anything else but a political 'naturalization' of Glissantian attitudes to nation and post-nation – but also his aim is to show that Glissant's abandonment of Martiniquan nationhood, in favour of chaotic and globalized relationism, can be rejected by a return to the nation state (2001, 126–32). However, just because Glissant today 'leaps over' the question of Martiniquan national liberation from French (colonial? postcolonial? neocolonial?) ownership, to reach a global totality, does this mean we have to counter this utopianism by returning to the nation state as a means of progress? It is precisely this national question that lies at the heart of Fanon's writing on Algeria.

Fanon's Atlantic credentials, as we have seen, are indisputable. They extend to the United States, where the Black Panthers were so influenced by Fanon that their forced exile in 1970 was arranged in Algiers. Indeed, the 'dialogue' between 'postcolonial' Martinique and Algeria may not be as 'deaf' as one might first imagine. Though Martinique, unlike Algeria, has not split with France, but rather perversely become integrated into the metropolitan post-colonial system, is it possible to say that much has changed, fundamentally, in Algeria since 1962? One may change the names and the dates, the players may have changed sides, but the 1990s have seen a civil war in Algeria every bit as bloody as the War of Liberation. The FLN government is now fully on the side of multinational and imperialist capital, sharing in the enormous profits from Algeria's minerals (gas and oil) in the south of the country; and the Islamists now seem to occupy a similar place and play a similar role to the one played by the FLN itself during the War of Independence. The extent to which the FLN government today will go to discredit the Islamists and deflect criticism is startling and frightening, as the account by an army officer-turned-critic has recently shown (Souaïdia 2001). The government allegedly organizes massacres in order to blame them on the Islamists – we might have had an inkling of the FLN's tactics today, given its attribution of the massacre of Messalistes at Melouza in 1958 to the French colonial army (Macey 2000, 354). But there is also little evidence to suggest that Algeria and other 'independent' nations are just that: independent.

Critiques of globalization notwithstanding, it is difficult to deny that the global economic system has Algeria in its tight grip: the FLN government today merely implements and then exploits the gross injustice meted out by the IMF and the World Bank with regards to the Algerian economy and population. Less 'neocolonial' (which implies little agency from the FLN government) than 'new colonialist', in which a more (though by no means completely) integrated world system works with a local army-backed dictatorship to continue exploitation by any means necessary, Algeria's 'postcolonial' status has, over forty years, scotched the potential for social liberation.

In light of this, I am certain that this Algeria is not the 'progressive' nation state that Hallward's critique of Glissant's post-nationalism is proposing. But it suggests that reliance on nation state-building, in the face of the global and international system, is a dangerous political and theoretical terrain to occupy. Similarly, Martinique is today no longer a colony (therefore, it is 'post-colonial' in the strict sense of the word). But its black population suffers similar if not the same discrimination and oppression as before departmentalization and incorporation into the French state. The failure of Algeria's independent but aligned path to freedom, peace and democracy raises questions then about Fanon's prognosis, and gestures towards the conditions of future liberation across the Atlantic in the French Antilles.

Fanon's political heritage

In his introduction to the new French edition of *The Wretched of the Earth*, Gérard Chaliand, an anti-colonialist activist and theorist of many years standing, offers a sharp but fraternal set of disagreements with Fanon (Chaliand 1991). Chaliand rightly rejects the argument that the (Fanonian) justification of violence results directly in the utter political and ethical bankruptcy of Algerian government since independence; the causes of the current dictatorship are to be found rather, he argues, in the 'confiscation' of power by the bureaucracy and the bourgeoisie. But Chaliand goes to the heart of the contradiction in Fanon's conception of the appropriate agent of Algerian liberation, the peasantry and the lumpen proletariat. On the one hand, Chaliand points out, Fanon sees the urban dispossessed as the 'fer de lance urbain' [urban spearhead], 'cette cohorte d'affamés détribalisées, déclassés' [this cohort of an undernourished, detribalized underclass], as 'les plus radicalement révolutionnaires d'un peuple colonisé' [the most radically revolutionary of the colonized people] (1991, 28). Only then, a few pages later, Fanon warns that this 'réserve humaine' [human reserve], if not organized immediately into the insurrection, 'se retrouvera comme mercenaires aux côtés de troupes colonialistes' [will find itself becoming mercenaries alongside colonial troops] (28). Chaliand suggests that Fanon 'oublie l'étroitesse des nationalismes lorsque ceux-ci cessent d'être opprimés' [forgets the narrowness of nationalisms once these are no longer oppressed] (35).

Chaliand's 'debate' with Fanon now touches on his 'volontarisme optimiste' [optimistic voluntarism]: 'Motivé par la soif de justice et de dignité' [motivated by a thirst for justice and dignity], suggests Chaliand, 'le tiers-mondisme de Fanon est plus moral que politique' [Fanon's third-worldism is more moral than political], 'un transfert utopique' [a utopian transfer] (35). Now we can begin to see similarities between Fanon and (*pace* Hallward's refusal of politics in literature) Glissant's political ideology. The tabula rasa view of history promoted by Fanon, in which 1954 becomes the new 'year zero' opening up the 'will' to become Algerian and to lay the basis of a 'new humanity', displays his view that History no longer locks in the anti-colonial insurgent (the origins of this can be found in the conclusion of *Black Skin, White Masks*). This voluntarism is evident in Glissant's current post-nationalist phase, and, though Fanon's voluntarism is very different from Glissant's, it is the 'leap' (perhaps, with the Maoist connotations) over and outside of History which characterizes their viewpoints, Fanon's post-personalist, Glissant's post-nationalist.

The other criticism by Chaliand concerns agency in Fanonian anti-colonial struggle, and the emphasis placed on the peasantry in his revolutionary politics. Chaliand points to the failure of Guevara's strategy of reliance on the 'foco' in South America, and to its coincidence with Fanon's 'welcoming of the peasantry' into the central revolutionary arena. But what Chaliand does not mention is the influence of Maoism. Here, Chaliand's fraternal 'argument' with Fanon is perhaps incomplete.

Under the influence of the anti-colonial struggle in Vietnam, theorized and led by Van Giap, the leadership of the Algerian drive to independence took on similar military formations, organizing the insurgents into 'katiba', as in the Viet Minh, of one hundred men, which avoided all contact with the French colonial authorities except in combat situations (Macey 2000, 266). This 'guerrilla swimming against the tide' activity had not just military similarities with Maoist forms of warfare, but also political relations.

Indeed, the peasantry – the archetypal force in Maoist revolutionary strategy – is treated in almost romantic terms by Fanon in *The Wretched of the Earth*, welcoming those forced out of Algiers into rural areas (Macey 2000, 314). Fanon's enthusiasm is such that he unfortunately decided to back Holden Roberto in Angola's struggle for independence, and not the MPLA, which he viewed as far too urban (Harbi, cited in Macey 2000, 391). Fanon's judgment was clouded by Holden's peasant support, to the extent that he was totally unaware of Holden's collaboration with the CIA.

Thus, for Fanon, as for the FLN leadership in general, the peasantry 'was the most revolutionary section of the population and contained inexhaustible numbers' (Macey 2000, 396). But, as Mohammed Harbi has pointed out, this view did not fit with reality: the peasant class in Algeria, largely proletarianized by 1954, 'contrairement à la Chine et au Viêt-nam, n'a pas connu de mouvement paysan' [unlike China and Vietnam, did not produce a peasant movement] (2001, 376–7). Indeed (paradoxically perhaps), the FLN practice of relying on the peasantry as 'professional revolutionaries' was merely an expedient tactic, rather than a planned strategy. There was very little attempt to organize agrarian reform, not to mention social revolution: the FLN relied precisely on the conservative tendencies of rural workers. And Harbi (2002) provides sufficient evidence of the Algerian peasantry's historical role as a non-revolutionary class.

Reliance on rural guerrilla forces was evident elsewhere too, especially in Cuba, with Castro's accession to power in 1959. But here, we must remember, no sections of the peasantry, nor of the Cuban working classes, were directly involved in overthrowing Batista's imperialist-backed regime. Much as the Cuban 'revolution' was progressive, its political content (to put it objectively) amounted to no more than an army coup led by intellectuals with the help of a rurally based army. So Fanon's 'tabula rasa', or 'année zéro', was, in political terms, anything but: its heritage was to follow the Maoist and Guevarist strategy, of constructing a loose amalgamation of the military and intellectuals, 'supported' by the rural poor. If this strategy proved fatal (quite literally for El Che), it was also to prove to stymie true liberation in Algeria.

A good example of interpreting Fanonian theory in this Third-Worldist direction can be seen in the pan-African movement, which, in good 1970s fashion, emphasized the appropriate aspect of Maoist politics to the situations pertaining in China and Vietnam, and for the future liberation of Mozambique (PANAF 1975, 147–58). It also influenced, as Abraham Serfaty points out (1998, 81), neighbouring Morocco in the near-insurrections of the late 1960s. Indeed, what is common to Maoist strategy is not only the reliance on a broad and socially ramshackle alliance of military, intellectual and rural actants, but also a mechanical view of social progress. It is not only the failure of total class revolution – where, as in Cuba, Vietnam, and China, state and capitalist power were never challenged – that has allowed power to be 'confiscated' in Algeria since Boumediène's 1965 coup. It is the reliance on a 'maoisant' political philosophy of 'stages' that failed to give Algerian revolution a proper leadership.

Despite Fanon's attempts to the contrary, *The Wretched of the Earth* is written within this 'stages' perspective (though it has to be acknowledged, written speedily and with fatal illness threatening). The 'stages' theory explicit in *The Wretched of the Earth* refers not to the intellectual 'stages' that Fanon describes, of individuals moving through assimilation to revolt (which is a fascinating account of a subjective radicalization process), but to an objective socio-political and historical category. Though, in the chapter 'On National Culture' of *The Wretched of the Earth*, Fanon is at pains to fight for not only pan-African solutions but world anti-colonialism (much more so than the provisional Algerian government, the GRPA), his perspective is clearly more transnationalist than internationalist. His belief that a pan-African unity need not pass through the 'bourgeois, chauvinist phase' of nationalism, relies on allegiances with other African states, and not on full-blown international revolution (Fanon, in Memmi 1971, 266). Fanon is clearly the most advanced of the FLN leadership in considering the need to dovetail Algeria's liberation struggle with Africa, often in the face of open FLN hostility to this widening of the struggle (see Macey 2001, 412–46). However, the key place to look for internationalist support was in France, among the working classes, in the heart of the colonialist beast as it were, a strategy that Third-Worldism could not entertain.

Though pan-Africanism, by its very nature, seemed to want to jump over the national cultures stages, it too believed, in practice, in a stagist approach, if only by default. By ignoring a strategy of true class solidarity, in the place where the exploited classes had the most power (France, Europe), Algerian (and African) liberation had chosen its camp, despite Fanon's attempts to steer a course between the two options. Thus, with international revolution deemed to be off the agenda (the European exploited were considered by Third-Worldist theory to be beneficiaries of continued colonial control), a cross-class alliance in decolonizing countries was bound to be led by a national(ist) bourgeoisie. Fanon's view that the 'Western dichotomy' of exploited workers versus exploiting bosses did not apply in Algeria, where it was a battle between colonizer and colonized (a view that implied crucially that French exploited classes actually benefited from the colonial set-up) could not but allow a heading-off, or a 'confiscation' of the Algerian revolution. No attempt to set up 'auto-gestion' after 1963, or to follow the non-aligned path that Algeria chose, could insulate it, truly and wholly, from world economic pressures. In practice, then, Fanonian (and Third-Worldist) decolonization strategy opted, though not by volition, for a 'stages' approach. The alternative to this is the theory of 'permanent revolution', devised by Trotsky months before the October Revolution in Russia in 1917.

Confiscation or deflection?

It is worth setting out briefly this conception of historical change, because it has important implications for the post-colonial world. The theory of permanent revolution is dialectical in that it stresses both the possibilities and limits of the prospect of liberation, in an imperialist-dominated world. Arguing that capitalism in the twentieth century is already a global system, in terms of its power if not of its physical implantation, permanent revolution nevertheless recognizes that advanced capitalist modes of production can sit alongside rural social organization (the Putilov factory in Moscow in 1917, at the time one of the most advanced industrial manufacturers in the world, sat 100 miles/160 km away from the most traditional and unchanged rural communities of Russia). This 'combined and uneven development' of world capitalism meant, for Trotsky and the Bolsheviks, that Russia, though largely rural in 1917, did not need to 'pass through' the bourgeois state system (as Western Europe and the United States had done over a number of centuries), but could move directly to socialist transformation. But, and this is very important, permanent revolution also stresses (against the Stalinist corruption of Marxism, and eventual direction of the Soviet Bloc under Stalin) that there can be 'no socialism in one country' (Löwy 1981).

This is all well and good in theory, but how did this theory apply to Algeria? How was it that the Algerian working classes did not lead a successful revolution for socialism, let alone participate *qua* social class in ejecting French colonial power? Many internationalist groups, following Trotsky's theory of permanent revolution, especially in France, were deeply involved in trying to influence Algeria beyond purely national, towards total social, liberation. The 'Fourth International' groups are a good example of this.

Despite the Fourth International's belief in permanent revolution – against the 'stages' perspective of Stalinism and Maoism – it could not make the theory fit the Algerian situation (see, for example, the writings of Michel Pablo in the *Quatrième International*). Time and again, there is, as with Cuba, a consistent attempt to paint post-independence Algeria, with its Yugoslavian model of workers' self-organization of the economy (autogestion), as socialist (this is evident to a lesser extent with post-independence Vietnam), despite socialism in one country being a mere illusion. Algerian isolationism was then promoted as the road to socialism, allowing nation state allegiances but as an independent 'socialist' state, leading to catastrophic results with Boumediène's 'confiscation' of power in 1965. For not only was the attempt by the *Charte d'Alger* to implement socialism (doomed to be) a failure, but also it was easy for an army coup to recuperate. This is amply illustrated by Clegg (1971). Though his critique of auto-gestion tends to ignore the international stage, Clegg is more perspicacious than Löwy, as the latter, though highly critical of the Algerian government's collaboration with multinational gas and oil companies, is blindly optimistic in considering Algeria's independent achievements as 'impressive' (Löwy 1981, 170–4). Such is the fundamental error in Löwy's 'orthodox' interpretation of permanent revolution that his natural instinct is to champion certain Third-World post-colonial nation states, thereby not seeing the confiscation of power by new indigenous ruling classes. Similarly, Craipeau (1982) ends up with this unsatisfactory 'stages' view of change. For even though he sees the post-independence Algerian government as a new bureaucratic ruling capitalist class, unlike Roberts (1982), he fails to update the theory of permanent revolution to explain the phenomenon of 'confiscation'.

Indeed, this 'confiscation' has been the classic direction of all post-colonial nation states, in one form or another: from Algeria to Zimbabwe, a new ruling class has usurped power (benignly, in the case of Nyerere's Tanzania, and less benignly in the case of Touré's Guinea, or Mugabe's Zimbabwe). Such is the power of international capital to dictate to the most isolationist of post-colonial countries (we need not dwell on the 'successful' examples of extreme isolationism, such as Cambodia and North Korea, for obvious reasons).

There are two dangers here. There is no space here to discuss the first, i.e. the pitfalls of denouncing this situation as 'neocolonial'. The other is that, since 'permanent revolution' did not adequately explain the trajectory of Algeria through the anti-colonial struggle to independence (the exploited masses did not even play a significant political role in liberation, the rural peasants' role being a purely military one), we are necessarily forced to return to a 'stagist' view of social progress, to valorize the nation state, in the manner that Hallward has done. However, the case of Algeria is instructive in rejecting a nation state approach. The Algerian military dictatorship's use of 'national security' after 11 September 2001 to repress the Islamists and thereby all other opposition, while the intense extraction of minerals and the associated lucrative spin-offs continue unabated, is example enough that 'nation state' politics is decidedly shaky. The alternative is to reformulate the permanent revolution theory.

In response to this 'problem' for the theory of permanent revolution, Tony Cliff devised in 1963, in the aftermath of Algerian independence, a crucial modification. Permanent revolution could, in certain situations, be 'deflected' toward a form of state capitalism, rather than socialism; in what we might call a 'post-trotskyist' perspective, Cliff's theory showed how a social revolution could be 'headed off' by a combination of social and political factors (1999, 60–9). In Algeria's case, these factors were subjective, and twofold.

Firstly, after the French army's routing of Algiers in 1957, trade union activity was severely impaired, and an already modest labour movement was now fragmented (contrast this with Russia in 1917, where a similarly modest working class was still able to take power). Secondly, and perhaps more importantly, the question of leadership, on an internationalist and class basis, was sorely lacking, something which C.L.R. James (1980 [1948]) thought he had resolved in his critique of Leninism. Even Fanon's instinctive internationalism was constrained by the 'maoisant' strategy adopted (consciously or not) by the FLN. This *de facto* 'nationalist' approach was compounded by the desperately poor anti-colonialist leadership of the international lynchpin of French colonialism, the French working and peasant classes, led by a French Communist Party keen to maintain links with capitalist power and thus to keep the Algerian liberation struggle at arm's length. (Indeed, there is a neat critique of Communist-Party attempts at keeping struggles isolated in Med Hondo's 1969 film *Soleil O*, where the trade union leader refuses the money given to him from abroad to support a strike in France!). Left to its own devices, isolated politically and internationally, Algeria could not fail to see the potential of social (and not just national) liberation confiscated by a clientelist-industrialist oligarchy (Harbi 2002), which, forty years on, is now happily integrated into the world economic system.

To return to our discussion of Fanon as Atlantic theorist – operating in Algeria, but from a Caribbean perspective – how then does the theory of a permanent revolution apply to the French Antilles, and specifically Martinique, where this revolution has neither been defeated nor deflected, for the simple reason that it has not taken place? Indeed, there is no inevitability about 'deflection': the social (and national) liberation of Martinique will ultimately depend on radical social change in France. As Algeria has shown, a 'liberated' Martiniquan nation state would not be a bulwark against IMF structural readjustment, even though Hallward would have us think otherwise (2001, 132): any national movement for Martiniquan liberation will have to consider this harsh economic fact as part of a permanent revolution to achieve true liberation. Otherwise, we will return to what W.E.B. Du Bois predicted in 1956, and which now pertains in Algeria. In a telegramme to the *Présence Africaine* conference in Paris, he warned that liberation should not 'go backward toward a new colonialism where hand in hand with Britain, France and the United States, black capital enslaves black labour' (cited in Macey 2000, 281).

Conclusion

It is perhaps ironic that we are back where we started with this chapter: the dilemma of examining the persistence of racism or that of imperialism. For what contemporary postcolonial debates around these two issues seem to have in common is precisely a universalist voluntarism, in which harsh political and economic determinants are drastically reduced if not ignored. This tendency is no doubt linked to a critique of essentialism and its attendant fatalism (see, for example, the dismissal of Ian Clegg's work on rural politics in Algeria by Lazarus 1999, 92–3). But it may also be a (para-doxical) form of pessimism. The peoples of Algeria and Martinique – on both sides of the Atlantic – are in no way better off than before the 1950s. In many ways, the situations are worse, except that they are (for what it is worth) 'post-colonial'.

But this cannot be an argument for going backwards either in political terms (to refound a truly independent nation state in both cases) or in theoretical terms (to return to a 'stagist' view of political progress). Therefore, far from the 'deflected' nature of permanent revolution being an internal, arcane argument within Trotskyist Marxism (just as the material roots of racism are not elements of an arcane argument over determinism and freedom), the future of liberation struggles – a 'counter-narrative of liberation', to quote Lazarus (1999, 143) – forty years after the (supposed) end of colonialism and imperialism is no less an imperative for political (and so-called post-colonial) analysis and praxis than it has ever been. The situations in Afghanistan and Algeria, in the ex-Zaire and Zimbabwe are as burning as ever, and suggest that a strictly Francophone understanding of either Fanon or of Atlantic theory is unhelpfully restrictive. Indeed, in the Middle East today, where liberation, new colonialism and violence appear to be deeply Fanonian, here too there is a danger of a 'stages' approach, whereby a two-state solution (imperialist-dominated rather than a secular, liberated Palestine, for Jews and Arabs) is the only (depressingly unrealistic) prospect on offer.

Thus, a 'deflected' view of permanent revolution is not some kind of 'virtual history' – asking, disinterestedly, 'what if?', in the past-conditional tense – precisely because it wishes to intervene in the future: the virtual is no friend of the potential. The only difference today from the decolonization period is that, as with the return of Fascism, we have no excuses for making the same mistakes: history is as present – and future – as ever.

POSTCOLONIAL THOUGHT AND CULTURE IN THE FRANCOPHONE WORLD

16

'Faire peau neuve' – Césaire, Fanon, Memmi, Sartre and Senghor

BY PATRICK WILLIAMS

One of the less remarked-upon aspects of the early phase of Francophone postcolonial theorizing has been the extent to which many of the key texts were written in relation or reaction to other work in the field. It might be something of an overstatement to regard this in the Bakhtinian sense as a fully dialogic space of theoretical production and elaboration, but it is important to counteract the idea of theorizing, especially anti-colonial theorizing, as a solitary practice, not least because the portrayal of opposition as isolated – therefore (implicitly) numerically insignificant, therefore unrepresentative and irrelevant – is very much the colonialist strategy. This interconnectedness could be understood in various ways: as the result of colonized intellectuals making what Edward Said calls 'the Voyage In' to the colonial metropolis (Said 1993); as the effect of the dispersions and displacements of the various stages of the black diasporas; as a natural consequence of the intercontinental flows of what Paul Gilroy has designated the Black Atlantic (Gilroy 1993); or as something a little more prosaic perhaps, such as the kind of linkage envisaged in Édouard Glissant's image of a network of roots floating in the sea, connecting the islands of the Caribbean, and extending beyond them into the world (Glissant 1981).

Among this particular group, the forms of connection are numerous: geographical (Martiniquan origin for Fanon and Césaire; North African location for Memmi and Fanon); disciplinary (background in psychology/psychiatry for Memmi and Fanon); political (varying degrees of left-wing affiliation for each of them); occupational (parliamentary roles for Senghor and Césaire) – though obviously what unites them all is their opposition to colonialism. Against this background, Fanon writes about Césaire and Senghor; Memmi writes about Fanon; Césaire writes about Senghor. At the same time, just as the colonial metropolis provides a focus, a point of connection in the midst of broader spatial movements, so a metropolitan intellectual – Sartre – provides a form of political and intellectual connection for all of these colonized theorists. As well as producing his own anti-colonial work, Sartre writes about all the others – Memmi, Césaire, Senghor, Fanon – and several of them in turn write about him. While the dialogue among the colonized intellectuals ranges from the comradely to the critical, Sartre's interventions are generally supportive, often taking the form of polemical articles or reviews which reappear as prefaces and introductions to the others' texts, promoting both the works themselves and the politics they espouse. The analyses they all produce range from those grounded in personal experience (the Fanon of *Black Skin, White Masks*, or the Memmi of *The Colonizer and the Colonized*) to those which offer a general or systemic critique (Césaire in *Discourse on Colonialism*, Fanon in *The Wretched of the Earth*, Sartre in 'Colonialism is a System'), and, within the space available, this chapter will aim to highlight just a few of the important aspects of this remarkable body of work, and, in particular, one of the less discussed areas of shared concern.

If there is one word in the Francophone postcolonial lexicon which instantiates those aspects to which we referred at the beginning – Black Atlantic or diasporic connections, metropolitan site of production, intellectual 'conversations' (comradely or not) – then that word is 'Negritude' (for discussion of Negritude, see Murphy, Chapter 20). In the half-century and more since the term was first used, it has been repeatedly argued over, often with great bitterness, though, while the arguments have not ceased, the position of some of its fiercest critics, such as Wole Soyinka, may have softened over time. Although Negritude's emergence in the 1930s may appear sudden, shocking or unlooked-for – as it no doubt was to many whites – it was (unsurprisingly) the product both of an ongoing process and of a particular conjuncture: political, cultural and personal. It is associated above all with the writings of Léon Gontran Damas from French Guyana, Aimé Césaire from Martinique and Léopold Sedar Senghor from Senegal, but they in turn were part of broader formations of politicized diasporic intellectuals, particularly in Paris, forming and reforming around groups such as the Ligue Universelle de Défense de la Race Noire, or journals like *L'Étudiant noir*, *La Voix des nègres* and *La Race nègre*. The longevity of the journals varied from *Légitime défense* which only brought out one issue (but nevertheless had a catalytic effect), to the enormously influential *Présence Africaine*, founded in 1947 and still published today. The lifespan of the groups was also variable – and often not extensive. The groups and journals in turn emerged from the broad context of Pan-African thinking and activism. Although the Pan-African movement is frequently regarded as an Anglophone phenomenon because of its association with figures such as W.E.B. Du Bois, George Padmore, C.L.R. James and Kwame Nkrumah, it also belongs to the Francophone world, marked by the fact that the 1919 Congress was held in Versailles.

That the term's first appearance is in a poem – Césaire's remarkable *Notebook of a Return to My Native Land* (1995 [1939]) – rather than a theoretical treatise, is an indication of the importance of the cultural in Negritude's anti-colonial and anti-racist stance, while the political importance of black poetry is forcefully argued by Sartre: 'black poetry in the French language is, in our time, the only great revolutionary poetry' (1988 [1948], 293–4). Although at one level it suits Sartre to be able to claim revolutionary status for Negritude embodied in poetry, it is important to give appropriate weight to such an assessment, bearing in mind that Negritude was subsequently felt by many commentators to represent something like the opposite of a revolutionary position, and was criticized for being – variously – retrogressive, essentialist or complicit with Eurocentric attitudes. While *Notebook of a Return to My Native Land* contains some forthright statements about Negritude, it is perhaps 'Black Orpheus', Sartre's Preface to Senghor's *Anthologie* (1948), which offers the first sustained attempt to theorize the phenomenon, an attempt which has in turn not always been regarded favourably: 'Senghor asked Sartre for a cloak to celebrate Negritude [...]. He was given a shroud' (Mudimbe 1988, 85). However, even if it had been Sartre's intention to stifle it in its infancy (which scarcely seems credible in view of what he says in 'Black Orpheus'), Negritude continued to thrive in the midst of criticism.

Even for Sartre, Negritude can appear contradictory and uncertain: 'Is Negritude necessity or liberty? For the authentic Negro, is it a matter of conduct deriving from essences? [...] Or is one a Negro in the way the religious faithful are believers?' (1988, 326). While Senghor wants to emphasize Negritude as African 'being' (with all its potentially problematic connotations of fixed identity and essential nature), for Sartre it can only make sense as 'becoming', part of a dialectical movement of transformation. In this context, whatever positive qualities Negritude has – and Sartre lists many – its role is to be transitory, a stage on the way to something greater, and it is no doubt this assertion of the need for self-transcendence on the part of Negritude which, if anything, lends support to Mudimbe's accusation. This (apparent) reduction of Negritude to something minor or ephemeral angers Fanon – at least the 'early' Fanon of *Black Skin, White Masks*, where he takes Sartre to task. The fact that Negritude is characterized as 'the minor term of a dialectical progression' (Fanon 1986 [1952], 133) he feels robs him of his last chance of claiming an identity via his blackness; and, while there is no longer an identity to be claimed, there is instead an imposed, pre-given 'meaning' to being black which is experienced as alien and constraining. Arguably, Fanon is misinterpreting Sartre, but the context is the chapter in which Fanon narrates his famous traumatic discovery of 'The Fact of Blackness', his status as Other, less than human, which makes his anger more understandable.

Charges of essentialism and complicity made against Negritude are generally founded on assertions by Senghor such as 'L'émotion est nègre,

comme la raison hellène' [Emotion is completely Negro, as reason is Greek],
or 'Negritude is nothing more or less than the [...] *the African personality*'
(1964, 24; 1993 [1977], 27; emphasis in original) While statements like
these do seem to give ammunition to the enemy, they clearly do not represent the totality of Senghor's views on Negritude. In addition, it is possible
to argue against the charges in various ways. For example, the apparent
complicity with standard colonialist or racist ideology ('Africans are
irrational') in the first quote can be regarded as an early form of that
strategy of appropriation and reversal of negative representations –
famously instantiated in the choice of the term Negritude – which became
so influential in the Black Power movement in the 1960s (with slogans such
as 'Black is beautiful') as well as second-wave feminism, and the gay and
lesbian movements. The essentializing generalization in the second quote
could also be regarded as a particular response to European racism:
'Colonialism did not dream of wasting its time in denying the existence of
one national culture after another. Therefore the reply of the colonized
peoples will be straightaway continental in its breadth' (Fanon 1967 [1961],
171). Fanon (the 'later' Fanon of *The Wretched of the Earth*) here understands the reaction of Senghor and those like him, and goes on to say,
echoing Senghor's words: 'The concept of Negroism [i.e. Negritude] was the
emotional if not the logical antithesis of that insult which the white man
flung at humanity' (1967, 171). Nevertheless, by this point Fanon is very
clear that Negritude represents a dead end, not least because it ignores the
fundamental historical differences not only between African cultures, but
more importantly between Africans and African-Americans, Caribbeans
and others in the diaspora.

Although for Fanon its method and assumptions may be flawed,
Negritude's project of remedying 'that insult which the white man flung at
humanity' is one which all the Francophone post-colonial thinkers share,
and one in which they participate in different ways, on the basis of their
differing theoretical perspectives. 'Who and what are we? Admirable
question', says Césaire (1972 [1955], 93). For black people, having had
their humanity denied for centuries, not least in order to justify the
inhumanity of the slave trade, one of the fundamental acts of post-colonial
resistance is the simple assertion of that humanity. Beyond that, however,
lies the task of analysing and constructing an ontology and an ethics: how
to be, how to behave as fully human. These may be less obvious than they
would appear.

The first step is the necessary rejection or repudiation of white claims to
superiority, and Césaire's *Discourse on Colonialism* is one of the most
remarkable examples of such repudiation. In 'Black Orpheus', Sartre had
examined some of the contradictions involved in black writers like Césaire
using the French language to denounce French racism or colonialism.
Césaire here takes things a stage further as he uses a typically French form –
the literary-philosophical-political essay – as a polemical, broadly high-

cultural weapon with which to destroy the claims of that culture. Césaire's starting point is that 'Europe is morally, spiritually indefensible', and that 'between *colonization* and *civilization* there is an infinite distance' (1972, 10, 11; emphasis in original). One of his principal tactics throughout the essay is to let the French condemn themselves, and he uses a range of writers, from the well known (including Ernest Renan, Jules Romains, Pierre Loti and Roger Caillois) to the completely unknown, to instantiate the varieties of arrogance, greed, racism and cynical brutality which would like to pass themselves off as the incontrovertible truths of white supremacy. For Césaire, it is important not to be taken in by the typical colonialist 'mystifications':

> They talk to me about progress, about 'achievements', diseases cured, improved standards of living.
> I am talking about societies drained of their essences, cultures trampled underfoot, institutions undermined, lands confiscated, religions smashed, magnificent artistic creations destroyed, extra-ordinary *possibilities* wiped out. (1972, 21; emphasis in original)

As well as powerfully reversing the typical colonialist assertion of the barbarism of the colonized, Césaire is concerned to demonstrate that the barbarism is something which Europe has progressively done to itself, that the daily facts of oppression and, even more so, the acts of brutality constitute a gradual slide into a condition of savagery whose apotheosis is Hitler. Rather than being a monstrous aberration, Hitler represents the logical end point of this European process of self-brutalization, and in Césaire's analysis Hitler's real crime in the eyes of Europeans is to have used on them those methods which they had previously reserved for colonized peoples.

The points which Césaire makes are taken up by others: Memmi and Fanon discuss the ways in which colonialism fundamentally damages the colonizer; Memmi argues that, even if the supposed benefits of colonization were a thousand times greater, they could not compensate for the damage done; in 'Colonialism is a System' (2001 [1964]), Sartre uses official French statistics to catalogue the organized impoverishment of the Algerian people by French colonialism (see Haddour, Chapter 6, for further discussion of this text); in 'A Victory' he discusses the (barbaric, systematic) use of torture in Algeria, which, to its shame, his nation refuses to acknowledge; Fanon also discusses torture, based on his experience of treating the psychological traumas of both the French perpetrators and the Algerian victims.

Having demonstrated the ways in which the colonizers dehumanize the colonized (and ultimately themselves) and in so doing destroy any pretensions to moral or cultural superiority, the next step for post-colonial thinkers is to delineate the paths by which the colonized might reassert their humanity. One of the main obstacles here is felt to be the Enlightenment category of humanism. Ostensibly universalist and egalitarian, it in fact operates strategies of exclusion, marginalization and hierarchization. In the name of 'the only race which is denied even the notion of humanity', Césaire rails against a narrow, biased 'pseudo-humanism', typified by Renan who calls for the widening of inequalities between peoples, not their removal (1972, 79), while, from the other side of the colonial divide, Sartre has this to say: 'with us there is nothing more consistent than a racist humanism, since the European has only been able to become a man through creating slaves and monsters' (2001, 151). The construction of the less-than-human slave or the non-human 'monstrous' secures the continuation of the (rather less than universal) 'human'. For Fanon, it is time to '[l]eave this Europe where they are never done talking of Man, yet murder men everywhere they find them' (1967, 251).

From a certain perspective, the process of rehumanization might already be achieved. Senghor, for example, proposes Negritude as the 'humanism of the twentieth century', and, to the extent that Negritude represents an actualized state of being for all black people, then there is no process of reclamation to be gone through, still less any sense of struggle. (This would also be another example of Negritude's problematic preference for static rather than dynamic concepts of identity.) Nothing could be further from Fanon's position, whether existential in *Black Skin, White Masks*, or revolutionary in *The Wretched of the Earth*. In both cases, the path to full human status – achieved, recognized – is long and arduous. In the earlier book, Fanon proposes a form of psychoanalytical practice on a huge scale: his aim is to counteract through critical analysis the alienating effects of white domination on black people. It is important to recognize the kind of shift being attempted here: Fanon takes an individualistic (some would say narcissistic) practice, and turns it into the means of collective liberation, arguing all the while that the grounds of the original alienation are primarily economic, rather than 'merely' a psychological complex. Although his aim is global – 'nothing short of the liberation of the man of colour from himself' (1986, 10) – his principal addressees are those from the Caribbean who have gone further down the road towards assimilating European culture and ideology. To this end, he analyses the myths and ideologies surrounding relations between black women and white men, and black men and white women, and the alienated forms which these relations take. He also devotes a chapter to dissecting Mannoni's theory that only those peoples with a 'dependency complex' end up being colonized – blaming the victims with a vengeance. In a move which recalls the earlier comments on the colonizers dehumanizing both the colonized and themselves, Fanon notes the extent to which both, rather than just the colonized, are alienated by the ideologies to which they are all subject. Each, as he says at the beginning, is 'sealed' into his whiteness or blackness; each requires liberation into a condition of full humanity. In this state where the alienation of one is implicated in the alienation of the other, the struggle for the self-liberation of black people would also entail liberating white people from their position as oppressors. This in turn would mean the emergence of a new humankind, bearers of a new humanism. The double, ultimately universal, process of liberation is the revolutionary reversal of the process of mutual dehumanization put in place by colonialism.

Many aspects of Fanon's analysis of current problems are shared by Memmi, but not his vision of future possibilities. For Memmi, since colonized people are still in the process of finding out who they are, 'to expect the colonized to open his mind to the world and be a humanist and internationalist would seem to be a ludicrous thoughtlessness' (1990 [1957], 201). Nonetheless, the double desire – for a new humanism, and its embodiment in a renewed humanity – runs literally from the first page of *Black Skin, White Masks* to the final words of *The Wretched of the Earth*: 'For Europe, for ourselves and for humanity, comrades, we must turn over a new leaf, we must work out new concepts, and try to set afoot a new man' (1967, 255). Here, the elaboration of an ontology and an ethics by Third-World people must not simply repeat European models, given the disastrous history of the latter, and the work is to be done in the name of, and for the benefit of, everyone – a fact powerfully embodied in the phrase 'faire peau neuve' ('turn over a new leaf', literally 'put on a new skin'), where the blighted racial-colonial epidermal histories and politics of black and white must be transcended for everyone's sake.

The hope centred on a new humanism and a renewed humanity is something Fanon shares with other post-colonial thinkers. In *Discourse on Colonialism*, Césaire, like Fanon, considers Europe currently incapable of foregoing its pseudo-humanism for a truer version, though his vision of a transformed humanity is different in emphasis. Although Césaire was, up until the Soviet invasion of Hungary in 1956, a member of the Communist Party, *Discourse on Colonialism* reads more like a catalogue of the West's moral failings than a Marxist critique of its imperialist practices. At the very end, however, looking (like Fanon) for a source of future salvation, Césaire finds it in a different form of universalism: not a revitalized, though undifferentiated, humankind, but 'the only class that still has a universal mission, because it suffers in its flesh from all the wrongs of history, from all the universal wrongs: the proletariat' (1972, 61). This is a position shared by Sartre in 'Black Orpheus' and elsewhere, and the reason for the downgrading of Negritude which so angered Fanon is that the racial claims of Negritude must give way to the universal class ones of the proletariat. In some ways, ending *Discourse on Colonialism* as he does is quite courageous of Césaire, because he considered that Marxism in general, and the Communist Party in particular, did not give enough weight to the difference which being black made. It also represents a certain form of loyalty, since increasingly the proletariat as typically construed within Marxism (i.e. as the 'urban' proletariat) was no longer regarded as the universal revolutionary class, especially in the Third World, where that role, as Fanon points out, falls to the peasantry.

While there may be something like unanimity among these post-colonial theorists over the need for a new humanism and a transformed humanity, there are relatively few of them who analyse in detail the stages by which these goals might be approached. Fanon is the significant exception here. As already mentioned, *Black Skin, White Masks* offers one model in its deployment and development of psychiatric practices as a process of disalienation on a massive scale. This involves a combination of the identification and analysis of the problems with a demonstration of these to the patients, aiming to change both the patients' behaviour and their understanding of the behaviour of others (with consequent change in the impact of the latter). As Memmi cryptically remarks, 'All analysis is, in the end, effective' (1990, 212). However, while that might have seemed an adequate approach at the beginning of the 1950s (and to someone with Fanon's particular disciplinary background), by the end of the decade, and in the context of a bitter war of national liberation, other methods were clearly called for – though, equally clearly, Fanon did not renounce his belief in the transformative potential of psychiatry. (It hardly needs to be stated that the belief is in psychiatry properly practised: Fanon notes the use of psychiatrists as supposedly friendly 'experts' in the cases of Algerian prisoners – all of whom ended up being guillotined.)

One of the methods by which the colonized peoples reconstitute themselves has led to Fanon being castigated as 'the apostle of violence' on the basis of the first chapter of *The Wretched of the Earth*, though an acknowledgement of violence was hardly confined to him alone: Memmi, for example, says that, rather than being surprised at violent anti-colonial revolts, we should be surprised that they are not more numerous and more violent. Colonialism, Fanon argues, both installs and maintains itself through violence, and its quotidian violence calls forth that of the colonized as the only available means of achieving freedom. Fanon certainly analyses the nature and causes of violence in the colonial context, and concludes – on the basis of solid historical evidence, he would argue – that 'decolonization is always a violent phenomenon' (1967, 27), though he himself was opposed to violence. (Whether the 'violence' of decolonization always and everywhere involves bloodshed is questionable, but Fanon's assessment of its inevitability in the Algerian situation, and others like it, is absolutely right.)

The violent colonial regime involves the creation of two types of people, the colonizer and the colonized. These are, for Fanon, material and ideological constructs, both false and unnatural, especially, perhaps, the colonized in their guise as 'native' or 'nigger'. These false, alienated modes of being must be done away with, and in the circumstances the most likely means of achieving this is revolutionary violence, which has a reconstitutive effect at every level, from the individual to the national and international. Fanon describes the impact on all aspects of the individual, from body rhythms to psychological states: 'At the level of individuals, violence is a cleansing force. It frees the native from his inferiority complex and from his despair and inaction; it makes him fearless and restores his self-respect' (1967, 74). At the level of social class, involvement in the anti-colonial struggle transforms the lumpen proletariat, the supposed dregs of society – and a non-class in effect – into a revolutionary force to fight alongside the new universal class, the peasantry. By this means, some of the most wretched of the earth – certainly some of the most despised – are rehumanized: 'These workless less-than-men are rehabilitated in their own eyes and in the eyes of history' (1967, 104). Another group, alienated and 'déclassé' in their own very different way – the intellectuals – are also brought into the struggle. Fanon's three-stage model, in the chapter 'On national culture', of the transformation of colonized intellectuals from assimilation via critical self-reflection to active participation in liberation is well known and influential. At the level of the nation, the (armed) struggle is the principal means by which national culture in all its forms is revitalized, and by which the nation gradually, eventually, constitutes itself as united, ultimately liberated.

At this decisive stage, two alienated, antagonistic and artificial forms of being – the colonizer and the colonized – cease to exist, because the colonial relationship which brought them into being no longer exists. The 'native' and the 'nigger' disappear with the disappearance of the power of those whose racist representations both constructed and constrained them. More fully human individuals and societies – autonomous and self-constituting – emerge from the ruins of the colonial system. That is Fanon's fervent hope, firm belief, analytical conclusion. It is a profoundly moving vision, but Fanon knows that things are not as simple as that. Firstly, such transfigurations do not merely happen, and Fanon devotes much of *The Wretched of the Earth* to discussing, among others, practical questions such as the need, in the context of the war, to replace 'spontaneity' with careful organization; or the roles of the mass of the people, the party, the intellectuals and the leader; or the problem of the indigenous bourgeoisie (Fanon's particular anxiety for the future).

Secondly, as the historian Basil Davidson says, 'The "transfer of power", in short, was above all a transfer of crisis' (1992, 190). Davidson sees this crisis in thoroughly negative terms, but for Fanon, as for others like Gramsci, crisis is a moment both of danger and opportunity. The danger is represented by the international capitalist system which created colonialism in the first place (and which has not disappeared), and, closer to home, by its ideologically co-opted offspring, the indigenous black bourgeoisie, which, Fanon (correctly) fears, may well become the post-independence ruling class. The opportunity is that things do not have to be like that. The corrupt, 'completely useless' black bourgeoisie are not the inevitable future of the nation, just the likely one, and part of not letting that happen is not regarding the nation – even a free one – as an end in itself. As important as the fight for national liberation is, it is as least as important to internationalize those politics, processes, movements which have created the nation, and to articulate the 'universalizing values' which the freedom struggle has encapsulated. As Fanon says, 'This new humanity cannot do otherwise than define a new humanism both for itself and for others' (1967, 198). At this point in Fanon's work, Francophone postcolonial theory arguably reaches its most powerful synthesis in the setting out of practical political strategies for the present, the internationalizing of anti-colonial and anti-capitalist struggle as the next stage, and finally the glimpsed, visionary, humanized future, all embodied in a language which is by turns descriptive, analytical, poetic.

It remains to sketch just a little of the subsequent fate of the various theorists and approaches, which can be instructive with regard to the vagaries of intellectual fortune and fashion, both within the field of post-colonial studies and, more often, outside it. With the (regrettable) exception of Sartre, all of the theorists discussed here have been acknowledged as significant influences – formative or ongoing – within postcolonial studies; however, the extent to which, and the areas in which, their work is drawn upon varies greatly.

There is an undoubted historical irony in the fact that at the moment when so much effort was being expended in post-colonial analysis grounded in or framed by Sartrean existentialist/humanist Marxism, the intellectual tide, especially in France, was moving in the opposite direction, with the growing influence of the 'objective' structuralism of Lévi-Strauss, and the 'scientific', partly structuralist-inflected, Marxism of Althusser, both of which were antithetical to the humanist assumptions in the work of Sartre and others. Both Lévi-Strauss and Althusser attacked Sartre on the grounds of – among others – subjectivism, ethnocentrism and historicism. At the same time, the anti-ethnocentric and anti-colonial Sartre, the advocate of Third-World liberation, went unnoticed – at least in this particular intellectual battle. Despite the subsequent fall from fashion of both structuralism and Althusser, Sartre has never recovered anything like his former status – and of course in certain quarters the status of Marxist theory and politics in general has sadly declined. (There is an interesting parallel with the situation a couple of decades later, when critics persuaded by the arguments of post-modernism, particularly Lyotard's assertion that the age of the 'grands récits' of human emancipation is definitively over, confronted those, especially from the post-colonial world, for whom such narratives remain a matter both of contemporary relevance and enormous importance.)

Senghorian Negritude, for its part, having endured a lengthy period in the intellectual wilderness, attacked even by those like Fanon who had previously embraced it, has more recently found favour in the general area of black identity politics, specifically, and perhaps somewhat unfortunately, in Molefi Kete Asante's 'Afrocentricity', which takes the putative essentialism of Senghor to extremes. At the same time, some former adversaries have changed their opinions: Wole Soyinka, who coined one of the most famous dismissals of Negritude ('A tiger does not proclaim his tigritude – he pounces') has devoted (perhaps in that very spirit of forgiveness) a substantial part of his recent book, *The Burden of Memory, The Muse of Forgiveness* (1999), to a reassessment of Senghor and Negritude.

Following his impact as a revolutionary thinker in the 1960s, when, as Eldridge Cleaver claimed, 'every brother on a rooftop can quote Fanon', Fanon was neglected in academic circles. Renewed interest in his work came especially with the emergence of postcolonial studies, though a particular moment in the renewal is marked by Homi Bhabha's introduction – 'Remembering Fanon' – to the reissued *Black Skin, White Masks*. Coming in the middle of a decade when academics and critics 'discovered' theory, Bhabha's introduction produced a problematic Fanon, seemingly tailored to Bhabha's own theoretical preferences and the poststructuralism of the moment. That apparent critical opportunism is one of the targets in Henry Louis Gates's 'Critical Fanonism' (1991), though Gates is also concerned about what he sees as the over-inflation of Fanon's importance. Over-inflation or not, critics (especially Anglophone critics) continue to find Fanon the most fertile and inspirational of the early postcolonial theorists.

And what of the great project for a renewed humanity, espousing a new humanism? At the level of post-colonial politics, the project failed as part of the general failure of the broad agenda of social liberation – as opposed to simply national liberation – which Fanon warned about, and which people like Davidson have analysed. At the level of theory – postcolonial and other – the climate of anti-humanism associated with structuralism, and subsequently poststructuralism, was deeply uncongenial to such ideas. At the same time, rather too many critics have been unable to get beyond the simple equating of humanism with the unsatisfactory Enlightenment version, thereby ignoring and jettisoning all that Césaire, Fanon and the others hoped for. One high-profile critic who has courageously stood out against this unfortunate trend has been Edward Said. In the face of repeated criticism for his endorsement of allegedly outdated and discredited concepts, Said has called for a new humanism stripped of 'the unpleasantly triumphalist freight that is carried with it' (1992, 230), and, as he makes clear in *Culture and Imperialism,* his model of humanism is very much that of Fanon and his contemporaries: critical, oppositional, inclusive – one of the most significant legacies of an important generation of thinkers.

17

Contesting contexts: Francophone thought and Anglophone postcolonialism

BY JOHN McLEOD

In 1997 Alec Hargreaves and Mark McKinney published what they believed to be the first collection of essays devoted specifically to minority postcolonial cultures in France. In the introduction the editors noted the dynamism of postcolonial studies in the English-speaking world, while decrying that in France 'the post-colonial problematic is seldom encountered in political or cultural discourse' (Hargreaves and McKinney 1997, 3). In their attempt to formulate a flexible and reflexive notion of the postcolonial that could be applied to the study of French minority cultural activity, Hargreaves and McKinney turned to debates among Anglophone theorists of the post-colonial for their conceptual tools and critical self-consciousness: Homi K. Bhabha, Anne McClintock, Stuart Hall, Ella Shohat, Arif Dirlik, Gayatri Chakravorty Spivak, Kwame Anthony Appiah and others. In so doing, and with an irony no doubt unintended, Hargreaves and McKinney rehearsed an intellectual 'detour' discernible in a number of ground-breaking scholarly works in Anglophone postcolonial studies. So many of the prominent figures in the field are indebted in fundamental ways to a variety of Francophone intellectuals that include in particular Frantz Fanon, Michel Foucault, Jacques Derrida and Jacques Lacan.

For better or worse, Anglophone postcolonial discourse is, according to Robert Young, a 'franglais mixture [that] has enabled the development of a new disciplinary field and theoretical apparatus for the analysis of colonialism' (2001, 18). This chapter aims to think critically about some of the important elements of this mixture. Part of my concern is to reveal the ways in which Anglophone postcolonial scholars are often in a creative and critical dialogue with the work of Francophone thinkers when constructing their models of the postcolonial. Yet this can involve a problematic disregard for the cultural and historical contexts of Francophone thought that is unacceptable to some critics.

Evidence of the critical encounter with Francophone thought can be found at the inception of postcolonialism in Edward Said's *Orientalism* (1978), the publication of which helped to inaugurate the postcolonial as an important and urgent area of study in the Anglophone world (Innes 2000; Loomba 1998; McLeod 2000; Moore-Gilbert 1997). As Bart Moore-Gilbert explains, *Orientalism* 'provided one of the first examples of a sustained application of [French "high theory"] to Anglophone cultural history and textual tradition', yet the nature of that application was always sceptical (1997, 34). Working closely with many ideas from Foucault's *The Order of Things* (1989 [1966]), *The Archaeology of Knowledge* (1972 [1969]) and *Discipline and Punish* (1979 [1975]), Said gave the term 'Orientalism' to a discursive system (especially dominant in the nineteenth century) that produces and conditions what can be said about the Middle Eastern lands known as the Orient (see also Forsdick, Chapter 4, for a discussion of Said). Importantly, Said's model is as much the product of his intellectual frustration with Foucault, which attempts to correct a number of alleged shortcomings, most notably Foucault's apparently Eurocentric enquiries into knowledge and power and lack of an account of historical change. As Said argues in his long and important essay 'Criticism between Culture and System', Foucault's account of power pays too little attention to the agents who seize, hold and use it intentionally. Foucault makes power seem to exist like 'a spider's web without the spider' (Said 1991 [1983], 221). Thus, *Orientalism* is in fact a highly un-Foucauldian attempt to explore 'the dialectic between individual text or writer and the complex collective formation to which [Foucault's] work is a contribution' (Said 1978, 24). Said attempts to reinstall human agency by turning to Gramsci as a corrective to Foucault and mobilizing a Gramscian attention to 'historical blocks, ensembles of relationship done from the perspective of an engaged political worker for whom the fascinated description of exercised power is never a substitute for trying to change power relations within society' (1991, 222). It is peculiar, then, that Said ultimately attends much more closely to the activities of the Orientalists and pays scant attention to the interventions of the colonized subaltern (Ahmad 1992; Porter 1983). Said provides the Foucauldian spider's web with its missing spiders, perhaps; but the ensnared flies remain invisible.

None the less, Said's attempt to deploy French thought in unanticipated ways was ultimately productive despite these failings: in opening up postcolonialism as a field, in asking Western scholars to reconsider the political and colonial contexts of their discipline and of key texts, as well as exposing the shortcomings of Foucault's achievement. In *Culture and Imperialism* (1993), Said replaced Gramsci's work on hegemony with Frantz Fanon's *The Wretched of the Earth* (1967 [1961]) as part of a reconceived attempt to bear witness to acts of resistance and change. Here Fanon is pitted against Foucault as a contemporaneous figure enjoying the same intellectual inheritance but purposefully exploring its relevance to the colonized world. Both

Foucault and Fanon draw upon Hegel, Freud, Nietzsche, Canguihelm, and Sartre, but only Fanon presses this material into anti-authoritarian service, while Foucault is accused of 'ignoring the imperial context of his own theories' (Said 1993, 336). For Said, as for so many others, Fanon comes to occupy moral, not just intellectual, higher ground – he is, perhaps, the most revered figure in Anglophone postcolonialism. Said also focuses on Fanon's warning in 'The Pitfalls of National Consciousness' that anti-colonial nationalism in the hands of the native bourgeoisie may quickly replicate the illiberalism and chauvinism of colonial authority and betray the revolutionary energies of the people. This makes Fanon important as a figure who 'expresses the immense cultural shift from the terrain of nationalist independence to the theoretical domain of liberation' (Said 1993, 324). Although seemingly aware of Fanon's locatedness in the Algerian struggle for independence, Said's manoeuvre threatens to displace Fanon from the bloody world of anti-colonial revolutionary nationalism in order to establish his primacy as a theoretical figure of post-national liberation. Consequently, Fanon's advocacy in *The Wretched of the Earth* of anti-colonial nationalism as a necessary and violent historical force of decolonization becomes of secondary importance. Said's reverential attitude to Fanon may appear sensitive to the specifics of Fanon's revolutionary career, but it actually ends up sacrificing the very contexts of resistance with which *Culture and Imperialism* is so anxiously concerned.

A much more irreverent appropriation of Fanon is found in the work of Homi K. Bhabha. Bhabha's thinking on the discourses of colonialism and postcolonialism (not always easily distinguishable, it has to be said) also owes a debt to Foucault's notion of the discursive system as the conjunction of power and knowledge. Yet Bhabha's theorizing of the operations of the discourse of colonialism is heavily inflected by Lacanian models of the unconscious and Derridean notions of the instability and slipperiness of language. In his collection of essays *The Location of Culture*, Bhabha draws upon the stylistic as well as intellectual resources of Lacan, Derrida, Lyotard and Foucault in an attempt to 'rename the postmodern from the position of the postcolonial' (1994, 175) by demonstrating the ways in which Francophone theory can service an Anglophone postcolonial critical project keen to revise received knowledge in terms of 'the subaltern history of the margins of modernity' (175). It is also, perhaps, a self-conscious attempt to resist empiricist modes of critique – modes that, as Antony Easthope has argued, are identifiable with Anglophone scholarship – deliberately by inflecting an English-language text with Francophone theoretical rhetoricity (Easthope 1998).

There is wilful ahistoricity about Bhabha's writing which might appear contemptuous of the cultural and historical contexts of the materials upon which he draws. Yet an empiricist reading of Bhabha fails to appreciate the spectacular possibilities of his particular version of 'franglais'. For example, his essay on mimicry (1994, 85–92) bewilderingly compresses (among others) Lacan, Freud, Fanon and Foucault, often turning unexpectedly between different thinkers to assemble a challenging collage from their ideas. Although Derrida is never cited during his essay, Bhabha's emphasis on mimicry as betraying the impossibility of fixing a stable image of the colonized subject in the discourse of colonialism is clearly indebted to Derrida's theorizing of the endless deferral of meaning in language. He also borrows Lacan's comment that mimicry, like camouflage, is not an attempt to harmonize with the background, but to blend in by becoming mottled – a 'seeming' rather than an identical copy (85). Mimicry is deemed part of a 'gaze of otherness' that, as Bhabha puts it a couple of pages later, 'shares the acuity of the genealogical gaze which, as Foucault describes it, liberates marginal elements and shatters the unity of man's being through which he extends his sovereignty' (89). Mimicry is also represented punningly as a 'fixation' of the discourse of colonialism: both in the Freudian sense of an obsession, but also in its sedentary sense. For this latter sense Bhabha borrows a quotation from Fanon's *For the African Revolution* (1970 [1964]) concerning the 'fixing' of colonial culture, in order to highlight the insurgent possibilities of the ambivalence of mimicry. So, eventually, when Bhabha writes that '[u]nder cover of camouflage, mimicry, like the fetish, is a part-object that radically revalues the normative knowledges of the priority of race, writing, history' (1994, 91), he simultaneously conjures and fuses in one sentence Lacanian notions of mimicry as camouflage, Freud's theorizing of the unconscious and the fetish, Foucault's genealogical (re)vision of history and Fanon's conception of colonial culture as radically insurgent. It is an extraordinary achievement perhaps, but one where the theoretical freight shouldered by the sentence threatens to overload and even annihilate its 'common sense' – which may be, of course, the point.

Bhabha's style and ideas have come in for heavy criticism by several critics unable or unwilling to see the creative possibilities of such intellectual adventurousness, keen instead to highlight his disregard for historical specificity and the privileging of the textual over the material (Parry 1987; Dirlik 1994). Much of this has centred on Bhabha's irreverent use of Fanon, and the fact that he dares both to critique Fanon's work and displace him from the context of the Algerian independence struggle. Bhabha claims that Fanon shifted 'the focus of cultural racism from the politics of nationalism to the politics of narcissism' (1994, 63). This remark, especially coming after a loving re-reading of Fanon's *Black Skin, White Masks* (1986 [1952]) which also chastises Fanon for turning at its conclusion to a banal existential humanism, seems deliberately to ignore Fanon's later work on the politics of nationalism and national consciousness. Bhabha seems eager to recast Fanon in the guise of a poststructuralist intellectual rather than revolutionary nationalist. In addition, Bhabha praises *Black Skin, White Masks* particularly because 'it rarely historicizes the colonial experience' (1994, 42); in general he has much less to say about Fanon's later work, especially *The Wretched of the Earth*. As Bart Moore-Gilbert argues, this is a way of reading Fanon 'backwards', and 'not so much of "remembering" as "dismembering" Fanon' (1997, 138), while Neil Lazarus argues that Bhabha thus distorts 'the testimony of Fanon's own evolution as a theorist' (1999, 79).

Indeed. But is there a 'true' or 'proper' way of reading Fanon? And why should Fanon be forever trapped within the historical moment of his work's emergence? In his writings on national culture, Fanon argues that the anti-colonial struggle must always shatter the ossification of received culture which is made to pursue new and unexpected directions under transformed circumstances. One might argue that Bhabha's appropriation of Fanon's ideas, wresting them from the Algerian past to the postcolonial present, is 'absolutely' Fanonian in its irreverent attitude to Fanon's hallowed and increasingly sedentary position as a cultural status symbol, walled in by the context of Algerian insurgency. In 'dismembering' Fanon, Bhabha perhaps betrays a specifically migrant tactic of reading Fanon by displacing him from the position of nationalist pedagogue and reinstalling him as a key explorer of the problematics of identity ('narcissism'), arguably the major fixation of the migrant mind. Bhabha applauds the ways in which Fanon attempted but never fully secured 'audacious, often impossible, transforma-tions of truth and value', often by exploring 'the edge' of his own thought which includes Hegelianism, existentialism and psychoanalysis (1994, 41). In this reading Fanon anticipates both the postcolonial migrant, standing at the 'overlap and displacement of domains of difference' (2) questioning the pedagogical authority of received wisdom (Fanon, of course, was also a migrant), and the poststructuralist philosopher attempting (but failing) to think beyond existing structures of knowledge too readily accepted in certain anti-colonial forms of resistance. Fanon comes to act as an interface which happily connects migrant, postcolonial and poststructuralist preoc-cupations – a narcissistic mirror for Bhabha, no less. If Fanon was 'fearful of his most radical insights' (61) and lapsed into existential humanism, then Bhabha seems eager to complete Fanon's unrealized, unfinished project of 'postcolonial contramodernity' (175).

Contrary to Said, then, Bhabha implies that Fanon's work might be cor-rected by, rather than a corrective for, subsequent French poststructuralist thought. The resulting image of Fanon at first seems similar: dismembered from the world of political action and revolutionary struggle and preserved in a kind of theoretical aspic first and foremost as an intellectual, more significant for (in this instance) deconstructing systems of thought rather than taking up arms. But, whereas Said effects this dismembering while seeming to remain obedient to the authority of historical context, Bhabha's reading of Fanon is much more daring, inventive and wilfully provocative in letting Fanon's work happily slip its Francophone moorings in order to create new analytical apparatus appropriate to the border lives of the late twentieth century. Here disobeying context may be a fundamentally impor-tant creative intellectual act – but at the cost of historical context, the price of which some critics remain unprepared to pay.

Gayatri Chakravorty Spivak's work is also noted for its transformative encounter with French poststructuralism (Childs and Williams 1997; Moore-Gilbert 1997), yet there is much less of an attempt to construct a theoretical 'franglais' where different critical influences combine to make new paradigms. In many ways, Spivak's work moves in the opposite direction by placing different intellectual traditions together not for the purpose of a new 'mixture' but to bring each other into crisis. As the English translator of Derrida's *Of Grammatology* (1976 [1967]), it should be no surprise that Derrida is a significant influence and a frequent source of inspiration. Deleuze and Guattari, Foucault, Kristeva, Lacan and Cixous are also important figures in her writing – yet so too are Marx, Engels, Gramsci, Rorty and others: Francophone thought is only one facet of Spivak's intellectual heritage. Spivak's enthusiasm for Derridean deconstruction contests the views of other postcolonial critics, such as Edward Said, who have argued that a Derridean approach 'will finally be unable to get hold of the local material density and power of ideas as historical actuality' (1991, 212). The opposition between the 'textualist' concerns of deconstruction and the 'materialist' concern of historicist or empiricist criticism is something that Spivak's work (like Bhabha's) forcefully and importantly attempts to break down.

Spivak frequently adopts a deconstructive approach as a way of laying bare the possibilities and limits of French theory for the study of postcolonial contexts, as well as enabling postcolonial contexts to cast critical light on poststructuralist theory – as in her essay 'A Literary Representation of the Subaltern: A Woman's Text from the Third World' (1987, 241–68) which reads the Bengali writer Mahasweta Devi's story 'Stanadayini' in part to expose the possibilities and limitations of 'First World' critical theory when engaging with 'Third World' texts. In probably her most influential essay 'Can the Subaltern Speak?' she juxtaposes a reading of Foucault and Deleuze with a discussion of nineteenth-century colonial attitudes towards 'sati', the practice of 'widow-burning' (1993a [1988]). In a Derridean spirit she warns against benign postcolonial attempts to retrieve the voice of the marginalized or subaltern, such as Indian women, from colonialism's archives, pointing out that the critic's approach will be inevitably overdetermined by the very structures of knowledge which rendered the subaltern as other in the first place. There exists no context untouched or uncompromised by the available structures of knowledge within which the subaltern as female can speak for herself, or be heard, on her own terms.

Of particular relevance to this chapter is Spivak's attention to the problems of translation. Spivak constantly attends to the difficulties in using translations in her work, not least because English struggles to capture adequately the French or German as she understands it. Often when quoting she resorts to inserting the source-language words in square brackets next to their English translations, and on many occasions she points out the inadequacy of the English translation of non-English terms. In an essay on

Foucault she complains that '[i]t is a pity that there is no word in English corresponding to *pouvoir* as there is "knowing" for *savoir*. *Pouvoir* is of course "power". But there is also a sense of "can-do"-ness in "*pouvoir*", if only because, in its various conjugations, it is the commonest way of saying "can" in the French language' (1993c, 34; emphasis in original). At such important moments Spivak complicates the appropriation of Francophone thought in Anglophone scholarship by hinting at the incommensurability between the source text and its translation. Anglophone scholars must beware working with ideas that are coded in a language which does not deliver the specifics of, in this instance, Foucault's thinking.

Spivak's meticulous attention to the inadequacy as well as necessity of translation reminds us that French theory as it is received, translated, understood and mobilized in Anglophone criticism may not be coincident with French theory in Francophone contexts. As Spivak puts it in her essay 'The Politics of Translation', 'the rhetorical nature of every language disrupts its logical systematicity' (1993c, 180). If language's 'logic' is that which allows us 'to jump from word to word by means of clearly indicated connections' (181), as I read it 'rhetoricity' functions in the opposite (Derridean) direction as a principle of 'random contingency' (180) that is part of the condition of possibility of that language, and unique to that language itself. In rhetoricity one finds ethics, agency, politics. These are effaced in a translation that prioritizes the production of logic at the expense of rhetoricity, and thus effaces the conditions of knowing out of which the original emerges. Spivak's essay serves as a warning that the Anglophone appropriation of French thought threatens to efface the specific conditions and contingencies of its emergence – one thinks immediately, perhaps, of Said's and Bhabha's appropriations of Fanon.

Wary of the thoughtless appropriation of Francophone thought, one that erases the conditions of its possibility, recent Anglophone postcolonial criticism has tended to approach historical and cultural contexts with much more sensitivity. Neil Lazarus has attempted to rescue Fanon's writings from the irreverent clutches of poststructuralism by returning them to the primary scenario of anti-colonial Algerian nationalism (1999, 68–122). Pleasingly, Lazarus's work on Fanon escapes glib genuflection and meditates critically on Fanon's ideas. Yet it remains caught up in a wearisome opposition in Anglophone postcolonial studies which has tended to feature critics sensitive to contextual specifics and sympathetic to Marxism and nationalism siding against poststructuralist models of the postcolonial deemed fatally compromised by their enthusiasm for Francophone thinking and alleged disregard for historical specifics (Ahmad 1996; Dirlik 1994; Lazarus 1999). The assumption that the Anglophone appropriation of Francophone thought, especially poststructuralism, sacrifices valuable material contexts and maintains the First World intellectual occupation of the Third remains at large, as in Arif Dirlik's complaint that postcolonial theory involves 'a reduction of social and political problems to psychological ones, and [...] the substitution of post-structuralist linguistic manipulation for historical and social explanation' (1994, 333).

One initiative, pursued by Robert Young, has attempted to uncover the inseparability of Marxian anti-colonial thought and French poststructuralism and go beyond this impasse – although not without controversy. This has involved a concerted attempt to establish the proper contexts for the writings of Fanon, Foucault, Derrida and others. In his *White Mythologies* (a title purloined from Derrida) Young points out that Sartre, Althusser, Derrida and Lyotard were all either born in Algeria or involved in the events of the war, before turning to Cixous's account of growing up as an Algerian French Jewish girl at the time (1990, 1–2). Just as Cixous claims that her critique of Western metaphysics is indebted to her childhood exposure to the arrogance of white French power in the colonized world, Young claims poststructuralism is also a direct intellectual product of the Algerian struggle for independence. French poststructuralism is deemed to discover its conditions of possibility wholly within the contexts of postcolonialism. In wiring up poststructuralism and postcolonialism so tidily, Young effectively short-circuits any alleged incompatibility between each paradigm.

This is an ingenious argument, but it runs into problems in Young's most recent book *Postcolonialism: An Historical Introduction* (2001). Several problems emerge in the remarkably deterministic narrative that is made concerning a thinker's identity or the location of their work, and the nature of the work itself. Young situates Foucault's life and work in the context of the Maghreb, and points out that he wrote *The Archaeology of Knowledge* while lecturing at the University of Tunis between 1966 and 1968 and living in the village of Sidi-Bou-Saïd (2001, 396). For Young, this book is one of the 'greatest examples of an ethnology of European institutional practices of power' (397) which aligns Foucault with those other exiled intellectuals writing critically about the country from which they are displaced. Rather than condemn Foucault for never writing explicitly about colonialism and race, Young presents an image of Foucault as involved in a form of critical intellectual work fundamentally indebted to, if not indeed formed by, postcolonial realities. This is in stark contrast to Said's complaint in *Culture and Imperialism* that Foucault never engages with French colonialism and resistances to it.

Young considers the significance of Foucault for Said, and suggests that the notion of discourse developed in *The Archaeology of Knowledge* has been misunderstood. Whereas Foucault's challenging model of discourse is concerned with the materiality of language, the ways in which languages and institutions intersect, in *Orientalism* Said understands discourse in the narrower sense as 'representations' and offers merely a reading of a number of imaginative texts, the materiality of which is lost in a more conventionally literary form of enquiry. Said's legacy has been to inaugurate a profoundly non-Foucauldian textualism in postcolonial theory where individual creative acts of the imagination are casually renamed as 'discourses', without any sustained attention to institutional or material systems. Hence, those that regard the textualist bent of postcolonial theory as an inevitable consequence of its Francophone influences are profoundly mistaken. In a remark which recalls Spivak's warnings about translation, Young suggests that the Anglophone appropriation of French theory has misrepresented Foucault, and '[t]he irony is that Foucault's own model of discourse in *The Archaeology of Knowledge* could be said to answer many of the fundamental objections that are made against colonial discourse' (394).

Perhaps. But Young neglects Said's placing of a Foucauldian attention to discursive systems quite deliberately in a dialectical relationship with the individual writer or text, although Foucault's work would scarcely admit the possibility of any such dialectic in the first place. If Said gets Foucault 'wrong' (which seems to be the case), then Young gets Said 'wrong' in neglecting Said's dialectical attempt to go beyond Foucault. Young wants Said to respect his French antecedent to the letter – to stay within Foucault's Francophone limits – but this makes it hard for him to value the specifics of Said's translative project. Advocates of context-sensitive criticism must beware blinding themselves to the creative potential of 'travelling theory' which, as Anglophone postcolonialism vividly demonstrates, can be enormously and urgently creative in breaking and making intellectual paradigms (Said 1991, 226).

Young also attempts to contextualize Derrida in relation to French postcolonial realities which are deemed the most important influence upon his work. In a chapter titled 'Subjectivity and History: Derrida in Algeria', Young seems to address Derrida directly and claims to have been conscious of Derrida's postcoloniality even before Derrida: 'when I sent you a copy of *White Mythologies* you remarked that I had indeed detected "a thread" that ran through your writings. [. . .] I knew it all along, for you showed it to me in your writings from the first' (2001, 412). Much is made of Derrida's childhood as a Jewish boy growing up and schooled in Algeria, arriving in Paris very much as an outsider to French culture in ways which recall Frantz Fanon's arrival from Martinique. It is then a short distance from the disorders of Derrida's identity to his subsequent deconstructive methods of bringing Western philosophy to crisis. So, with Derrida safely installed as a 'colonized subject', a 'Marranized crypto-Jew, coming from Algeria' who dares 'to challenge the canonical traditions of the west' Young proceeds to make a number of reorientations of poststructuralism (419, 425). Poststructuralism came 'from the south' and is better thought of as 'Franco-Maghrebian theory' (413, 414). It has been 'a form of cultural and intellectual decolonization', born entirely among French colonials and pitted against the propriety of Western rationality (421). Deconstruction becomes quintessentially postcolonial; and because Derrida is deemed to speak the same language as the oppressed minorities, his writing 'reconceptualized the world from their perspective and asserted the power of the marginalized in the heartlands of western institutions' (426).

These are major claims, to be sure, but one might be uncomfortable with the way Derrida is placed alongside people like Fanon simply because he 'like so many of those who led the independence movements, travelled to the imperial capital for [his] university education' (422). This is a point of resemblance, no doubt, but Derrida has (to my knowledge) never led an independence movement nor been involved in an armed struggle alongside the wretched of the earth against their oppressors – which is not to invalidate Derrida's work, of course, but to point out the differences between his intellectual project and the resistance of others. Where is Young's sensitivity to context now? Also, if Derrida is a colonized subject (and Cixous, and others), is he colonized in the same way and with the same consequences as Fanon, Aimé Césaire or Léopold Senghor? Young's attempt to recontextualize French poststructuralism may be inversely analogous to Bhabha's provocative resituating of Fanon, while the second-person address of the chapter might suggest that Young's intention is laced with levity for polemical effect. Yet he remains in danger of resurrecting a remarkably glib notion of context in his attempt to make poststructuralism postcolonial, one that in many ways short-circuits the creative innovations of so many Anglophone postcolonial thinkers.

As we have briefly seen, Anglophone postcolonial scholarship has been fundamentally inspired by French thought and remains in critical dialogue with it – it is certainly a 'franglais' – but the issue of context and the legitimacy of Francophone thought remains a problem for some. A definite wariness has arisen in Anglophone appropriations of the Francophone today, in part created by the often deliberately decontextualizing propensity that has come to be identified with much Anglophone postcolonial theory. But it seems inappropriate to rule out all such encounters on the grounds that French and British colonial contexts are incommensurable and thus that one is being ahistorical or disrespecting context when using Francophone thought in Anglophone postcolonialism; although contexts are not to be simply ignored. As Edward Said rightly argues, '[l]ike people and schools of criticism, ideas and theories travel – from person to person, from situation to situation, from one period to another' (1991, 226). Hargreaves's and McKinney's recent welcome initiative is another passage on a continuously exciting series of fertile exchanges from which postcolonialism – Anglophone and Francophone – draws so much of its creative energy.

|18|

Francophone women writers and postcolonial theory

BY ANNE DONADEY

Postcolonial theory has overwhelmingly been an English studies endeavour. Originating from Commonwealth studies, it has tended to take as its object of inquiry any works from the former British empire, as well as any works written in English that even remotely deal with issues of colonization. Thus, former white settler colonies such as Canada, Australia, and New Zealand have been included from the beginning (Ashcroft *et al.* 1989) in spite of subsequent criticisms (McClintock 1993 [1992]). More recently, questions as to the postcoloniality of the United States have been at the forefront (King 2000; Singh and Schmidt 2000). The majority of postcolonial theorists and critics themselves originate from former British colonies. A few of them do comparative work in languages other than English.

The most important influence of the Francophone sphere on postcolonial studies has been Martiniquan political theorist, psychiatrist and activist Frantz Fanon, a precursor whose works have become enshrined in post-colonial studies (Bhabha 1983, 1986 and 1994; Gates 1991; Lazarus 1993). Another major French-language import has been poststructuralist theory, which has intertwined very closely with postcolonial theory (Lacan and Bhabha, Derrida and Spivak, Foucault and Said). Strangely enough, very few postcolonial theorists have taken into account the works of Francophone writers and philosophers besides Fanon. Founder of the Negritude movement Aimé Césaire is occasionally mentioned, as is Fanon's contemporary Albert Memmi, but more recent thinkers such as Moroccan Abdelkebir Khatibi and Martiniquan Édouard Glissant – major influences on Francophone studies – have been strangely ignored by postcolonial theory, even though their theoretical insights make a major contribution to the study of linguistic and cultural hybridity with which postcolonial studies so largely concerns itself (Lionnet 1989). Khatibi and Glissant are both creative writers and theorists, but only a selection of Glissant's most influential theoretical treatises have been translated into English (1989, 1997a) and Khatibi's central theoretical work, *Maghreb pluriel*, still remains untranslated (on this subject, see also Woodhull, Chapter 19). Both Francophone literature – whether by women or men – and Francophone studies as an academic field are equally ignored by postcolonial theory, with several significant exceptions such as the work of Appiah (1992), Lionnet (1989, 1995a), Miller (1990, 1998), Spivak (1992, 1993a, 1994), and Trinh (1989). In turn, with the exception of Lionnet's pathbreaking work, Francophone studies as a field is only slowly beginning to interface with postcolonial theory (Britton 1999; Donadey 2001; Miller 1998; Murdoch 2001; Murphy 2002).

Given this situation, it may be more accurate to speak of a certain confluence of interests between Francophone women writers and postcolonial theory, rather than a direct contribution of the former to the latter. Lionnet and others argue that fiction by black and postcolonial women writers performed 'the kind of cultural critique which some contemporary philosophers later set out to theorize' (1995b, 169). Similarly, bell hooks notes that '[l]ong before feminist theorists began to think in terms of race, gender, and class, black women writers had created work that spoke from this previously unarticulated standpoint' (1999, 200). This is what Barbara Christian (1990) calls 'theorizing'; in other words, this literature anticipated many of the findings of postcolonial theory. It should be therefore read as theorizing, as a first articulation of problems, as a hermeneutic gesture.

I will first discuss two areas in which postcolonial theory could profitably learn from the theorizing of Francophone women writers: the first is postcolonial theory's lack of a focus on gender issues, which is particularly evident in the work of Homi Bhabha (although the same criticism could be levied at many others). Another blind spot of postcolonial theory is its single-minded emphasis on issues of hybridity and its concomitant distaste for national(ist) narratives, which have the consequence of ignoring a whole range of issues relevant to postcolonial nations and making migrant literature the only true representative of postcolonial concerns (Lazarus 1993; Miller 1998, 1–7; Spivak 1999, 255–6). I will then focus on a central postcolonial theorist, Gayatri Spivak, whose comparative work has engaged both Anglophone and Francophone theoretical and literary productions. This discussion will show the confluence of interests between her works and those of a major Francophone woman writer, Assia Djebar.

Gender and postcoloniality

While there is a growing corpus of feminist postcolonial theorists such as Spivak, Mohanty, Trinh, Lionnet, Mani, Loomba, McClintock and Stoler, most of the male critics have yet to address gender issues. Bhabha, for one, repeatedly – and literally – relegates gender to a footnote. Cixous's remark that the footnote can be seen as 'a typographical metaphor of repression' is pertinent here (1976, 537). A perfect illustration is the only footnote to

Bhabha's essay 'Remembering Fanon' (1986, xxvi), to which a few brief comments on gender and Fanon are relegated. Both Bergner (1995, 84–5) and McClintock (1997, 95–6) comment on the process of deferral of gender at work in the footnote. Parts of this essay are reprinted in Bhabha's 'Interrogating Identity' (1994, 40–65), but here, the revelatory footnote has disappeared. In 'The Other Question', class joins gender in the list of deferred topics in the first footnote (Bhabha 1983, 18). The itinerary of this footnote is interesting. It was already present in an early version of the essay, as Robert Young notes – also in a footnote (Young 1990, 210). In the reprint of 'The Other Question' in *The Location of Culture*, the footnote itself has disappeared. The trace of the repressed has once again been erased. While Bhabha begins the essay by mentioning the importance of 'an articulation of forms of difference – racial and sexual', in the very next paragraph this double articulation has symptomatically morphed into 'forms of racial/ cultural/historical otherness' (1994, 67).

The trace of the repressed reappears in another significant place in Bhabha's work. In 'The Other Question', he analyses Fanon's chapter 'The fact of Blackness' in *Black Skin, White Masks* in terms of a racial primal scene. Whereas Freud postulated a sexual primal scene – the moment in which the child witnesses/fantasizes his (gender inflexion intended) parents engaging in the sexual act, Fanon, according to Bhabha, borrows this model to apply it to the situation of a black man who discovers the overdeterminations of his skin colour in a white context. For Fanon, this racial primal scene is encapsulated in the first time he hears a white child exclaiming within his earshot: 'Look, a Negro!'. Like the sexual primal scene, this racial primal scene causes its protagonist to experience disorientation, nausea (a term repeated twice by Fanon), and shame (repeated six times in the French original). The exclamation 'Look, a Negro!' takes on the force of an incantation in Fanon's chapter, as it is repeated nine times in the first five pages (in the French original). In 'The Fact of Blackness', this white child is explicitly gendered as male three times (1986, 114). Yet, in Bhabha's version, the male perpetrator has turned into a female one (1983, 28)! The slip – which is repeated twice in Bhabha's text – is present again in the reprint of this important essay in *The Location of Culture* (Bhabha 1994, 76; see Bergner 1995, 86 n.14; and Holmlund 1991, 7–8).

This slip is part of a broader difficulty Bhabha has in conceptualizing gender issues in general. His only discussion of the topic in 'The Other Question' is in criticism of an essay by Stephen Heath for too strong a focus on gender difference. In this critique, which ironically could be applied to his own work as well, Bhabha comments that 'seeing only one possible articulation of the differential complex "race-sex"' prevents one from seeing the 'collusion between racism and sexism as a *mixed economy*' (1994, 69; emphasis in the original). Monistic articulations of difference and oppression are problematic in both the feminist and postcolonial contexts. They are barriers to an understanding of the specific situations of women 'of colour' and women in the 'Third World' (King 1990). Perhaps one reason for Bhabha's inability to include gender in an otherwise dazzling analysis of the colonial stereotype has to do with his analogical reading of Freud (which he borrows from Fanon). Sexual articulations of the primal scene, fetishism, desire and the regime of the scopic drive are translated – literally carried across – into racial ones. While this rearticulation of psychoanalysis goes a long way towards illuminating the complex role of racial stereotypes in colonial discourse and in identity formation, it also follows its psychoanalytic model in its inability to account for female subjectivity. Whereas Fanon's use of a psychoanalytic framework leads him explicitly to objectify female desire and bolster male subjectivity, in Bhabha, the apparent absence of the subject, or its transparency, returns as male (see Holmlund 1991, 1–2, 6–8; King 1990; Stepan 1986; Burnham 1994).

Bhabha chooses to focus on Fanon's earlier work for two main reasons. The first is disciplinary. *Black Skin, White Masks* makes a psychoanalytic argument that reorients Lacan's insights to shed light on the psychology of the colonial context. Fanon also uses literary texts to support his position. In turn, Bhabha is working at the intersection of psychoanalysis and literary analysis. The main reason for Bhabha's preference, however, is that *Black Skin, White Masks* is a much more ambivalent text than Fanon's later work, *The Wretched of the Earth*. Since Bhabha is intent on demonstrating the internal ambivalence of colonial discourse, he must shy away from Fanon's last book (Donadey 2001, xxii–iv; see also P. Williams, Chapter 16, and McLeod, Chapter 17). In so doing, he is also avoiding the issue of violence, which Fanon dealt with in a controversial manner in *The Wretched of the Earth*. In contrast, Francophone women writers have taken up issues of violence and written back to Fanon. Not only have they contended with colonial violence (Lacrosil 1961; Bugul 1983; Djebar 1985; Donadey 2001), they have also brought to the forefront a variety of other types of violence, particularly sexual and familial, which Fanon never thought of addressing (Schwarz-Bart 1972; Beyala 1987, 1988; Djebar 1992 [1980]; Pineau 1995; Kalisa 1999).

It is interesting to note that academic feminism has been more readily interested in Francophone women writers than postcolonial studies. For example, Mariama Bâ's *So Long a Letter* (1981 [1979]) is taught in many Women's Studies classes in the US, to the extent that it has become a somewhat emblematic text in the field. The politics of such inclusion are, however, problematic. Bâ's book is often taught in ways that tokenize it as the only text from Africa or the Muslim world – or the only literary text – on the syllabus. While *So Long a Letter*, with its focus on gender issues, has received such attention, a novel such as Aminata Sow Fall's *The Beggars' Strike* (1981 [1979]), which presents women's issues as being intricately connected to neocolonialism, religion, economic and class issues, is rarely taught in Women's Studies and is now out of print in its English translation, despite the fact that both books have generated a large number of critical articles. In spite of such problems, the broader influence of academic feminism on the study of Francophone women writers has been a positive one overall. The literary output of Francophone women writers – which has been increasing in both quantity and quality since the 1970s – is now central to the field of Francophone studies in the US. Indeed, it is one of the few fields in which there is parity in the critical attention directed toward female and male writers.

Home and migration

Feminist theory has shown that one's location is inexorably bound up with one's perspective, an important insight with respect to the question of 'home' versus 'diasporic' intellectuals. Vijayasree argues that many of the themes developed by postcolonial theorists and writers – a focus on 'multiple and shifting identities' (1996, 225), difference, ambivalence, hybridity, displacement, home and homelessness, an 'almost obsessive preoccupation with the past' (226) – are also the function of an 'expatriate consciousness' (222; see also Shohat 1992, 108–9; and Hall 1994, 402). For historical and political reasons, postcolonial women writers often tend to be diasporic. Exile is unfortunately more and more common among Algerian intellectuals, male and female, as violence has escalated there since 1992 (see Woodhull, Chapter 19). Some diasporic writers such as Djebar primarily locate their fiction in Algeria and highlight Algerian issues, others like Sebbar focus on the situation of migrants in France, refiguring dominant versions of homogeneous Frenchness into a patchwork of heterogeneous (European and non-European) migrations (Djebar 1985, 1992; Sebbar 1982, 1984).

I see a diasporic literature of 'métissage' as being one of two main types of postcolonial literature. I would call the other type national postcolonial literature. In this second category of texts, the problematics of hybridity are much less central. This literature tends to emphasize issues of national importance such as neocolonialism, governmental corruption, women's issues, poverty, unemployment and social problems. Works representative of this second type of postcolonial literature include those of Anglophone writers Ama Ata Aidoo from Ghana and Tsitsi Dangarembga from Zimbabwe, and of Francophone authors Aminata Sow Fall and Ousmane Sembene from Senegal (see Murphy, Chapter 20, for a discussion of Sembene's work). They also tend to have a more Marxist approach to issues, which may explain postcolonial theory's lack of interest in this literature overall.

'Can the Subaltern Speak?'

A critic who has engaged both forms of postcolonial literature, the diasporic and the national, is Gayatri Spivak. In one of her most famous essays, 'Can the Subaltern Speak?', Spivak braids three strands of argument into a negative response to the question posed in her title. To begin with, she focuses on the double meaning of the term 'representation', both as 'Vertretung' (the political sense of proxy, speaking for, substitution, and persuasion) and as 'Darstellung' (the artistic or economic sense of portrait, trope, staging, signification, or scene of writing) (1993a, 70–4). She also discusses the dangers inherent in having intellectuals pretend that their position is transparent and that they can let the oppressed speak for themselves (73–90). Finally, she makes the controversial statement that in an overdetermined context, between the twin discourses of imperialism and nativism, the subaltern woman cannot speak (93–104).

Spivak thus rejects the idea that subalterns can speak for themselves unproblematically outside of representation, because this would 'restore the category of the sovereign subject' (73) which, like Bhabha, she is bent on deconstructing. She argues that the idea of subaltern speech generally elides the intellectual's position as mediator between the subaltern and the public. Indeed, this issue is crucial not only in the context of white, first-world women mediating the voice of the 'subaltern', but also in the context of postcolonial nations such as Algeria in which the woman from the educated elite wonders how to speak to and 'close to' rather than for or about subaltern women (Djebar 1992, 2).

For Spivak, the task of the female intellectual is not to speak for the subaltern, but to expose the mechanisms by which she is silenced: 'The point is not to recover a lost consciousness, but to see [...] the itinerary of the silencing rather than the retrieval' (1990a, 31). The female intellectual must also learn to speak to the subaltern woman in ways that will make sense to her and will engage with her issues (1990a, 42, 56). The strong wording, 'The subaltern cannot speak' (1993a, 104), illuminates both Spivak's allegiance to deconstruction and her impatience with the avalanche of books titled '... Women Speak' (1986, 229). She does not seem to believe that it is possible to destroy or go outside the imperialist/patriarchal script. Rather, in good deconstructive fashion, Spivak feels that one can only undermine or unsettle this script from within. Young rightly points out that '[t]he problem is not that the woman cannot speak as such, that no records of the subject-consciousness of women exist, but that she is assigned no position of enunciation' (1990, 164). In the Algerian context, for example, women's participation in the war of national liberation (1954–62) can be interpreted as a subaltern instance because it is ideologically represented in ways that are overdetermined both by imperialist and nativist patriarchal discourses. Djebar's works seek to create a mediated position of enunciation for Algerian women while navigating prior overdeterminations.

There is a certain kind of ambivalence in Spivak between making such radical statements as 'the subaltern cannot speak', presumably putting all postcolonial women writers in the category not of the subaltern, but of the indigenous elite, and her repeated insistence on the works of two postcolonial women writers, Djebar and Mahasweta Devi, who do much more than trace 'the itinerary of the silencing' of the subaltern woman (Spivak 1990a, 31). I have shown elsewhere how Djebar focuses on the gaps and silences of history and reinscribes women (including 'subaltern' women) into history while foregrounding her own status as mediator in the process (Donadey 2001, 43–62). Subaltern voices are present in her texts, although always in mediated form, which leads one to wonder to what extent there is not some nostalgia for unmediated speech at play when Spivak claims that 'the subaltern cannot speak'.

Spivak is of course using the term as a catachresis,[1] in a metaphorical way that, in Gramsci's definition of the term subaltern, allows it to accommodate different concepts of oppressed and exploited classes (the urban proletariat, peasant women, tribal people, the scheduled castes, the colonized) (see Young 1990, 159–60). This is the way historians from the Subaltern Studies group in India have defined the term. The word 'subaltern' thus operates much like the concept of the 'Other' in philosophy and theory – although, as Spivak herself points out, 'subaltern' does not mean the same thing as the 'Other', which is more of a theoretical concept (2000, xx). To use an analogy, the 'subaltern' appears to be to the 'elite' what the 'Other' is to the 'Same' (Spivak 1999, 271). In spite (or perhaps because) of the fact that the term subaltern can refer to so many different groups, it also exhibits a certain fixity in Spivak's text, which is probably what leads Parry to critique it as monolithic (1987, 35). Indeed, in a revised version of 'Can the Subaltern Speak?' Spivak draws a distinction between the '"true" subaltern group' (the non-elite) and an intermediate group that would be composed of those in an indeterminate situation, for example belonging to the elite in terms of class and to the subaltern in terms of gender (1999, 272–3).

Spivak's powerful formulation is marred by what could be interpreted as a dismissal of both everyday and organized resistance through a rhetorical move that leads her to argue that as soon as the subaltern begins to speak and be heard, s/he is no longer a subaltern (presumably, s/he would then become an (elite) intellectual, who must in turn avoid 'speaking for' other subalterns). The formulation is useful in that it is a way to remind those who speak up always to remain vigilant, but it also returns us to a binary division between intellectual and subaltern that I find somewhat problematic. It is not because a 'subaltern' speaks up and begins to be heard that her material conditions of existence suddenly change for the better. Focusing on lack of speech or lack of being heard as the sole marker of the subaltern denies that the exploitation of the 'subaltern' who speaks will most likely continue, and

---

[1]   Spivak (1999) defines catachresis in the following ways: 'abuse or perversion of a trope or metaphor' (14); 'a false but useful analogy' (179); 'a (conceptually) false metaphor, and/or a (metaphorically) compromised concept' (322). In an earlier essay, she defined it as '[a] concept-metaphor without an adequate referent' (1990b, 225).

elides the dangers of violent repression s/he will most likely incur as well. Finally, to say that the subaltern cannot speak or be heard leads to the question of who cannot (or will not) hear her. Who is the implied 'deaf' audience? Spivak suggests that the 'subaltern' cannot be heard by the hegemonic dominant, i.e. within imperialist and patriarchal parameters. The question of whether the subaltern is heard by other subalterns does not seem to be an issue. Loomba notes: 'To say that if the subaltern could speak she/he would not be a subaltern is a neat enough formulation, but somewhat inadequate if the "Third World" is not to be, yet again, theorized into silence' (1994, 320). For her, 'the choice between [...] romanticizing subaltern resistance or effacing it is not particularly fertile' (308).

Of all of Spivak's work, the essay on the subaltern is the one that has generated the most commentary (Moore-Gilbert 2000; Parry 1987; Varadharajan 1995, 90–9; Young 1990, 163–73). Responding to scholars such as Parry who criticized her position for its pessimism, Spivak revised the essay in *A Critique of Postcolonial Reason*. In particular, she deleted the sentence that had drawn the most fire, 'There is no space from which the sexed subaltern subject can speak' (Spivak 1993a, 103; 1999, 306) and called that remark 'inadvisable' (1999, 308). Her conclusion attempted to be more optimistic about the possibility of subaltern speech, while still highlighting the potential complicity of the postcolonial elites as well as that of First World feminist and liberal intellectuals in the silencing process (1999, 309).

In the last instance, Spivak's essay is more powerful in what it has to say to the intellectual (researcher, activist, leader) than about the subaltern, which is consistent with her refusal of 'speaking for' (Moore-Gilbert 2000, 464). In the preface to her translation of some of Mahasweta Devi's short stories, Spivak elaborates on the task of the intellectual vis-à-vis the subaltern. S/he must:

> establish ethical singularity with the subaltern [which] is neither 'mass contact' nor engagement with 'the common sense of the people'. [...] [T]he responses come from both sides: this is responsibility and accountability. [...] [I]t is impossible for all leaders (subaltern or otherwise) to engage every subaltern in this way, especially across the gender divide. This is why *ethics is the experience of the impossible.* [...] *[T]here is no victory, but only victories that are also warnings.* [...] I look for post-colonial woman [*sic*] writers cognizant of the aporias or ethico-historical dilemmas in women's decolonization. (1995, xxiv–vii; my emphasis)

In the overture to her *Women of Algiers in their Apartment*, Djebar called for a new way of relating to Spivak's 'subaltern' women: 'not to claim to "speak for" or, worse, to "speak on", but barely speaking *next to*, and if possible *very close to*' (1992, 2; italics in the original). Djebar's entire work reflects the impossibility of letting the 'Other' woman speak outside of the circulation of power, especially in a postcolonial context. The Algerian author's heightened awareness of this impossibility and her desire to stage 'ethical responsibility' in her writing (Spivak 1999, 286 n.134) partly explain Spivak's interest in her work (1992, 1993b and 1994). As I have shown elsewhere, the dialogue between women in Djebar's work inscribes itself precisely in the interstices between sisterhood and appropriation, in the shuttling between 'speaking for' and 'speaking very close to' (Donadey 2001, 43–62). The fact that Djebar highlights the elite writer's mediation of subaltern women's voices as well as the concomitant impossibility of 'letting the subaltern speak' in any transparent way evince a clear commonality of preoccupations between her and Spivak. Herein resides the most direct confluence between postcolonial theory and Francophone women writers.

19

Postcolonial thought and culture in Francophone North Africa

BY WINIFRED WOODHULL

Given the scattering of Francophone North African writers and intellectuals across the globe, as well as new modes of writing that bear witness to the sweeping economic and social changes of the past twenty years, it is incumbent upon us to develop fresh theoretical approaches to the postcolonial thought and culture of North Africans, wherever they may be living and working. The approach I would like to propose takes into account the current context of economic globalization, characterized by cross-border flows of finance capital, labour and commodities, and by migrations of peoples, cultures and ideas. It takes into account, too, the fact that in today's world, political and cultural identities, including those of North Africa, are more overdetermined and more fluid than ever and that they constantly take on new meanings that are inevitably shaped by growing disparities of power and well-being, not only between the North and the South but also between the rich and the poor within each of those arenas. I want to suggest that the multicultural societies of North Africa can fruitfully be analysed in a global frame that enables us to extend a promising line of recent critical inquiry concerned with globalization. It is an approach that takes seriously the repressive effects of that process, which stem in no small part from the operations of minimally regulated, exploitative multinational corporations. It also takes seriously the devastating effects of the political and economic policies of the world's wealthiest nations, and of the rich countries' daunting control over flows of information and culture through vast media networks spanning the entire planet.

Yet, while it acknowledges the harm inflicted by globalization, this approach is none the less committed to exploring its potentially liberatory dimensions as well. A recent example of this type of inquiry by D.N. Rodowick focuses on 'the media state', understood as 'a virtual information "territory"' which, in conjunction with the 'deterritorialized transnational communities' spawned by hegemonic forces, produces a 'cosmopolitan public sphere' (2002, 13–23). This new public sphere is capable of fostering innovative forms of political activism despite its genesis by the very communication technologies, migratory flows and processes of transculturation that make possible state-of-the-art modes of domination. A transnational space fraught with contradiction, it is noticeably eroding the traditional functions of the state, sometimes in emancipatory ways.

An important dimension of the cosmopolitan public sphere is 'defined by the global reach of electronic communication and entertainment networks' (Rodowick 2002, 14). While global media forms may themselves elude state regulation and restrict both the content and the dissemination of information in ways that undermine democracy the world over, they are not monolithic; rather, 'they are heterogeneous and contradictory with respect to their source (print, film, television, video, radio, and the varieties of computer-mediated communication) and to modes of reception' (Rodowick 2002, 14). Media conglomerates create networks (by means of satellite communications, cellular phones and the internet, for instance) whose velocity and global range offer myriad possibilities for political intervention on the part of activists operating independently of repressive states. They provide technological resources that can be taken up by alternative media and channelled into new circuits, and can help to generate new modes of identification and forms of collective action that are consonant with democratic politics.

Until 11 September 2001, political intervention on the part of activists operating independently of repressive states was considered almost exclusively on the left in relation to 'progressive' political activity, such as high-profile protests against environmentally hazardous, dehumanizing forces of globalization, demands for decent wages and working conditions for labourers everywhere, and media activism – for example, innovative uses of video that double as art and cultural criticism. Today, however, critics and activists across the political spectrum are keenly aware of the frightening possibilities now open to religious and political 'conservatives', notably the young men allegedly responsible for the spectacularly successful attacks on the World Trade Center in New York. These men, and many others with whom they were associated, evaded control by nation states and used global electronic communication networks to build and mobilize a transnational community of Islamic militants as well as to plan, fund and carry out acts of mass destruction. It seems evident that all those interested in the potentially liberatory political effects of North African cultural production should consider that production in relation to the wider transnational public sphere to which al-Qaida and other Islamic militants have so dramatically drawn attention. As I will show later, many North African writers and artists are already doing so. Basic questions to consider in this connection concern the role of literature and culture in today's world and how effective they can be in countering the destructive uses to which new communication technologies and new modes of community building can be put.

Maghreb pluriel

The most interesting and productive North African theoretical and cultural texts from the early 1980s to the present offer radical reformulations of North African identity and culture. The best recent works eschew the notion of a pre-colonial Maghrebian cultural essence at the same time as they chart a new historical course that carries reflection beyond the quest for national identity. This had been articulated mainly in relation to French colonialism on the one hand – most famously in Kateb Yacine's *Nedjma* (1956) and Albert Memmi's *Portrait of the Colonized* (1990 [1957]) in the 1950s – and to the repressive, newly independent states of North Africa on the other (for example, in the novels of Nabile Farès, Rachid Boudjedra and Tahar Ben Jelloun dating mainly from the 1970s and 80s). Abdelkebir Khatibi's *Maghreb pluriel* (1983a), probably the most important and influential text in this category, combines theory and cultural criticism in its reflections on the future of North Africa. Written in the wake of the overthrow of the Shah and the establishment of an Islamic theocracy in Iran in 1979, *Maghreb pluriel* resonates, later in the decade, with the Ayatollah Khomeini's fatwa against Salman Rushdie following his publication of *The Satanic Verses* (1988). Khatibi urges the Third World to reject both the universalizing, imperializing reason of the West and the unreason that the West attributes to the non-West, and to find a 'third way' of thinking, speaking, and acting on a planetary scale.

Moving beyond the confines of the Maghreb-France dyad that had for so long shaped the thinking of Francophone scholars, particularly in the two or three decades following independence in Morocco and Tunisia (1956) and in Algeria (1962), Khatibi reconceptualizes North African culture in terms of its relation to the Mediterranean and Middle Eastern worlds at large, a relation manifested, for example, not only in the many languages that circulate in the Maghreb (Berber, Arabic, French, Italian, etc.) but in the traces left by one language in another and in the complex weave of imperial, cultural and religious histories that has shaped the region from ancient times to the present day. Conquests by Romans, Arabs, Ottoman Turks, French and Italians make of the Maghreb (which means 'West' in Arabic) a veritable mosaic of cultures. As such, according to Khatibi, it could well become a privileged site for the cultivation of cosmopolitan forms of 'hospitality' that allow an array of languages, cultures and histories to inter-mingle and to speak through one another without any one of them silencing or effacing the other.

Aspects of this 'plural Maghreb' had already been glimpsed in the work of Kateb and Memmi in the colonial period. They also found expression in Abdelwahab Meddeb's *Talismano* (1979) and Khatibi's *Amour bilingue* (1983b). However, it was not until the 1990s that a significant number of writers and critics fully embraced the idea of a 'plural Maghreb'. They did so at that time in response to Islamic fundamentalists' growing power in many parts of the Middle East and Africa, particularly Algeria, where the bloody civil war that was sparked in 1991 continues to this day. Islamist movements in Algeria, like those in other countries, have tried to dehistoricize religion and culture. They maintain that their interpretation of Islam is the eternal truth, and that their understanding of Algerian culture as essentially Arab and Muslim constitutes the essence of Algeria. They stake their claim to political legitimacy not only on the broad-based support that would have brought them to power in 1991 if the government had not cancelled national elections, but above all on their supposed religious and cultural purity. At the same time as they assert their own legitimacy, they try to discredit and to destroy all secular forces in the country. The Islamists' targets range from the profoundly corrupt government and military to liberal professionals (physicians, lawyers, teachers, journalists and writers) who are repaid for their defence of democratic values by being murdered, disfigured or forced to live in fear of these extreme forms of violence. The other key targets – when the violence is not randomly perpetrated on civilians in cities, suburbs or villages – are feminist activists such as Khalida Messaoudi, or simply women who exercise their right to work for pay outside the home or to traverse public space unveiled and unchaperoned. In short, the Islamists' reductive, ahistoric and repressive views have been violently imposed on the people of Algeria.

A number of international groups responded to the generalized terror reigning in Algeria – for example, the International Committee in Support of Algerian Intellectuals and the League of Human Rights, which together issued an appeal in 1994 for civil peace in Algeria. At one of the groups' public meetings, Jacques Derrida, a Sephardic Jew who was born in Algeria and did not leave there until the age of nineteen, read his text 'Taking a stand for Algeria' (1998b [1995]), in which he takes a stand for four basic principles: a new international solidarity that would not detract from Algeria's autonomy; an electoral agreement; the effective dissociation of the political and the theological; and a new Third Estate in Algeria, meaning all Algerian citizens who feel represented neither by the state nor by the organizations struggling against it by means of killing or threats of violence. There followed in 1997 another peace initiative, sponsored by the platform of the Association pour l'information sur l'Algérie and published in the July 1997 issue of the journal *Esprit*. This one criticized not only the political and civil deterioration in Algeria (signalled for instance by growing hostility toward the use of the Berber and French languages) but France's restrictive visa policy as well, and it called upon France and the European Union to put pressure on the Algerian government to promote democratic freedoms.

At about the same time, Francophone writers and scholars working outside North Africa concentrated their efforts on producing texts that testify to the Maghreb's long history of linguistic, religious, cultural and political diversity and to the futility – as well as the depravity – of attempting to eradicate it. Examples of literary work along these lines include Nabile Farès's poem 'Histoire de l'homme qui avait perdu son âme' (1998), Hélène Cixous's 'Letter to Zohra Drif' (1998), and many texts by Assia Djebar, such as *Oran, langue morte* (1997), *Le Blanc de l'Algérie* (1995a), and *Vaste est la prison* (1995b). The latter novel is especially notable for its 'pluralizing' effects. It beautifully traces the intricate relations between North Africa on the one hand and a host of other Mediterranean cultures on the other, from ancient Greece, Rome and Carthage, through the period of Arab conquest in the ninth century, into early modern times when Andalusian Moors and Spanish Jews crossed and re-crossed the Mediterranean (along with writers like Cervantes), and on into the periods of French colonial conquest, anti-colonial war and the current state of exile imposed on Djebar and many of her compatriots. *Vaste est la prison* restores polyphony to Algeria while at the same time relating histories in which women are significant actors. This strategy is important not just in the general sense of affirming women's potency as real-world agents and inventors of social meanings. It is also a crucial means of countering the near exclusion of women from Algerian political life, initially as a result of the 1984 Family Code, which reduced women to second-class citizens, and later as a result of the civil war.

A related feminist strategy that was deployed even before the civil war erupted in Algeria is evident in the fiction of Djebar and the scholarship of Moroccan sociologist Fatima Mernissi. It consists in exploring the history of Islam and of women's participation in early Islamic communities as a way of fostering democratic values and thereby countering Islamists' claims to possess the only valid interpretation of the Koran and other sacred texts. Feminist work reveals the error, hypocrisy, and intolerance of fanatics who pretend to be obeying divine law in enforcing the subjection of women and in attempting to impose their brand of authoritarian rule in the Maghreb and elsewhere. Key examples are Djebar's *Loin de Médine* (1991) and Mernissi's *The Veil and the Male Elite* (1991 [1987]) as well as her *Forgotten Queens of Islam* (1993 [1990]). Together with critics such as Marie-Aimée Hélie-Lucas, Djebar and Mernissi show that, somewhat paradoxically, the male proponents of the one true faith in the Maghreb in fact borrow from myriad conflicting historical interpretations of Islam and from diverse cultural practices around the Muslim world in expounding their views and forcibly imposing them on North African women and men.

Scholarship on these issues, all of which concern the 'plural Maghreb', abounds in the 1990s. Derrida's *Monolingualism of the Other* (1998a [1996]), which brings theory to bear on human rights, reflects personally and politically on the effects of the colonial education system in Algeria. Hélène

Cixous's 'My algeriance, in other words to depart not to arrive from Algeria' (1996), recalls her youth in Algeria and evokes the ways in which Algeria 'returns' to her, decades later, in France through her friendships with Algerian women, activists who are persecuted and forced to live in hiding. Both these texts, and many others, are discussed in a very engaging piece by Emily Apter entitled '"Untranslatable" Algeria' (1998b), published in an issue of the journal *Parallax* entitled 'Translating "Algeria"'. This same issue features essays by North African intellectuals based in Britain and the US, who reflect on Algeria as a contested space both in the colonial period and during the post-colonial civil war. Other collections that focus on these questions are *Algeria in Others' Languages* (Berger 2002), edited by Cixous's daughter, and *Tunisie plurielle* (Bouraoui 1997), edited by a Toronto-based Tunisian poet and scholar. Finally, the most theoretically sophisticated and comprehensive study to appear in recent years is *Queer Nations: Marginal Sexualities in the Maghreb* (Hayes 2000), a pioneering analysis of sexual dissidence and other forms of political contestation as they are figured in the literature of all three Maghrebian nations over a period of several decades. The energy of Hayes's writing and the acuity of his readings provide a fresh and illuminating perspective on both colonial and postcolonial culture, showing that many of the most frequently read North African texts compellingly stage the interplay of sexuality, gender, class and ethnicity in the ubiquitous and ongoing reconfiguration of national identities.

Questions for French, Francophone and Postcolonial Studies

Recent North African writing implicitly demands that we stop conducting business as usual in French departments and Postcolonial Studies pro-grammes and rethink our critical task in light of the current contexts of cultural production and reception. However many studies may have emerged in the past twenty years emphasizing the heterogeneity of North African cultures, the focus in the overwhelming majority of scholarly books and articles remains terribly restricted in two respects. Firstly, even in the criticism published in France, which is still quite formalist and shies away from historically grounded readings (on the unfounded pretext that such readings can only be 'sociological' or reduce the literary text to the status of an ethnographic document), most work addresses texts drawn from a single national context – Moroccan, Algerian, or Tunisian. And, whether or not the corpus comprises works from various parts of the Maghreb, the inter-pretive frame that is adopted rarely relates North African texts to any socio-cultural reality beyond the France–Maghreb nexus. Clearly, this interpretive frame dates from and is symptomatic of the colonial period; indeed colonial relationships deeply structure French and Francophone Studies to this day.

This brings me to my second point about the narrow focus of scholarship on North African cultural production. I believe that the French colonial legacy, together with the entrenchment of outmoded disciplinary structures in universities (not to mention in the minds of people who work in those settings) perpetuate the compartmentalization of French Studies (see also Hargreaves, Chapter 13, on this point). They police the borders between North African, sub-Saharan African, Caribbean, and South-East Asian literature, ensuring that texts from different parts of the former French empire be considered in isolation from one another, as if the old imperative to divide and conquer were destined eternally to shape critical inquiry. This habit is the more perverse since the groundbreaking work of writers like Kateb, Memmi, Léopold Sédar Senghor and Aimé Césaire between 1945 and 1965 was often at pains to bridge the distance between subjected peoples, not only within the French empire but in other parts of the world as well. For example, Kateb wrote on the establishment of Israel, Fanon wrote volumes about Algeria and West Africa, and the *Présence Africaine* group, which included the African-American novelist Richard Wright, adopted an explicitly internationalist stance during the Cold War years when the concept of the 'Third World' emerged. In sum, the peoples consigned to the Third World, as well as American blacks, actively and publicly sought ways to support each other while resisting control by the two superpowers and their imperial masters alike. So why should scholars persist in rigorously separating texts emanating from various parts of the Francophone world?

This applies equally to scholarship on the literatures of immigration in France, which are invariably considered in terms of carefully segregated ethnic groups, even in the best recent work. Here I am thinking, for example, of *Cultures transnationales de France* (Gafaïti 2001), edited by a Texas-based North African scholar. Although it tries to open a dialogue on the theories, methods, objects and aims of Francophone literary criticism by bringing together scholars from France, North Africa, Britain and the USA, the volume looks exclusively at texts by North African and 'Beur' writers, whereas its title seems to promise a broader scope. There is much to be gained by putting the many Francophone literatures of immigration in dialogue with each other, rather than restricting each of them, defined in terms of the ethnicity of their author, to a 'tête-à-tête' with 'French' identity, whose whiteness/Europeanness usually remains untheorized, except in the exemplary work of Étienne Balibar (1988).

Even more to the point at present, why should we persist in segregating the Francophone world from the rest of the planet in our thinking about literature and culture, particularly when the most interesting North African writers of our time are expressly drawing connections between North Africa and other parts of the world, and when so many North African literary scholars are living and writing in countries outside the French-speaking world? I believe that recent North African writing suggests some new directions not only for French/Francophone studies but for postcolonial studies generally, which have, by and large, focused on relations between a colonized or formerly colonized space and a corresponding imperial or neoimperial metropole, drawing on the centre-periphery model favoured in political theory of the 1960s and 1970s. In the age of transnationalism, it seems more fruitful to shift our sights and to look at both minoritarian writing's relations to an array of 'metropolitan' locations and its relations to other minoritarian spheres, that is, relations of margin to margin. It is also important to link North African literature to other types of cultural production, as is now more frequently being done in immigration studies, for instance, in *Post-Colonial Cultures in France* (Hargreaves and McKinney 1997), which features essays on television, raï, hip-hop, commercial film, comics and other popular cultural forms.

The World, the North African text and the critic

A number of the most prominent North African writers have lately made a clear effort to establish ties between their own work and a public sphere that extends beyond France and the Maghreb. For example, Tahar Ben Jelloun, who resides in France, wrote a collection of stories based on his travels through the zones inhabited by undocumented workers in southern Italy. Entitled *Dove lo stato non c'è: racconti italiani*, the collection was originally commissioned by *Il mattino*, then published in Turin in collaboration with Egi Volterrani (1991). This gesture signals the Moroccan writer/scholar's cross-border concerns with underclass North African immigrants (and others) who have been settling in Italy in recent years.

Like Ben Jelloun, Assia Djebar has moved beyond the French-North African sphere. One of the Maghreb's most accomplished writers, she is now based in New York. While she publishes mainly in Paris, she receives significantly more critical attention in the US, Canada and Germany than she does in France. In a prize-winning collection of her writings published in Montreal, *Ces Voix qui m'assiègent: en marge de ma francophonie* (1999), she evokes a host of writers from all over the world who have sparked her imagination, including a number of expatriates such as Marguerite Duras (Indochina/France), Mohammed Khaïr-Eddine (Morocco/France), Nuruddin Farah (Somalia/Britain) and Salman Rushdie (India/Pakistan/ Britain), whose experiences of permanent exile overlap in some ways with her own. She also refers to Pier Paolo Pasolini who, like her compatriot Tahar Djaout, fell victim to political assassins in his own country. Finally, Djebar not only links her creative project to the lives and struggles of the women of Algeria, as she has always done, but explicitly ties it as well to the lives of today's female immigrants in wealthy countries – North Africans, but also Malians and Zairians in France, Turks in Alsace, Germany and Holland, and Indians and Pakistanis in Britain. She expresses her concern that current scholarly attention to the work of literate young immigrants of the 'second generation' may bar from view the immigrant women of the first generation, many of whom know no European languages and live in dispiriting isolation. She worries that their inability to communicate and their social marginality may be interpreted by Europeans in utterly inappropriate 'romantic' terms, that is, in terms of 'mystery' (1999, 198).

In this respect, Djebar's project resembles that of Leïla Sebbar in her early novels, such as *Fatima ou les Algériennes au square* (1981), which deals not only with the trials of a young Algerian girl living in France but also with those of the girl's mother and her women friends, who do not read or write and who are even more cut off from the French mainstream than their children. Djebar's project also has something in common with that of Yamina Benguigui, whose documentary film *Mémoires d'immigrés: l'héritage maghrébin* (1998) movingly recalls the painful experiences of North African men who emigrated to France as manual labourers in the 1950s and 1960s. Benguigui's filmed interviews with these men, who were elderly when the film was shot in the 1990s, evoke the squalid conditions in which they lived, the indignities to which they were routinely subjected, and the loneliness from which they suffered over long periods of time. Because of its emphasis on the subjective process of remembering these experiences and of assigning them a place in personal and collective histories, the film offers a view of immigration that is unique to the men of that generation.

To be sure, at least one early 'Beur' novel, Azouz Begag's *Le Gone du chaâba* (1986), evokes the migrant camps where Begag and other younger people (who are now middle-aged) lived as children once the French government permitted the immigrant labourers of their fathers' generation to bring their wives and families to France. But the 'Beur' text does not convey the adults' experiences of anger, guilt and despair that come across so poignantly in Benguigui's film. And of course most immigrants of the older generation – indeed, most immigrants of all ages – do not have the possibility (fraught with ambivalence, to be sure) of telling their story and having it circulated beyond a narrow circle of friends and family. I want to emphasize that, however important it may be to affirm the Beurs' resourcefulness in negotiating their relationship to French language, culture and nationality in novels and in real life, or to highlight the inventiveness of the Berber diaspora in using home videos, e-mail and websites ('CouscousNet') to maintain existing social ties as well as to forge new communities (Merolla 2002), it is crucial to keep in view the many underclass immigrant women and men who are excluded from these social circuits, and who have no meaningful way to participate in the new public sphere. The critical force of Djebar and Benguigui lies in their ability to enter into the new public sphere, to channel their work into worldwide circuits and to use those resources in such a way as to convey, in a concrete, moving and unpatronizing manner, the life world of people who derive little benefit from digital cosmopolitanism. In these artists' work we can see clearly that for people whose mobility is forced upon them by the transnational labour market, and who do not enjoy citizenship in the country where they live and work, the privileges and pleasures of virtual travel and sociability are out of reach.

For the reader of Mohammed Dib's latest novel, *Comme un bruit d'abeilles* (2001), making one's way through the text very much resembles an experience of virtual travel. As if clicking to open a long series of surprising new windows on a computer screen, one moves abruptly from one depressing yet strangely intriguing locale to another. In a tangle of narratives set in present-day Russia, Algeria and the Czech Republic, Dib's novel relates the current civil war in Algeria to the worldwide drama of the twentieth century: on the one hand, the hopes inspired by socialism, the progressive struggles they fuelled, and the disastrous outcomes of those struggles in the Gulag and in Algeria; and, on the other, the failed promises of democracy in the West and in the rest of the world.

Yet, despite its concern with the imminent implosion of the author's mother country, Dib's text also signals the possibility of a new start for Algeria. For example, recurrent figures of rebellious young women link Algeria to the Czech Republic, specifically to 'Satellite Info' in the capital, an organization that recalls the old Prague of the Soviet bloc as well as the present-day city, a contradictory space of uncertainty, foreboding and promise. In turn, Satellite Info links all of these sites to France and the US. *Comme un bruit d'abeilles* thus provides the symbolic cables to connect Algeria to a digital universe, a virtual territory with no fixed boundaries, where new, life-affirming transnational communities could perhaps be generated. Whether they will in fact be generated depends on political activity that can mobilize sufficient support for democratic institutions the world over. One important type of political activity will involve transforming the imaginative, affective and ethical landscape so that democracy may be genuinely desired and valued – which is where literature and culture come in. They can redirect energies that may otherwise fuel the compulsion to return repeatedly to the deadly questions of origin and identity, figured by Dib in references to the myth of Oedipus. And, like the ardent young women in *Comme un bruit d'abeilles*, literature and culture can stir things up, pose provocative questions, invent new modes of identification, and encourage egalitarian forms of affiliation that are local and global at the same time.

|20|

Beyond tradition versus modernity: postcolonial thought and culture in Francophone sub-Saharan Africa

BY DAVID MURPHY

The archetypal image of French colonialism in sub-Saharan Africa is that of African schoolchildren in remote villages, learning the history of 'nos ancêtres, les Gaulois' [our ancestors, the Gauls]. This powerful image is based on the premise that France's colonial policy was one of assimilation, turning the 'primitive natives' into 'civilized, assimilated' Frenchmen (women were largely excluded from the colonial education process). Indeed, French colonial propaganda consistently stressed that France was engaged in a 'mission civilisatrice' [civilizing mission] in its colonies, in opposition to the 'brute mercantilism' of the British. However, much important historical work has been carried out in recent decades, underlining the distance between the rhetoric of assimilation and colonial reality: for instance, throughout most of the colonial period, less than 2 per cent of children attended French schools (Miller [1998] uses this historical work to reassess early twentieth-century African literature).

The notion of assimilation none the less retains a strong grip on the imagination of artists and critics in their work on France's former colonial possessions in sub-Saharan Africa. Consequently, the vision of a Francophone sub-Saharan Africa attempting to balance the influences of its French and African heritages – sometimes successfully, but more often with tragic consequences – has been central to much African cultural production, particularly literature, over the past few decades. Most commonly, this debate has pitched 'tradition versus modernity' (the oppositional 'versus' indicating the predominant motif of conflict). This chapter will examine briefly the evolution of this tradition-modernity model over the past forty years, revisiting some of the received ideas about French colonial policy in Africa, especially the notion of assimilation. It will also challenge the privileged position occupied by Senegalese colonial and post-colonial culture in such debates, assessing the danger of adjudging one African country to be 'representative' of the whole continent. The main focus will be on 'literature' (including historical writing and philosophy) and cinema, which have been the principal subjects of postcolonial criticism, but it will also widen discussion to include elements of popular culture – music and sport – that have hitherto been neglected (Barber 1997).

There are many reasons for the predominance of the Senegalese model in discussions of Francophone Africa. Senegal was France's oldest African colony, the French 'presence' on the coast dating from the seventeenth century. By the mid-nineteenth century, the 'old colony' of Senegal comprised the 'quatre communes' of Gorée, Saint-Louis, Rufisque and Dakar. In 1871, the Third Republic gave these four communes the right to elect a deputy to the French parliament, thus assimilating them into metropolitan France in a manner that would be systematically denied to all of France's other sub-Saharan African possessions – acquired between 1870 and 1900 – until after the Second World War. The four communes were thus a testing ground for assimilation, but their example emphasizes the limited nature of France's ability or desire to 'assimilate' Africans. The inhabitants of the communes who enjoyed the status of 'citizens' were numbered in the thousands while the millions of 'Senegalese' in the remainder of the colony were mere 'subjects' of French imperial rule, who could be made to carry out forced labour, and were governed by the arbitrary diktats of 'l'indigénat', or direct colonial military rule. Essentially, the 'Senegalese model' of assimilation was not widespread even in Senegal itself.

This situation was mirrored in France's other sub-Saharan possessions, each of which produced a small, French-educated elite to staff the colonial service as teachers and civil servants. For much of the period between 1914 and the independence of France's sub-Saharan colonies in 1960, political struggle was based on extending the full rights of French citizenship to all Africans. This process gained force in the aftermath of both world wars when thousands of African troops, mainly uneducated men from rural areas across Africa – but misleadingly called 'tirailleurs sénégalais' – were enlisted to help save 'la patrie' [the homeland]. Having fought to defeat France's enemies, these Africans believed they had earned a right to become citizens. Between 1944 and 1960 the process of assimilation finally reached a large number of Africans: each of the colonies gained political representation in Paris, and the difference between citizens and subjects was abolished in 1946. The irony was that assimilation appeared to be reaching fruition just as the empire was in terminal decline.

France's colonies in sub-Saharan Africa negotiated their independence in 1960 (except Guinea in 1958). This peaceful accession to independence meant that decolonization did not bring about a radical rupture with France, which for some was a boon to these new states, while others described the process as a mere sham with France becoming a neocolonial power that continued to dominate its former possessions economically and militarily (French troops are still stationed in many former colonies in sub-Saharan Africa). Senegal, the most politically stable (if far from the most economically successful) of these emergent countries, was a major target for these claims of neocolonialism in the early decades of independence when it was ruled by the Francophile president, Léopold Sédar Senghor. Best remembered as the poet of Negritude, the positive expression of an essential black identity, Senghor was also the chief theorist of 'francité', a way of expressing the world shared by all French-speakers (Senghor 1964). Negritude and 'francité' were complementary notions, the emotion and spirituality of 'black culture' gaining from its contact with the clarity and logic of French culture and language: in Senghor's famous phrase – 'assimiler, ne pas être assimilé' – French colonialism allowed Africans 'to assimilate' French culture, and 'not to be assimilated' by it. For Senghor, the culture of France's former African colonies – especially that of Senegal – was, consequently, marked by a profound Franco-African hybridity. (Senghor was, unsurprisingly, a key player in founding an institutional Francophonie in the 1960s: see Parker, Chapter 8.)

Two novels written in the dying stages of French colonialism have proven hugely influential in thinking about culture and identity in post-independence Africa, placing the 'tradition/modernity' model on a seemingly unshakable pedestal. *The African Child* (1959 [1953]) by the Guinean author Camara Laye is a nostalgic evocation of the African village, written from the perspective of a young, educated African who has made the trip from village to town to colonial metropolis. Compensation for the loss of the 'traditional' world of the African village is found in the writing of the (French) literary text. Although now living in the harsh world of materialistic modernity, the African must maintain his (Negritude's Africa was almost exclusively male) personality by 'putting his soul in a safe place' (one of Senghor's favourite sayings).

An alternative vision of the educated African's trajectory is found in Cheikh Hamidou Kane's *Ambiguous Adventure* (1972 [1961]). An exponent of Negritude, Kane was close to Senghor both culturally and politically, serving as a minister in several of the latter's governments. However, the novel presents a much darker vision of the process of assimilation than any of Senghor's work. Kane's tragic hero, Samba Diallo, is torn between the 'spirituality' of African culture and the 'rationality' of Europe, or in other terms, between (African) 'tradition' and (European) 'modernity'. The intellectual and spiritual voyage from Koranic school to French school creates a split personality that can lead to madness, as in the case of 'le fou'

– an ex-tirailleur traumatized by his experience of war – or to death, as happens to Samba Diallo when he is murdered by le fou for refusing to renounce the influence of Europe.

Samba Diallo's obsession with learning the colonizer's language has been repeated in many Francophone African texts. Compare this with the focus on religion as a determining factor in alienating educated young Africans from their parents in *Things Fall Apart* (1958) by Nigerian author Chinua Achebe. The secular French Republic seduced its African schoolchildren with the all-encompassing embrace of its universal language and values, not the loving embrace of Jesus (French Catholic schools were very much in a minority). French colonial administrators, unlike their British counterparts, rejected the use of 'indigenous' languages in the education of young Africans. Francophone states in Africa continued the policy of teaching in French after independence, and Francophone authors have not been tempted to follow Ngugi's lead in adopting African languages in their work (Ngugi 1981).

The 1960s saw the heyday of Negritude, but it came under increasing criticism from the early 1970s as its underlying essentialism was challenged by young African philosophers and artists. Negritude played a key role in developing a sense of self-worth primarily among educated Africans but its monolithic vision of a homogenous African culture, although strategically important in the struggle against colonialism (see P. Williams, Chapter 16), was simply not representative of the wide array of ideas and beliefs held in Africa. Even at its height, there was never a unanimous consensus behind the notion (or even a consensus among supporters as to what it meant). Philosophers such as Towa and Adotévi criticized Negritude from a materialist perspective, rejecting the binary opposition between Africa and the West, and the notion that black African culture was characterized by its emotional, spiritual nature (Towa 1971; Adotévi 1972). This materialist trend has remained central to much thinking in African philosophy but there has also been a strong vein of support for the notion of 'ethno-philosophy' – i.e. that African ethnic groups have specific modes of thought that must be examined as coherent philosophical systems distinct from Western thought (Appiah 1992, 85–106). In the 1990s, this debate took a new turn under the influence of poststructuralist theories about epistemology and meaning, which questioned the 'universality' of dominant Western modes of thought. 'Ethnic systems of thought' were given a new legitimacy, with the debate focusing on the notions of 'endogenous' and 'exogenous' knowledge, a variation on the old debate about 'tradition' and 'modernity' (Hountondji 1994). The work of V.Y. Mudimbe in particular has provided a complex and insightful analysis of the issues surrounding knowledge and its representation in post-colonial Africa (Mudimbe 1988).

The lack of consensus around Negritude's philosophical vision has been mirrored by the debate surrounding African history. From the 1950s, Cheikh Anta Diop's exploration of the black roots of Egyptian culture –

thus positing black people as the 'source' of Greek civilization (i.e. European civilization) – proposed an alternative vision of the African past to that of Negritude (Diop 1954). Since the 1960s, Negritude's version of African history and culture has been challenged from both 'modernist' and 'traditionalist' positions. For Senegalese historian, Mamadou Diouf, Senghor's 'traditional Africa' was a timeless place that provided a striking range of symbols and metaphors for the poet-president, but which bore little relation to the contemporary 'realities' of African rural and urban life (Diouf 1989). Within Senegal, Senghor's 'sensual' vision of Africa was simply ignored by writers intent on tracing the sociocultural history of specific ethnic groups (Sylla 1978). More importantly, Islam – and not France – increasingly came to be seen as the defining influence on Senegalese culture (Samb 1971).

In terms of fiction, the earliest and most consistent challenge to the cultural hegemony of Negritude came from Senegalese author and film-maker Ousmane Sembene, who wrote a series of novels and short stories that explicitly rejected the main premises of Negritude. His major novel, *God's Bits of Wood* (1995 [1960]), tells the story of the 1947–8 railway strike on the Dakar-Bamako line. The male strikers and their female relations are not simply looking to earn better pay, they are engaged in a struggle to create a new Africa, claiming the benefits of 'Western' modernity as their own. A committed Marxist, Sembene rejects the facile amalgama-tion of 'modernity' with capitalism, and his African characters demand the right to adapt those elements of 'Western modernity' that will be useful in the creation of egalitarian African societies.

By the late 1960s, new, critical and distinctive literary voices were emerg-ing. In 1968, both Ahmadou Kourouma and Yambo Ouologuem published their debut novels, casting a jaundiced eye on the African societies emerging from the mess of decolonization. Kourouma's *The Suns of Independence* employed a startlingly hybrid French, laden with direct translations from Malinke, in relating the tragicomic tale of a former prince fallen on hard times in the new Africa of the one-party state. Ouologuem's *Bound to Violence* was an even more striking novel, using an array of styles in a devastating satire of the African nobility, cast as the true oppressors of the common African. For Kwame Appiah, Ouologuem's novel represents a 'post-national' stage in African writing, when the dream of national libera-tion from empire was replaced by the nightmare of so many failed independ-ent African states (Appiah 1992, 150–2).

This 'post-national' stage saw satire and an imaginative escape from 'reality' become the dominant motifs of fiction in the 1970s and 1980s. Writers no longer believed their works could change the world, so instead they attempted to change how their world was represented and imagined. As Jacques Chevrier argues: 'À une écriture de la politique succède une politique de l'écriture' [Political writing has given way to a writing policy] (1989, 64). The playful texts of Sony Labou Tansi (1979), Emmanuel

Dongala (1982) and Tierno Monénembo (1997) are indicative of the post-ideological literature of the past twenty years. The work of Labou Tansi also belongs to a category of African fiction in which the shocking violence that has marked many post-colonial African states is given full reign. In particular, authors from the former Belgian Congo (Democratic Republic of the Congo, formerly Zaire), such as V.Y. Mudimbe and Pius Ngandu Nkashama, have presented nightmarish visions of post-independence, depicting societies where extreme violence has become daily reality and the principal means of imposing state authority. Critics have often viewed these authors as emblematic of contemporary 'African' writing but the same nihilism and despair is simply not to be found in more peaceful and stable regions of Africa. The novels of Nkashama and Mudimbe (and of their neighbours from the former French Congo, Labou Tansi in particular) are primarily a reflection of the legacy left by the brutality of the Belgian regime, which led directly to the thirty-year reign of the kleptocratic dictator Mobutu Sese Seko. This issue highlights the dangers of trying to impose a unified theory of African literature/culture (as well as underlining the need for closer examination of the differences between the literature of former Belgian and French colonies), and the past two decades have seen an often polemical debate between those African literary critics who advocate the study of 'national literatures' and those in favour of the study of 'African literature' (Huannou 1989; Midiohouan 1982).

The most significant development in African literature in the past twenty years has been the emergence of writing by women. In the mid-1970s, a number of autobiographies by women appeared, chronicling their experience living under colonialism and in the early years of independence (Diallo 1976). In 1979, Mariama Bâ published her landmark novel, *So Long a Letter*, in which the expression of female concerns was inextricably linked with the process of writing and education. There now exists a wide spectrum of female voices articulating different concerns in vastly different styles – from the conservatism of Aminata Sow Fall's novels to the lyrical, experimental work of Werewere Liking (Hitchcott 2000). As well as expressing the opinions and concerns of African women, these female authors have underlined the 'crisis of masculinity' that had already been evoked in some earlier African fiction by men. However, despite the challenges to male authority in African fiction, it is significant that many female authors are based in Europe – e.g. the Cameroonian Calixthe Beyala and the Ivorian Véronique Tadjo – where they have more liberty from the social constraints that continue to mark most women's lives in sub-Saharan Africa. (Beyala has often explored in her novels the liberating effects of emigration to Europe for African women: see Hargreaves, Chapter 13, and Ní Loingsigh, Chapter 14, for discussion of her work.)

It is not only African women that are forced to seek intellectual and personal liberty outside of Africa. Many male authors have long been based in France where most African novels are published (although new African-based publishers are emerging after the failed experiments of the 1970s). However, a remarkable feature of the past decade has been the increasing attraction of the United States for African artists and academics – for example, the novelists/academics Emmanuel Dongala, Pius Ngandu Nkashama and V.Y. Mudimbe are all based in the USA. This indicates that the former colonial centre is no longer the pole of attraction that it once was, suggesting a broadening of horizons for African authors and an escape from the dichotomies of colonizer–colonized relationships. However, there is also concern that the current 'brain drain' of academics to North America reflects the demands of the process of (US-dominated) globalization, serving to undermine the already fragile education systems in African countries. This contrast between the positive (increased hybridity) and negative (economic exploitation) effects of globalization echoes one of the key post-colonial debates of the past decade, opposing Homi K. Bhabha (1994) and his critics (Brennan 1997; Lazarus 1999). This debate has reworked the 'tradition/modernity' opposition, taking cultural métissage as a given, but disagreeing about the nature and extent of the process.

Many of the ideas that are central to African literature in French have also been explored in cinema from Francophone Africa (see Diawara 1992; Ukadike 1994; Givanni 2000). However, the two forms have not evolved in identical fashion. Unlike African authors of the 1950s and 1960s who were, by and large, well-educated products of the colonial system seeking to understand their own position between 'tradition' and 'modernity', many pioneers of African cinema were left-wing radicals who rejected received ideas about identity. Throughout the 1960s and 1970s, the films of Ousmane Sembene and Med Hondo (Mauritania) were openly critical of colonialism and the neocolonial order. In Sembene's *The Money Order* (1968) and *Xala* (1974), the crisis of independent Africa is exposed in a style that merges social realism with Brechtian distancing techniques and African oral narrative structures (Murphy 2000, 67–123). Sembene's films also first charted the move from French to 'indigenous' African languages, attempting to make direct contact with the African masses unable to read his fiction. Hondo's work has been more experimental than Sembene's: e.g. *Soleil O* (1968) is a visually stunning film essay on slavery, colonialism and the plight of African immigrants in France. However, perhaps the most gifted African director was the late Djibril Diop Mambéty (Senegal), who eschewed political commitment in favour of a highly poetic and experimental vision. His masterpiece, *Touki-Bouki* (1973), combines elements of the road movie with oral narratives to create a remarkable vision of the hybridity and confusion of urban culture in Dakar, a world where values and cultural signifiers swirl around in a heady and unsettling brew.

The chief irony in the development of Francophone African cinema is that it has been almost entirely dependent on the financial support of the French authorities (although better-known directors such as Sembene can now avail of independent sources of finance). French government

investment has allowed this cinema to survive but hardly to thrive.
(Anglophone African cinema, by comparison, which has received no British
support, has only emerged in the past fifteen years.) Films are made but
rarely seen in Africa where cheap foreign imports – American action films,
Kung-Fu blockbusters from Taiwan, and Bollywood song-and-dance spec-
taculars – dominate screens.

There have been notable exceptions to this rule – Sembene's *Xala* was a
huge success in West Africa in 1975 – and many younger African directors
have made a conscious effort to produce films that are less consciously
political, and (thus potentially) more 'popular' to a wide African audience.
The work of the Malian director Souleymane Cissé acts as a bridge between
the radical period and today. His early films – e.g. *Baara* (1978) – were
social realist movies with a strong political message. However, in *Yeelen*
(1987) he adopted a different style, combining elements of mythology and
parable to relate his ideas, a mix that proved successful with African and
Western audiences. In a less experimental vein, Gaston Kaboré and Idrissa
Ouédraogo (Burkina Faso) have developed a popular cinema, through the
use of simple narratives dealing with moral issues – e.g. Kaboré's *Wend
Kuuni* (1982), or Ouédraogo's *Tilaï* (1990). In the past two decades, a host
of younger directors – Cheikh Oumar Sissoko, Adame Drabo, Jean-Pierre
Bekolo – has emerged. (Some young women directors have also finally
emerged to join pioneers such as Safi Faye: Fanta Nacro is perhaps the best
known.) In their work, and particularly that of a director such as the
Congolese Balufu Bakupa-Kanyinda – see his film *Le Damier* (1996) – it is
possible to see a new, brashly confident aesthetic at work in which a prominent role is given to those elements of Western popular culture that have
taken root in Africa.

Without doubt, the most commercially successful and widespread form
of cultural production in Africa is popular music, often generically termed
as 'Afropop' (Frith 1989; Ewens 1991). This music should not be confused
with African folk musics, which have developed as an expression of specific
local cultures. On the contrary, Afropop is the expression of a modern,
urban African sensibility that merges various Western and African elements
to form something radically different. African pop music is marked by a
profound syncretism of diverse 'African' and 'Western' elements in terms of
musical style and lyrical content, as well as in the image projected by bands
to their audience. For example, in the 1970s and early 1980s, the Malian
musician/vocalist Salif Keïta, in his work with the *Rail Band* and *Les
Ambassadeurs*, helped to create a startlingly hybrid form of music. Their
songs featured a lilting guitar sound that modified the phrasing of the
previously dominant Afro-Cuban rumba to create a cascading spiral of
notes in imitation of the kora (a 24-stringed West African instrument, often
compared to a harp). The guitar was punctuated by Afro-Cuban brass
sections, and the songs were driven by Keïta himself with his soaring,
Islamic-inflected vocals and often deeply traditional lyrics, expressing the

values of Mande culture. In terms of lyrical content, these groups might have appeared traditional but their syncretic music projected an image of vibrant modernity which was very attractive, particularly to a young African audience, both in Mali and further afield. In the 1980s, the centre of 'Afropop' may have shifted from the regional economic centre of Abidjan to the old colonial centres of London and Paris but the original commercial and artistic development of this music was the result of networks that cannot be defined purely by old colonizer-colonized binaries.

Essentially, for its African audience, Afropop constitutes a dynamic and effervescent cultural practice that is both resolutely 'modern', while also recognizably 'African' (Irele 1993; Lazarus 1999, 196–225). Such a state-ment does not seek to elide the major cultural differences between different regions of Africa. However, many African popular musics – for example, the Congolese rumba of the 1950s and its successor soukous in the 1980s – cross ethnic and political boundaries within Africa and come to be seen as an expression of a popular 'African' culture, as well as acting as expressions of specific ethnic or national cultures. Afropop with its myriad forms and styles thus provides a fascinating example of the way in which the local/national and the 'African' are negotiated throughout Africa.

The exploration of forms such as Afropop has generally been limited to Africanists or to cultural studies departments. This work highlights the need to expand the study of Francophone African culture beyond literature (and a side interest in film). The issues central to an educated elite writing in French need to be balanced against the issues illustrated in forms of popular culture such as music, comic books, sport, in which the role of French language and culture are often far less prominent (which does not imply that one set of issues is more 'authentic' than the other). The emerging field of sports studies seems particularly rich for an exploration of postcolonial Africa and its relationship with France. During the colonial era, Raoul Diagne, son of Blaise Diagne, first black African deputy to the French Assembly, was a famous footballer who played eighteen times for France, while the current president of the International Amateur Athletics Federation (IAAF), Lamine Diack, represented France in athletics (Deville-Danthu 1997). Through sport, the 'lesser peoples' of the colonies could become 'honorary Frenchmen' representing the grandeur of 'la Plus Grande France'. This discourse re-emerged in 1998 when the French football team won the World Cup with a team comprising several players from France's African immigrant communities. Problematic immigrants were suddenly (and temporarily) transformed into heroic examples of the country's diversity.

The 2002 World Cup provided an even more fascinating illustration of postcolonial relationships between France and sub-Saharan Africa. On 31 May 2002, the French football team faced Senegal, playing in their first ever World Cup, in the opening match of the tournament. The social, cultural and historical network linking the two countries was made evident in various ways. One of France's best players, Patrick Vieira, was born in Senegal but moved to France as a young child, while several of the Senegalese players were actually born in France to Senegalese parents, and virtually the entire Senegal team was plying its trade in the French football championship. (To round off this complex set of relationships, Senegal's coach was a Frenchman.) These factors led the French press to dub Senegal 'France B' or 'Les Sénefs' (Sénégalais-Français), in a rather patronizing tone, which proved singularly misplaced when the Senegalese beat France 1–0, leading to great rejoicing in Senegal, and the mass slaughter of cockerels – the symbol of the French team – throughout the country. At the level of symbolic action, the former colony had firmly underlined its independence.

I would like to conclude with an image from the end of this football match, which featured on the front pages of newspapers around the world the following day. In this photograph, Senegal's best player, El Hadji Diouf, is dancing on the pitch with some teammates. With bleach-blond hair and a gold earring, he appears every bit the modern, wealthy, sporting superstar. However, he has removed his jersey to reveal a t-shirt bearing the picture of a shrouded figure, Cheikh Amadou Bamba, founder of the Mourides, one of the largest Islamic brotherhoods in Senegal, of which Diouf is a member. A devout Muslim (the title, 'El Hadji', denoting a person who has undertaken the pilgrimage to Mecca) with a taste for expensive clothes and cars, who spent his formative teenage years at the French football club Rennes in Brittany, Diouf provides a remarkable example of the contradictions and complexity of contemporary African culture: an adherence to certain 'local' practices and beliefs, an attraction to the rampant consumerism introduced by globalization, and an ambiguous relationship with the former colonial power. The exploration of this complex culture in all its various expressions is the principal task of postcolonial studies of sub-Saharan Africa in the coming years.

21

Postcolonial thought and the Francophone Caribbean

BY J. MICHAEL DASH

One of the more striking omissions from the founding theoretical work of postcolonial studies, *The Empire Writes Back* (Ashcroft *et al.* 1989), is the Francophone Caribbean. Celia Britton, in *Édouard Glissant and Postcolonial Theory*, one of the rare attempts to situate a major writer and thinker from the Francophone Caribbean in relation to the major ideas of postcolonial theorists, laments this deficiency: 'Postcolonial theory [...] includes considerable discussion of writers from the English-speaking world – Brathwaite, Wilson Harris, Derek Walcott, etc. – but, again apart from Fanon, has little to say about writers and intellectuals of the French Caribbean' (1999, 4–5). In contrast, as she points out, the Anglophone Caribbean is singled out for relatively extensive treatment as an entire region that Ashcroft *et al.* declare to be 'the crucible of the most extensive and challenging post-colonial literary theory' (1989, 145). It is certainly also true that the omission of the Hispanophone Caribbean is even more glaring as it is not mentioned even once. It is only much later that one of the authors of *The Empire Writes Back* will make the case for a Latin American post-coloniality (Ashcroft 1998). However, the Republic of Haiti, independent longer than any of the countries discussed in *The Empire Writes Back* and presumably wrestling with a post-colonial reality since 1804, inexplicably gets short shrift.

Nevertheless, the Francophone Caribbean maintains a shadowy yet powerful presence in the formulation of postcolonial thought. It would have been quite impossible to attempt a definition of postcolonial practice and leave out of account the major anti-colonial movement that such a practice must transcend, i.e. Negritude. This movement's Caribbean roots are not explored, however, and no mention is made of the Haitian sociologist Jean Price-Mars, who was recognized by the Negritude writers as a key precursor. Negritude is essentially read through its critics. As Britton mentioned above, Frantz Fanon is central to the early theorizing of post-colonial theory because of his insight into the binary nature of colonialist discourse and the appeal of his theory of radical deracination. The Manichean colonial world of centre/periphery, black/white, colonizer/ colonized was shown by Fanon to be a crippling legacy for those who attempt to dismantle colonial domination. Fanon's critique of Negritude as ideologically derivative and blindly ethnocentrist is, therefore, vital to advancing the emancipatory possibility of a postcolonial theory.

Fanon's importance derives from his rejection of an understanding of identity grounded in difference, which he saw as the product of a Manichean colonial discourse. In demystifying the exercise of power within a colonial relationship, his demonstration that colonial domination was not merely economic, political or rational had enormous consequences for anti-colonial or postcolonial thought. It is his investigation of the anxiety and ambivalence of the colonial relationship that makes Fanon so acutely aware of the flawed nature of the liberation movements and ideologies that set out to dismantle colonialism. His critique of the mimetic drive and the lack of what he calls 'ontological resistance' on the part of the alienated colonial subject is crucial to the postcolonial critique of utopian theories of counter-colonial resistance built around race and nation. In this regard, he serves the same purpose as the only other Francophone Caribbean writer who gets some treatment in postcolonial thought, the Haitian novelist, Jacques-Stephen Alexis. Alexis's theory of Marvellous Realism points the way to the exploration of more ambiguous and tactical forms of opposition explored by one of the iconic writers of postcolonial theory, Wilson Harris, in his theoretical exploration of cross-culturality.

It is not that the theorists of *The Empire Writes Back* have misunder-stood or misrepresented the main thrust of the ideas of either Alexis or Fanon. The problem lies rather in the selective and generalizing use of these major figures from the Francophone Caribbean. In its pursuit of an anti-essentialist agenda, postcolonialism suppresses the specific dynamic of a region that is considered central to the critique of colonialism. In so doing, it may well mask the ways in which these and other writers from the region may or may not adhere to a postcolonial orthodoxy. The selective, non-contextual use of writers from the region may have also become so established as to make the opportunistic use of similar writers standard practice in postcolonial theory. It is this treatment of Fanon as a 'global theorist in vacuo' that drives Henry Louis Gates to regret the fact that Fanon has become 'a Rorschach blot with legs', and to urge postcolonial theorists 'not to elevate him above his localities of discourse as a trans-cultural, transhistorical Global Theorist' (Gates 1991, 17).

The aversion to national or regional constructs and the consequent desire to privilege all thought that apparently promotes hybrid identities and interstitial spaces continue to marginalize questions of historical and geographical particularity in postcolonial thought. As postcolonial theory has entered a new triumphalist phase, the selective use of French Caribbean theorists whose work has been translated into English has continued unabated. This headlong rush to impose a postcolonial orthodoxy of nomad identities has led, for instance, Christopher Miller to sound the alarm at the use of Édouard Glissant's ideas in order to impose a doctrinaire glorification of prescriptive hybridity. Postcolonial readings of Glissant, he complains, now have a critical monopoly in his field: 'Through the influence of Deleuze on Édouard Glissant and thinkers like him, the ideas of deterritorialization and nomadology have, so to speak, taken root and become almost a dogma' (1998, 5). It is unlikely that Ashcroft *et al.* envisaged in 1989 the inexorable spread of prescriptive hybridity when they launched the once liberating theories of cross-culturality and creolization. However, not only has such a critical orthodoxy emerged, but so has a procrustean temptation to tailor placeless theories and global theorists, emptied of their specificity, to fit the prevailing dogma.

The apparent lack of interest in or knowledge of postcolonial theory by French intellectuals as a whole has done nothing to help this problem of mutual incomprehension. As Emily Apter recently concluded, 'Many French intellectuals seem to have difficulty in grasping the pertinence of postcolonial theory to the contemporary politics of culture, despite their recognition that Maghrebian, Caribbean, West African and Indochinese exclusion from mainstream "francité" continues to inflect internal political and cultural affairs as well as the export of French culture abroad' (1995, 169–70). The French reluctance to confront the ghosts of its colonial past may explain this reticence, but even major Francophone writers whose works have been translated into English seem unaware of postcolonial theory. Maryse Condé, arguably the Francophone Caribbean writer whose work has been most often read through a postcolonial lens, makes no mention of it in her extensive interview with Françoise Pfaff in 1991 (Pfaff 1993). Nor does Patrick Chamoiseau, who has been promoted in a *New York Times* review of *Texaco* as 'the Salman Rushdie of the Caribbean', seem particularly aware of postcolonial thought despite the relevance of some of its concepts to his 'créolité' movement.

If the main thrust of postcolonial theory is to demystify the logic of identitarian thought with its rhetoric of alterity and its dream of nativist resistance, the Francophone Caribbean does not fit easily into this postcolonial problematic. Too uncritical a reading of Frantz Fanon himself may ironically have encouraged the thorough-going scepticism that is apparent in postcolonial thought. Fanon's explosive identity politics, with its complete disavowal of what he saw as the emasculated Caribbean as well as his rejection of all Caribbean writing before the radicalism of the 1930s, may well have led to simplifications of place and tradition within the Caribbean region. The resultant ideal of free-floating hybridities and fluid cultural diversity tends to downplay the situational density and the complicating dynamics of cultural interaction in a region where issues of identity or specificity are never easily silenced. Joël Desrosiers raised the issue of postcolonialism's scepticism on the subject of constructing identities with

Édouard Glissant when he asked him to comment on Edward Said's claim that all identities were imaginary constructions. It is clear that Glissant is unaware of Said's work and his answer does not address the question. If anything, the answer was given in Glissant's preceding lecture where he declares that identity means living 'la totalité-monde à partir du lieu qui est le sien' [the world's totality from the perspective of the place that is one's own] (Glissant 1996, 67). Even when Desrosiers raises the question again later in *Introduction à une poetique du divers*, Glissant returns to the question of the relation of place to identity when he asserts that 'le lieu est incontournable. [...] Le lieu n'est pas un territoire: on accepte de partager le lieu, on le conçoit et le vit dans une pensée de l'errance, alors même qu'on le défend contre toute dénaturation' [place cannot be circumvented. [...] Place is not territory: one accepts sharing place, one conceives of it and lives it within the concept of errancy just as one defends it against any disfigurement] (Glissant 1996, 105).

Glissant's fear is that, if the ideas of difference and specificity are lost or diluted, then everything risks collapsing into a uniform sameness. He is by no means suggesting a reversion to an unproblematic glorification of rootedness, but restating the importance of a dialectical situatedness in a system of relations fraught with the tensions, disruptions and anxieties of a globalizing modernity. In Glissant's model of relational rootedness, the loci of Caribbean culture are numerous, widespread, eccentric. Their meanings can never be exhausted by any one voice. In this regard, it is well worth our while to pay attention to the persistence of the island trope in Glissant's writing. The island is a floating symbol for that zone of anxiety where individual consciousness enters history, a secretive marker within an undecipherable sea of global change – 'l'île, qui est secrète s'accomplit dans son rayonnement. Diamant des contraires' [the island, that is secret, finding its fulfillment in its radiance. Diamond of contradictions] (1957, 42). The 'Diamond of contradictions' referred to here is not just a poetic image, but refers to that modest monolith Diamond Rock off the south coast of Martinique. It is the logic of a poetics of (dis)location that leads Glissant to an increased fascination with the dark monolith which is both marine and volcanic, scintillating in association yet opaque in reality. 'Diamant' is dense with the tensions of Glissant's relational model. It both preserves the past of Martinique and negates it, allowing it to be more fully integrated into the archepelic space of the Caribbean Sea and the crushing force of the Atlantic. In his most recent work, the island becomes a basic unit in his vision of a 'Tout-Monde' where intolerant, continental masses symbolically break down into 'des îles, des isthmes, des presqu'îles, des avancées, terres de mélange et de passage, et qui pourtant demeurent' [islands, isthmuses, peninsulas, headlands, lands in which you are mixed up and those you pass through, and which nevertheless endure] (1997b, 181).

The irony here is that the very Caribbean writer who is seen by Christopher Miller as guilty of spreading the gospel of borderless identities and happy hybridity emphatically adheres to ideas of difference, location and particularity. It is precisely this open insularity, the shifting ground between lived opacity and fated relationality, that characterizes Francophone Caribbean writing. Glissant's point is not that hybridity represents the triumph of a new nomadic postcolonial identity. Rather he imagines a confluence of cultures whose creative energies are generated from the tense interdependency of specific cultures. Throughout his essays, versions of the following formulation are repeated: 'La poétique de la relation suppose qu'à chacun soit proposée la densité (l'opacité) de l'autre. Plus l'autre résiste dans son épaisseur ou sa fluidité (sans s'y limiter), plus sa réalité devient expressive, et plus la relation féconde' [the poetics of relatedness supposes that each one must face the density (opacity) of the other. The more the other resists in his thickness or fluidity (without being confined to this), the more expressive his reality, and the more fruitful the interrelating] (1969, 24).

In such a scheme of things, colonialism is merely one manifestation of a process of globalizing modernity, which has been demonized in the past but is part of that which energizes what he calls the Caribbean's irruption into modernity. It is his way of shifting away from the reifying polarities of colonial discourse towards a system in which irreducible difference is in a constant state of flux but never absent. Identity is, therefore, stripped of its particularizing exclusiveness but is not thrust into a state of postcolonial groundlessness. Also, in such a system, there is no stable equilibrium that holds together centres and peripheries. There can no longer be a simple counter-discursive rewriting of the European canon. It is this paradoxical double consciousness or doubling of identity that can be seen to characterize the most radical redefinition of postcolonial space, which is marked by trajectories that no longer follow the lines of the imperial project.

This problematizing of ground as irreducible yet borderless in Francophone Caribbean writing seems to have emerged with particular urgency in the recent writing of the Haitian diaspora. The status of inter-American wanderer has been acquired by almost all major Haitian writers today as the Haitian diaspora spreads through the hemisphere. Two of these writers in particular, Dany Laferrière, seen as much as a Quebecois as a Haitian novelist, and the Haitian-American Edwidge Danticat, have recently revisited this question of Haitian space in their works. Two novels in particular write back to earlier works that explored Haiti in terms of a redemptive modernist poetics. This is not a postcolonial manoeuvre but a transversal undoing of narratives defined by colonizing centres. It is one in which the Empire (or department or ex-colony) does not always predictably write back to the centre (or metropole).

In Laferrière's *Pays sans chapeau*, the native land of Haiti is not awaiting the fiery ideological inscription of the returning visionary. In this regard, the novel can be read as an indirect satire of Jacques Roumain's *Masters of the Dew* in particular and all Caribbean narratives of return in general, as the narrator who returns to Haiti in Laferrière's novel is no saviour but simply a confused subject who cannot adjust to the changes that have taken place in the native land. The precariousness of the regarding subject is constantly stated in this fictive ethnography. He writes – literally sitting at 'une petite table bancale sous un manguier' [a shaky little table under a mango tree] (Laferrière 1996, 13) – at the mercy of the arbitrary falling fruit, with no distance between him and the invasive, bustling density of reality. In an effort to suggest the elusiveness of reality to which he belongs, 'le pays réel', he declares in the opening pages and at the end of *Pays sans chapeau* that he is an 'écrivain primitif' [primitive writer] (1996, 15). In so doing, he points to the well-known tradition of Haitian painting as well as raising the issue of opacity on which a changing Haitian identity can be based. In so doing, he questions the cultural nationalism promoted by earlier generations but not in terms of a postnational postcoloniality.

The difficulty of fixing Caribbean space in terms of absolute belonging or comprehension is also a major theme in Edwidge Danticat's works. Her first novel *Breath, Eyes, Memory* (1995) is haunted by the problems of mothering as it is by the absent space of the motherland. Her most recent novel, *The Farming of Bones* (1998), returns to these anxieties but this time in the guise of historical fiction. This novel can be read as the rewriting of the famous novel by Jacques-Stephen Alexis, *Compère Général Soleil* (1955), which also traces the history of the massacre of Haitian cane cutters in the Dominican Republic. Instead of the apocalyptic denouement when the hero greets the rising militant General Sun at the frontier of his 'terre natale' [native land], Danticat's protagonist with her ambiguous ancestry, as much Dominican as Haitian, is immersed in the Massacre River, a river which has witnessed the massacre of Haiti's indigenous people by the Conquistadors. The battered body of her heroine finds itself in this liquid borderland between two spaces frozen in mutual hostility because of their nationalist impulses. The site of the river is as much amniotic fluid allowing a new consciousness to be born as a location of nightmarish memory which projected Haiti irrevocably into a history of violent colonization. The warm water 'with the pebbles of the riverbed scouring my back' caresses her naked body (Danticat 1998, 310).

To borrow the words of Danticat's title, it is really about farming bones. Where we bury our dead is usually the surest indication of belonging and community. A triumphalist postcolonialism is reminded that carefree nomadism is always haunted by the need for the individual to be buried somewhere. We should also be aware that locating and excavating the bones of the dead is not about communing with the ancestors and putting them to rest. The dead in the borderlands between Haiti and the Dominican Republic demonstrate the extent to which this zone is inter-American space, cruelly configured from the dislocations of the US Occupation, the greed of the Haitian elite and Dominican racism projecting the ambiguities of the past into the present. Massacre River like Diamond Rock is a manifestation of totalizing enrootedness, seemingly marginal locales that are zones of historical inter-American convergence.

Enigmatic islets, bones at border crossings, situational opacities all consistently point to the persistence to an irrepressible reflex in identitarian thought in the region that resists static polar identities as well as reductive ideals of transparency, mutation and formlessness. It is a question of an emancipatory opacity, as Celia Britton perceptively points out in relation to this key concept launched by Glissant: 'Opacity is also a defence against understanding at least in the hierarchical, objectifying way in which this usually operates between the West and the Third World [...]. The right to opacity, which Glissant claims is more fundamental than the right to difference, is a right not to be understood' (Britton 1999, 19; see also Forsdick, Chapter 4). Instead of reading the Francophone Caribbean in terms of essentialist mystifications that must be undone by an enlightened postcolonialism, it might be more useful to approach the Francophone Caribbean in terms of the way in which the right to opacity is negotiated at various times and the way in which it can become derailed into essentialist narratives of redemptive wholeness. Caribbean writing in the twentieth century is filled with such movements. Negritude, 'noirisme', 'créolité' are three major instances of the way in which liberating opacity can congeal into essentialist myths. They are the reductive generalizations that grew out of attempts to conceptualize a local specificity that ultimately became enmeshed in the binaries of colonialist discourse. In their assertion of cultural separateness they provide valid targets for a demystifying postcolonial critical practice but also mask their specific, complex theoretical and historical origins.

The point of departure for this theorizing of global cultural blocs, whether neo-African or Creole, at least at the outset, resisted abstract formulations of identity. The issues of otherness, alterity and specificity were raised in the 1920s in Haiti and in the 1930s for France's Caribbean colonies in the context respectively of the nationalist reaction against the American Occupation and the push for decolonization fed by an European avant-garde. In the case of Haiti, it was not necessary for Haitians to demonstrate to the American marines that they were black and proud to be so. The dynamic of the nationalist movement of the 1920s in Haiti was much more driven by a class and colour dynamic which meant that it was a matter of demonstrating to the light-skinned Francophile elite the value of the peasantry. After all, the theoretician of this movement, Jean Price-Mars, was much more interested in reforming and modernizing the Haitian elite than in propagating a global theory of a monolithic black culture. He was in his early fifties when the indigenous movement was launched and his use of anthropological sources in *Ainsi parla l'oncle* (1928) was not meant to prove the separateness of black culture but to point out the extent that Haitian society was debilitated by a neocolonial system of apartheid that both spurned and exploited the peasantry.

It is surely a similar desire to reform the elite to which Jacques Roumain, the best-known product of Haitian indigenism, unswervingly adhered throughout his short career as a militant and novelist. It is almost certainly with this corrective intent in mind that he wrote his celebrated novel *Masters of the Dew* (1947 [1944]). This story of the political triumph of requited love is fundamentally concerned with nation building and constructing a fraternal vision of national identity. Yet Roumain appears in his short literary career to avoid generalizing truths regarding the Haitian peasantry at a time when the indigenous movement was predisposed to lyrical evocations of black beauty or the wonders of peasant ritual. The themes of solidarity with the poor and the earthy embrace of the 'terre-femme' were explored by other members of *La Revue indigène* who saw themselves as bohemian 'poètes maudits'.

Roumain's work was initially aimed at the fecklessness and parochialism of the elite and its corrupt politicians. When he turned to depicting the peasantry it was certainly not to prepackage peasant culture for the consumption of the local elite or foreign visitors. In a little-known article published in *Regard* (Roumain 1937), he fiercely chastised the Haitian poet Léon Laleau for doing precisely this, namely for presenting exotic generalizing images ('simple, amusante , souriante' [simple, amusing, smiling]) of the peasantry for foreign consumption. He did not simply want to become a spokesman for the Haitian peasantry. Rather his work in the 1930s suggests the elusiveness and inscrutability of this world, which resists the reductiveness of indigenist ideology. In an early travel piece written in 1930, Roumain confesses that '[l]a chaleur et la monotonie sans cesse renouvelée des bayahondes et des cactus accablent l'esprit' [the heat and the unceasingly repeated monotony of the acacias and the cactus overwhelm the mind] (1930, 1). This is not a world that can easily summon up spiritual plenitude. It seems to resist literary as much as ideological representation: 'C'était un paysage irréel, noir et tumultueux, empli de bruits confus, de murmures et par intervalles de la stridulation cristalline des anolis; c'était un paysage chaotique sans contours, toutes perspectives perdues, qui s'éveillait, entre d'obscures montagnes' [It was an unreal landscape, dark and disorderly, filled with confused sounds, murmurs punctuated by the crystalline grating of ground lizards; it was a chaotic, formless landscape, all perspective obscured, which was awakening, between dark mountains] (1930, 1).

The problem of literary representation, which Roumain sensed strongly in 1930, is illustrated in his short story 'La Montagne ensorcelée'. This tale of peasant tragedy can be read as a study in collective hysteria, which is built around the deepening paranoia felt by a peasant community that cannot explain a series of tragic events that take place in the village. The author even seems deliberately to undo the lyricism of the opening pages as the image of the snake-like path leading to the old woman's home is later used by one character as evidence of her diabolical nature. This is a world susceptible to collective delirium, which is presented neither in terms of human melodrama nor of an ideological paradigm. After Roumain's return to Haiti from exile, his ethnographic reports on peasant religious ritual, prepared for the 'Bureau d'ethnologie' that he had founded in 1941, again emphasize the specificity of Haitian peasant culture and there is no evidence of broad generalizing with regard to black culture. This approach coincided with the work of Surrealist writer Pierre Mabille who also was involved with the 'Bureau d'ethnologie'. The travel pieces written by Mabille (1981) also show a similar reticence to generalize on Haitian popular religion. Mabille's role in Haiti at this time is remarkably different from that of his fellow French writer Jean-Paul Sartre and the Negritude movement. Mabille's reluctance to explain Haitian peasant culture is as marked as Sartre's theorizing of Negritude as the negative moment in the Hegelian dialectic.

This dynamic and complex view of otherness and specificity, in which can be traced the nationalist roots of Haitian 'noirisme', can also be found in ideas of the *Tropiques* group in Martinique during the Second World War. The ideas of this group predate the spread of Negritude in the 1950s and again point to the way in which a subtle notion of cultural difference later congeals into an essentialist, anti-colonial rhetoric. The relationship between those who collaborated in this journal and the Negritude movement is a complicated one. It was Césaire who founded the *Tropiques* group, but, as Michael Richardson very astutely points out, approaches to culture and identity were not uniform in the movement: 'For Ménil and for Suzanne Césaire [...] surrealism was more of a critical tool, a means of reflection that would provide them with a critical foundation from which to explore their own cultural context. For Ménil in particular, as a philosopher, it was surrealism's ideas that were most important, and especially its Hegelian basis' (Richardson 1996, 7–8). Ménil himself admits that the various texts in *Tropiques* 'do not reflect a single unified philosophy' (1996, 75), and his ideas in particular can be read as anticipating those of Glissant on the subject of opacity and the reductiveness of universal truths.

Both Césaire's wife, Suzanne Césaire, and René Ménil refused to reduce the question of identity to anti-colonial polemic. They looked beyond the colonial relationship to problematize identity in terms of the shaping forces of cultural contact. They insisted on the view that identity was sustained by a constantly shifting sense of otherness to avoid being blandly assimiliationist either in terms of a totalizing white or totalizing black ideal. Neither spoke of a black sensibility or bought into the negative wish fulfilment of Negritude. In the writing of both Suzanne Césaire and Ménil there was a consistent awareness of the importance of a concrete historical context and a reluctance to objectify cultural difference.

For Suzanne Césaire, Surrealism was a point of departure for thinking through the oppositional binaries of the colonial situation. Her appropriation of Surrealist thought as well as her refusal of the organic stereotypes of

Negritude are striking. In her essay '1943: Surrealism and Us', she contemplates a tomorrow where:

> des millions de mains noires, à travers les ciels rageurs de la guerre
> mondiale vont dresser leur épouvante [...]. Notre surréalisme lui
> livrera alors le pain de ses profondeurs. Il s'agira de transcender enfin
> les sordides antinomies actuelles: blancs-noirs, européens-africains,
> civilisés-sauvages [...]. Retrouvée notre valeur de métal, notre
> tranchant d'acier, nos communions insolites. (Césaire 1996, 126)

> millions of black hands will thrust their terror into the raging skies of
> world war [...]. Our surrealism will then deliver the bread of its
> depths. Finally those sordid contemporary antinomies of black/white,
> European/African, civilized/savage will be transcended [...]. Our value
> as metal, our cutting edge of steel, our amazing communions will be
> rediscovered.

Similarly, Ménil values highly the Surrealist emphasis on the irreducible alterity of other cultures, which was for him a way of freeing them from predetermined meanings. Menil's comments on the question of exoticism are very revealing:

> Les rapports humains dans l'exotisme sont ceux de deux consciences
> différentes face à face, saisies du sentiment de la différence de leurs
> mœurs respectives. La vision exotique est une vue de l'homme prise 'de
> l'autre coté' du dehors et par-dessus les frontières géographiques.
> Malheureusement, la tendance naturelle, dans l'exotisme, est de rater
> le 'sérieux' et l'authenticité du drame (de l'autre) pour s'en tenir à une
> vision idyllique, superficielle [...]. Ce n'est qu'en brisant les limites de
> cette conscience idyllique que l'étranger atteint l'étranger dans son
> drame, comme sujet profond et riche. (Ménil 1999, 20-1)

> Human relations in exoticism are those of two different conscious-
> nesses brought face to face and seized with a sense of the difference
> between their respective customs. The exotic vision is a view of
> humanity taken 'from the other side', from outside and beyond
> geographical frontiers. Unfortunately, the natural tendency in
> exoticism is to miss the 'seriousness' and authenticity of the drama (of
> the other) and to confine oneself to an idyllic and superficial vision
> [...]. It is only through breaking through the bounds of this idyllic
> consciousness that the stranger can approach the stranger in this
> dramatic moment, as a profound and rich subject.

What is striking in both extracts is the emphasis on the importance of recognizing otherness without attempting to fix it any way and the value of such a methodology for issues of identity, which are constantly open to reinvention.

The emphasis on the polarities of difference as opposed to hybrid post-colonial forms has been a powerful reflex in identitarian thought in the Francophone Caribbean. While postcolonial demystification of essentialist ideologies has been a welcome corrective to the excesses of noirisme and Negritude, the promotion of free-floating identities obscures the important emphasis on cultural difference as it has emerged in the Francophone Caribbean. Rather than a triumphalist progression that takes us from colonial through anti-colonial to postcolonial, it might be much more useful to conceive of a system of spatial interplay of difference as Glissant proposes in the concept of transversality. Such a non-centrist web of relations is central to a disruption of networks that once linked the centre to the Empire and allows the oppressed to speak in the present from their specific locations and peculiar opacities.

22

Resisting colonialism? Gabrielle Roy and the cultural formation of Francophones in Manitoba

BY ROSEMARY CHAPMAN

Je me souviens du vif intérêt que je pris à la littérature anglaise aussitôt que j'y eus accès. Et pour cause: de la littérature française, nos manuels ne nous faisaient connaître à peu près que Louis Veuillot et Montalembert. (Roy 1996, 71)

I remember the strong interest I took in English literature as soon as I had access to it. And with good reason: as far as French literature went, our manuals offered little beyond the works of Louis Veuillot and Montalembert.

Je ne m'étonnais pas d'ailleurs que ce fût en Angleterre [...] que je naissais enfin peut-être à ma destination, mais sûrement en tout cas à mon identité propre que jamais plus je ne remettrais en question. (Roy 1996, 392)

Besides, I was not surprised that it was in England [...] that I was finally awakening if not to my goal in life, then certainly at least to my individual identity, that I would never again question.

These two quotations from the autobiography of Manitoban-born writer Gabrielle Roy give some insight into the linguistic and cultural situation of a minority Francophone population within an Anglophone province of Canada in the interwar years. (In 1921, people of French-speaking origin represented 7 per cent of the population of Manitoba, but 47 per cent of the population of Saint-Boniface, Roy's home town.) The first quotation indicates Roy's failure to identify with the French literature she studied at the Académie Saint-Joseph in Saint-Boniface, and her love of English literature. The second recalls her recognition in her late twenties that the French language was nevertheless an essential part of her identity and that in future she would write only in French. Her upbringing and education as a Francophone in the Prairie province of Manitoba explain not only how Roy came to have such a mixed cultural and linguistic allegiance, but also the layers of significance the choice of a preferred language can have. In addition to economic factors (publication, distribution, readership), there are personal factors that are significant, in particular the ambivalent relationship between Roy and her mother, and the effect this might have had on Roy's eventual choice of her mother('s) tongue. Such psychological or psychoanalytical approaches are both fascinating and plausible, but my current focus lies elsewhere. For Roy's origins within a specific linguistic minority mean that questions of individual linguistic and cultural identity also need to be understood in relation to a range of collective, cultural and ideological factors. More specifically, her choice of language was made within a complex, colonial framework.

The aim of this chapter is to explore Roy's choice as a response to a very particular kind of 'bicultural straddle' (Healy 1992, 70) which resulted from the education system operating in Manitoba in the years when Roy was firstly a pupil (1915–28), then a trainee teacher (1928–9), and finally an elementary school teacher (1929–37). Education was one of the key tools of colonialism and Roy's case is indicative of the situation for many Francophones in pre-1960s Canada. Teacher training, the curriculum, the methods of examination and the choice of textbooks all play their part in shaping patterns of thinking: 'Education is perhaps the most insidious and in some ways the most cryptic of colonialist survivals, older systems now passing, sometimes imperceptibly, into neo-colonialist configurations' (Ashcroft *et al.* 1995, 425). Education is a site of competing notions of identity and of culture (Imperial, Anglo-Canadian, Franco-Canadian, Franco-Manitoban, Catholic, secular, humanist) and open to a variety of responses. With reference to British colonialism in India, Loomba speaks of 'the complex interface of nationalism and colonial authority', in which 'particular subjects may contribute to diverse and even conflicting traditions of anticolonialism, nativism and collaboration' (1993, 314). In the very different 'Second World' (Slemon 1990) context of the Francophone settler populations of Canada, the same complexity of response to the authority of the British and the Anglo-Canadians as well as to emerging strands of Anglo-Canadian and French-Canadian nationalism can be found. Education not only serves as a means of acculturation and assimilation. It can also be the site of various techniques of resistance and survival.

Gabrielle Roy's education and subsequent career as a teacher in Manitoba coincide with the period when the linguistic rights of the Francophone minority were severely challenged. The details of the

Manitoba Schools question are complex and explored in detail elsewhere (Morton 1979; Jaenen 1984; Blay 1987; Taillefer 1988). The key elements are as follows. Article 23 of the 1870 Manitoba Act, based on the 1867 British North America Act, guaranteed the linguistic rights of Francophones and Anglophones in Manitoba. Article 22 confirmed the establishment of a denominational education system, with a Catholic and a Protestant section. In 1890 both the status of French as an official language and the dual system of denominational education were abolished. In 1896 the Laurier-Greenway compromise was negotiated and enacted in 1897 as an amendment to the School Act. This allowed teaching to be conducted in a minority language (thus opening the field to French and other languages) according to the bilingual system, and religious education to be taught between 3.30 and 4.00 p.m. where numbers were sufficient. But the new Liberal government in Manitoba in 1915 was committed to reforming the education system, making school attendance obligatory and reducing the proportion of time devoted under the bilingual system to the teaching of minority languages. In 1916 the bilingual clause was removed from the School Act despite vigorous opposition from French members and the Ukrainian member (but with the support of the representatives of the Icelandic and Scandinavian communities who favoured assimilation). The French members' response was that the legislation was 'an attempt on our national life' (Morton 1979, 9). The Francophone Liberal, Talbot, declared: 'The French are a distinctive race, and we will not be assimilated, whether you like it or not' (Morton 1979, 9). At the heart of this controversy lay the question of assimilation of the language, culture and ideology of the Anglophone majority. The outbreak of the Great War saw a heightening of racial tensions between groups of different national origins in Canada, not all of which felt equal allegiance to the British Empire. It was felt that increased emphasis on the learning of English could hasten the emergence of a common (Anglo-)Canadian identity. But, of course, English was still the language of Empire and the teaching of English still entangled with the practices of that Empire. The Franco-Manitobans' own colonial past and their stubborn assertion of difference were perceived as obstacles to these various processes.

The loss of the bilingual system meant that after 1916 no teaching in French was allowed. Under the bilingual system some teaching had been allowed in a minority language from Grade 1 onwards, but most subjects still had to be taught and examined in English. After 1916 the French language could only be taught at secondary level as a second language and religious education, as between 1897 and 1916, was permitted only in the half-hour after the official end of the school day (where numbers justified it). With the abolition of the bilingual system all teacher training was delivered in English. Francophones from Saint-Boniface, such as Gabrielle Roy, now had to attend the Provincial Normal School in Winnipeg (whereas three of her older sisters had trained as bilingual teachers in neighbouring Saint-Boniface).

Yet the apparent defeat of the bilingual system of schooling in Manitoba in 1916 was only partial. When the French-Canadian nationalist and historian Lionel Groulx visited Manitoba in 1928 to research the history of the education of minority Francophone populations, he was struck by the vigour of Franco-Manitoban culture, their institutions and their education system, which he declared to be examples of 'la résistance constructive' [constructive resistance] (1979, 242), and an excellent means of defence against Anglophone domination. What Groulx found on his visit to Saint-Boniface was evidence of a clandestine parallel system of education administered by the Association d'Éducation des Canadiens-Français du Manitoba (AECFM). This organization came into being as a response to the announcement of the 1916 legislation and only disbanded in 1968 when the principle of bilingual education had been reinstated in provincial legislation (Bill 59, 1967).

For most Franco-Manitobans in 1916 the Catholic faith was part of their history and of their future survival. The AECFM relied on this link, acting as 'le véhicule d'une résistance ayant pour but la conservation de la langue gardienne de la foi' [the vehicle for a resistance aimed at preserving the language, which was guardian of the faith] (Blay 1987, 46). The relationship between the lay founders of the Association and the Catholic Church was close, and the authority and patronage of the Church strengthened the control of the Association over the parents, teachers and pupils. The Association acted as a parallel Department of Education, instructing its schools on matters of curriculum, set texts, school library provision and classroom displays. In 1922 the Association appointed two school visitors, shadowing the role of the Department's inspectors, but concentrating on the teaching of French and of religion in schools (Taillefer 1988, 283). Teachers were expected to teach the French syllabus in addition to the official English syllabus as set out in the Department of Education Program of Study. All pupils were to sit the Department of Education examinations (prior to the 1916 legislation this had not been a legal requirement). From 1923 to 1967 the Association ran a 'concours', which was effectively an examination of the parallel curriculum in French language, literature, history and religious instruction, from Grade IV to Grade XII (see Minutes of the meeting of the comité du fonctionnement scolaire, 31.3.1925, AECFM 42/232/58). Teachers were encouraged to enter all their pupils, not just the best, for the examination (see letter from J.-H. Daignault, AECFM secretary, to J.L. Hacault, 24.1.1928, AECFM 42/279/1110). Association correspondence reveals the amount of work that the organization of the 'concours' required, notably in the constant search for sponsors of the numerous prizes (AECFM 42/279/1108–12). The French-language newspaper *La Liberté* published the results and other news from the Association's activities (so helping to ensure the high profile of the Association's work in the Franco-Manitoban population). The Association relied on grass-roots support from its members, in the form of annual donations, and a small levy on each pupil.

Although the unofficial French Programme d'études is not available for the period 1916–37, there are many references to its existence and some details of set texts, given in minutes and correspondence for this period. Initially the AECFM recommended that schools continue to use French text-books as before (Taillefer 1988, 282). After a period of adjustment to their clandestine status a new syllabus was prepared by two of the nuns teaching at Gabrielle Roy's school (Taillefer 1988, 282). According to secretary J.-H. Daignault in a letter to the President of the Association St Jean-Baptiste in Quebec City in 1927, the curriculum 's'inspire du programme suivi dans les écoles primaires de Québec' [is inspired by the syllabus followed in primary schools in Quebec] (AEFCM 42/279/1109). Many of the textbooks were written by members of religious orders, notably the Frères de l'instruction chrétienne, the Frères des écoles catholiques and the Clercs Saint-Viateur.

For the unofficial bilingual system to thrive there had to be a secure supply of future 'institutrices' [primary school teachers]. The convents were an important source of recruits – Gabrielle Roy's sister Bernadette was herself a teaching nun. The Association took on the role of encouraging, and policing, the lay recruits. The 'concours' served to reward success and bestow value on the French-language element of the pupils' education. Prizes at the higher level were conditional upon the winners taking up places at Winnipeg Normal School. The prize money was payable to the Department of Education to pay the fees for the course. A system of loans to Francophone trainee teachers also helped to encourage young women into the profession. The Association actively monitored the students' progress and required them to attend a parallel 'cours pédagogique' and 'cours d'apologétique' with a separate examination. Circulars reminded the 'normaliennes' of their duty to attend 'si vous voulez être en mesure de lutter efficacement contre les tendances pernicieuses de la philosophie matérialiste de l'école normale' [if you want to be equipped to resist effectively the pernicious tendencies of the materialist philosophy of the Normal School] (Circular 20.1.1927, AECFM 44/234/117). Local priests were also given the names of the Association's newly qualified 'institutrices' and asked to keep a strict eye on their behaviour and contacts. An annual summer school was held at the Académie Saint-Joseph in Saint-Boniface which covered both pedagogical and religious topics and was preceded by a five-day retreat. In every area of the Association's activity moral and spiritual concerns can be seen to go hand in hand with their pedagogical and linguistic aims. In this educational context it is interesting to note Roy's phrasing when she states in her autobiography: 'Ce dut être vers l'âge de quatorze ans que j'entrai en étude comme on entre au cloître' [It must have been when I was about 14 years old that I entered the world of learning like one enters a convent] (1996, 67).

To dwell on the details of the AECFM's work can give the impression that the Catholic Church's control of schools and the teaching profession in Manitoba in the interwar years was as strong as in Quebec. Certainly

Franco-Manitobans received an education strongly imbued with the tenets of Catholicism, loyal to the spirit of those colonizing missionaries who introduced education in New France. But Manitoba is not Quebec (where denominational schooling was the norm until the 1960s and the Quiet Revolution). This was only part of the story in what was a curious form of cultural resistance. All those involved in the delivery of an alternative French education had to play a double game. In correspondence the AECFM reminds teachers of the need for secrecy and subterfuge. For example, in Minutes of the Comité du fonctionnement scolaire of 31.8.1926, a recommendation concerning the provision of supplementary reading for pupils is accompanied by the words 'mais de prendre soin que ces livres ne soient pas vus de l'inspecteur' [but to take care that those books are not seen by the inspector] (AECFM 42/232/59). Groulx likens the development of parallel French-language establishments to the spreading of an invasive plant through a flowerbed (1979, 131). To use an alternative metaphor, French and Catholic ideology and practice were woven or knitted into the existing system, fitting into the interstices of the existing fabric. But the fabric remained and it was British in form and content. So, while children in 1930 would be taught to respond correctly to the *Catéchisme des trois provinces* in Grade III, they would also be studying *The Canadian Reader*, Book III, with its mix of Canadian and British ideology in images, texts and messages.

In many other ways it is clear that education was regarded as an arm of imperial governance. As now, education was a provincial not a federal responsibility, so the Department of Education reported not to Ottawa but to the Lieutenant Governor of Manitoba, the King's representative. All those seeking a teacher's licence were required to swear an oath of allegiance to the Crown and non-British citizens were only allowed a temporary licence. In the half-yearly records of attendance returned to the Department of Education each teacher had to sign two declarations: firstly, that there had been no religious education taught in school apart from in the half-hour period after 3.30 p.m., in accordance with the law; secondly, that 'the regulations respecting the flying of the "Union Jack" at the school have been complied with during the present term and that the said "Union Jack" in use in the said School District is now in good condition and repair' (Provincial Archives of Manitoba, Department of Education: Half-yearly returns of attendance, 1930–1, District 1188). Roy explicitly mentions the flying of the British flag in *La Petite Poule d'eau* (1951). In the late 1920s, when Roy attended Normal School, the mastery of English was an overriding concern for the Department of Education. All candidates for Normal School had to pass both a medical examination and a test of English proficiency comprising an oral examination and silent reading. The introduction to the Program of Studies 1927–8 states that: 'every lesson should be a language lesson' (2) and the Report of the Department of Education 1928–9 confirms: 'One of the greatest needs of the Elementary and High Schools is attention to

English speech' (3). Whether this concern arises from the continuing flow of allophone immigrants to Manitoba or from the AECFM's campaign is not clear. It is striking that the annual reports make almost no overt references to the Francophone population. For example, in 1929–30 (the year before Gabrielle Roy joined the staff as Reception Class teacher) the École Provencher opened a brand new wing, offering eight extra classrooms. The Report records this proudly, with a photograph, but with no reference to the fact that much of the teaching there was carried out in French. It would seem that discussion of the teaching in Francophone school districts was a taboo subject in official reports (as the question of First Nations' residential schools also seems to have been). The AECFM archives reveal that there was a certain amount of contact, lobbying (on matters like school libraries), and even consultation (on curriculum reviews) with the Department of Education. Some inspectors were sympathetic to the bilingual cause. But the law had to be seen to be obeyed.

The curriculum is of course a key aspect of educational control, which is why the AECFM sought to counterbalance it. The school curriculum and the status of the literary text have been the subject of numerous contributions to the field of postcolonial studies. Many of these have focused on British colonial rule in India and Africa (Bhabha 1994, 102–22; Loomba 1993; Ngugi 1993), some on other settler colonies (Docker 1995; Slemon 1990) and a few on Canada (Mukherjee 1986). But the relatively unusual cohabitation of two settler populations makes Manitoba's case more complex. Here, two colonial visions and two emergent nationalisms confront each other in an unequal battle. As demonstrated by the account above, the purpose of the French language and literature in the curriculum of Franco-Manitobans was specifically to reinforce the link between 'la foi' [faith] and 'la langue' [language]. That link in turn harks back to Quebec's chosen route to survival, based on 'la terre, la foi et la langue' [land, faith and language], in defiance of British rule and in keeping with the collective narrative of French Canada's sacred mission. The fervour surrounding the language of instruction which Roy and others have recalled (Roy 1970, 75) would seem to arise from the thrill of subterfuge and resistance rather than the exciting nature of the subject matter. Otherwise the resistance of the AECFM is clearly conservative in cultural and political terms.

This conservatism is evident when one looks at evidence of the curriculum that Roy herself studied during 1925–8. The standard French-literature manual used at that time for Grades X–XII was Edmond Procès, *Modèles français: extraits des meilleurs écrivains avec notices*. References to it appear both in the Department of Education Program of Studies and in AECFM correspondence. The two authors Roy targets for her strongest criticism, Veuillot and Montalembert, are both Catholic authors. Veuillot was a militant journalist, in favour of ultramontanism and, according to Gérard Tougas, 'l'écrivain français le plus universellement admiré au Canada français pendant le Second Empire' [the French author most universally admired in Francophone Canada during the Second Empire] (1974, 67–8). Montalembert was a publicist, politician and liberal Catholic. Roy's memories of the curriculum are expressed in negative terms and emphasize the limited range of authors studied: 'Quelle idée pouvions-nous avoir de la poésie française ramenée presque entièrement à François Coppée, à Sully Prudhomme et au "Lac" de Lamartine, si longtemps rabâché qu'aujourd'hui par un curieux phénomène – de rejet peut-être – je n'en saurais retrouver un seul vers' [What idea could we have had of French poetry, restricted as it was to little more than François Coppée, Sully Prudhomme and to Lamartine's 'The Lake', which we'd recite time and time again so that today by some strange phenomenon – perhaps a process of denial – I would not be able to recite a single line of it] (1996, 71). The (official) examination papers of the period reveal that Roy would also probably have studied some French-Canadian writers, notably *L'Oublié* by Laure Conan, one of her many historical and hagiographical works, regularly set at Grade X, plays by Racine (*Esther* and *Athalie* both set in the 1920s have Biblical subjects) at Grade XI and Corneille's *Polyeucte* (the 1682 edition of which bears the full title, *Polyeucte. Martyr. Tragédie chrétienne*). On the evidence it seems safe to generalize that 'French literature' was mostly from France and chiefly an expression or exploration of Catholic beliefs. Among the French authors studied, only Daudet is remembered with pleasure. The omissions from the syllabus are given as much space in Roy's account as the inclusions. She cites Zola, Flaubert, Maupassant and Balzac, and later adds Rimbaud, Verlaine, Baudelaire and Radiguet. By contrast the account of her early study of English literature is expressed very positively: 'La littérature anglaise, portes grandes ouvertes, nous livrait alors accès à ses plus hauts génies' [English literature, its doors wide open, gave us access to its greatest geniuses] (1996, 71). She lists Hardy, Eliot, the Brontës, Austen, Keats, Shelley, Byron, the Lake poets and above all, perhaps, Shakespeare. Roy's 'English' education is evident not just in her bilingualism, but also in the imprint of a typically British taste for universalism and humanism. It is worth noting that in the 1920s the canon of English and French literature studied at school remained firmly Eurocentric, but that a few Canadian texts were being included, particularly through readers but also at Grade XI, which for many pupils was their final year.

So, both the material that Roy studied and the context in which she studied encouraged her to adopt different modes of cultural identification. Her education was in effect bilingual, but divided into different zones, which Roy represents retrospectively as follows: 'Nous étions en quelque sorte anglaises dans l'algèbre, la géométrie, les sciences, dans l'histoire du Canada, mais françaises en histoire du Québec, en littérature de France et, encore plus, en histoire sainte' [We were in a way English in algebra, geometry, science, Canadian history, but French in the history of Quebec, in French literature and especially scripture] (1996, 71). This division seems to create a divide between reason and faith, between the tools of Anglophone power and the affective, so less powerful, sphere of the Francophone mother tongue. The passage continues: 'Cela nous faisait un curieux esprit, constamment occupé à rajuster notre vision' [That gave us a curious mentality, constantly having to readjust our vision] (71). Rather than producing the kind of tunnel vision discussed by Blaut in his study of history teaching (2000), it could be argued that this double curriculum confronts the pupil with 'twin tunnels'. Caught between two cultural instances, Roy needed to play the game very well to succeed. In fact her academic achievements and later success in gaining teaching posts relied on her being perfectly bilingual (Ricard 1996, 131–2). In her autobiographical accounts of her schooldays, cultural identity becomes a game, willingly played by Roy, by the teaching staff, perhaps even by the Department of Education. A visit from the school inspector exemplifies the kind of bicultural role-play expected: 'Il me demanda si je connaissais quelque passage de la pièce. Je ne perdis pas une minute, imprimai sur mon visage le masque de la tragédie et me lançai à fond de train: Is this a dagger...' [He asked me whether I knew any passages from the play. Without a moment's hesitation my expression took on the mask of tragedy and I launched myself at full pelt into 'Is this a dagger...'] (Roy 1996, 74). Roy then comments on the pleasure this ritual seems to produce: 'C'était la première fois que je découvrais à quel point nos adversaires anglophones peuvent nous chérir, quand nous jouons le jeu et nous montrons de bons enfants dociles' [It was the first time that I discovered just how much our Anglophone adversaries can cherish us when we play the game and act like good obedient children] (75). The scene confirms power relations between Anglophone and Francophone in Manitoba (Franco-Manitobans as children and Anglophone power justified by the Shakespearean text). It is essentially a colonial scene: 'Recitation of literary texts [...] becomes a ritual act of obedience, often performed by a child before an audience of admiring adults, who, in reciting that English tongue, speaks as if s/he were the imperial speaker/master rather than the subjectified colonial so often represented in English poetry and prose' (Ashcroft *et al.* 1995, 426). Roy's text suggests that this bicultural role-play was a game she played consciously, in a mode she refers to as 'un petit côté cabotin, peut-être en partie entretenu par notre sentiment collectif d'infériorité, et qui me faisait rechercher l'approbation de tous côtés' [a slight tendency to play to the gallery, perhaps partly sustained by our collective feeling of inferiority, and which made me seek approval from all sides] (1996, 73).

This last quotation reveals what I believe to be a significant tension in Roy's autobiographical recreation of her youth. This 'playing to the gallery' seems much more significant for her in the interwar years than any collective sense of revolt. Identity for Roy personally was more of a game than a cause. The pleasures of mimicry, of recitation, of play-acting for Anglophone and Francophone alike form a thread through Roy's education, her teaching career, her social life and leisure activities. In all spheres she was successfully bilingual. At school she was a leading pupil not just in French, but also in English. Her teaching at the Institut Provencher (1930–7), a boys' school in the heart of Catholic Saint-Boniface, was in the Reception Class for non-Francophones whom she taught in English. Her literary culture encompassed a wide range of French and English literature and other European authors in translation (Gagné 1973, 275–82). In her early attempts at writing (short stories, journalism and screenplays) she used both French and English. Throughout the 1930s Roy was active in amateur dramatic groups, notably the Cercle Molière, but also English-language groups in Winnipeg. The Cercle Molière offered a very different route into culture from that of the clerical nationalist AECFM. Many of its members were first- or second-generation immigrants from France, with European taste, accents and education. As Jean-Pierre Dubé writes, in its first phase (1925–41) the Cercle Molière's aim was to be recognized beyond Saint-Boniface, by educated Anglophones and Francophones alike: 's'inscrire dans une tradition européenne d'inspiration universelle, où la langue française est particulièrement respectée' [to inscribe ourselves in a universal, European tradition, in which French is particularly respected] (2001, 7). Involvement in the theatre helped to widen Roy's social circle beyond Saint-Boniface and gave her an entrée into a bourgeois, cosmopolitan world. It allowed her to travel, touring the Prairie province, but also twice to Ottawa to take part in the Dominion Drama Festival (Roy 2000, 28–31). Whereas for her mother the Provencher Bridge (between Saint-Boniface and Winnipeg) marked a divide, for her bilingual daughter it was a link to the wider world, and a route she would take easily, adapting to the expectations on both sides. When she left Manitoba for Europe in 1937 she spent time in both London and Paris, feeling much more at home in Britain than in France. It was only after her year living in England that the choice of language (quoted at the outset) crystallized. It is possible that it was only away from Manitoba that she could choose the French language, her mother's tongue, which she had experienced as the language of religious obedience and of inferiority.

The term 'bicultural straddle' is a useful one to apply to Roy's case and that of the Franco-Manitoban minority more generally, facing 'the complex interface of nationalism and colonial authority' (Loomba 1991, 314). Healy characterizes biculturalism as 'a talent made necessary by the imbalance of power that exists in these boundary situations. […] a technique of survival in someone else's world' (1992, 70). While there certainly was, and is, an imbalance of power between Anglophone and Francophone populations in Manitoba, the boundary is nevertheless between a colonial and a former colonial power, not between a colonial power and an indigenous, 'black' population. The resisting minority had considerable cultural and institutional resources at its disposal. As a result of the AECFM's efforts, pupils of Roy's generation were literally between cultures, between two colonial pasts and a range of nationalist discourses. Model pupil, Roy absorbed and recited, but the duality of her culture and the duplicity with which pupils were encouraged to counter Anglophone domination served perhaps to highlight the contradictions between cultures, not the absolute value of one culture. The clerical nationalism of the AECFM certainly presented an instance of resistance to Anglophone hegemony, but for Roy it seems to have had the quality of a 'masque' not a 'peau' (Fanon 1986 [1952]). She was in many ways the product of her education, but not the product intended by fervent Franco-Manitobans for whom 'l'héritage de foi et de langue ancestrale [...] allaient de pair' [the heritage of faith and language [...] went hand in hand] (Roy 1970, 74). The conservative aspects of the AECFM's activities in the interwar years doubtless did much to preserve a French-speaking presence in Manitoba. But Roy's successful negotiation between cultures perhaps offers a more flexible model of bilingualism and biculturalism for today.

23

Colonial undercurrents: the motif of the Mekong in Marguerite Duras's 'Indochinese' texts

BY JULIA WATERS

Colonial Indochina, the space of Marguerite Duras's birth and early life, occupies a privileged position in the author's literary universe, returning with haunting regularity, throughout her lengthy career, as contextual, thematic and psychological source of inspiration. Yet Duras's established status as a canonical, 'mainstream' French writer, and her pivotal contribution to some of twentieth-century France's most influential literary, intellectual and theoretical debates, have meant that the important, non-metropolitan, (post)colonial aspects of her works have, until very recently, received little critical attention.

Over the last decade, in line with the general growth of interest in Francophone Postcolonial Studies, a number of critics have begun to focus upon Duras's literary and filmic representations of Indochina and her texts' shifting engagements with colonial ideology. Often building on the feminist and gender-focused approaches that have dominated Duras studies, these postcolonial theoretical readings have shed fascinating new light on some of the author's best-known texts. Yet critics are strikingly divided as to the precise nature of Duras's treatments of the colonial context: while some – Dugast-Portes (1990), Holmlund (1991), Chester (1992) and Hsieh (1996) – celebrate the writer's transgressive disruption of social and colonial hierarchies, others – Norindr (1996), Bécel (1997) and Ha (2001) – argue that, for all their textual experimentation, Duras's texts ultimately reflect, or even reinforce, imperialist ideology's racial and class divisions. In her recent book, *Postcolonial Duras* (2001), Winston rejects oppositional readings of Duras as either pro- or anti-colonial. Borrowing the notion of the 'border-zone' or 'borderlands' from studies by Gloria Anzaldúa (1987) and Renato

Rosaldo (1993), she argues instead for an inclusive recognition of Duras's in-between position. Winston's study is, however, based primarily on the historical and biographical context of postwar France, rather than on Duras's writing itself.

Despite such recent interest in the (post)colonial aspects of Duras's work and life, virtually no critical attention has been paid to date to the heavily propagandist text, *L'Empire français*, that Duras co-wrote with Philippe Roques in 1940, while working at the Ministère des Colonies. (This work was written under Duras's original, birth surname. She did not adopt the pseudonym of 'Duras' until the publication of her first novel, *Les Impudents*, in 1943.) Yet the existence of this non-fictional precursor to Duras's novels and films offers particularly fertile ground for the exploration of possible connections between two very different discourses – propaganda and fiction – articulated by the same author. Indeed, Duras's lengthy career, spanning the colonial and post-colonial eras, and her personal trajectory – from child of impoverished 'colons' to major French intellectual and literary celebrity – make her work singularly appropriate material for exploring the relationship between the colonial and the post-colonial.

This chapter aims to explore the textual reflections of such a relationship, by focusing on the reworkings of the central, recurrent motif of the river Mekong in Duras's work – from her non-fictional *L'Empire français* of 1940, to her 'Indochinese' novels, *Un Barrage contre le Pacifique* (1950), *The Lover* (1985 [1984]) and *The North China Lover* (1994 [1991]). Duras highlighted, in interview, the formative and enduring importance of the Mekong in her imagination, when claiming: 'Ce Mékong auprès duquel j'ai dormi, j'ai joué, j'ai vécu, pendant dix ans de ma vie, il est resté' [This river, the Mekong, beside which I slept, played and lived for ten years of my life, it has stayed with me] (Duras and Gauthier 1974, 137). Given the inherent mobility and fluidity of the river motif, what descriptive or symbolic roles are ascribed to it in Duras's various works, spanning over half a century? In exploring the intertextual transposition of the motif from early pro-colonial, propagandist text to post-colonial, heterogeneous literary works, what picture do we gain of the development of Duras's retrospective reconstruction of Indochina?

According to Panivong Norindr, '"Indochine" is an elaborate fiction, a modern phantasmatic assemblage invented during the heyday of French colonial hegemony in Southeast Asia. It is a myth that has never existed and yet endures in our collective imaginary' (1996, 1). Norindr is here not only referring to France's conquest and annexation of previously distinct regions under the umbrella of the neologistic and geographically artificial entity of 'Indochine'. He is also stressing the prevalent depiction of both geography and people in terms of unifying, exoticizing and picturesque clichés which, through their proliferation, collectively construct a fantastic, mythical image of an already artificial place. An inextricable link therefore exists, in the construction of 'Indochina', between French imperialist practice and colonialist discourse. *L'Empire français* is an archetypal example of just this kind of mythologizing, pro-colonialist discourse. Written in 1940 (and thus certainly after the heyday of French imperialism), the book presents the French Empire as a source of patriotic reassurance and of material aid in the face of war. The contemporary threat to France's status as a world power can be seen to underpin the text's somewhat anachronistic recourse to consistently optimistic, clichéd images of its colonies and to euphemistic references to the 'noble motives' underlying France's 'civilizing mission' (Donnadieu [Duras] and Roques 1940, 45). The myth that *L'Empire français* constructs of Indochina is of that of 'la plus belle des colonies françaises' [the most beautiful of the French colonies] (116), with the Mekong portrayed as a superlatively majestic, defining feature.

Rivers provided colonial powers with the practical means of accessing, exploring and subjugating the inland areas of foreign countries. In tandem with this extension of colonial hegemony into the interior, the mapping of the routes taken into the interior asserted discursive control over subjugated lands. In *L'Empire français*, the centrality of geography and cartography to the discursive creation of the myth of 'Indochina' is evident both in the inclusion of a map of the colony, on which the Mekong is a prominent, named feature, and in the long description of the river's source, length and tributaries, the towns and areas it runs through and the rites and festivals associated with it.

Rivers not only allowed the colonial power to explore and annex the interior, bringing to it the 'benefits' of their 'civilizing mission', but also, inversely, to carry away goods, produce and workers from inland to other parts of the Empire. Casting such exploitative practices in a characteristically positive and euphemistic light, *L'Empire français* describes the Mekong as providing 'un merveilleux moyen de communication jusqu'à la mer' [a wonderful means of communication to the sea] (106). The Mekong's picturesque, superlative attributes of majesty and power are thus shown as simultaneously vital to the economic infrastructure of the colony.

The assertion of colonial control over the colonized land by means of economic exploitation is nowhere more keenly felt than in the description in *L'Empire français* of the Mekong's annual flooding. While the power of the river is again emphasized, its potential destructiveness is negated by the text's optimistic, pro-colonial agenda:

Le fleuve charrie de la terre et des matériaux en suspens dans ses eaux. Au moment maximum de la crue, à son point mort, ceux-ci se déposent lentement et forment une couche que couvre et que fixe l'année suivante une abondante végetation semi-aquatique, dont les joncs et les palétuviers sont en Indochine les spécimens les plus répandus. Peu à peu, ces terrains se colmatent et se superposent; les terres gagnent sur la mer. (107–8)

The river carries along soil and other debris suspended in its waters. When the flood reaches its very highest point, just before it begins to subside, these slowly settle to form a thick layer. This layer is fixed in place, the following year, by abundant, semi-aquatic plants, such as rushes and mangroves, the most common varieties in Indochina. Gradually, these areas are silting over, layer on layer: the land is gaining ground on the sea.

Even the destructive power of the river and the disastrous annual flooding of the Mekong Delta – the cause of much personal suffering for Duras's family and the subject of her novel *Un Barrage contre le Pacifique* – are glossed over in the text's assertion of France's control over the colony's natural resources. The floods are seen, by their moving and depositing of fertile debris, as enabling the cultivation, appropriation and pacification of Indochinese land, so ensuring and justifying the extension of French colonization.

Throughout the depiction of the geography of Indochina, inextricable and essentialist links are established between the 'natives' and their surroundings: the flat and monotonous flood plains are portrayed as determining the inhabitants' indolent and passive character. In opposition to the industrious Europeans, such links deny the 'native' the possibility of affinity with more powerful and destructive elements of the landscape, such as the flooding Mekong. The pacification of both the river and the people, and the assertion of a formative link between the two, can be seen, for instance, in the following description of the city of Pnom-Penh: 'Bâtie au plus large du Mékong, elle a toute la douceur de la cité fluviale. Le calme, l'immuabilité de son atmosphère tient au caractère silencieux et paisible de ses habitants' [Built at the widest point of the Mekong, it has the characteristic tranquillity of a riverside city. Its calm and unchanging atmosphere stems from the quiet, peaceful character of its inhabitants] (114). Just as the power of the Mekong is portrayed as being harnessed, so too are the people discursively pacified and controlled, in a characteristically colonialist manner, by their mythical association with what Abdul JanMohamed has called 'some magic essence of the continent' (1985, 68).

Written just ten years after *L'Empire français*, in 1950, Duras's *Un Barrage contre le Pacifique* in many ways represents a rejection and reversal of the ideological stance of its precursor. Exploiting many of the same descriptive elements as *L'Empire français*, the novel repeatedly turns them upon themselves, so making explicit the binary oppositions and racial stereotypes on which the myth of colonial Indochina was constructed. The novel centres on the vain battles of a family of poor white 'colons' both against the floodwater that annually invades the Mekong Delta and against the corrupt colonial officials who sold them their worthless plot of land. The Mekong is here shown as a destructive, unstoppable force that thwarts the family's hubristic attempts to hold it back. Reversing the qualities of fertility and productivity attributed to it in *L'Empire français*, the Mekong is now seen to invade the colonial world, eroding its edges and threatening its very foundations.

In the novel's depiction of the colonial city of Saigon, the busy, muddy river presents a stark contrast to the domesticated order of the 'haut quartier' [European district]. At the heart of the class and racial segregation on which the colonial system is based, lies the very different relationship that each distinct social group has with the river. The colonial town-planning of the European district is portrayed as maintaining an artificial separation between on the one hand its spotless and regimented avenues and on the other the chaotic indigenous areas by the dirty river. The essential whiteness, of skin and clothes, that crucially distinguishes the rich 'colons' from both 'natives' and poor Europeans, is shown as reliant on the constant use of purified and sanitized riverwater:

> Dès qu'ils arrivaient, ils apprenaient à se baigner tous les jours [...] et à s'habiller de l'uniforme colonial, du costume blanc, couleur d'immunité et d'innocence. Dès lors, le premier pas était fait. La distance augmentait d'autant, la différence première était multipliée, blanc sur blanc, entre eux et les autres, qui se nettoyaient avec la pluie du ciel et les eaux limoneuses des fleuves et des rivières. (Duras 1950, 167–8)

> As soon as they arrived, they would learn to bathe every day [...] and to dress in the colonial uniform of a white suit, the colour of immunity and innocence. From that moment on, the first step had been taken. White on white, the distance increased all the more, and the initial difference, between them and the others, who washed in rainwater and the silty water of the river and its tributaries, intensified.

The rich 'colons' exploit the water to maintain their lush gardens, fill their swimming pools and preserve the ordered cleanliness and whiteness on which the colonial structures depend, but they simultaneously maintain a self-protective distance from the less salubrious river from which it is drawn.

The 'indigènes', on the other hand, as in the above quotation, are repeatedly characterized by their contact with the river, living near or on it, swimming and washing in it, drinking from it, and diverting it to supply the paddy-fields that provide their living. Their daily immersion in the riverwater is even portrayed as influencing their physical characteristics. As in *L'Empire français*, a formative link is established between the 'natives' and their surroundings. This link in turn establishes a binary opposition between their association with mud, squalor, wildness and contamination and the colonizers' association with cleanliness, innocence, domestication and immunity.

As poor whites, on the lower rungs of the colonial ladder, Suzanne and her family in many ways embody the hidden or forgotten middle ground between colonizer and colonized. This in-between status is mirrored by the family's relationship with the river and its water. Suzanne is repeatedly depicted as passing the time, sitting on the bridge or beside the water. Her mother, in a more humble variant of the rich settlers' obsessive cleanliness, intermittently washes their decrepit bungalow with extravagant quantities of riverwater. When the family visits Saigon, they stay at the Hôtel Central, which occupies a site beyond the edges of the European district, between the delineating tramlines and the muddy river, bustling with native boats. The family's social status in the colonial hierarchy is matched by their relationship with the Mekong: dependent upon, though threatened by it, their proximity stands mid-way between the rich settlers' distance from, and the indigenous population's immersion in, the riverwater.

Arguably reflecting the disillusionment and self-questioning of the postwar years, *Un Barrage contre le Pacifique* refutes and complicates the neat certainties of the colonial era, as presented in *L'Empire français* just a decade earlier. Yet, in keeping with the inherent fluidity of the river motif, areas of ambivalence still exist. The native inhabitants remain silent and virtually faceless throughout, and the proximity of the disaffected white family with the river could be seen to imply their contamination, by association with the poverty and squalor of the 'natives'. The portrayal of Indochina in *Un Barrage contre le Pacifique* does indeed muddy its colonial structures, but it does not offer an outright rejection of them.

When Duras returns, over thirty years later, to the territory of her childhood in Indochina, in her semi-autobiographical novel *The Lover*, the Mekong is again a recurrent motif. Meandering its way through the many-layered, heterogeneous text, the central motif of the Mekong here takes on multiple symbolic and stylistic meanings. Some of its many, interlocking associations are present in the following, early reference to the young girl's crossing of the river, a pivotal, recurrent scene in the novel:

> I look at the river. My mother sometimes tells me that never in my whole life shall I ever again see rivers as beautiful and big and wild as these, the Mekong and its tributaries going down to the sea [...]. In the terrible current I watch my last moments. The current's so strong it could carry everything away – rocks, a cathedral, a city. There's a storm blowing inside the water. A wind raging. (Duras 1985, 14)

As in *L'Empire français*, reference is made to the Mekong's superlative, majestic beauty and to its many tributaries; yet this is combined here with an emphasis on the threat that the river's power poses to man-made, colonially imposed structures – rocks, a cathedral, a city. In addition, the use of the first-person narrative and the insistence on the act of watching establish a link between the river's destructive potential and the girl's story, between the water's swift, unstoppable flow and the passing of time, to which the autobiographical writing bears witness.

Throughout *The Lover*, the girl's identity becomes inextricably associated with the Mekong. The crossing of the river represents her crossing of the boundaries between different zones and her disruption of conventional order, while her contemplative gaze at its turbulent flood-water underlines her affinity with the motif's multiple meanings. As the novel progresses, the symbolic links between the girl and the river are expanded to include the force of desire. Just as the floodwater threatens to sweep away colonial society's physical structures, so too here does the young white girl's affair with the Chinese lover of the novel's title trans-gress its moral and ethnic boundaries. Not only do the age, class and ethnic differences between them make their affair scandalous, but the fact that the lover is Chinese, rather than 'Indochinese', further disrupts easy binary oppositions between colonizer and colonized. In the novel's description of the young girl's first meeting with her lover on the Vinh-Long ferry over the Mekong, the force of the couple's latent desire and the inevitability of their affair are signalled implicitly by the inclusion of the following reference to the river:

> The river's picked up all it's met with since Tonle Sap and the Cambodian forest. It carries everything along, straw huts, forests, burned-out fires, dead birds, dead dogs, drowned tigers and buffaloes, drowned men, bait, islands of water hyacinths all stuck together. Everything flows towards the Pacific, no time for anything to sink, all is swept along by the deep and head-long storm of the inner current, suspended on the surface of the river's strength. (25–6)

Here, *L'Empire français*'s description of the debris carried along by the floodwater, quoted earlier, is lyrically expanded and, far from stressing its settling and the area's subsequent fertility and potential exploitation, the novel's reworking of the motif emphasizes the river's (and, by association, desire's) unstoppable, unpredictable dizzying power and open-endedness. The girl's discovery of the power of sexual desire, mirrored textually in the river's irrepressible force, leads to her rejection of her family's and society's rules and to her transition from childhood to adulthood. The repeated references to death in the above passage also underline the river's symbolic association with the passing of time, signalling the inevitable temporal gap between the aged writing self and the young autobiographical self, as remembered and reconstructed in the text. A complex network of inter-connected and ever-proliferating associative links is thus implicitly set in motion, by means of the motif of the Mekong, between writing, place, time, self, desire and death.

In *The North China Lover*, written seven years after *The Lover* and in many ways a reworking of the same autobiographical material, the transgressive link between the young white girl of the earlier book and the river is taken a step further. Whereas, in the previous text, the girl's relationship to the river emphasized her ability to cross and disrupt colonial boundaries of class and race, the later novel establishes a defining link between the land of her birth and the young girl's identity. The novel repeatedly refers to her native command of Vietnamese and her repulsion for all but Vietnamese food. More than birthplace, diet or language, however, contact with water is shown as forming the overriding basis for the girl's claim to an Indochinese identity. Just as the indigenous people, in *Un Barrage contre le Pacifique* or *The Lover*, were portrayed as being formed by their constant immersion in water, so too the young white girl's non-Caucasian appearance and complexion are shown to have been formed, as her lover says to her, by her contact with rainwater: 'You have the rain skin of Asian women' (Duras 1994, 74). This claim to a non-European identity and appearance, via association with the river, echoes Duras's own claim, in an interview, that she was often mistaken for a mixed-race child. Countering accusations that her mother might have had an affair with a local, she argues that 'le métissage vient d'ailleurs. [...] Notre appartenance indicible à la terre des mangues, à l'eau noire du sud, des plaines à riz' [our métissage comes from something else. [...] From our inexpressible sense of belonging to the land of mangos, to the dark water of the south, the rice plains] (Duras 1984, 278).

While the river is repeatedly evoked in *The North China Lover*, it occupies a less central position than in *The Lover*: rather than being the key symbolic motif, linking the various levels of the text via its embodiment of flux, desire and transgression, it becomes confounded with other motifs, such as rain, paddy-fields or the sea, to form a watery, symbolic subtext or backdrop. Indeed, many of the Mekong's symbolic associations can only be fully deduced by reading them in intertextual association with those of *The Lover*. For instance, the key scene of the ferry crossing is portrayed in the following, highly allusive passage:

This is the river.

This is the ferry across the Mekong. The ferry in the books.
On the river.
There on the ferry is the native bus, the long black Léon Bollée cars,
    the North China lovers, looking.

The ferry sets out.
Once it departs, the child gets off the bus. She looks at the river. She
    also looks at the elegant Chinese who is inside the big black car.
She is made up, the child, dressed like the young girl in the books.

(1994, 25)

As in *The Lover*, the figures on the ferry are juxtaposed with the river below. Yet the implicit link with the destructive force of desire underlying this juxtaposition, and hinted at through the girl's gaze, is not descriptively expanded and can only be constructed by reference, via the phrases 'the ferry in the books' and 'the young girl in the books', to the motif's network of interrelated symbolic associations in the earlier text.

The Mekong becomes, in *The North China Lover*, a shortcut form of intertextual self-reference, even further distanced from an original geographic and historical location than in previous works. Indeed, Duras has warned against over-referential readings of her depictions of 'real' places, referring to the techniques she uses as 'descriptions par touches de couleur' [descriptions by brushstrokes of colour] (Knapp 1971, 655): that is, rather than construct a detailed, mimetic description, she would focus on just four or five signs or objects that encapsulated what she saw as a place's essence. The following extract, in which the river is included as just one of several signs or 'repères' [reference points] in a rapid sketch of colonial Saigon, seems to embody just such an abstract, tangentially referential approach:

> Across the city. Two or three landmarks, right off the list: the Charner Theater, the Cathedral, the Eden Cinema, the Chinese restaurant for whites. The Continental, the most beautiful hotel in the world. And the river, that incantation, always, day or night, empty or crowded with junks, calls, laughter, songs, and sea birds coming up from the Plain of Reeds. (Duras 1994, 86)

At the end of the novel, Duras describes an appended series of descriptive images – many of which are of the river or of rain – 'as an exterior to the film, a "country", the one the people in this book are from, the world of the film. And of the film alone, with no attempt to reproduce reality' (227). Although the novel's central character is repeatedly portrayed as having an essential, formative affinity with the place of her birth through association with its natural elements, Duras simultaneously uses such elements to construct a fictional, mythical space, far removed from its original autobiographical or geographic source.

As we have seen, while the descriptive motif of the river Mekong is an enduring one throughout Duras's 'Indochinese' texts, it undergoes a series of major intertextual transformations. In the propagandist *L'Empire français*, the Mekong is predictably portrayed as a central, picturesque element of the landscape and as a powerful but containable ally in the colonial economic infrastructure. In *Un Barrage contre le Pacifique*, ten years later, however, the river's floodwater is portrayed as threatening the stability and order of colonial structures and hierarchies. In *The Lover*, the destructive potential of the Mekong – a key symbolic trope – is expanded to include not only the transgression of class and race boundaries, but also the unstoppable power of desire and death. The portrayal, in *The North China*

Lover, of the central character's 'métissage', based primarily on essential links with water, seems to present a further step in the blurring of racial boundaries and the disruption of colonial hierarchies. Yet this is countered by the use of the river as a picturesque 'brushstroke' in the construction of a non-referential, 'imaginary' Indochina, implying a return to a position of spectatorial, even neocolonial, distance from, and appropriation of, the original source.

The intertextual, symbolic transformations that the Mekong motif undergoes between Duras's various works in many ways reflect more general shifts, during the period, in France's relationship to its colonial past: from wartime patriotic assertion of its status as a world power, to postwar disillusionment and anti-colonial struggles, to postcolonial self-questioning tinged with nostalgia. Yet Duras's particular position – as a canonical French author, although born in Indochina, to a family of poor 'colons' – embodies further levels of paradox and ambiguity in the relationship between France and its former colonies.

All of Duras's 'Indochinese' texts, from *L'Empire français* of 1940 to *The North China Lover* (originally published in 1991), were written in France, at a spacial, and increasingly temporal, distance from their original geographic context. Duras never returned to the land of her birth after leaving it in 1933, and her only first-hand experience of it was under colonial rule. Although written in a postcolonial era, Duras's later, semi-autobiographical novels consistently reconstruct a colonial world that no longer exists. In recollecting, in literary form, the land of her childhood, Duras concomitantly draws on the anachronistic structures and discourse of that time. Our examination of the transformative and emulative intertextual reworkings of the Mekong motif, from the propagandist *L'Empire français* to Duras's later novels, not only illustrates the inherent fluidity and ambiguity of this particular motif, but also highlights the continued influence of tropes of colonial discourse in apparently transgressive, postcolonial, literary texts. Just as the Mekong's meanderings through Duras's works blur narrative boundaries, so too do they underline the impossibility of ever truly separating the post-colonial from its colonial past.

Bibliography

ACHEBE, Chinua. 1958: *Things Fall Apart*. London: Heinemann.

ADIAFFI, Jean-Marie. 1980: *La Carte d'identité*. Paris: Hatier.

ADOTÉVI, Stanislas. 1972: *Négritude et négrologues*. Paris: Plon.

AECFM ARCHIVES. Consulted at the Centre du patrimoine franco-manitobain, Saint-Boniface.

AGACINSKI, Sylviane. 2001: *Politique des sexes et mise au point sur la mixité*. Paris: Seuil.

AGER, Dennis. 1999: *Identity, Insecurity and Image: France and Language*. Clevedon: Multilingual Matters.

AGERON, Charles-Robert. 1968: *Les Algériens musulmans et la France (1871–1919)*. Paris: PUF.

AGERON, Charles-Robert. 1997: 'L'Exposition coloniale de 1931: Mythe républicain ou mythe impérial?'. In NORA (ed.), I, pp. 493–515.

AHMAD, Aijaz. 1987: 'Jameson's rhetoric of otherness and the "national allegory"'. *Social Text* 17, pp. 3–27.

AHMAD, Aijaz. 1992: *In Theory: Classes, Nations, Literatures*. London and New York: Verso.

AHMAD, Aijaz. 1996: 'The politics of literary postcoloniality'. In Padmini MONGIA (ed.), *Contemporary Postcolonial Theory: A Reader*. London: Arnold, pp. 276–93.

ALAN, John, and Lou TURNER. 1986: *Frantz Fanon, Soweto and American Black Thought*. Chicago: News and Letters.

ALEXIS, Jacques-Stephen. 1955: *Compère Général Soleil*. Paris: Gallimard.

AMIROU, Rachid. 1995: *Imaginaire touristique et sociablilités du voyage*. Paris: PUF.

ANDREW, Dudley. 1995: *Mists of Regret: Culture and Sensibility in Classic French Film*. Princeton: Princeton UP.

ANDREW, Dudley. 1997: 'Praying Mantis: enchantment and violence in French cinema of the exotic'. In BERNSTEIN and STUDLAR (eds), pp. 232–52.

ANONYMOUS. 2000 [1740]: *Histoire de Louis Anniaba*, ed. Roger LITTLE. Exeter: University of Exeter Press (Textes littéraires 108).

ANTOINE, Régis. 1992: *La Littérature franco-antillaise*. Paris: Karthala.

ANZALDÚA, Gloria. 1987: *Borderlands/La Frontera: The New Mestiza*. San Francisco, CA: Aunt Lute Books.

APPIAH, Kwame Anthony. 1992: *In My Father's House: Africa in the Philosophy of Culture*. Oxford and New York: Oxford UP.

APTER, Emily. 1995: 'French Colonial Studies and postcolonial theory'. *Sub-Stance* 76–7, pp. 169–80.

APTER, Emily. 1998: '"Untranslatable" Algeria'. *Parallax* 7, pp. 47–59.

APTER, Emily. 1999: *Continental Drift: From National Characters to Virtual Subjects*. Chicago and London: University of Chicago Press.

AQUIN, Hubert. 1988: 'The cultural fatigue of French Canada', trans. L. Shouldice. In Anthony PURDY (ed.), *Writing Quebec: Selected Essays by Hubert Aquin*. Edmonton: University of Alberta Press, pp. 19–48. [First published as 'La fatigue culturelle du Canada français', 1962.]

ARAC, Jonathan. 1997: 'Shop window or laboratory: collection, collaboration and the Humanities'. In E. Ann KAPLAN and George LEVINE (eds), *The Politics of Research*. New Brunswick, NJ: Rutgers UP, pp. 116–26.

ASHCROFT, Bill. 1996: 'On the hyphen in "post-colonial"'. *New Literatures Review* 32, pp. 23–31.

ASHCROFT, Bill. 1998: 'Modernity's first born: Latin America and post-colonial transformation'. *ARIEL* 29.2, pp. 7–29.

ASHCROFT, Bill, Gareth GRIFFITHS and Helen TIFFIN. 1989: *The Empire Writes Back: Theory and Practice in Post-Colonial Literatures*. London and New York: Routledge.

ASHCROFT, Bill, Gareth GRIFFITHS and Helen TIFFIN (eds). 1995: *The Post-Colonial Studies Reader*. London and New York: Routledge.

ASHCROFT, Bill, Gareth GRIFFITHS and Helen TIFFIN. 1998: *Key Concepts in Post-Colonial Studies*. London and New York: Routledge.

AUGUST, Thomas G. 1985: *The Selling of the Empire: British and French Imperialist Propaganda, 1890–1940*. Westport, CT, and London: Greenwood Press.

BÂ, Ahmadou Hampâté. 1973: *L'Étrange destin de Wangrin*. Paris: UGÉ.

BÂ, Ahmadou Hampâté, and Lilyan KESTELOOT (eds). 1969: *Kaïdara: récit initiatique peule*. Paris: Julliard.

BÂ, Mariama. 1981: *So Long a Letter*, trans. Modupe Bode-Thomas. London and Portsmouth, NH: Heinemann. [First published as *Une si longue lettre*, 1979.]

BADINTER, Elisabeth. 1996: 'Non aux quotas de femmes'. *Le Monde* 12 June, p. 15.

BADINTER, Elisabeth, Régis DEBRAY, Alain FINKIELKRAUT, Elisabeth DE FONTENAY and Catherine KINTZLER. 1989: 'Profs, ne capitulons pas!'. *Le Nouvel Observateur* 23–9 November.

BADOU, Gérard. 2000: *L'Enigme de la Vénus Hottentote*. Paris: Lattès.

BAKHTIN, Mikhail. 1981: *The Dialogic Imagination*. Austin: University of Texas Press.

BALIBAR, Étienne, and Immanuel WALLERSTEIN. 1988: *Race, nation, classe: les identités ambiguës*. Paris: La Découverte.

BALIBAR, Renée. 1985: *L'Institution du français: Essai sur le colinguisme des Carolingiens à la République*. Paris: PUF.

BALZAC, Honoré de. 1957 [1829]: *Les Chouans*, ed. Maurice Regard. Paris: Garnier Frères.

BANCEL, Nicolas, Pascal BLANCHARD, Gilles BOETSCH, Eric DEROO and Sandrine LEMAIRE (eds). 2002: *Zoos humains: de la Vénus hottentote aux reality shows*. Paris: La Découverte.

BARBER, Karin. 1991: *I Could Speak Until Tomorrow: Oriki, Women and the Past in a Yoruba Town*. Edinburgh: Edinburgh UP.

BARBER, Karin. 1995: 'African-language literature and postcolonial criticism'. *Research in African Literatures* 26.4, pp. 3–30.

BARBER, Karin (ed.). 1997: *Readings in African Popular Culture*. Oxford: James Currey; Bloomington: Indiana UP.

BARBER, Karin, Alain RICARD and John COLLINS. 1997: *West African Popular Theater*. Bloomington: Indiana UP.

BARDOLPH, Jacqueline. 2001: *Études postcoloniales et littérature*. Paris: Champion.

BARTHÉLEMY, Gérard. 2000: *Créoles-Bossales: Conflit en Haïti*. Petit-Bourg, Guadeloupe: Ibis Rouge.

BARTHES, Roland. 1957: *Mythologies*. Paris: Seuil.

BASSNETT, Susan. 1993: *Comparative Literature: A Critical Introduction*. Oxford: Blackwell.

BASSNETT, Susan, and Harish TRIVEDI. 1999: *Post-Colonial Translation: Theory and Practice*. London and New York: Routledge.

BAUMGART, Winfried. 1982: *Imperialism: the Idea and Reality of British and French Colonial Expansion, 1880–1914*. Oxford: Oxford UP.

BÉCEL, Pascale. 1997: 'From *The Sea Wall* to *The Lover*: Prostitution and Exotic Parody'. *Studies in Twentieth-Century Literature* 21.2, pp. 417–32.

BEER, William R. 1980: *The Unexpected Rebellion: Ethnic Activism in Contemporary France*. New York: New York UP.

BEGAG, Azouz. 1986: *Le Gone du Chaâba*. Paris: Seuil.

BEGAG, Azouz. 1989: *Béni ou le paradis privé*. Paris: Seuil.

BELCHER, Stephen. 1999: *Epic Traditions of Africa*. Bloomington: Indiana UP.

BENALI, Abdelkader. 1998: *Le Cinéma colonial au Maghreb*. Paris: Éditions du Cerf.

BENIAMINO, Michel. 1999: *La Francophonie littéraire: essai pour une théorie*. Paris: L'Harmattan.

BEN JELLOUN, Tahar. 1984: *Hospitalité française*. Paris: Seuil.

BEN JELLOUN, Tahar, with Egi VOLTERRANI. 1991: *Dove lo stato non c'è: racconti italiani*. Turin: Einaudi.

BENOT, Yves. 1989: *La Révolution française et la fin des colonies*. Paris: La Découverte.

BENOT, Yves, and Marcel DORIGNY (eds). 2000: *Grégoire et la cause des Noirs (1789–1831)*. Paris: Société française d'histoire d'outre-mer.

BERGER, Anne-Emmanuelle (ed.). 2002: *Algeria in Others' Languages.* Ithaca, NY: Cornell UP.

BERGNER, Gwen. 1995: 'Who is that masked woman? or the role of gender in Fanon's *Black Skin, White Masks*'. *PMLA* 110.1, pp. 75–88.

BERNABÉ, Jean, Patrick CHAMOISEAU and Raphaël CONFIANT. 1993 [1989]: *Éloge de la créolité.* Paris: Gallimard.

BERNARDIN DE SAINT-PIERRE, J.-H. 1995 [1818]: *Empsaël et Zoraïde, ou les Blancs esclaves des Noirs à Maroc*, ed. Roger LITTLE. Exeter: University of Exeter Press (Textes littéraires 92).

BERNHEIMER, Charles (ed.). 1995. *Comparative Literature in an Age of Multiculturalism.* Baltimore, MD, and London: Johns Hopkins UP.

BERNSTEIN, Matthew, and Gaylyn STUDLAR (eds). 1997: *Visions of the East: Orientalism in Film.* London and New York: I.B. Tauris.

BERTHO, Catherine. 1980: 'L'invention de la Bretagne: genèse sociale d'un stéréotype'. *Actes de la recherche en sciences sociales* 35, pp. 45–62.

BERY, Ashok, and Patricia MURRAY (eds). 1999: *Comparing Postcolonial Literatures: Dislocations.* Basingstoke: Macmillan.

BEYALA, Calixthe. 1987: *C'est le soleil qui m'a brûlée.* Paris: Stock.

BEYALA, Calixthe. 1988: *Tu t'appelleras Tanga.* Paris: Stock.

BEYALA, Calixthe. 1992. *Le Petit Prince de Belleville.* Paris: Albin Michel.

BEYALA, Calixthe. 1993: *Maman a un amant.* Paris: Albin Michel.

BEYALA, Calixthe. 2000: *Lettre d'une Afro-française à ses compatriotes.* Paris: Mango document.

BHABHA, Homi K. 1983: 'The Other question ... Homi K. Bhabha reconsiders the stereotype and colonial discourse'. *Screen* 24.6, pp. 18–36.

BHABHA, Homi K. 1986: 'Remembering Fanon'. Introduction to FANON, pp. vii–xxv.

BHABHA, Homi K. (ed.). 1990: *Nation and Narration.* London and New York: Routledge.

BHABHA, Homi K. 1994: *The Location of Culture.* London and New York: Routledge.

BIONDI, Jean-Pierre, and Françoise ZUCCARELLI. 1989: *16 pluviôse an II: les colonies de la Révolution.* Paris: Denoël.

BLANCHARD, Pascal, and Nicolas BANCEL. 1998: *De l'indigène à l'immigré.* Paris: Gallimard, Découvertes.

BLANCHARD, Pascal, Nicolas BANCEL and Sandrine LEMAIRE. 2001: '1931! Tous à l'Expo'. *Manière de voir* 58, pp. 46–9. [Special issue entitled 'Polémiques sur l'histoire coloniale'.]

BLANCHARD, Pascal, Eric DEROO and Gilles MANCERON. 2002: *Le Paris noir.* Paris: Hazan.

BLAUT, James M. 2000: 'History inside out: the argument'. In Diana BRYDON (ed.), *Postcolonialism: Critical Concepts.* London and New York: Routledge, pp. 1692–738.

BLAY, Jacqueline. 1987: *L'Article 23: les péripéties législatives et juridiques du fait français au Manitoba, 1870–1986*. Saint-Boniface: Les Éditions du Blé.

BLOCHE, Patrick. 1999: *Le Désir de France*. Paris: La Documentation Française.

BODY-GENDROT, Sophie. 2001: 'Culture et politique: nouveaux défis'. In WIEVIORKA and OHANA (eds), pp. 42–9.

BOEHMER, Elleke. 1995: *Colonial and Postcolonial Literature*. Oxford and New York: Oxford UP.

BONGIE, Chris. 1991: *Exotic Memories: Literature, Colonialism, and the Fin de Siècle*. Stanford, CA: Stanford UP.

BONGIE, Chris. 1998: *Islands and Exiles: The Creole Identities of Post/Colonial Literature*. Stanford, CA: Stanford UP.

BONN, Charles. 1974: *La Littérature algérienne de langue française et ses lectures*. Quebec: Naaman.

BONN, Charles. 1985: *Le Roman algérien de langue française: Vers un espace de communication littéraire décolonisé?* Paris and Montreal: L'Harmattan–PUM.

BORGOMANO, Madeleine. 1998: *Ahmadou Kourouma: le 'guerrier' griot*. Paris: L'Harmattan.

BOURAOUI, Hédi. 1997: *Tunisie plurielle*. 2 vols. Tunis: L'Or du temps.

BOURDIEU, Pierre, Jacques DERRIDA, Didier ERIBON, Michelle PERROT, Paul VEYNE and Pierre VIDAL-NAQUET. 1996: 'Pour une reconnaissance légale du couple homosexuel'. *Le Monde* 1 March.

BOUTHILLETTE, Jean. 1997 [1971]: *Le Canadien français et son double*. Quebec: Lanctôt.

BRAHIMI, Denise, and Anne TREVARTHEN. 1998: *Les Femmes dans la littérature africaine: portraits*. Paris and Abidjan: Karthala–Ceda.

BRÄNDLE, Rea. 2002: 'La monstration de l'Autre en Suisse: plaidoyer pour des micro-études'. In BANCEL *et al.* (eds), pp. 221–6.

BRENNAN, Timothy. 1997: *At Home in the World: Cosmopolitanism Now*. Cambridge, MA, and London: Harvard UP.

BRITTON, Celia. 1996: 'Eating their words: the consumption of French Caribbean Literature'. *ASCALF Yearbook* 1, pp. 15–23.

BRITTON, Celia. 1999: *Édouard Glissant and Postcolonial Theory: Strategies of Language and Resistance*. Charlottesville: UP of Virginia.

BRITTON, Celia, and Michael SYROTINSKI. 2001: 'Introduction'. *Paragraph* 24.3, pp. 1–11. [Special issue entitled 'Francophone Texts and Postcolonial Theory'.]

BUCK-MORSS, Susan. 2000: 'Hegel and Haiti'. *Critical Inquiry* 26.4, pp. 821–65.

BUGUL, Ken. 1983: *Le Baobab fou*. Abidjan: NÉA.

BURNHAM, Linda. 1994: 'Race and gender: the limits of analogy'. In Ethel TOBACH and Betty ROSOFF (eds), *Challenging Racism and Sexism:*

Alternatives to Genetic Explanations. New York: The Feminist Press, pp. 143–62.

BURTON, Richard. 1993: '"KI MOUN NOU YE": The idea of difference in contemporary French West Indian thought'. *New West Indian Guide* 67.1, pp. 5–32.

CABANEL, Patrick. 2002: 'Protestantisme et laïcité: réflexion sur la trace religieuse de l'histoire contemporaine de la France'. *Modern and Contemporary France* 10.1, pp. 89–103.

CAERLÉON. 1969: *La Révolution bretonne permanente*. Paris: La Table Ronde.

CALVET, Louis-Jean. 1974: *Linguistique et colonialisme: petit traité de glottophagie*. Paris: Payot.

CALVET, Louis-Jean. 1999 [1987]: *La Guerre des langues et les politiques linguistiques*. Paris: Hachette.

CAMUS, Albert. 1948: *The Plague*, trans. Stuart Gilbert. London: Hamish Hamilton. [First published as *La Peste*, 1947.]

CAMUS, Albert. 1953: *The Rebel*, trans. Anthony Bower. London: Hamish Hamilton. [First published as *L'Homme révolté*, 1951.]

CAMUS, Albert. 1962: 'The Guest'. In *Exile and the Kingdom*, trans. Justin O'Brien. Harmondsworth: Penguin, pp. 65–82. [First published as 'L'Hôte'. In *L'Exil et le royaume*, 1957.]

CAMUS, Albert. 1965 [1958]: *Actuelles III: Chroniques algériennes (1938–1958)*. In Albert CAMUS, *Essais*, ed. Roger QUILLIOT and Louis FAUCON. Paris: Gallimard, Bibliothèque de la Pléiade, pp. 887–1018.

CANNON, Steve. 1997: '*Paname City Rapping*: B-Boys in the "banlieues" and beyond'. In HARGREAVES and McKINNEY (eds), pp. 150–66.

CÉLESTIN, Roger. 1996: *From Cannibals to Radicals: Figures and Limits of Exoticism*. Minneapolis and London: University of Minnesota Press.

CERQUIGLINI, Bernard. 1999: 'La Charte européenne des langues régionales ou minoritaires'. In CLAIRIS *et al.* (eds), pp. 107–10.

CÉSAIRE, Aimé. 1972: *Discourse on Colonialism*, trans. Joan Pinkham. New York: Monthly Review Press. [First published as *Discours sur le colonialisme*, 1955.]

CÉSAIRE, Aimé. 1981 [1961]: *Toussaint Louverture: La Révolution française et le problème colonial*. Paris: Présence Africaine.

CÉSAIRE, Aimé. 1995: *Notebook of a Return to My Native Land*, trans. Mireille Rosello with Annie Pritchard. Newcastle: Bloodaxe. [First published as *Cahier d'un retour au pays natal*, 1939.]

CÉSAIRE, Suzanne. 1996 [1943]: '1943: Surrealism and us'. In RICHARDSON (ed.), pp. 123–6.

CHALAYE, Sylvie. 1998: *Du Noir au nègre: l'image du Noir au théâtre de Marguerite de Navarre à Jean Genet (1550–1960)*. Paris: L'Harmattan.

CHALIAND, Gérard. 1991: 'Frantz Fanon, à l'épreuve du temps'. In FANON, pp. 9–36.

CHAMBERLAND, Paul. 1983 [1964]: 'De la damnation à la liberté'. In Paul CHAMBERLAND, *Un Parti pris anthropologique*. Montreal: Parti pris, pp. 79–129.

CHAMOISEAU, Patrick. 1993: *Une Enfance créole 1: Antan d'enfance*. Paris: Gallimard.

CHAMOISEAU, Patrick. 1994: *Une Enfance créole 2: Chemin-d'école*. Paris: Gallimard.

CHAMOISEAU, Patrick. 1997: *Écrire en pays dominé*. Paris: Gallimard.

CHAMOISEAU, Patrick. 2002: *Biblique des derniers gestes*. Paris: Gallimard.

CHAMOISEAU, Patrick, and Raphaël CONFIANT. 1991: *Lettres créoles: tracées antillaises et continentales de la littérature*. Paris: Hatier.

CHAMPAUD, Claude. 1977: *Le Séparisianisme*. Rennes: Armor.

CHESTER, Suzanne. 1992: 'Writing the subject: exoticism/eroticism in Marguerite Duras's *The Lover* and *The Sea Wall*'. In Sidonie SMITH and Julia WATSON (eds), *Decolonizing the Subject*. Minneapolis: University of Minnesota Press.

CHEVALIER, Jean-Claude. 1997: '*L'Histoire de la langue française* de Ferdinand Brunot'. In NORA (ed.), III, pp. 3385–411.

CHEVRIER, Jacques. 1974: *Littérature nègre*. Paris: A. Colin.

CHEVRIER, Jacques. 1989: 'Roman africain: le temps du doute et des incertitudes'. *Jeune Afrique* 1 March, pp. 62–4.

CHIKH, Slimane. 1981: *L'Algérie en armes*. Algiers: Office des Publications Universitaires.

CHILDS, Peter, and Patrick WILLIAMS. 1997: *An Introduction to Post-Colonial Theory*. London: Prentice Hall/Harvester Wheatsheaf.

CHRISTIAN, Barbara. 1990: 'The race for theory'. In Gloria ANZALDÚA (ed.), *Making Face, Making Soul. Haciendo caras: Creative and Critical Perspectives by Feminists of Color*. San Francisco, CA: Aunt Lute Books, pp. 335–45.

CinémAction. 1990: 'Cinémas métis: De Hollywood aux films beurs'. 56.

CIXOUS, Hélène. 1976: 'Fiction and its phantoms: a reading of Freud's *Das Unheimliche* (the "uncanny")'. *New Literary History* 7.3, pp. 525–48.

CIXOUS, Hélène. 1996: 'My algeriance, in other words to depart not to arrive from Algeria'. Unpublished lecture delivered at the 'Algeria in and out of France' conference, Cornell University. Cited in APTER 1998, p. 58, note 22.

CIXOUS, Hélène. 1998: 'Letter to Zohra Drif'. *Parallax* 7, pp. 189–96.

CLAIRIS, Christos, Denis COASTAOUEC and Jean-Baptiste COYOS (eds). 1999: *Langues et cultures régionales de France: état des lieux, enseignement, politiques*. Paris: L'Harmattan.

CLANCY-SMITH, Julia, and Frances GOUDA (eds). 1998: *Domesticating the Empire: Gender and Family Life in French and Dutch Colonialism*. Charlottesville and London: UP of Virginia.

CLEGG, Ian. 1971: *Workers' Self-Management in Algeria*. London: Allen Lane.

CLEGG, Ian. 1979: 'Workers and Managers in Algeria'. In Robin COHEN, Peter GUTKIND and Phyllis BRAZIER (eds), *Peasants and Proletarians: The Struggles of Third World Workers*. London: Hutchinson, pp. 223–47.

CLIFF, Tony. 1999: *Trotskyism after Trotsky*. London: Bookmarks.

CLIFFORD, James. 1988: *The Predicament of Culture: Twentieth-century Ethnography, Literature and Art*. Cambridge, MA: Harvard UP.

CLIFFORD, James. 1992: 'Travelling Cultures'. In Lawrence GROSSBERG, Cary NELSON and Paula A. TREICHLER (eds), *Cultural Studies*. New York and London: Routledge, pp. 96–112.

CLIFFORD, James. 1997: *Routes: Travel and Translation in the Late Twentieth Century*. Cambridge, MA, and London: Harvard UP.

LE CODE NOIR. 1742: *Le Code Noir, ou Recueil des réglemens rendus jusqu'à présent concernant le gouvernement, l'administration de la justice, la police, la discipline et le commerce des nègres dans les colonies françoises, et les conseils et compagnies établis à ce sujet*. Paris: Prault.

COHEN, William B. 1980: *The French Encounter with Africans: White Responses to Blacks*. Bloomington: Indiana UP.

COLLECTIVE. 2002: *ContreOffensive*. Paris: Pauvert.

COMBE, Dominique. 1995: *Poétiques francophones*. Paris: Hachette.

COMPAGNON, Antoine. 2000: 'L'Exception française'. *Textuel* 37, pp. 41–52.

CONDÉ, Maryse. 1979: *La Parole des femmes: essai sur des romancières des Antilles de langue française*. Paris: L'Harmattan.

CONDÉ, Maryse. 1993: 'Order, disorder, freedom and the West Indian writer'. *Yale French Studies* 82–3, pp. 121–35.

CONFIANT, Raphaël. 1993a: *Aimé Césaire: Une traversée paradoxale du siècle*. Paris: Stock.

CONFIANT, Raphaël. 1993b: *Ravines du devant-jour*. Paris: Gallimard.

CONKLIN, Alice. 1997: *A Mission to Civilize: The Republican Idea of Empire in France and West Africa, 1895–1930*. Stanford, CA: Stanford UP.

COOPER, Frederick, and Ann STOLER (eds). 1997: *Tensions of Empire: Colonial Cultures in a Bourgeois World*. Los Angeles and London: University of California Press.

COOPER, Nicola. 2001: *France in Indochina: Colonial Encounters*. Oxford: Berg.

CORONIL, Fernando. 1997: *The Magical State: Nature, Money and Modernity in Venezuela*. Chicago: University of Chicago Press.

CRAIPEAU, Yvan. 1982: *Ces Pays que l'on dit socialistes*. Paris: Études et Documentation Internationales.

CRAWSHAW, Carol, and John URRY. 1997: 'Tourism and the photographic eye'. In Chris ROJEK and John URRY (eds), *Touring Cultures:*

Transformations of Travel and Theory. New York and London: Routledge, pp. 176–95.

CRONIN, Michael. 2000: *Across the Lines: Travel, Language, Translation.* Cork: Cork UP.

DADIÉ, Bernard. 1959: *Un Nègre à Paris.* Paris: Présence Africaine.

DAENINCKX, Didier. 1984: *Meurtres pour mémoire.* Paris: Gallimard, Série noire.

DAENINCKX, Didier. 1998: *Cannibale.* Lagrasse: Verdier.

D'ALLEMAGNE, André. 1966: *Le Colonialisme au Québec.* Montreal: Éditions R-B.

DANTICAT, Edwidge. 1995: *Breath, Eyes, Memory.* London: Abacus.

DANTICAT, Edwidge. 1998: *The Farming of Bones.* New York: Soho.

DASH, J. Michael. 1998: *The Other America: Caribbean Literature in a New World Context.* Charlottesville and London: UP of Virginia.

DAUPHINÉ, Joël. 1998: *Canaques de la Nouvelle-Calédonie à Paris en 1931: de la case au zoo.* Paris: L'Harmattan.

DAVET, S., and V. MORTAIGNE. 1996: 'Les réseaux FM protestent contre les quotas de chansons francophones'. *Le Monde* 10 January, p. 27.

DAVIDSON, Basil. 1961: *Black Mother: Africa and the Atlantic Slave Trade.* Harmondsworth: Pelican Books.

DAVIDSON, Basil. 1992: *The Black Man's Burden: Africa and the Curse of the Nation-State.* Oxford: James Currey.

DEBOST, Jean-Barthélémy. 1993 'Publicité: des images noires'. *Mscope* 4, pp. 47–52.

DE CERTEAU, Michel. 1984: *The Practice of Everyday Life*, trans. Steven Rendall. Berkeley and London: University of California Press. [First published as *L'Invention du quotidien*, 1980.]

DE CHAMBERET, Georgia (ed.). 1999: *XciTés: The Flamingo Book of New French Writing.* London: Flamingo.

DELSHAM, Tony. 1998: *Gueule de journaliste.* Schoelcher: Éditions MGG.

DENIAU, Xavier. 1983: *La Francophonie.* Paris: PUF.

DEPARTMENT OF EDUCATION ARCHIVES. Consulted at the Department of Education Library (IRU), Winnipeg, and the Provincial Archives of Manitoba, Winnipeg.

DE RAYMOND, Jean-François. 2000: *L'Action culturelle extérieure de la France.* Paris: Documentation française.

DERDERIAN, Richard L. 2002: 'Algeria as a *lieu de mémoire*: ethnic minority memory and national identity in contemporary France'. *Radical History Review* 83, pp. 28–43.

DERRIDA, Jacques. 1976: *Of Grammatology*, trans. Gayatri Chakravorty Spivak. Baltimore, MD: Johns Hopkins UP. [First published as *De la Grammatologie*, 1967.]

DERRIDA, Jacques. 1998a: *Monolingualism of the Other, or the Prosthesis of Origin*, trans. Patrick Mensah. Stanford, CA: Stanford UP. [First published as *Le Monolinguisme de l'autre*, 1996.]

DERRIDA, Jacques. 1998b: 'Taking a stand for Algeria', trans. Boris Belay. *Parallax* 7, pp. 17–23. [First published as 'Parti pris pour l'Algérie', 1995.]

DEVATINE, Flora. 1998: *Tergiversations et rêveries de l'écriture orale*. Papeete: Au Vent des Îles.

DEVILLE-DANTHU, Bernadette. 1997: *Le Sport en noir et blanc: du sport colonial au sport africain dans les anciens territoires français de l'Afrique occidentale (1920–1965)*. Paris: L'Harmattan.

DIAGNE, Souleymane Bachir. 2001: Unpublished public lecture. University of Indiana, Bloomington, 11 April.

DIALLO, Nafissatou. 1976: *De Tilène au plateau: une enfance dakaroise*. Dakar: NÉA.

DIAWARA, Manthia. 1992: *African Cinema: Politics and Culture*. Bloomington: Indiana UP.

DIB, Mohammed. 2001: *Comme un bruit d'abeilles*. Paris: Albin Michel.

DIENG, Bassirou, and Lilyan KESTELOOT. 1997: *Les Épopées d'Afrique noire*. Paris: Karthala.

DIOP, Birago. 1985: *Tales of Amadou Koumba*, trans. Dorothy S. Blair. London: Longman. [First published as *Les Contes d'Amadou Koumba*, 1947.]

DIOP, Boubacar Boris. 1997: *Le Cavalier et son ombre*. Paris: Stock.

DIOP, Cheikh Anta. 1954: *Nations nègres et culture*. Paris: Présence Africaine.

DIOUF, Mamadou. 1989: 'Représentations historiques et légitimités politiques au Sénégal (1960–1987)'. *Revue de la Bibliothèque Nationale* [Paris] 34, pp. 14–23.

DIOUF, Mamadou. 1991: 'L'invention de la littérature orale: les épopées de l'espace soudano-sahélien'. *Études littéraires* 24.2, pp. 29–39.

DIRLIK, Arif. 1994: 'The Postcolonial Aura: Third World Criticism in the Age of Global Capitalism'. *Critical Inquiry* 20, pp. 328–56.

DJEBAR, Assia. 1985: *L'Amour, la fantasia*. Paris: J.-C. Lattès.

DJEBAR, Assia. 1991: *Loin de Médine*. Paris: Albin Michel.

DJEBAR, Assia. 1992: *Women of Algiers in their Apartment*, trans. Marjolijn de Jager. Charlottesville: Caraf Books/University Press of Virginia. [First published as *Femmes d'Alger dans leur appartement*, 1980.]

DJEBAR, Assia. 1995a: *Le Blanc de l'Algérie*. Paris: Albin Michel.

DJEBAR, Assia. 1995b: *Vaste est la prison*. Paris: Albin Michel.

DJEBAR, Assia. 1997: *Oran, langue morte*. Arles: Actes Sud.

DJEBAR, Assia. 1999: *Ces Voix qui m'assiègent: en marge de ma franco-phonie*. Montreal: Presses de l'Université de Montréal.

DOCKER, John. 1995 [1978]: 'The neocolonial assumption in university teaching of English'. In ASHCROFT *et al.* (eds), pp. 443–6.

DONADEY, Anne. 1996: '"Une certaine idée de la France": the Algeria syndrome and struggles over "French" identity'. In UNGAR and CONLEY (eds), pp. 215–32.

DONADEY, Anne. 2001: *Recasting Postcolonialism: Women Writing between Worlds*. Portsmouth, NH, and London: Heinemann.

DONGALA, Emmanuel. 1982: *Jazz et vin de palme*. Paris: Hatier.

DONNADIEU [DURAS], Marguerite, and Philippe ROQUES. 1940: *L'Empire français*. Paris: Gallimard.

DRAKE, David. 1999: 'Sartre, Camus and the Algerian War'. *Sartre Studies International* 5.1, pp. 16–32.

DRUON, Maurice. 1994: *Lettre aux Français sur leur langue et leur âme*. Paris: Julliard.

DUBÉ, Jean-Pierre. 2001: *Le Cercle Molière: 75ᵉ anniversaire*. Winnipeg: Le Cercle Molière.

DUBOIS, Laurent. 1998: *Les Esclaves de la République*. Paris: Calmann-Lévy.

DUBOIS, Laurent. 2000: '*La République Métissée*: Citizenship, Colonialism, and the Borders of French History'. *Cultural Studies* 14.1, pp. 15–34.

DUBOIS, Laurent. 2004: *A Colony of Citizens: Revolution and Slave Emancipation in the French Caribbean, 1787–1804*. Chapel Hill: University of North Carolina Press [forthcoming].

DUCHET, Michèle. 1971: *Anthropologie et histoire au siècle des Lumières: Buffon, Voltaire, Rousseau, Helvétius, Diderot*. Paris: Maspero.

DUGAST-PORTES, Francine. 1990: 'L'Exotisme dans l'œuvre de Marguerite Duras'. In *Le Roman colonial*. Paris: L'Harmattan, pp. 147–57.

DUHAMEL, Maurice. 1929: *La Question bretonne dans son cadre européen*. Paris: André Delpeuch; Rennes: Breiz Atao.

DURAS, Marguerite. 1943: *Les Impudents*. Paris: Plon.

DURAS, Marguerite. 1950: *Un Barrage contre le Pacifique*. Paris: Gallimard.

DURAS, Marguerite. 1984 [1976]: 'Des enfants maigres et jaunes'. In Marguerite DURAS, *Outside*. Paris: P.O.L, pp. 277–9.

DURAS, Marguerite. 1985: *The Lover*, trans. Barbara Bray. London: Flamingo. [First published as *L'Amant*, 1984.]

DURAS, Marguerite. 1994: *The North China Lover*, trans. Leigh Hafrey. London: Flamingo. [First published as *L'Amant de la Chine du nord*, 1991.]

DURAS, Marguerite, and Xavière GAUTHIER. 1974: *Les Parleuses*. Paris: Minuit.

DURHAM, John George, Earl of Lambton. 1963 [1838]: *Lord Durham's Report: An Abridgement of Report on the Affairs of British North America*, ed. G.M. CRAIG. Toronto: McClelland & Stewart.

DURMELAT, Sylvie. 1998: 'Petite histoire du mot *beur*'. *French Cultural Studies* 9.2, pp. 191–207.

DYER, Richard. 1997: *White*. London: Routledge.

EASTHOPE, Antony. 1998: *Englishness and National Culture*. London and New York: Routledge.

ESSOMBA, Jean-Roger. 1996: *Le Paradis du Nord*. Paris: Présence Africaine.

EWENS, Graeme. 1991: *Africa O-Ye! A Celebration of African Music*. Enfield: Guinness.

EZRA, Elizabeth. 2000: *The Colonial Unconscious: Race and Culture in Interwar France*. Ithaca, NY, and London: Cornell UP.

FABIAN, Johannes. 1983: *Time and the Other: How Anthropology Makes its Object*. New York: Columbia UP.

FALL, Aminata Sow. 1981: *The Beggars' Strike, or the Dregs of Society*, trans. Dorothy S. Blair. London: Longman. [First published as *La Grève des Battù*, 1979.]

FALL, Aminata Sow. 1993a: *L'Appel des arènes*. Dakar: NÉA.

FALL, Aminata Sow. 1993b: *Le Jujubier du patriarche*. Dakar: Khoudia.

FANON, Frantz. 1967: *The Wretched of the Earth*, trans. Constance Farrington. Harmondsworth: Penguin. [First published as *Les Damnés de la terre*, 1961.]

FANON, Frantz. 1970. *For the African Revolution*, trans. Haakon Chevalier. Harmondsworth: Penguin. [First published as *Pour la Révolution africaine*, 1964.]

FANON, Frantz. 1986: *Black Skin, White Masks*, trans. Charles Lam Markmann. London: Pluto. [First published as *Peau noire, masques blancs*, 1952.]

FANON, Frantz. 1991 [1961]: *Les Damnés de la terre*. Paris: Gallimard, Folio.

FARÈS, Nabile. 1998: 'Histoire de l'homme qui avait perdu son âme'. *Parallax* 7, pp. 67–9.

FASSIN, Didier. 2000: 'The politics of PACS in a translatlantic mirror: same-sex unions and sexual difference in France today'. *Sites* 4.1, pp. 55–64.

FERRETTI, Andrée, and Gaston MIRON (eds). 1992: *Les Grands Textes indépendantistes: Écrits, discours et manifestes québécois 1774–1992*. Montreal: L'Hexagone.

FICK, Carolyn. 1990: *The Making of Haiti: The Saint-Domingue Revolution from Below*. Knoxville: University of Tennessee Press.

FINKIELKRAUT, Alain. 1987: *La Défaite de la pensée*. Paris: Gallimard.

FONKOUA, Romuald. 2002: *Essai sur une mesure du monde au XXe siècle: Édouard Glissant*. Paris: Champion.

FORD, Caroline. 1993: *Creating the Nation in Provincial France: Religion and Political Identity in Brittany*. Princeton: Princeton UP.

FORSDICK, Charles. 1997: 'Edward Said, Victor Segalen and the implications of post-colonial theory'. *Journal of the Institute of Romance Studies* 5, pp. 323–39.

FORSDICK, Charles. 2000: 'L'exote mangé par les hommes: from the French Kipling to *Segalen le partagé*'. In Charles FORSDICK and Susan MARSON (eds), *Reading Diversity*. Glasgow: University of Glasgow French and German Publications, pp. 1–22.

FORSDICK, Charles. 2001a: 'Introduction'. In Charles FORSDICK (ed.), *Travel and Exile: Postcolonial Perspectives*. Liverpool: ASCALF Critical Studies in Postcolonial Literature and Culture, 1, pp. v–ix.

FORSDICK, Charles. 2001b: 'Travelling concepts: postcolonial approaches to exoticism'. *Paragraph* 24.3, pp. 12–29.

FORSDICK, Charles. 2002: 'A persistent concept: exoticism today'. *Journal of Romance Studies* 20, pp. 101–10.

FOUCAULT, Michel. 1972: *The Archaeology of Knowledge*, trans. A.M. Sheridan Smith. London: Tavistock. [First published as *L'Archéologie du savoir*, 1969.]

FOUCAULT, Michel. 1979: *Discipline and Punish: The Birth of the Prison*, trans. Alan Sheridan. London: Penguin. [First published as *Surveiller et punir: Naissance de la prison*, 1975.]

FOUCAULT, Michel. 1989: *The Order of Things: An Archaeology of the Human Sciences*. London: Routledge. [First published as *Les Mots et les choses: une archéologie des sciences humaines*, 1966.]

FREEDMAN, Jane, and Carrie TARR. 2000: 'Introduction'. In Jane FREEDMAN and Carrie TARR (eds), *Women, Immigration and Identities in France*. Oxford: Berg, pp. 1–10.

FRITH, Simon (ed.). 1989: *World Music, Politics and Social Change*. Manchester and New York: Manchester UP.

FROSTIN, Charles. 1975: *Les Révoltes blanches à Saint-Domingue aux XVIIème et XVIIIème siècles*. Paris: L'École.

FUMAROLI, Marc. 1997: 'Le "génie" de la langue française'. In NORA (ed.), III, pp. 4623–85.

GAFAÏTI, Hafid (ed.). 2001: *Cultures transnationales de France*. Paris: L'Harmattan, Études transnationales, francophones et comparées.

GAGNÉ, Marc. 1973: *Visages de Gabrielle Roy*. Montreal: Librairie Beauchemin.

GALLAGHER, Mary. 1994: 'Whence and whither the French Caribbean *créolité* movement?' *ASCALF Bulletin* 9, pp. 3–19.

GALLET, Dominique. 1995: *Pour une ambition francophone: Le désir et l'indifférence*. Paris: L'Harmattan.

GARRETT, Mitchell Bennett. 1916: *The French Colonial Question, 1789–1791*. Ann Arbor, MI: Wahr.

GASPARD, Françoise, Anne LE GALL and Claude SERVAN-SCHREIBER. 1992: *Au pouvoir citoyennes! Liberté, Égalité, Parité!* Paris: Seuil.

GASPARD, Françoise, and Farhad KHOSROKHAVAR. 1995: *Le Foulard et la République*. Paris: Découverte.

GATES, Henry Louis, Jr. 1991: 'Critical Fanonism'. *Critical Inquiry* 17, pp. 457–70.

GAUTHIER, Florence. 1995: 'Le rôle de la députation de Saint-Domingue dans l'abolition de l'esclavage'. In Marcel DORIGNY (ed.), *Les Abolitions de l'esclavage de L.F. Sonthonax à V. Schoelcher, 1793, 1794, 1848*. Paris: Presses Universitaires de Vincennes, pp. 199–212.

GAUVIN, Lise. 1997: *L'Écrivain francophone à la croisée des langues: Entretiens*. Paris: Karthala.

GAUVIN, Lise. 2000: *Langagement: l'écrivain et la langue au Québec*. Montreal: Les Éditions Boréal.

GEGGUS, David. 1982: *Slavery, War and Revolution*. Oxford and New York: Oxford UP.

GEGGUS, David. 1989a: 'The Haitian revolution'. In Franklin KNIGHT and Colin PALMER (eds), *The Modern Caribbean*. Chapel Hill: University of North Carolina Press, pp. 21–50.

GEGGUS, David. 1989b: 'Racial equality, slavery and colonial secession during the Constituent Assembly'. *American Historical Review* 94.5, pp. 1290–308.

GEGGUS, David. 1997: 'Slavery, war and revolution in the Greater Caribbean, 1789–1815'. In David GASPAR and David GEGGUS (eds), *A Turbulent Time: The French Revolution and the Greater Caribbean*. Bloomington: Indiana UP, pp. 1–50.

GEGGUS, David (ed.). 2001. *The Impact of the Haitian Revolution in the Atlantic World*. Columbia: University of South Carolina Press.

GIKANDI, Simon. 1991: *Reading Chinua Achebe: Language and Ideology in Fiction*. London: James Currey; Portsmouth, NH: Heinemann.

GILDEA, Robert. 1994: *The Past in French History*. London and New Haven, CT: Yale UP.

GILROY, Paul. 1993: *The Black Atlantic: Modernity and Double Consciousness*. London: Verso.

GILROY, Paul. 2000: *Against Race: Imagining Political Culture beyond the Color Line*. Cambridge, MA: Harvard UP.

GIRARDET, Raoul. 1972: *L'Idée Coloniale en France de 1871 à 1962*. Paris: Hachette.

GIRARDET, Raoul. 1983: *Le Nationalisme français: Anthologie, 1871–1914*. Paris: Seuil.

GIVANNI, June (ed.). 2000: *Symbolic Narratives/African Cinema: Audiences, Theory and the Moving Image*. London: BFI.

GLISSANT, Édouard. 1957: *Soleil de la conscience*. Paris: Seuil.

GLISSANT, Édouard. 1969: *L'Intention poétique*. Paris: Gallimard.

GLISSANT, Édouard. 1981: *Le Discours antillais*. Paris: Seuil.

GLISSANT, Édouard. 1989: *Caribbean Discourse: Selected Essays*, trans. and introduced by J. Michael Dash. Charlottesville: UP of Virginia.

GLISSANT, Édouard. 1990: *Poétique de la Relation*. Paris: Gallimard.

GLISSANT, Édouard. 1996: *Introduction à une poétique du divers*. Paris: Gallimard.

GLISSANT, Édouard. 1997a: *Poetics of relation*, trans. Betsy Wing. Ann Arbor, MI: University of Michigan Press.

GLISSANT, Édouard. 1997b: *Traité du Tout-Monde*. Paris: Gallimard.

GONTARD, Marc. 1981: *Violence du texte: la littérature marocaine de langue française*. Paris: L'Harmattan.

GONTARD, Marc. 1990: *Victor Segalen: une esthétique de la différence.* Paris: L'Harmattan.

GONTARD, Marc. 1995: "Pour une littérature bretonne de langue française". *Plurial 5*, pp. 17–31.

GONTARD, Marc. 2000: *Le Moi étrange: littérature marocaine de langue française.* Paris: L'Harmattan.

GREEN, Mary Jean, Karen GOULD, Micheline RICE-MAXIMIN, Keith L. WALKER and Jack A. YEAGER (eds). 1996: *Postcolonial Subjects: Francophone Women Writers.* Minneapolis and London: University of Minnesota Press.

GREER, Allan. 1993: *The Patriots and the People: The Rebellion of 1837 in Rural Lower Canada.* Toronto: University of Toronto Press.

GROULX, Lionel. 1972: *Mes Mémoires.* Montreal: Fides.

GROULX, Lionel. 1979: *L'Enseignement français au Canada: Les écoles des minorités.* II. Montreal and Paris: Éditions Leméac/Éditions d'aujourd'hui.

GUIOMAR, Jean-Yves. 1987: *Le Bretonisme: les historiens bretons au XIXe siècle.* Mayenne: Imprimerie de la Manutention.

HA, Marie-Paule. 2000: *Figuring the East: Segalen, Malraux, Duras, and Barthes.* New York: State University of New York Press.

HA, Marie-Paule. 2001: 'Durasie: women, natives, and other'. In James WILLIAMS (ed.), *Revisioning Duras.* Liverpool: Liverpool UP, pp. 95–111.

HADDOUR, Azzedine. 2000: *Colonial Myths: History and Narrative.* Manchester: Manchester UP.

HAIGH, Sam. 2000: *Mapping a Tradition: Francophone Women's Writing from Guadeloupe.* Leeds: Maney/MHRA.

HALIMI, Gisèle. 1994: *Plaidoyer pour une démocratie paritaire.* Paris: Gallimard.

HALIMI, Gisèle. 1999: *Fritna.* Paris: Plon.

HALL, Stuart. 1993: 'Cultural identity and diaspora'. In WILLIAMS and CHRISMAN (eds), pp. 392–403.

HALLWARD, Peter. 2001: *Absolutely Postcolonial: Writing between the Singular and the Specific.* Manchester: Manchester UP.

HARBI, Mohammed. 2001: *Une Vie debout: Mémoires politiques, 1945–1962.* Paris: La Découverte.

HARBI, Mohammed. 2002: 'Et la violence vint à l'Algérie'. *Le Monde diplomatique 580*, pp. 14–15.

HARE, Geoff. 1997: 'The quota of French language songs on radio'. *Modern and Contemporary France 5.1*, pp. 73–5.

HARGREAVES, Alec G. 1996: 'A Deviant Construction: The French Media and the "Banlieues"'. *New Community 22.4*, pp. 607–18.

HARGREAVES, Alec G. 1997: *Immigration and Identity in Beur Fiction: Voices from the North African Community in France.* Oxford and New York: Berg.

HARGREAVES, Alec G., and Mark McKINNEY (eds). 1997: *Post-Colonial Cultures in France*. London and New York: Routledge.

HARRISON, Nicholas. 2003: *Postcolonial Criticism: History, Theory and the Work of Fiction*. Cambridge: Polity Press.

HAY, Jean (ed.). 2000: *African Novels in the Classroom*. Boulder: Rienner.

HAYES, Jarrod. 2000: *Queer Nations: Marginal Sexualities in the Maghreb*. Chicago: University of Chicago Press.

HAZARD, Paul. 1935: *La Crise de la conscience européenne (1680–1715)*. Paris: Boivin.

HEALY, J.J. 1992: 'The melting of the mosaic: landscape, power and ethnicity in Post-Confederation Canada'. In Jean BURNET, Danielle JUTEAU, Enoch PADOLSKY, Anthony RASPORICH and Antoine SIROIS (eds), *Migration and the Transformation of Cultures*. Toronto: Multicultural History Society of Ontario, pp. 55–89.

HITCHCOTT, Nicki. 1997: 'Calixthe Beyala and the Post-Colonial Woman'. In HARGREAVES and McKINNEY (eds), pp. 211–25.

HITCHCOTT, Nicki. 2000: *Women Writers in Francophone Africa*. Oxford and New York: Berg.

HODEIR, Catherine, and Michel PIERRE. 1991: *L'Exposition coloniale*. Brussels: Complexe.

HOFFMANN, Léon-François. 1973: *Le Nègre romantique: personnage littéraire et obsession collective*. Paris: Payot.

HOLLAND, Patrick, and Graham HUGGAN. 1998: *Tourists with Typewriters: Critical Reflections on Contemporary Travel Writing*. Michigan: University of Michigan Press.

HOLMLUND, Christine. 1991: 'Displacing limits of difference: gender, race, and colonialism in Edward Said and Homi Bhabha's theoretical models and Marguerite Duras's experimental films'. *Quarterly Review of Film and Video* 13.1, pp. 1–22.

HOOKS, bell. 1992: *Black Looks: Race and Representation*. Boston: South End Press.

HOOKS, bell. 1999: *Remembered Rapture*. New York: Henry Holt.

HOROWITZ, Donald L., and Gérard NOIRIEL. 1992: *Immigrants in Two Democracies: French and American Experience*. New York: New York UP.

HOUNTONDJI, Paulin J. 1994: *Les Savoirs endogènes: pistes pour une recherche*. Dakar: CODESRIA.

HOUNTONDJI, Paulin J. 1998: 'Réponse d'attente'. *Interventions* 1.1, pp. 28–9.

HOWE, Stephen. 1999: *Afrocentrism: Mythical Pasts and Imagined Homes*. London: Verso.

HSIEH, Yvonne Y. 1996: 'L'Évolution du discours (anti-)colonialiste dans *Un barrage contre le Pacifique*, *L'Amant* et *L'Amant de la Chine du Nord* de Marguerite Duras'. *Dalhousie French Studies* 35, pp. 55–65.

HUANNOU, Adrien. 1989: *La Question des littératures nationales en Afrique noire*. Abidjan: CEDA.

HUE, Bernard. 1994: 'Du mythe à la réalité'. *Plurial* 4, pp. 5–6.

HUE, Bernard. 1995: 'Le temps des évidences'. *Plurial* 5, pp. 11–15.

HUGGAN, Graham. 2001: *The Postcolonial Exotic: Marketing the Margins*. London and New York: Routledge.

HUGO, Victor. 2004 [1826]: *Bug-Jargal*, trans. Chris Bongie. Peterborough, ONT: Broadview Press [forthcoming].

INNES, C.L. 2000: 'Postcolonial Studies and Ireland'. In BERYand MURRAY (eds), pp. 21–30.

IRELE, Abiola. 1993: 'Is African Music Possible? In an age after modernism, what role is left for local difference?' *Transition* 61, pp. 56–71.

IRELE, Abiola. 2001: *The African Imagination: Literature in Africa and the Black Diaspora*. Oxford and New York: Oxford UP.

JACQUEMIN, Jean-Pierre. 2002: 'Les Congolais dans la Belgique "impériale"'. In BANCEL *et al.* (eds), pp. 253–8.

JAENEN, Cornelius J. 1984: 'Le français au Manitoba: fruit de l'histoire ou d'une contrainte extérieure?'. *Langue et société* 13, pp. 3–16.

JAMES, C.L.R. 1963 [1938]: *The Black Jacobins: Toussaint L'Ouverture and the San Domingo Revolution*. New York: Vintage.

JAMES, C.L.R. 1980 [1948]: *Notes on Dialectics. Hegel, Marx, Lenin*. London: Allison & Busby.

JAMESON, Fredric. 1986: 'Third-World literature in the era of multinational capitalism'. *Social Text* 15, pp. 65–88.

JANMOHAMED, Abdul R. 1985: 'The economy of Manichean allegory: the function of racial difference in colonialist literature'. *Critical Inquiry* 12.1, pp. 59–87.

JANMOHAMED, Abdul R., and David LLOYD (eds). 1986: 'Introduction: Towards a theory of minority discourse: What is to be done?'. In Abdul R. JANMOHAMED and David LLOYD (eds), *The Nature and Context of Minority Discourse*. Oxford and New York: Oxford UP, pp. 1–16.

JEANCOLAS, Jean-Pierre. 1983: *Quinze ans d'années trente*. Paris: Stock.

JEANSON, Francis. 1952: 'Albert Camus ou l'âme révoltée'. *Les Temps Modernes* 79, pp. 2070–90.

JELEN, Christian. 1997: 'Enquête sur la République'. *Libération* 22 January.

JENSON, Deborah. 2001: *Trauma and its Representations: The Social Life of Mimesis in Post-Revolutionary France*. Baltimore, MD: Johns Hopkins UP.

JEYIFO, Biodun. 1984: *The Yoruba Travelling Theatre of Nigeria*. Lagos: Nigeria Magazine.

JONES, Rufus M. 1911: *The Quakers in the American Colonies*. London: Macmillan.

JOUSSE, Thierry. 1995: 'Le banlieue-film existe-t-il?' *Cahiers du Cinéma* 492, pp. 37–9.

JULIEN, Eileen. 1992: *African Novels and the Question of Orality*. Bloomington: Indiana UP.

JULIEN, Eileen. 2003: 'The extroverted African novel'. In Franco MORETTI (ed.), *Il Romanzo*. IV. Turin: Einaudi [forthcoming].

KAGANSKI, Serge. 2001: '*Amélie* pas jolie'. *Libération* 31 May.

KALISA, Marie-Chantal. 1999: 'Violence, Memory and Writing in Francophone African and Caribbean Women's Fiction'. Unpublished Ph.D, University of Iowa.

KANE, Cheikh Hamidou. 1972: *Ambiguous Adventure*, trans. Katherine Woods. London: Heinemann. [First published as *L'Aventure ambiguë*, 1961.]

KANE, Mohamadou. 1974: 'Sur les formes traditionnelles du roman africain'. *Revue de littérature comparée* 48, pp. 536–68.

KANE, Mohamadou. 1982: *Roman africain et tradition*. Dakar: NÉA.

KATEB, Yacine. 1956: *Nedjma*. Paris: Seuil.

KAZADI, Ntole. 1991: *L'Afrique afro-francophone*. Paris: Didier Érudition.

KEGINER, Kristian. 1972: *Un Dépaysement, précédé d'une Mise au point et suivi d'un Point de départ (Une poésie révolutionnaire bretonne existe)*. Preface by Paol Keineg. Paris: P.J. Oswald.

KEINEG, Paol. 1969: *Hommes liges des talus en transes, réédition augmentée de Le poème du pays qui a faim, et suivi de Vent de Harlem*. Preface by Gwenc'hlan Le Scouëzec. Paris: P.J. Oswald.

KEINEG, Paol. 1971: *Chroniques et croquis des villages verrouillés, comprenant, en édition bilingue, Barzhonegou-trakt (poèmes-tracts)*. Preface by Yves Rouquette. Honfleur: P.J. Oswald.

KHATIBI, Abdelkebir. 1983a: *Maghreb pluriel*. Paris: Denoël.

KHATIBI, Abdelkebir. 1983b: *Amour bilingue*. Montpellier: Fata Morgana.

KHATIBI, Abdelkebir. 1985: 'Double criticism: the decolonization of Arab sociology'. In Halim BARAKAT (ed.), *Contemporary North Africa: Issues of Development and Integration*. Washington, DC: Center for Contemporary Arab Studies, pp. 9–19.

KHATIBI, Abdelkebir. 1987: *Figures de l'étranger dans la littérature française*. Paris: Denoël.

KHOSROKHAVAR, Farhad. 2001: 'La fin des monoculturalismes'. In WIEVIORKA and OHANA (eds), pp. 17–30.

KING, C. Richard. 2000: *Postcolonial America*. Urbana: University of Illinois Press.

KING, Deborah. 1990: 'Multiple jeopardy, multiple consciousness: the context of a Black feminist ideology'. In Micheline R. MALSON, Jean F. O'BARR, Sarah WESTPHAL-WIHL and Mary WYER (eds), *Feminist Theory in Practice and Process*. Chicago: University of Chicago Press, pp. 75–105.

KNAPP, Bettina. 1971: 'Interview with Marguerite Duras'. *The French Review* 44.4, pp. 653–9.

KONSTANTARAKOS, Myrto. 1999: 'Which Mapping of the City? *La Haine* (Kassovitz, 1995)'. In POWRIE (ed.), pp. 159–71.

KOUROUMA, Ahmadou. 1981: *The Suns of Independence*, trans. Adrian Adams. London: Heinemann. [First published as *Les Soleils des indépendances*, 1968.]

KPOMASSIE, Tété-Michel. 1981: *Un Africain à Groenland*. Paris: Flammarion.

LACROSIL, Michèle. 1961: *Cajou*. Paris: Gallimard.

LAFERRIÈRE, Dany. 1996: *Pays sans chapeau*. Quebec: Lanctot.

LAFITAU, Joseph-François. 1994 [1724]: *Mœurs des sauvages américains comparées aux mœurs des premiers temps*, ed. Edna Hindie LEMAY. Paris: La Découverte.

LAFONT, Robert. 1967: *La Révolution régionaliste*. Paris: Gallimard.

LAFONT, Robert. 1974: *La Revendication occitane*. Paris: Flammarion.

LAGNY, Michèle, Marie Claire ROPARS and Pierre SORLIN. 1986: *Générique des Années Trente*. Paris: Presses Universitaires de Vincennes.

LAHONTAN, Louis-Armand de Lom d'Arce, baron de. 1990 [1703]: *Suite du Voyage de l'Amérique, ou Dialogues de Monsieur le baron de Lahontan et d'un sauvage dans l'Amérique*, ed. Réal OUELLET and Alain BEAULIEU. In *Œuvres complètes*, II. Montreal: Presses de l'Université de Montréal.

LALANNE-BERTOUDICQ, Philippe. 1998: 'Faut-il défendre la langue française?'. Lecture dated 19 November, posted on: http://www.langue-francaise.org/Articles_Dossiers/Defendre_la_langue.html [No indication of venue, circumstances or audience given. Last consulted on 8 May 2003.]

LAMCHICHI, Abderrahim. 1999: 'Identité religieuse, laïcité républicaine et islam de France'. In Tariq RAGI and Sylvia GERRITSEN (eds), *Les Territoires de l'identité*. Paris: L'Harmattan, pp. 187–216.

LAMONDE, Yvan, and Claude CORBO (eds). 1999: *Le Rouge et le Bleu: Une anthologie de la pensée politique au Québec de la Conquête à la Révolution tranquille*. Montreal: Presses de l'Université de Montréal.

LARZAC, Jean. 1972: *L'Étranger du dedans et autres poèmes politiques*. Paris: P.J. Oswald.

LAYE, Camara. 1959: *The African Child*, trans. James Kirkup. London: Fontana. [First published as *L'Enfant noir*, 1953.]

LAYE, Camara. 1980: *The Guardian of the Word*, trans. James Kirkup. London: Fontana. [First published as *Le Maître de la parole*, 1978.]

LAZARUS, Neil. 1990: *Resistance in Postcolonial African Fiction*. New Haven, CT, and London: Yale UP.

LAZARUS, Neil. 1993: 'Disavowing decolonization: Fanon, nationalism, and the problematic of representation in current theories of colonial discourse'. *Research in African literatures* 24.4, pp. 71–98.

LAZARUS, Neil. 1999: *Nationalism and Cultural Practice in the Postcolonial World*. Cambridge: Cambridge UP.

LEBESQUE, Morvan. 1970: *Comment peut-on être Breton? Essai sur la démocratie française*. Preface by Gwenc'hlan Le Scouëzec. Paris: Seuil.

LEBOVICS, Herman. 1992: *True France: The Wars over Cultural Identity, 1900–1945*. Ithaca, NY: Cornell UP.

LE BRIS, Michel. 1995: *Fragments du royaume*. Vénisseux: Paroles d'Aube.

LECOINTE-MARSILLAC [published anonymously]. 1968 [1789]: *Le More-Lack, ou essai sur les moyens les plus doux et les plus équitables d'abolir la traite et l'esclavage des Nègres d'Afrique, en conservant aux colonies tous les avantages d'une population agricole*. Paris: EDHIS.

LEVEAU, Rémy, Khadija MOHSEN-FINAN and Catherine WIHTOL DE WENDEN. 2001: *L'Islam en France et en Allemagne: Identités et citoyennetés*. Paris: Documentation française.

LIKING, Werewere. 1983: *Elle sera de jaspe et de corail*. Paris: L'Harmattan.

LIONNET, Françoise. 1989: *Autobiographical Voices: Race, Gender, Self-Portraiture*. Ithaca, NY: Cornell UP.

LIONNET, Françoise. 1995a: *Postcolonial Representations: Women, Literature, Identity*. Ithaca, NY: Cornell UP.

LIONNET, Françoise. 1995b: 'Spaces of comparison'. In BERNHEIMER (ed.), pp. 165–74.

LIONNET, Françoise. 1998: 'Reframing Baudelaire: literary history, biography, postcolonial theory, and vernacular languages'. *Diacritics* 28.3, pp. 63–85.

LITTLE, Roger. 1995: *Nègres blancs: représentations de l'autre autre*. Paris: L'Harmattan.

LITTLE, Roger. 2001a: *Between Totem and Taboo: Black Man, White Woman in Francographic Literature*. Exeter: University of Exeter Press.

LITTLE, Roger. 2001b: 'Boulle plays Marivaux'. *French Studies Bulletin* 81, pp. 14–17.

LITTLE, Roger. 2002a: 'Fictional negroes in eighteenth-century France'. In Nicolas CRONK (ed.), *Remapping the Rise of the European Novel, 1500–1800*. Oxford: Voltaire Foundation [forthcoming].

LITTLE, Roger. 2002b: 'The Oroonoko Syndrome'. *ASCALF Bulletin* 24, pp. 33–53.

LONGLEY, Kateryna Olijnyk. 2002: 'Fabricating Otherness: Demidenko and Exoticism'. In SANTAOLALLA (ed.), pp. 21–39.

LOOMBA, Ania. 1993: 'Overworlding the "Third World"'. In WILLIAMS and CHRISMAN (eds), pp. 305–23.

LOOMBA, Ania. 1998: *Colonialism/Postcolonialism*. London and New York: Routledge.

LOWE, Lisa. 1991: *Critical Terrains: French and British Orientalisms*. Ithaca, NY: Cornell UP.

LÖWY, Michael. 1981: *The Politics of Combined and Uneven Development: The Theory of Permanent Revolution*. London: Verso.

LYNCH, Deidre, and William B. WARNER (eds). 1996: *Cultural Institutions of the Novel*. Durham, NC, and London: Duke UP, pp. 47–72.

MAATOUK, Frédéric. 1979: 'Le Théâtre des travailleurs immigrés en France'. Unpublished Doctorat d'état, UER Sciences de l'Homme, Université François-Rabelais, Tours.

MABILLE, Pierre. 1981: 'Souvenirs d'Haïti'. In Pierre MABILLE, *Messages de l'étranger*. Paris: Plasma, pp. 7–28.

MACCANNELL, Dean. 1992: *Empty Meeting Grounds: The Tourist Papers*. New York and London: Routledge.

MACEY, David. 2000: *Frantz Fanon: A Life*. London: Granta.

MACHEREY, Pierre. 1978: *Pour une théorie de la production littéraire*. Paris: Maspero.

MAIGNE, Vincenette. 1985: 'Exotisme: évolution en diachronie du mot et de son champ sémantique'. In R. ANTONIOLI (ed.), *Exotisme et création: Actes du colloque international de Lyon, 1983*. Lyons: Hermès, pp. 9–16.

MARTEL, Frédéric. 1996: *Le Rose et le noir: les homosexuels en France depuis 1968*. Paris: Seuil.

MASPERO, François. 2002: *Les Abeilles et la Guêpe*. Paris: Seuil.

MASPERO, François, and Anaïk FRANTZ. 1994: *Roissy Express: A Journey Through the Paris Suburbs*, trans. Paul Jones. London: Verso. [First published as *Les Passagers du Roissy-Express*, 1990.]

MAZAMA, Ama. 1996: 'Critique afrocentrique de *l'Éloge de la créolité*'. In Maryse CONDÉ and Madeleine COTTENET-HAGE (eds), *Penser la créolité*. Paris: Karthala, pp. 85–100.

McCLINTOCK, Anne. 1993 [1992]: 'The angel of progress: pitfalls of the term "post-colonialism"'. In WILLIAMS and CHRISMAN (eds), pp. 291–304.

McCLINTOCK, Anne. 1997: '"No longer in a future heaven": gender, race, and nationalism'. In Anne McCLINTOCK, Aamir MUFTI and Ella SHOHAT (eds), *Dangerous Liaisons: Gender, Nation, and Postcolonial Perspective*. Minneapolis: University of Minnesota Press, pp. 89–112.

McLEOD, John. 2000: *Beginning Postcolonialism*. Manchester: Manchester UP.

McNEE, Lisa. 2000: *Selfish Gifts: Senegalese Women's Autobiographical Discourse*. New York: State University of New York.

MEDDEB, Abdelwahab. 1979: *Talismano*. Paris: Bourgois.

MEMMI, Albert. 1971: 'La vie impossible de Frantz Fanon'. *Esprit* 406, pp. 248–72.

MEMMI, Albert. 1972: *Portrait du colonisé*. Montreal: Éditions Étincelle.

MEMMI, Albert. 1990: *The Colonizer and the Colonized*, trans. Howard Greenfeld. London: Earthscan. [First published as *Le Portrait du colonisé précédé de Portrait du colonisateur*, 1957.]

MENGOUCHI and RAMDANE. 1978: *L'Homme qui enjamba la mer*. Paris: Henri Veyrier.

MÉNIL, René. 1996: 'For a Critical Reading of *Tropiques*'. In RICHARDSON (ed.), pp. 69–78.

MÉNIL, René. 1999: *Antilles déjà jadis*. Paris: Jean-Michel Place.

MERCIER, Roger. 1962: *L'Afrique noire dans la littérature française: les premières images (XVIIᵉ et XVIIIᵉ siècles)*. Dakar: Université de Dakar.

MERNISSI, Fatima. 1991: *The Veil and the Male Elite: a Feminist Interpretation of Women's Rights in Islam*, trans. Mary Jo Lakeland. Reading, MA: Addison-Wesley Pub. Co. [First published as *Le Harem politique: le prophète et les femmes*, 1987.]

MERNISSI, Fatima. 1993: *Forgotten Queens of Islam*, trans. Mary Jo Lakeland. Minneapolis: University of Minnesota Press. [First published as *Sultanes oubliées: femmes chefs d'état en islam*, 1990.]

MEROLLA, Daniela. 2002: 'Digital imagination and the "landscape of group identities": Berber diasporas and the flourishing of theater, home videos, and CouscousNet'. Unpublished paper presented at the annual meeting of the African Literature Association, San Diego, CA, 3–7 April.

MESCHONNIC, Henri. 1997: *De la langue française*. Paris: Hachette.

MIDIOHOUAN, Guy Ossito. 1982: 'Le Phénomène des "littératures nationales" en Afrique'. *Peuples noirs/Peuples africains* 27, pp. 57–70.

MILLER, Christopher L. 1985: *Blank Darkness: Africanist Discourse in French*. Chicago and London: University of Chicago Press.

MILLER, Christopher L. 1990: *Theories of Africans: Francophone Literature and Anthropology in Africa*. Chicago and London: University of Chicago Press.

MILLER, Christopher L. 1998: *Nationalists and Nomads: Essays on Francophone African Literature and Culture*. Chicago and London: University of Chicago Press.

MISHRA, Vijay, and Bob HODGE. 1993 [1991]: 'What is post(-)colonialism?'. In WILLIAMS and CHRISMAN (eds), pp. 276–90.

MOI, Toril. 1994: *Sexual/Textual Politics*. London: Routledge.

Le Monde. 1999: 'Comment les Anglais voient notre littérature'. 27 August.

MONÉNEMBO, Tierno. 1997: *Cinéma*. Paris: Seuil.

MOORE-GILBERT, Bart. 1997: *Postcolonial Theory: Contexts, Practices, Politics*. London: Verso.

MOORE-GILBERT, Bart. 2000: 'Spivak and Bhabha'. In SCHWARZ and RAY (eds), pp. 451–66.

MORETTI, Franco. 2000: 'Conjectures on World Literature'. *New Left Review* (2nd series) 1, pp. 54–68.

MORGAN, Janice. 1994: 'In the Labyrinth: Masculine Subjectivity, Expatriation, and Colonialism in *Pépé le Moko*'. *The French Review* 67.4, pp. 637–47.

MORTON, Patricia A. 2000: *Hybrid Modernities: Architecture and Representation at the 1931 Colonial Exposition, Paris*. Cambridge, MA: MIT Press.

MORTON, W.L. 1979: 'Manitoba schools and Canadian nationality,

1890–1923'. In David C. JONES, Nancy M. SHEEHAN and Robert M. STAMP (eds), *Shaping the Schools of the Canadian West*. Calgary, Alberta: Detselig Enterprises, pp. 3–13.

MOURA, Jean-Marc. 1992a: *L'Image du tiers monde dans le roman français contemporain*. Paris: PUF.

MOURA, Jean-Marc. 1992b: *Lire l'exotisme*. Paris: Dunod.

MOURA, Jean-Marc. 1999: *Littératures francophones et théorie postcoloniale*. Paris: PUF.

MOURALIS, Bernard. 1984: *Littérature et développement*. Paris: Silex.

MOURALIS, Bernard. 1993: *L'Europe, l'Afrique et la folie*. Paris: Présence Africaine.

MOURALIS, Bernard. 1999: *République et colonies: Entre histoire et mémoire: la République française et l'Afrique*. Paris: Présence Africaine.

MUDIMBE, V.Y. 1979: *L'Écart*. Paris: Présence Africaine.

MUDIMBE, V.Y. 1988: *The Invention of Africa: Gnosis, Philosophy and the Order of Knowledge*. London: James Currey.

MUKHERJEE, Arun P. 1986: 'Ideology in the classroom: a case study in the teaching of English literature in Canadian universities'. *Dalhousie Review* 66.1–2, pp. 22–30.

MUNFORD, Clarence J. 1991: *The Black Ordeal of Slavery and Slave Trading in the West Indies, 1625–1715*. 3 vols. Lampeter: Mellen.

MURDOCH, H. Adlai. 2001: *Creole Identity in the French Caribbean Novel*. Gainesville: UP of Florida.

MURPHY, David. 2000: *Sembene: Imagining Alternatives in Film and Fiction*. Oxford: James Currey; Trenton, NJ: Africa World Press.

MURPHY, David. 2002: 'De-centring French studies: towards a postcolonial theory of Francophone cultures'. *French Cultural Studies* 13.2, pp. 165–85.

NEWELL, Stephanie. 2002: *Readings in African Popular Fiction*. Bloomington: Indiana UP.

Newsweek. 1996: 'Street Culture'. 26 February, pp. 36–45.

NGUGI WA THIONG'O. 1981: *Decolonising the Mind*. London: Heinemann.

NGUGI WA THIONG'O. 1993: *Moving the Centre: the Struggle for Cultural Freedoms*. London: James Currey; Portsmouth, NH: Heinemann.

NIANE, Djibril Tamsir. 1970: *Sundiata: An Epic of Old Mali*, trans. G.D. Pickett. London: Longman. [First published as *Soundjata ou l'épopée mandingue*, 1960.]

NKASHAMA, Pius Ngandu. 1987: *Vie et mœurs d'un primitif en Essonne quatre-vingt-onze*. Paris: L'Harmattan.

NKASHAMA, Pius Ngandu. 1989: *Écritures et discours littéraires: études sur le roman africain*. Paris: L'Harmattan.

NKASHAMA, Pius Ngandu. 1997: *Ruptures et écritures de violence: études sur le roman et les littératures africaines*. Paris: L'Harmattan.

NORA, Pierre (ed.). 1997: *Les Lieux de mémoire*. 3 vols. Paris: Gallimard/Quarto.

NORINDR, Panivong. 1996: *Phantasmatic Indochina: French Colonial Ideology in Architecture, Film and Literature*. Durham, NC, and London: Duke UP.

NORINDR, Panivong. 1999: 'Mourning, memorials, and filmic traces: reinscribing the *Corps étrangers* and Unknown Soldiers in Bertrand Tavernier's Films'. *Studies in 20th Century Literature* 23.1, pp. 117–41. [Special issue entitled 'Empire and Occupation in France and the Francophone Worlds', ed. Anne DONADEY *et al.*]

OBIECHINA, Emmanuel. 1975: *Culture, Tradition and Society in the West African Novel*. Cambridge: Cambridge UP.

OBIECHINA, Emmanuel. 1993: 'Narrative proverbs in the African novel'. *Research in African Literatures* 24.4, pp. 123–40.

O'BRIEN, Charles. 1997: 'The "Cinéma colonial" of 1930s France: film narration as spatial practice'. In BERNSTEIN and STUDLAR (eds), pp. 207–31.

OGEDE, Ode S. 2001: '*African Novels in the Classroom*, ed. Margaret Jean Hay'. *Research in African Literatures* 32.4, pp. 224–5.

OSBORN, Andrew. 2002: 'Pygmy show at zoo sparks disgust'. *The Observer* 11 August, p. 19.

O'SHAUGHNESSY, Martin. 1996: '*Pépé le Moko* or the impossibility of being French in the 1930s'. *French Cultural Studies* 7.3, pp. 247–58.

O'SHAUGHNESSY, Martin. 2000: *Jean Renoir*. Manchester and New York: Manchester UP.

OUOLOGUEM, Yambo. 1971: *Bound to Violence*, trans. Ralph Manheim. London: Heinemann. [First published as *Le Devoir de violence*, 1968.]

OYONO, Ferdinand. 1966: *Houseboy*, trans. John Reed. London: Heinemann. [First published as *Une Vie de boy*, 1956.]

PANAF. 1975: *Frantz Fanon*. London: Panaf Books.

PARKER, Gabrielle. 2002a: 'The Fifth Republic and the Francophone Project'. In SAHLI (ed.), pp. 15–30.

PARKER, Gabrielle. 2002b: 'France and Southern Africa: culture, cooperation and language policy'. In SAHLI (ed.), pp. 231–46.

PARRY, Benita. 1987: 'Problems in current theories of colonial discourse'. *Oxford Literary Review* 9.1–2, pp. 27–58.

PEABODY, Sue. 1996: '*There are No Slaves in France': The Political Culture of Race and Slavery in the Ancien Régime*. New York and Oxford: Oxford UP.

PETREY, Sandy. 1988: *Realism and Revolution: Balzac, Stendhal, Zola, and the Performances of History*. Ithaca, NY: Cornell UP.

PFAFF, Françoise. 1993: *Entretiens avec Maryse Condé*. Paris: Karthala.

PICQ, Françoise. 2002: 'Parité, la nouvelle "exception française"'. *Modern and Contemporary France*, 10.1, pp. 13–23.

PICQUENARD, Jean-Baptiste. 1804 [1800]: *Zoflora; or, The Generous Negro Girl: A Colonial Story*. 2 vols. London: Lackington, Allen & Co.

PIGAULT-LEBRUN [pseud. of C.A.G. Pigault de l'Épinoy]. 2001 [1795]:

Le Blanc et le Noir, drame en quatre actes et en prose, ed. Roger LITTLE. Paris: L'Harmattan (Autrement Mêmes 4).

PINEAU, Gisèle. 1995: *L'Espérance-macadam*. Paris: Stock.

PIRIOU, Yann-Ber. 1971: *Défense de cracher par terre et de parler breton: poèmes de combat (1950–1970: Anthologie bilingue)*. Paris: P.J. Oswald.

PORTER, Dennis. 1983: 'Orientalism and its problems'. In Francis BARKER (ed.), *The Politics of Theory*. Colchester: University of Essex Press, pp. 179–93.

PORTER, Roy, and G.S. ROUSSEAU. 1990: *Exoticism in the Enlightenment*. Manchester: Manchester UP.

POUPINOT, Yann. 1961: *Les Bretons à l'heure de l'Europe*. Paris: Nouvelles Éditions Latines.

POWRIE, Phil (ed.). 1999: *French Cinema in the 1990s: Continuity and Difference*. Oxford: Oxford UP.

PRATT, Mary Louise. 1992: *Imperial Eyes: Travel Writing and Transculturation*. New York and London: Routledge.

PRICE, Richard, and Sally PRICE. 1999: 'Shadowboxing in the mangrove: the politics of identity in postcolonial Martinique'. In Belinda EDMONDSON (ed.), *Caribbean Romances: the Politics of Regional Representation*. Charlottesville and London: UP of Charlottesville, pp. 123–62.

PRICE-MARS, Jean. 1928: *Ainsi parla l'oncle*. Compiègne: Imprimerie de Compiègne.

QUILLIOT, Roger. 1962: 'Albert Camus's Algeria'. In Germaine BRÉE (ed.), *Camus*. Englewood Cliffs, NJ: Prentice Hall, pp. 38–47.

RADAKRISHNAN, R. 1992: 'Nationalism, gender and the narrative of identity'. In Andrew PARKER, Mary RUSSO, Doris SOMMER and Patricia YAEGER (eds), *Nationalisms and Sexualities*. London and New York: Routledge, pp. 77–95.

RAYNAL, Guillaume-Thomas. 1981 [1770]: *Histoire philosophique et politique [du commerce et des établissments des Européens] d[ans l]es deux Indes: avertissement et choix de textes par Yves Benot*. Paris: Maspero.

REECE, Jack E. 1977: *The Bretons against France: Ethnic Minority Nationalism in Twentieth-Century Brittany*. Chapel Hill: University of North Carolina Press.

RENARD, Raymond. 2000: *Une Éthique pour la francophonie: Questions de politique linguistique*. Paris: Didier Érudition.

REYNAERT, François. 1993: 'Y a-t-il une culture beur?' *Le Nouvel Observateur* 2 December, p. 18.

RICARD, François. 1996: *Gabrielle Roy: une vie*. Montreal: Boréal.

RICHARDSON, Michael (ed.). 1996: *Refusal of the Shadow: Surrealism and the Caribbean*. London: Verso.

RIVAROL. 1784: *De l'universalité de la langue française*. Paris: Dessenne.

ROBBINS, Louise E. 2002: *Elephant Slaves and Pampered Parrots: Exotic*

Animals in Eighteenth-Century Paris. Baltimore, MD, and London: Johns Hopkins UP.

ROBERTS, Hugh. 1982: 'The Algerian bureaucracy'. *Review of African Political Economy* 24, pp. 39–54.

RODOWICK, David N. 2002: 'Introduction: mobile citizens, media states'. *PMLA* 117.1, pp. 13–23.

ROMIEU, Auguste. 1831: 'Basse Bretagne'. *Revue de Paris* 30, pp. 145–54.

RONY, Fatimah Tobing. 1996: *The Third Eye: Race, Cinema, and Ethnographic Spectacle*. Durham, NC, and London: Duke UP.

ROSALDO, Renato. 1993: *Culture and Truth: The Remaking of Social Analysis*. London: Routledge.

ROSELLO, Mireille. 2001: *Postcolonial Hospitality: the Immigrant as Guest*. Stanford, CA: Stanford UP.

ROSS, Kristin. 1995: *Fast Cars, Clean Bodies: Decolonization and the Reordering of French Culture*. Cambridge, MA: MIT Press.

ROUANET, Marie (ed.). 1971: *Occitanie 1970: Les Poètes de la décolonisation/Occitania 1970: los poètas de la descolonizacion: anthologie bilingue*. Paris: P.J. Oswald.

ROUMAIN, Jacques. 1930: 'Port-au-Prince–Cap Haitien'. *Haiti-Journal* 3 April, p. 1.

ROUMAIN, Jacques. 1931: *La Montagne ensorcelée*. Port-au-Prince: Imp. Chassaing.

ROUMAIN, Jacques. 1937: 'Dans la mer Caraïbe, une tragédie haïtienne'. *Regards* 18 November, pp. 4–6.

ROUMAIN, Jacques. 1947: *Masters of the Dew*, trans. Langston Hughes and Mercer Cook. New York: Reynal & Hitchcock. [First published as *Les Gouverneurs de la rosée*, 1944.]

ROUQUETTE, Yves. 1972: *Rouergue, si, précédé de Ode à saint Aphrodise et suivi de Messe pour les cochons, édition bilingue*. Paris: P.J. Oswald.

ROUSSO, Henri. 1987: *Le Syndrome de Vichy (1944–198…)*. Paris: Stock.

ROY, Gabrielle. 1951: *La Petite Poule d'eau*. Paris: Flammarion.

ROY, Gabrielle. 1970: 'Mon Héritage du Manitoba'. *Mosaic* 3.3–4, pp. 69–79.

ROY, Gabrielle. 1996: *La Détresse et l'enchantement*. Montreal: Boréal.

ROY, Gabrielle. 2000: *Le Pays de Bonheur d'occasion et autres récits autobiographiques épars et inédits*. Montreal: Boréal, Les Cahiers Gabrielle Roy.

RUSHDIE, Salman. 1988: *The Satanic Verses*. London: Viking.

SABBAH, Laurent. 1997: *Écrivains français d'outre-mer*. Paris: ADPF.

SAHLI, Kamal (ed.). 2002: *French in and out of France: Language Policies, Intercultural Antagonisms and Dialogue*. London: Peter Lang.

SAID, Edward W. 1978: *Orientalism: Western Conceptions of the Orient*. London: Routledge & Kegan Paul.

SAID, Edward W. 1991 [1983]: *The World, The Text, and The Critic*. London: Vintage.

SAID, Edward W. 1992: 'Interview'. In Michael SPRINKER, (ed.), *Edward Said: A Critical Reader*. Oxford: Blackwell, pp. 221–64.

SAID, Edward W. 1993: *Culture and Imperialism*. London: Chatto & Windus.

SAID, Edward W. 2000 [1994]: 'Travelling theory reconsidered'. In Edward W. SAID, *Reflections on Exile and Other Literary and Cultural Essays*. London: Granta, pp. 436–52.

SAINT-LAMBERT, J.-F. de. 1997 [1769]: *Ziméo*. In Roger LITTLE (ed.), *Contes américains: L'Abenaki, Ziméo, Les Deux Amis*. Exeter: University of Exeter Press (Textes littéraires 99).

SALA-MOLINS, Lluis. 1992: *Les Misères des Lumières: sous la raison, l'outrage ...* Paris: Laffont.

SAMB, Amar. 1971: 'L'islam et l'histoire du Sénégal'. *Bulletin de l'IFAN* série B 33.3, pp. 461–507.

SAND, George. 1994: *Indiana*, trans. S. Raphael. Oxford: Oxford UP. [First published as *Indiana*, 1832.]

Sans Frontière. 1985: 'La "Beur" Génération'. 92–3.

SANTAOLALLA, Isabel (ed.). 2000: *'New' Exoticisms: Changing Patterns in the Construction of Otherness*. Amsterdam: Rodopi.

SARTRE, Jean-Paul. 1964: 'Réponse à Albert Camus'. *Situations IV*. Paris: Gallimard, pp. 90–125.

SARTRE, Jean-Paul. 1967 [1961]: 'Preface'. In FANON, pp. 7–26.

SARTRE, Jean-Paul. 1976: *Critique of Dialectical Reason*. London: NLB. [First published as *Critique de la raison dialectique*, 1960.]

SARTRE, Jean-Paul. 1988: 'Black Orpheus'. In *'What is Literature?' and Other Essays*. Cambridge, MA: Harvard UP, pp. 289–330. [First published as 'Orphée noir'. In SENGHOR, 1948.]

SARTRE, Jean-Paul. 2001: *Colonialism and Neocolonialism*, trans. Azzedine Haddour, Steve Brewer and Terry McWilliams. London and New York: Routledge. [First published as *Situations V: Colonialisme et néo-colonialisme*, 1964.]

SCEMLA, Jean-Jo. 2001: 'La littérature dans le Pacifique: le cas tahitien'. *Notre Librairie* 143, pp. 112–23.

SCHEUB, Harold. 1985: 'A review of African oral traditions and literature'. *African Studies Review* 28.2–3, pp. 559–75.

SCHMIDT, Hans. 1985 [1972]: *The United States Occupation of Haiti, 1915–1934*. New Brunswick, NJ: Rutgers UP.

SCHWARZ, Henry, and Sangeeta RAY (eds). 2000: *A Companion to Postcolonial Studies*. Oxford: Blackwell.

SCHWARZ-BART, Simone. 1972: *Pluie et vent sur Télumée Miracle*. Paris: Seuil.

SEBBAR, Leïla. 1981: *Fatima ou les Algériennes au square*. Paris: Stock.

SEBBAR, Leïla. 1982: *Shérazade, 17 ans, brune, frisée, les yeux verts*. Paris: Stock.

SEBBAR, Leïla. 1984: *Le Chinois vert d'Afrique*. Paris: Stock.

SEEBER, Edward Derbyshire. 1936: 'Oroonoko in France in the XVIIIth century'. *PMLA* 51, pp. 953–9.

SEEBER, Edward Derbyshire. 1937: *Anti-Slavery Opinion in France during the Second Half of the Eighteenth Century.* Baltimore, MD: Johns Hopkins Press.

SEGALEN, Victor. 1995: *A Lapse of Memory,* trans. Rosemary Arnoux. Mount Nebo: Boombana Publications. [First published as *Les Immémoriaux,* 1907.]

SEGALEN, Victor. 2002: *Essay on Exoticism: An Aesthetics of Diversity,* trans. and ed. Yaël Rachel SCHLICK. Durham, NC, and London: Duke UP. [First published as *Essai sur l'exotisme,* 1978.]

SÉGUIN, Robert-Lionel. 1964: *La Victoire de Saint-Denis.* Ottawa: Parti pris.

SEMBENE, Ousmane. 1995: *God's Bits of Wood,* trans. Francis Price. London: Heinemann. [First published as *Les Bouts de bois de Dieu,* 1960.]

SENGHOR, Léopold Sédar. 1948: *Anthologie de la nouvelle poésie nègre et malgache.* Paris: PUF.

SENGHOR, Léopold Sédar 1964: *Liberté 1: Négritude et humanisme.* Paris: Seuil.

SENGHOR, Léopold Sédar. 1990: *Œuvre poétique.* Paris: Seuil.

SENGHOR, Léopold Sédar. 1993: 'Negritude, a humanism of the twentieth century'. In WILLIAMS and CHRISMAN (eds), pp. 27–35. [First published as 'La Négritude est un humanisme du XXe siècle'. In *Liberté 3: Négritude et civilisation de l'universel,* 1977.]

SERFATY, Abraham. 1998: *Le Maroc, du Noir au Gris.* Paris: Éditions Syllepse.

SETH, Sanjay, Leela GANDHI and Michael DUTTON. 1998: 'Postcolonial studies: a beginning'. *Postcolonial Studies* 1.1, pp. 7–11.

SEYDOU, Christiane. 1972: *Silâmaka et Poullori: récit initiatique peul.* Paris: A. Colin.

SHAPIRO, Ron. 2000: 'In defence of exoticism: rescuing the literary imagination'. In SANTAOLALLA (ed.), pp. 41–9.

SHELLER, Mimi. 2000: *Democracy After Slavery: Black Publics and Peasant Radicalism in Haiti and Jamaica.* Gainesville: University Press of Florida.

SHOHAT, Ella. 1992: 'Notes on the "post-colonial"'. *Social Text* 31–2, pp. 99–113.

SIBLOT, Paul, and Jean-Louis PLANCHE. 1986: 'Le 8 Mai 1945: élément pour une analyse des positions de Camus face au nationalisme algérien'. In Jean-Yves GUÉRIN (ed.), *Camus et la politique.* Paris: L'Harmattan, pp. 160–74.

SINGH, Amritjit, and Peter SCHMIDT (eds). 2000: *Postcolonial Theory and the United States: Race, Ethnicity, and Literature.* Jackson: UP of Mississippi.

SLAVIN, David Henry. 1996: 'Heart of Darkness, Heart of Light: the civilizing mission in *L'Atlantide*'. In UNGAR and CONLEY (eds), pp. 113–35.

SLAVIN, David Henry. 2001: *Colonial Cinema and Imperial France, 1919–1939: White Blind Spots, Male Fantasies, Settler Myths*. Baltimore, MD and London: Johns Hopkins UP.

SLEMON, Stephen. 1990: 'Unsettling the Empire: resistance theory for the Second World'. *World Literature Written in English* 30.2, pp. 30–41.

SLEMON, Stephen. 1991: 'Modernism's Last Post'. In Ian ADAM and Helen TIFFIN (eds), *Past the Last Post: Theorizing Post-Colonialism and Post-Modernism*. Hemel Hempstead: Harvester Wheatsheaf, pp. 1–11.

SOCÉ, Ousmane. 1937: *Mirages de Paris*. Paris: Nouvelles Éditions Latines.

SOUAÏDIA, Habib. 2001: *La Sale Guerre*. Paris: La Découverte and Syros.

SOYINKA, Wole. 1999: *The Burden of Memory, The Muse of Forgiveness*. Oxford: Oxford UP.

SPIVAK, Gayatri Chakravorty. 1986: 'Imperialism and sexual difference'. *Oxford Literary Review* 8.1–2, pp. 225–40.

SPIVAK, Gayatri Chakravorty. 1987: *In Other Worlds: Essays in Cultural Politics*. London and New York: Routledge.

SPIVAK, Gayatri Chakravorty. 1990a: *The Post-Colonial Critic: Interviews, Strategies, Dialogues*. London and New York: Routledge.

SPIVAK, Gayatri Chakravorty. 1990b: 'Poststructuralism, marginality, postcoloniality and value'. In Peter COLLIER and Helga GEYER-RYAN (eds), *Literary Theory Today*. Ithaca, NY: Cornell UP, pp. 219–44.

SPIVAK, Gayatri Chakravorty. 1992: 'Acting bits/identity talk'. *Critical Inquiry* 18.4, pp. 770–803.

SPIVAK, Gayatri Chakravorty. 1993a [1988]: 'Can the Subaltern Speak?' In WILLIAMS and CHRISMAN (eds), pp. 66–111.

SPIVAK, Gayatri Chakravorty. 1993b: 'Echo'. *New Literary History* 24.1, pp. 17–43.

SPIVAK, Gayatri Chakravorty. 1993c: *Outside in the Teaching Machine*. London and New York: Routledge.

SPIVAK, Gayatri Chakravorty. 1994: 'Examples to fit the title'. *American Imago* 51.2, pp. 161–96.

SPIVAK, Gayatri Chakravorty. 1995: 'Translator's preface'. In Mahasweta DEVI, *Imaginary Maps: Three Stories*, trans. Gayatri Chakravorty Spivak. London and New York: Routledge, pp. xxiii–xxix.

SPIVAK, Gayatri Chakravorty. 1999: *A Critique of Postcolonial Reason: Toward a History of the Vanishing Present*. Cambridge, MA: Harvard UP.

SPIVAK, Gayatri Chakravorty. 2000: 'Foreword: upon reading the *Companion to Postcolonial Studies*'. In SCHWARZ and RAY (eds), pp. xv–xxii.

STEPAN, Nancy. 1986: 'Race and gender: the role of analogy in science'. *ISIS* 77, pp. 261–77.

STORA, Benjamin. 1991: *La Gangrène et l'oubli*. Paris: La Découverte.

STROOBANTS, Jean-Pierre. 2002: 'Polémique sur les Pygmées qui dansent le long de la Meuse wallonne'. *Le Monde* 31 July, p. 1.

SUGNET, Charles J. 2001: 'Dances with Wolofs'. *Transition* 87, pp. 138–59.

SUK, Jeannie. 2001: *Postcolonial Paradoxes in French Caribbean Writing: Césaire, Glissant, Condé*. Oxford: Clarendon Press.

SYLLA, Assane. 1978: *La Philosophie morale des Wolof*. Dakar: Sankoré.

TADJO, Véronique. 1999: *Champs de Bataille et d'amour*. Abidjan: NÉI; Paris: Présence Africaine.

TAI, Hue-Tam Ho. 2001: 'Remembered realms: Pierre Nora and French national Memory'. *History Cooperative* 106.3, 38 pars. <http://www.historycooperative.org/journals/ahr/ 106.3/ah000906.html>.

TAILLEFER, J.-M. 1988: 'Les Franco-manitobains et l'éducation 1870–1970: une étude quantitative'. Unpublished Ph.D, University of Manitoba.

TANSI, Sony Labou. 1979: *La Vie et demie*. Paris: Seuil.

TARR, Carrie. 1999: 'Ethnicity and Identity in the *cinema de banlieue*'. In POWRIE (ed.), pp. 172–84.

TAVERNIER, Yves. 2000: *Du Global à l'universel: Les enjeux de la francophonie*. Paris: Librairies-Imprimeries Réunies, Rapport d'information à l'Assemblée Nationale, 2592.

TCHEUYAP, Alexie. 2001: 'Creolist mystification: oral writing in the works of Patrick Chamoiseau and Simone Schwarz-Bart'. *Research in African Literatures* 32.4, pp. 44–60.

TÉTU, Michel. 1997: *Qu'est-ce que la Francophonie?* Paris: Hachette Édicef.

TÉVANIAN, Pierre. 2001: *Le Racisme républicain: réflexions sur le modèle français de discrimination*. Paris: L'Esprit frappeur.

THIESSE, Anne-Marie. 1991: *Écrire la France: le mouvement littéraire régionaliste de langue française entre la belle époque et la libération*. Paris: PUF.

THIESSE, Anne-Marie. 1999: *La Création des identités nationales: Europe, XVIIIe–XXe siècle*. Paris: Seuil.

THOMAS, Dominic. 2001: 'Daniel Biyoula: exile, immigration and transnational cultural productions'. In Susan IRELAND and Patrice J. PROULX (eds), *Immigrant Narratives in Contemporary France*. Westport, CT: Greenwood Press, pp. 165–76.

THORNTON, John K. 1991: 'African Soldiers in the Haitian Revolution'. *Journal of Caribbean History* 25.1–2, pp. 58–80.

THORNTON, John K. 1993: 'I am the subject of the King of Kongo: African political ideology and the Haitian revolution'. *Journal of World History* 4.2, pp. 181–214.

TINE, Alioune. 1985: 'Pour une théorie de la littérature africaine écrite'. *Présence Africaine* 133–4, pp. 99–121.

TODOROV, Tzvetan. 1982: *La Conquête de l'Amérique: la question de l'autre*. Paris: Seuil.

TODOROV, Tzvetan. 1993: *On Human Diversity: Nationalism, Racism and Exoticism in French Thought*, trans. Catherine Porter. Cambridge, MA: Harvard UP. [First published as *Nous et les Autres: la réflexion française sur la diversité humaine*, 1989.]

TOUGAS, Gérard. 1974: *La Littérature canadienne-française*. Paris: PUF.

TOURAINE, Alain. 1997: *Pourrons-nous vivre ensemble? Égaux et différents*. Paris: Fayard.

TOURNIER. Michel. 1986: *La Goutte d'or*. Paris: Gallimard.

TOWA, Marcien. 1971: *Léopold Sédar Senghor: Négritude ou servitude?* Yaoundé: CLE.

TRINH, T. Minh-ha. 1989: *Woman, Native, Other: Writing Postcoloniality and Feminism*. Bloomington: Indiana UP.

TRIVEDI, Harish. 1999: 'The postcolonial or the transcolonial? Location and Language'. *Interventions* 1.2, pp. 269–72.

TROUILLOT, Michel-Rolph. 1990: *State Against Nation: The Legacy and Roots of Duvalierism*. New York: Monthly Review Press.

TROUILLOT, Michel-Rolph. 1995: *Silencing the Past: Power and the Production of History*. Boston, MA: Beacon Press.

TRUDEAU, Pierre Elliott. 1962: 'La nouvelle trahison des clercs'. *Cité libre* 46, pp. 3–16.

TUTUOLA, Amos. 1952: *The Palm-Wine Drinkard*. London: Faber & Faber.

UKADIKE, Nwachukwu Frank. 1994: *Black African Cinema*. Berkeley, Los Angeles, London: University of California Press.

UNGAR, Steven. 1996: '*La Maison du Maltais* in Text and Document'. In Dina SHERZER (ed.), *Cinema, Colonialism, Postcolonialism: Perspectives from the French and Francophone Worlds*. Austin: University of Texas Press, pp. 30–50.

UNGAR, Steven, and Tom CONLEY (eds). 1994: *Identity Papers: Contested Nationhood in Twentieth-Century France*. Minneapolis: University of Minnesota Press.

URBAIN, Jean-Didier. 1993: *L'Idiot du voyage: histoires de touristes*. Paris: Plon.

URRY, John. 1995: *Consuming Places*. New York and London: Routledge.

VARADHARAJAN, Asha. 1995: *Exotic Parodies: Subjectivity in Adorno, Said, and Spivak*. Minneapolis: University of Minnesota Press.

VERGÈS, Françoise. 1999: *Monsters and Revolutionaries: Colonial Family Romance and Métissage*. Durham, NC: Duke UP.

VIDEAU, André. 2001: 'Écrans métis: satisfaction mitigée'. *Hommes et migrations* 1231, pp. 67–9.

VIEIRA, Else R.P. 1999: 'Postcolonialisms and the Latin Americas'. *Interventions* 1.2, pp. 273–81.

VIJAYASREE, C. 1996: 'The politics and poetics of expatriation: the Indian version(s)'. In Harish TRIVEDI and Meenakshi MUKHERJEE (eds), *Interrogating Post-Colonialism: Theory, Text and Context*. Rasgtrapati Nivas, Shimla: Indian Institute of Advanced Study, pp. 221–9.

VINCENDEAU, Ginette. 1998: *Pépé le Moko*. London: BFI.

VINCENTHIER, Georges. 1983: *Histoire des idées au Québec: Des troubles de 1837 au référendum de 1980*. Montreal: VLB.

WALCOTT, Derek. 1998: *What the Twilight Says*. London and New York: Faber.

WARNIER, Jean-Pierre. 1999: *La Mondialisation de la culture*. Paris: La Découverte.

WEBER, Eugen. 1997: 'L'Hexagone'. In NORA (ed.), I, pp. 1171–90.

WIEVIORKA, Michel (ed.). 1996: *Une Société fragmentée? Le multiculturalisme en débat*. Paris: Découverte.

WIEVIORKA, Michel. 1997: *Commenter la France*. Paris: Éditions de l'aube.

WIEVIORKA, Michel. 2001a: 'Introduction'. In WIEVIORKA and OHANA (eds), pp. 7–14.

WIEVIORKA, Michel. 2001b: *La Différence*. Paris: Balland.

WIEVIORKA, Michel, and Jocelyne OHANA (eds). 2001: *La Différence culturelle: une reformulation des débats*. Paris: Balland.

WILLIAMS, David. 1999: 'Condorcet and the politics of black servitude'. In James DOLAMORE (ed.), *Making Connections: Essays in French Culture and Society in Honour of Philip Thody*. Bern: Peter Lang, pp. 67–80.

WILLIAMS, David. 2002: 'Tableaux des souffrances négrières au siècle des Lumières'. In Roger LITTLE (ed.), *Interculturel francophonies 2: Aperçus du Noir: regards blancs sur l'autre*. Lecce: Alliance française, pp. 53–69.

WILLIAMS, Heather. 2003: 'Writing to Paris: poets, nobles and savages in nineteenth-century Brittany'. *French Studies* [forthcoming].

WILLIAMS, Patrick, and Laura CHRISMAN (eds). 1993: *Colonial Discourse and Post-Colonial Theory: A Reader*. Hemel Hempstead: Harvester Wheatsheaf.

WILLIAMS, Patrick. 2001: 'Nothing in the post? – Said and the problem of post-colonial intellectuals'. In Patrick WILLIAMS (ed.), *Edward Said*. 4 vols. London: Sage, I, pp. 314–34.

WINSTON, Jane Bradley. 2001: *Postcolonial Duras: Cultural Memory in Postwar France*. New York and Basingstoke: Palgrave.

WOODHULL, Winifred. 1993: *Transfigurations of the Maghreb: Feminism, Decolonization, and Literatures*. Minneapolis and London: University of Minnesota Press.

WOODSON, Drexel. 1990: 'Tout Mounn Se Mounn, Men Tout Mounn Pa Menm: Microlevel Sociocultural Aspects of Land Tenure in a Northern Haitian Locality'. Unpublished Ph.D, University of Chicago.

YEAGER, Jack. 1987: *The Vietnamese Novel in French: A Literary Response to Colonialism*. Hanover: University of New England Press.

YEE, Jennifer. 2000: *Clichés de la femme exotique*. Paris: L'Harmattan.

YOUNG, Robert J.C. 1990: *White Mythologies: Writing History and the West*. London and New York: Routledge.

YOUNG, Robert J.C. 1995: *Colonial Desire: Hybridity in Theory, Culture and Race*. London and New York: Routledge.

YOUNG, Robert J.C. 2001: *Postcolonialism: An Historical Introduction*. Oxford: Blackwell.

Index